TAMING THE ANARCHY

Groundwater Governance in South Asia

TUSHAAR SHAH

Resources for the Future
Washington, DC, USA
International Water Management Institute
Colombo, Sri Lanka

TD
302.9
.S53
2009

An RFF Press book
Published by Resources for the Future
1616 P Street NW
Washington, DC 20036–1400
USA
www.rffpress.org

A copublication of Resources for the Future (www.rff.org) and the International Water Management Institute (www.iwmi.cgiar.org)

Library of Congress Cataloging-in-Publication Data

Shah, Tushaar.
Taming the anarchy : groundwater governance in South Asia / Tushaar Shah.
p. cm.
978-1-933-115-60-3
Includes bibliographical references.
1. Groundwater—Government policy—South Asia. 2. Irrigation—South Asia—Management. I. Resources for the Future. II. Title.
TD302.9.S53 2009
333.91'30954—dc22

2008040547

978-1-933-115-60-3

About Resources for the Future
and RFF Press

Resources for the Future (RFF) improves environmental and natural resource policymaking worldwide through independent social science research of the highest caliber. Founded in 1952, RFF pioneered the application of economics as a tool for developing more effective policy about the use and conservation of natural resources. Its scholars continue to employ social science methods to analyze critical issues concerning pollution control, energy policy, land and water use, hazardous waste, climate change, biodiversity, and the environmental challenges of developing countries.

RFF Press supports the mission of RFF by publishing book-length works that present a broad range of approaches to the study of natural resources and the environment. Its authors and editors include RFF staff, researchers from the larger academic and policy communities, and journalists. Audiences for publications by RFF Press include all of the participants in the policymaking process—scholars, the media, advocacy groups, NGOs, professionals in business and government, and the public.

The mission of the **International Water Management Institute (IWMI)** is to improve the management of water and land resources for food, livelihoods, and nature in developing countries, with a vision for a "water for food secure world." IWMI conducts a worldwide research and capacity-building program to improve water and land resources through better technologies, policies, institutions, and management. Since its inception, the organization has developed a comprehensive understanding on the management of water in the agriculture sector through research in key areas such as water productivity from field to basin scales; water access, allocation and distribution; groundwater management and conjunctive use of groundwater and surface water; environmental flows and wetland management; and wastewater irrigation. IWMI is a non-profit organization with headquarters in Colombo, Sri Lanka, and offices in over 10 countries across Asia and Africa. It is one of 15 international research centers supported by the network of 60 governments, private foundations, and international and regional organizations collectively known as the Consultative Group on International Agricultural Research (CGIAR).

CONTENTS

About the Author vi
Preface vii
Introduction 1
1. The Hydraulic Past: Irrigation and State Formation 5
2. Rise of the Colossus 34
3. The Future of Flow Irrigation 59
4. Wells and Welfare 91
5. Diminishing Returns? 122
6. Aquifers and Institutions 151
7. Can the Anarchy be Tamed? 187
8. Thriving in Anarchy 208
Endnotes 245
Glossary of Hindi and Other Terms 269
References 271
Index 305

ABOUT THE AUTHOR

Tushaar Shah is a senior adviser to the director general at the International Water Management Institute in Colombo, Sri Lanka. His previous books include *Groundwater Markets and Irrigation Development: Political Economy and Practical Policy*. He was formerly director of the Institute of Rural Management in Anand, India (1988-1995), and was chair of the Governing Board of the Professional Assistance for Development Action (PRADAN), a New Delhi-based NGO that helps promote and strengthen the livelihoods of rural poor people, including marginal farmers and tribal groups.

PREFACE

In 2000, I managed to persuade Frank Rijsberman, then the director general of the International Water Management Institute (IWMI), Colombo, and Sudhir Rao of Sir Ratan Tata Trust, Mumbai, to jointly fund an open-ended, collaborative water policy research program for India. This partnership between an international research center and an Indian foundation gave birth to IWMI-Tata Water Policy Program (ITP). Because IWMI did not have an office in India, IWMI left it to me to choose a location for setting up the ITP office, and I happily settled for Anand, a smallish but upbeat and well-connected town in Gujarat where I knew and could lean on everyone, almost. With an unusual concentration of research centers and NGOs in its neighborhood, Anand also offered an ideal base for building collaborations to work on the entire array of water scarcity problems, of which Gujarat had more than its fair share.

Over the next few years, ITP grew into a remarkable, if somewhat unruly, knowledge institution, attracting every year scores of young researchers and students from India and elsewhere. Prodigious in its output, eclectic in its research methods, ITP evolved a distinctive work culture of its own. It worked on a broad research canvas and was ever ready to team up with any local researcher, student, or NGO with an interesting question to ask. Peers often bemoaned the short shrift that young ITP researchers sometimes gave to methodological rigor, yet ITP's annual partners' meetings teemed with hundreds of eager participants, including dozens of policymakers, who came to it for the bold—at times seemingly reckless—ideas that ITP youngsters brought to the water policy discourse. With all these angularities, ITP also produced more refereed research per dollar of IWMI money than many other projects. Much reviewed, it was held out by many as an exemplar.

For someone with abiding curiosity about what makes knowledge communities thrive, I found ITP a wonderful study. As a senior IWMI researcher, I was so occupied with my own research that the ITP team of a dozen or so youngsters and countless partners was surprisingly undermanaged and lightly led. If ITP followed anything like a research strategy, it changed on a quarterly basis. Arun Pandhi, who succeeded Sudhir Rao at SRTT, kept fuming about ITP's "strategic fluidity," but decided "if it ain't broke, don't fix it." Frank Rijsberman put up with, even defended, ITP's wayward ways and allowed the juggernaut to meander for some years before it was finally "mainstreamed," having finally strayed too far.

This book is both a tribute to and a celebration of that wayward, unruly, self-directing ITP. It revels in the big-picture analysis that was the ITP hallmark. Many ideas in this book took shape in the ITP dialectics of yesteryear. Like much other ITP research, it presents an alternative reading of available evidence to understand broad trends in South Asia's irrigation economy and where it is headed. In exploring these trends, it strives to be broadly right rather than precisely wrong. The book is written to provoke—and its reviewers agreed that, if nothing else, it will do just that. Many readers will find it difficult to fully agree with some of its arguments. Indeed, I would be surprised if critiques and counterpropositions do not pop out from ITP itself, as has been its vogue from the start. But the irreverent will find a sympathetic cord. In any case, the often inconvenient evidence that the book adduces in support of some of its key propositions does need to be explained and properly rehabilitated.

Expressing gratitude for this book means thanking all those who made that wayward ITP possible. For the material support and encouragement throughout the early ITP years, I must thank Sir Ratan Tata Trust's and

IWMI's leaders. Frank Rijsberman and Arun Pandhi provided much support and encouragement. Even after moving on from ITP, Colin Chartres, Frank's successor at IWMI, continued to support my water policy research of the genre ITP represented. Christopher Scott, then IWMI's India director, also provided support and encouragement, and he contributed greatly to my evolving understanding and thinking on groundwater governance issues in two spells of fieldwork we did together in Guanajuato in Mexico. Jinxia Wang made two similar fieldwork opportunities possible in the North China Plains, and Intizar Hussain took me to an extended and illuminating fieldtrip to Pakistan Punjab. Thanks are due to more than 50 young researchers—masters and Ph.D. students and collaborators from a host of Indian NGOs and research institutions—for creating and sustaining that intellectual "high" in the ITP ideas manufactory at Anand, some of whose contributions inform this work.

I would like to acknowledge comments from an IWMI internal reviewer and eight referees who reviewed the manuscript for the RFF Press. Avinash Kishore, Aditi Mukherji, Sanjiv Phansalkar, Maria Saleth, the late Anil Shah, Amrita Sharma, Hugh Turral, and Ship Verma provided extensive comments on an earlier draft, and I have thankfully incorporated their suggestions as best as I could. Dinesh Kumar contributed by challenging many of my ideas. Many others not directly involved in this book still helped shape the ideas in it; these include Shamjibhai Antala, Jacob Burke, Mark Giordano, Rajnarayan Indu, Sunderrajan Krishnan, Marcus Moench, Arvind S. Patel, Madar Samad, R. Sakthivadivel, and Frank van Steenbergen. Ramon Llamas needs particular mention as a source of constant remote support and advice; Ramon also made possible two productive visits to Spain. In an IWMI workshop, I boasted that groundwater governance is a work-in-progress throughout the world, including in the United States. This caused my friend John Peck of the University of Kansas to organize an extremely productive day-long conference at the Kansas Law School, where I had opportunities to learn about the U.S. experience from the groundwater managers themselves. I still hold the same view but admit Kansas is an exception that shows how transaction-costly institutional groundwater management can be for countries in South Asia. Among my IWMI colleagues, I would like to acknowledge Upali Amarasinghe, Deborah Bossio, David Molden, Bharat Sharma, and Peter McCornick for being supportive and understanding. Kanu Patel and Rajnarayan Indu helped with several of the diagrams; Sham Davande, R. Ravindranath, and O.P. Singh helped with the maps. And scores of local research partners helped with studies—such as on the impact of the *Jyotirgram* scheme in Gujarat and the effect of soaring diesel prices on smallholder irrigation in the Indo-Gangetic basin. I have liberally drawn on these studies, and their insights, at various places in this book. Don Reisman and Ellen Davey of the RFF Press deserve special thanks for their patience and indulgence; so does Sally Atwater, whose excellent copy editing has made this book a whole lot easier to read than the manuscript I had turned in.

By far the major partner in this book project has been Reghu, my secretary, who pursued it to the end with more vigor and fervor than I could muster myself. His contributions have been so diverse and decisive that instead of trying to recount them, I would just say, "Thank you."

TUSHAAR SHAH
ANAND

INTRODUCTION

Irrigation has always been central to life and society in the plains of South Asia. According to Alfred Deakin, a three-time Australian prime minister and an irrigation enthusiast of early 20th century who toured India in 1890, the region had 12 million hectares (ha) of irrigated land compared with three million ha in the United States, two million ha in Egypt, 1.5 million ha in Italy and a few hundred thousand ha each in Ceylon (Sri Lanka), France, Spain, and Victoria (Australia) (*The Age* 1891). Although Egypt and Sri Lanka are better known as hydraulic civilizations, a century ago British India was the world's irrigation champion.

During the past 40 years, however, much of what was British India has witnessed more development in irrigation than in the preceding two centuries. Available statistics—better today than a hundred years ago—suggest that in 2002, the world had some 300 million ha under irrigation,[1] and of these, more than 90 million ha was in today's India, Pakistan, and Bangladesh—lands that were the bulk of British India before 1947.

This book is about the growing anarchy in South Asia's irrigation econ-omy. From antiquity until the 1960s, water mobilization and management for agriculture were predominantly the affair of village communities or the state. Today, however, the region's agriculture has come to depend on explo-sive growth in irrigation from individually owned groundwater wells, and the current irrigation regime is wholly new. The resulting groundwater stress poses an environmental threat, but it also raises questions about the future of a vast agrarian system founded on a boom that seems destined to go bust.

Large swaths of western and southern South Asia are withdrawing much more water from underground aquifers than man and nature can put back into them, and society has yet to find a way of restoring the balance. The hard-rock aquifers in inland peninsular India offer so little scope for large-scale groundwater use that hydrogeologists would consider intensive irrigation with groundwater suicidal in these regions; nevertheless, smallholder agricul-ture in these parts has come to depend heavily on groundwater wells. Along the coasts, pumping groundwater on a large scale tips the precarious balance between coastal aquifers and the sea, threatening saltwater intrusion; never-theless, many coastal areas are witnessing a runaway groundwater boom. In the Indus basin in the northwest, even though vast alluvial aquifers are recharged by the network of canals from the Indus Basin Irrigation System, farmers pumping groundwater bring up the salts accumulated thousands of years ago, when most of the region was under the sea, and deposit them on the fields, progressively reducing the productivity of soils. When fields are drained, these salts enter the river system and help make the Indus a salt-laden drain by the time it arrives in Sind. Only in the Ganga-Brahmaputra-Meghna basin on the eastern front—where the alluvium is 600 meters deep and the annual runoff exceeds 1,400 km^3 (Shiklomanov 1993, 16)—did there seem an opportunity for large-scale groundwater irrigation without major collateral damage. In recent years, however, arsenic has shown up in groundwater.

Drained wetlands and low-flowing rivers, falling water levels and rising pumping costs, deteriorating groundwater quality and new public health hazards—these are all consequences of South Asia's anarchic groundwater development. Agricultural opportunism has been the driving force, and intel-ligent resource governance, a casualty. There are fervent calls to end the anar-chy, but this is more easily said than done. This book explores why. It describes how irrigation has enhanced the welfare of the region's poor even as the groundwater boom threatens to create "illfare" on a comparable scale. It con-siders irrigation's changing nature, drivers, and impacts on South Asia's still predominantly agrarian society. Above all, it asks how South Asia will manage this irrigation anarchy.

The book begins by tracing the ascent of water-managed agriculture to situate irrigation today in its historical context. This prelude is essential for understanding the forces that drive South Asia's irrigation economy, and for analyzing how public policies and institutions can bring order to this chaotic economy without undermining its stupendous benefits. When we compare the South Asian situation with the experience of other irrigating countries of the world, the historical background becomes critical to developing the central policy argument of the book: that to be effective, irrigation policies in South Asia must address the unique socioecological characteristics of the region and its people.

Here is a brief tour of the book. Chapter 1 traces the evolution of irrigation in South Asia, and elsewhere in the world, with emphasis on the progression of events during the nineteenth and twentieth centuries. Chapter 2 analyzes the unique dynamic of South Asia's groundwater boom and explains why it must be understood as a phenomenon in itself rather than as part of the global socioecology of groundwater irrigation. Chapter 3 analyzes how gravity-flow irrigation is shrinking in South Asia and why it will continue to do so, absent any change in policy. Chapter 4 recounts the welfare that groundwater irrigation has created for South Asia's agrarian poor. Chapter 5 deals with the disaster it threatens to create unless the region implements an effective strategy for managing this runaway groundwater irrigation economy. Chapter 5 also analyzes how the groundwater irrigation boom is silently reconfiguring river basins, upsetting old calculations and challenging received wisdom on river basin management. It suggests that establishing effective river basin management in South Asia may depend on understanding how farming communities respond to groundwater development in different aquifer conditions. Chapter 6 proposes a set of hypotheses to facilitate such an understanding and adduces evidence in their support. Chapter 7 presents a comparative analysis of other countries' experience in managing the demand for groundwater and describes how nascent efforts at demand management in South Asia are driven to chart their own distinctive course. Chapter 8 concludes the book by arguing for a practical, short- to medium-term groundwater governance strategy for South Asia that is society-centric rather than state-centric.

A note about geographical terms: Thus far I have used both "British India" and "South Asia" to refer to the vast landmass that is the stage of the drama described in this book. In reality, however, there is little groundwater irrigation in the middle Himalayas or in Bhutan and Burma (Myanmar), or in India's northeastern states, except Assam. The "groundwater anarchy" is occurring in what were the princely state of Hyderabad, in a cluster of more than 200 small princely states of Kathiawar, in the Terai areas of Nepal, and in northern and eastern areas of Sri Lanka—none of which were part of British India. Throughout this book, then, I use "South Asia" to describe what is happening in the plains of Bangladesh, India, Nepal and Pakistan, while taking an occasional look at the rapidly growing groundwater irrigation in northern Sri Lanka.

And finally, a note about the approach and methodology. The book takes a broad sweep to describe and analyze broad trends in South Asian irrigation that may overlook local details. It proposes several new hypotheses and introduces evidence in their support but does not necessarily offer rigorous tests for them. Its approach is intuitive more than formal, its aim being to design a frame that can center the current reality of South Asia's irrigation economy. The Streeten-Kuhn maxim (Kuhn 1962) underlines the approach taken: a model (or framework) is never defeated by facts, however damaging, but only by another model.

CHAPTER 1

THE HYDRAULIC PAST: IRRIGATION AND STATE FORMATION

Irrigation makes you free; irrigation makes you rich.
— *Document dated 1243, Catalonia, Spain*

Over the millennium past, the history of South Asian irrigation has undergone three distinct yet overlapping phases: the era of *adaptive irrigation*, up to 1800; the era of *constructive imperialism*, from 1800 to 1970; and the era of *atomistic irrigation*, from 1970 to date. This opening chapter attempts a broad-brush narrative, based on a review of the literature, of the evolution of South Asian irrigation over these three eras, as the historical backdrop against which the current problem needs to be viewed.

Accounts of the evolution of irrigation in India are often wholly preoccupied with the great works of kings, overlords and colonial engineers. From the Sudarshan reservoir, built and rebuilt in Saurashtra by Mauryans, to the 2,000-year-old overflow irrigation systems built by the Chola kings in Bengal and recreated in Tanjore, to the irrigation systems of Zainul Abidin in Kashmir, the ancient earthen dams on Cauvery and Vaighai in the south, and later the great canal systems extended from Jamuna by the Delhi sultans and renovated from time to time by the Mughals, the Porumamila tank of Cuddappah in the

Vijayanagar empire and the ancient tank cascades of Sri Lanka—in recounting these accomplishments, history textbooks seldom tire of the audacious irrigation adventures of ancient and medieval India's kings and overlords.

Indeed, preoccupation with these large, state-constructed irrigation works led great thinkers like Marx to regard centrally managed irrigation as the defining feature of the "Asiatic mode of production" and ancient and medieval Indian society and politics. "One of the material bases of the power of the state over the small disconnected producing organisms in India," said Marx famously, "was the regulation of the water supply. The Mohammedan rulers of India understood this better than their English successors" (Marx cited in Habib 1999, 297, n. 47).

Unlike Deakin, who had firsthand experience of the Indian irrigation scene, Marx's inferences were from secondhand accounts. However, the idea that irrigation dictated politics and early state formation in India, China, and other eastern civilizations continued to hold sway decades after Marx. The imperatives of managing large-scale irrigation works became the leitmotif of Karl Wittfogel's once hugely influential book, *Oriental Despotism: A Comparative Study of Total Power* (1957). In irrigation, Wittfogel was searching for the answer to an epochal question: why, through the first 1,500 years after Christ, eastern absolutism was so much more comprehensive and oppressive than in western societies. In understanding the harshest forms of total power that oriental despotism represented, Wittfogel, like Max Weber and Karl Marx, was particularly impressed by two features of oriental societies: the large waterworks maintained for irrigation and communication, and the fact that the government was often the biggest landowner.

According to Wittfogel, construction and maintenance of large irrigation systems—required in the arid Orient but not in temperate Europe—necessitated a political and social structure capable of forceful extraction of labor, which led to despotism[1] and a different social and political organization in China, India, Egypt, Yemen, Ceylon, and Mesopotamia. Hydraulic management necessitated a structured bureaucratic organization under centralized control, and the building and maintenance of irrigation systems forced people to become unequal leaders. As the systems grew, leadership was required to build new canals, maintain existing ones, and ensure efficient distribution of water.

How accurate and valid were Wittfogel's and Marx's characterization of irrigation as the central determinant of state formation and "oriental despotism?" In Indian history, evidence of an irrigation bureaucracy with responsibility for measuring land and regulating water supply at sluices is found only in Mauryan kingdoms and, to some extent, in the reign of Firoz Shah Tughlak, who built the first Jumna canal (Randhawa 1982). India had some great ancient irrigation works; however, much farming in ancient and medieval India was, in Wittfogel's terms, *hydro-agriculture* with a strong role of village communities rather than *hydraulic farming* under state domination. The great works were constructed at disparate times over the course of 2,000 years; it is unlikely that at any given point in time, these were a significant presence in a typical Indian peasant household. Farming here was organized as a family enterprise, whereas water mobilization and distribution had a strong tradition of local community management. The compilation by the Delhi-based Centre for Science and Environment in *Dying Wisdom* (Agarwal and Narain 1997) of myriad small, indigenous water harvesting and irrigation systems in different parts of South Asia supports the view that decentralized, community-based hydro-agriculture, not centralized hydraulic farming, dominated the region. Around 1800, water was being artificially applied to some six million ha in India; of that land, perhaps no more than a few hundred thousand ha depended on works centrally controlled by the state through an elaborate bureaucracy. Irfan Habib, the eminent historian of Mughal India, suggests, "Despite the urgings of Marx, sufficient evidence does not exist to warrant the belief that the state's construction and control of irrigation works was a prominent factor in the agrarian life of Mughal India" (Habib 1999, 297).[2] However, much evidence indicates that a tradition of community-level cooperation in mobilizing and managing water for flow irrigation—superimposed over the family as a farming unit—was a prominent aspect of agrarian life in Mughal and earlier periods.[3]

Discredited as Wittfogel's thesis remains today,[4] his analysis offers deep and powerful insight into the gradual but persistent atrophy of present-day public and community gravity-flow irrigation in South Asia, and perhaps elsewhere in the developing world, as we examine in Chapter 3.

Irrigation in Mughal India and Earlier

Although South Asia, along with China and Europe, were the most densely populated regions of the world in 1700 (Klein and Ramankutty 2004), farming land went abegging here until 150 years ago. Villages tended to settle at sites hydraulically most opportune for stable and productive agriculture. Riverine areas that were not so low as to be flooded were preferred. The popular notion that civilizations formed around watercourses aptly described settlement patterns of those times.

The state as well as the people lived off the land. Since farming was the primary source of government revenue, the intercourse between the state and the peasants was broad as well as deep, and the apparatus for land revenue administration substantial and prominent. Peasants had few property rights, if any. In Mughal India, no one could sell, mortgage, or bequeath land.[5] All land belonged to the emperor, who was also the heir to every subject. Commonly, land was held by the village community, and land went back to the community if its tiller died heirless. Rights were given only to till the land and to collect the emperor's share of the produce of land, which except during Akbar's rule was generally higher than one-third, closer to one-half, of the output.

Helping the peasant produce as large a surplus over his subsistence needs was a prime motive of the state right up to the colonial period.[6] The desire to maximize land revenue is what created incentives to invest in irrigation, not any interest in improving the welfare of the peasant, as today. The South Asian village was far less "settled" and permanent than we know it today; and *begar*, the institution of forced labor, was widely prevalent. When demand for land tax and *begar* from the ruling classes became excessive, or during times of war, peasants would desert their lands en masse, depopulating whole villages and migrating with their cattle to forests or hills or to neighboring provinces where revenue demands were lower.[7] The mobility of peasants was the only check against unbridled rent-seeking by overlords, who had no use for territory without peasants. Hard pressed to keep peasants on their lands, feudal lords sometimes used force but were often more successful by offering wet lands in river valleys or along the banks of the rivers, or by helping (or coercing) peasant communities to build embankments, or bunds, and channels that offered a modicum of water control.

This suited the adaptive strategies of farming communities, and agriculture as well as human settlements intensified and grew in regions that offered natural water control, typically in well-drained wetlands. As Ludden (1999, 49) points out,

> In Punjab, as in general through out the northern basins, the long term geographic spread of intensive agriculture moved outward from places where drainage is simpler to harness to places where more strenuous [water] controls are necessary . . . from naturally wetter into drier areas; where as in flood plains and humid tropics, it moved initially from higher and drier parts of the low

lands into the more waterlogged areas at the river's edge. Everywhere, agriculture also moved up river valleys into the highlands. In the Yamuna-Ganga basin, the general trend of expansion of intensive agriculture has been from east to west and upland from low lands; and in the Punjab, from north-east to south-west.

There must have been little by way of pure dryland or rain-fed farming in the sense we understand today—that is, crop cultivation based on rainfall and soil moisture alone in arid and semiarid environments where extensive pastoralism was the customary livelihood. But there was also little of the kind of water control that modern irrigation implies, with its well-managed canals and tube wells. Like basin irrigation that dominated Egyptian agriculture, the inundation or overflow irrigation in Mughal India is best understood as minimalist, adaptive, nonintrusive irrigation that entailed minimal human footprint on the basin hydrology. This involved spreading river floods over nearby arable lands, allowing the water to soak in, and then draining them. As Agnihotri (1996, 42) suggests for northwestern India, farming involved "maximizing the utilization of *sailab* (floods) as well as digging up watercourses and making minor bunds. The idea being . . . to raise the area as well as the productivity of riverine cultivation."[8] The *ahar-pyne* systems in eastern India and water tanks of southern India and Bengal had the same purpose. Upon his first visit to northern India in the early sixteenth century, Babur, the founder of the Mughal Empire, was surprised that people left rivers alone but used shallow wells and tanks for irrigation (Bagchi 1995). This was, however, less the case farther east, where floodwaters were used extensively to grow crops.

Wells played an important though supplemental role in water-managed agriculture in northern and western India. There is extensive evidence of the use of open-lined and unlined wells in Vedic literature primarily for domestic water needs but also for supplementary irrigation. The Satwahanas introduced ring wells—dug wells whose shafts were lined with concentric terracotta or sometimes wooden rings—for domestic use and brick wells for irrigation use. Well irrigation, and its productivity-enhancing potential, was firmly established in the revenue calculus of ancient and medieval rulers. Well construction was actively encouraged through incentives and tax remissions, but lands irrigated with wells were also assessed at a higher rate than rain-fed lands from the time of Arthashastra (third century B.C.) to the Mughal rulers during the sixteenth to eighteenth centuries A.D. and, still later, during the colonial era (see, e.g., Hardiman 1998). Wells were preferred because earthen dams were easy prey to marauding armies (Ludden 1999). The significance

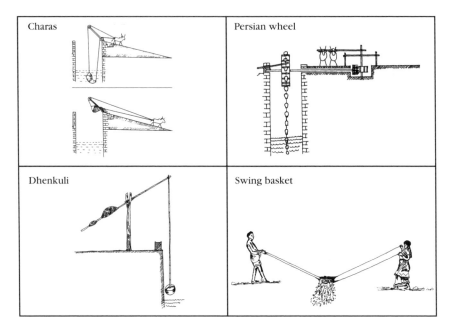

Figure 1.1   Traditional water-lifting devices used in India

of well irrigation was growing, in quantitative terms, during the Mughal as well as the colonial eras. Yet as Agarwal and Narain (1997, 285) note, ". . . little else is known about the long term history of wells because they were family enterprises, and their fortunes went unrecorded." We may surmise that around two million ha of farmland was irrigated by wells around 1800, and the total quantity of ground (and soil) water lifted during a typical year was around eight to 10 km³. The number of bullock pairs and the human effort needed to irrigate larger areas than this using leather buckets would be too large for the available peasant labor.

For centuries, the use of well irrigation was limited by the laborious technologies for lifting water: the leather bucket *(charasa)*, the swing basket, and the bamboo basket *(dhenkuli)* (see Figure 1.1). The introduction of the Persian wheel *(sakiya,* or *rahat)* by West Asians to northern India's peasantry hastened the spread of well irrigation (Hardiman 1998).[9] A system powered by oxen driven in a circle, the Persian wheel became the universal mode of lifting water from wells or canals in many northern and western parts of South Asia (Islam 1997). Abu-l-Fazl asserted that "most of the province of Lahore is cultivated with well-irrigation," an assertion repeated by a chronicler of the late seventeenth century who himself lived in that province (Habib 1999, 29).

The Persian wheel was widely preferred because it could be operated with four or six bullocks whereas the *charasa* required six or eight. Moreover, even a child or a woman could operate the Persian wheel; the *charasa* required two able-bodied men, one to drive the bullocks and the other to empty the bucket. The Persian wheel could also be adapted to lift different volumes of water and work effectively at different depths of water level. As a result, the Persian wheel commanded a larger area and was more widely used than other devices (Islam 1997). Four major improvements occurred in the Persian wheel during the nineteenth century: the wooden frame was replaced by iron; the heavy earthen buckets were exchanged for lighter aluminum ones; the use of metal roller bearings reduced friction and increased automatic lubrication of moving parts; and finally, toward the end of the nineteenth century, animal power was replaced by diesel engines and electric motors (Islam 1997).

Most irrigation wells in northern India were *kuchcha*, or earthen, and made afresh every year, which suggests that groundwater levels remained at predevelopment levels during most parts of a year with a normal monsoon season. In the early nineteenth century, as statistics of irrigated areas began to be compiled, it was striking that well digging increased during drought years, as it does even today. Wells were used more as insurance against drought or a dry spell. In years of successive drought, however, the falling water levels severely tested the power of manual lifting devices.

Collective action at the community level, common in flow irrigation, was widespread in well irrigation, too. The groundwater institutions we find in South Asia today were incipient in the early years of the nineteenth century and fully operational in its later decades. Jointly owned wells in nineteenth century Punjab (Islam 1997) operated much as tube well companies of North Gujarat (Shah and Bhattacharya 1993) and Punjab (Tiwari 2007) do today, as well as the *wara bandi* (rotational) system in canal irrigation systems in the Indus basin. Dividing waters among owners was done in proportion to shares owned. Each share entitled the bearer to a certain number of *waris* (turns), each *wari* divided into a *prahara* (one-eighth of a day) of three hours. The number of shares were usually in proportion to the holder's land in the command (Islam 1997). Far from the complex, state-controlled irrigation machine that Marx attributed to the Mughal Empire, water-managed agriculture involved local cooperation and community rulemaking and enforcement. Historians are unanimous in noting the spread and significance of well irrigation in northwestern and western India as a tradition extending from West Asia.[10] Even with major public investments in canal irrigation during the second half of the nineteenth century, private capital investment in well irrigation remained substantial in these parts.[11]

However, we seldom hear about irrigation by wells on a large scale in eastern, central and southern India during the Mughal as well as the colonial era, except perhaps in the Coimbatore and Tanjore areas in Madras, where wells acquired some importance in the late nineteenth century (Roy 2000). By far the best account of irrigation in peninsular and eastern India around 1800 comes from Francis Buchanan, a medical officer on the rolls of the East India Company. Irrigation by wells is conspicuous by its absence in Buchanan's travelogue, which is otherwise detailed and incisive in describing agrarian conditions, including the means for irrigation. In today's Tamilnadu, Karnataka, Kerala, and parts of Andhra Pradesh, which he toured extensively in the early nineteenth century, Buchanan reported on vibrant "water-managed"[12] agriculture around tanks and reservoirs but found well irrigation as rare as tanks were ubiquitous (Dutt 1904).[13] In the hard-rock geology of peninsular India, digging wells was far costlier and more laborious than in alluvial areas of the Indo-Gangetic plains, and it was equally costly and laborious to bale out water "from deep wells of Rayalaseema by three to four robust adult males working with a pair or two of strongly built bullocks" (A. Reddy 1990, *621*).

A few years later, from Patna, Buchanan noted that although large reservoirs and long canals were used for irrigation, the "greater portion of winter crops, vegetables, and sugarcane was irrigated from wells" (Dutt 1904, Part I, *153*). However, over the next seven years, in his travels to Shahbad, Bhagalpur, Gorakhpur, Dinajpur, Purnia, and Assam districts, Buchanan seldom mentioned well irrigation. Only in Gorakhpur did he find some land watered with wells; leather buckets and swing baskets were used to raise the water.[14]

In a set of four lectures delivered c. 1910, Sir William Willcocks (1984), a brilliant colonial engineer who worked on irrigation projects in India as well as Egypt, drew the similarities between the extensive systems of overflow irrigation that prevailed in Bengal[15] until the decline of the Moghul Empire and those he had seen in Babylon and Egypt. Willcocks asserted that the broad, shallow, long and parallel earthen canals extending from rivers like Bhagirathi and Damodar—which the British engineers thought were stagnant pools of water—were the remnants of a hydraulic civilization that had supported irrigated agriculture in central and eastern parts of the Ganga-Brahmaputra-Meghana basin for close to 2,000 years.[16] In building an elegant case for reviving this system of overflow irrigation, Willcocks offered a detailed description of the water-managed agriculture he saw in Bengal, but like Buchanan, he failed to mention irrigation by wells even once.

L. S. S. O'Malley, a prolific and celebrated writer of district gazetteers, was explicit in noting the insignificance of well irrigation in Bengal around 1900. In 1908, in Bankura, he found well irrigation in upland areas but only "to a small extent" (O'Malley 1995a, 97), and in 1910, he noted that "well irrigation is not practiced except in the case of garden produce" in Birbhum (O'Malley 1996, 60–61). For Santhal Paragana, he wrote, "There is very little well irrigation in this district" (O'Malley 1999, 191), and of Murshidabad, he said simply, "Irrigation wells . . . do not exist" (O'Malley 1997, 116). In 1886, W. W. Hunter (1997, 105) had averred that "Wells are not used for irrigation purposes in Midnapur District;" a quarter-century later, in 1911, O'Malley (1995b, 101) confirmed that the situation in this respect had not changed: "there is little or no irrigation from wells" in Midnapore.

All those accounts suggest that although well irrigation on a large scale was a feature of agrarian life in western and northwestern India, in eastern and southern India it was largely absent around 1800 and very limited around 1900. Tanks supplied water for agriculture in the southern parts, and overflow systems of the *ahar-pyne* type (Pant 1998) that Willcocks described in Bengal and southern Bihar were the chief means of irrigation in eastern India.

The Cotton-Cautley Era of Canal Construction, 1830–1947

The 1830s marked a quantum leap in Indian irrigation, pioneered in the south by Sir Arthur Cotton and in the north by Major Proby Cautley. The East India Company, which by now ruled over much of India, was beginning to perceive a great opportunity in irrigation to combine the "interests of charity and the interests of commerce" (Whitcombe 2005, 677) in repairing and expanding the great irrigation works of Tanjore and Delhi. Improving preexisting irrigation systems proved so profitable in achieving these twin objectives that the company and British merchants in India began raising commercial loans in London to finance some new irrigation works[17] (A. Reddy 1990). The reconstruction of the Grand Anicut in 1838 and the Jumna canals soon thereafter launched a phase of frenzied canal construction activity that reflected a paradigm shift in irrigation thinking.

The new irrigation ideology that took root was a clean break from the past. Instead of adaptive, minimalist, unobtrusive ways of improving local water control along rivers and streams, where farming was then concentrated, the colonial irrigation ideology boldly sought opportunities for opening up vast—often unpeopled—areas for farming by manipulating large untapped rivers and reconfiguring basin hydrology. Controlling rivers and reshaping river basins were considered goals befitting an empire. Grandiosity was at the heart of the colonial irrigation ideology, described by S. B. Saul (1957, *174*) as "constructive imperialism:" "arid lands were the instruments" of imperialism and "irrigation the methodology" (Worster cited in Gilmartin 2003a, 2). Rather than merely helping communities build and manage local irrigation systems, the new ideology created centralized structures for constructing and managing large irrigation systems on commercial lines, often to grow cash crops like cotton for export. This was a considered strategy of unbalanced irrigation development, without regard for regional equity. The focus was on exploiting hydraulic opportunity for intensive irrigated agriculture, rather than all-round, regionally balanced development of agriculture. Accordingly, colonial works, especially in northwestern India, made it possible to sustain vast areas of productive "colony agriculture" in arid lands used thus far only for extensive pastoralism. Elsewhere in the world, notably in the United States and Australia, irrigation development in the nineteenth century was still in the private domain. The colonial irrigation ideology in India advocated—and successfully demonstrated—the role that only the state could play in partnership with science in taming rivers to improve human welfare on a massive scale. This ideology survived the end of the Empire and dominated irrigation thinking in the independent states of India and Pakistan that succeeded British India in 1947.

Enthusiasm for new irrigation projects waned somewhat around 1920, and public investments in irrigation experienced relative stagnation thereafter compared with the 1870–1910 period. The Great Depression that engulfed the whole world also hit the Indian economy and public expenditure. Moreover, as the Indian Independence movement gathered momentum, the colonial government was increasingly unsure about the wisdom of undertaking projects with long gestation periods. Despite this slowdown, at the colonial government's initiative, the irrigation profile of India changed beyond recognition, especially in Punjab, United Provinces, and Madras (Table 1-1). In 1948, of the net sown area of 116.8 million ha in undivided India, 28.2 million ha was irrigated—15.2 million ha by canals, 6.6 million

Table 1-1   Irrigated area as proportion of cultivated area in major provinces of British India, 1885–1939

| Region | 1885–86 | 1938–39 | Percentage increase in irrigated area due to | |
			Government canals	Wells
Punjab	29.3	57.4	95.5	9.3
Madras	24.1	23.5	49.6	18.6
United Provinces	19.3	26.6	57.0	37.2
Rest of British India (excluding Burma)	6.0	12.5	31.3	10.7

Source: (Roy 2000, 59)

ha by wells, 3.3 million ha by tanks, and 3.1 million ha by other sources (Bagchi 1995).

By the end of colonial rule, the British had established the commercial viability of canal irrigation (Whitcombe 2005). However, its overall impact on the performance of Indian agriculture was—and continues to be—a matter of much debate. As Napoleon once quipped, history is nothing but a fable agreed upon; however, canal irrigation's impact on agriculture in British India is one story about which there is little agreement. Some, like Mason (2006), argue that canal irrigation made famines history. Others argue that the strategy of "unbalanced irrigation development"—concentrating irrigation investments in Punjab, Madras, and United Provinces—failed to help feed the rest of India.

During the period 1900–1946, when India's population growth rate jumped from 0.51 percent per year to 0.87 percent and its food requirements rose accordingly, the pace of urbanization declined, and as a result, pressure on agriculture increased inexorably. Investments in irrigation were expected to come to the country's rescue in these hard times. Yet India's agriculture stagnated like never before. Net domestic product from agriculture grew at a mere 0.31 percent per year during this period, compared with more than one percent during 1868–1898, and India's real per capita income experienced a negative growth rate (Roy 2000). All of the colonial investment in irrigation and railways—justified on the grounds of preventing famine—could not prevent the great Bengal famine of 1942 and the starvation deaths of four million people. In *Late Victorian Holocausts*, Mike Davis (2001) counted 31 serious famines in 120 years of British rule compared with 17 in the 2,000 years before British rule. True, famines in colonial India were more the result of repressive and discriminatory colonial economic policies and a paucity of exchange entitlements than a consequence of food supplies; however, it appears that irrigation works were unable even to soften the misery.

Undivided Punjab was cited as the exemplar of the success of colonial irrigation ideology. However, despite receiving 40 percent of the total colonial irrigation investments in India before 1920, and despite the resulting increase in irrigated acreage to 50 percent of the total cropped area, food production in British Punjab increased only 0.7 percent per year from 1904–05 to 1944–45. This was barely keeping pace with the growth in the population of Punjab itself—from 7.55 million in 1901 to 9.6 million in 1944–45—not to mention feeding the rest of British India (Bhalla 1995).

Irrigation Adventures Elsewhere

When colonial irrigation enterprises began in India, large-scale irrigation development was already underway elsewhere in the arid and semiarid world, mostly engineered by Europeans. South Asia was but one of five irrigation development contexts. The second was West Asia and North Africa, where for millennia, civilizations had risen and fallen around irrigation enterprises (Christensen 1998). Sustaining irrigation here was a constant struggle with salinity, and continuous maintenance and repair were needed to arrest the atrophy in this region's surface irrigation systems. During the middle of the first millennium of the Christian era, the great Sassanian Empire built ambitious irrigation systems, complete with dams and canals, which brought Mesopotamia (modern-day Iraq) great riches and wealth. However, the massive upkeep and persistent salinization got the better of the Sassanians as well as their Muslim successors.

Such cycles of rise and decline in bold irrigation enterprises, and the civilizations that flourished around them, played out repeatedly in different regions until the nineteenth century, when the British brought modern irrigation technologies to revitalize irrigation in Egypt and elsewhere. Even though Wittfogel's thesis, built on the Middle-Eastern irrigation experience, stands discredited today, the ruling elites did make massive use of forced labor in construction and maintenance of irrigation systems, and the motive in state irrigation initiatives was enhancing the land revenue, which in Sassanian Mesopotamia was by far the most important source of state income. "There is no reason to believe that some sort of population pressure constituted the real 'prime mover' " (Christensen 1998, *18*). Because the state had revenue interests in irrigation systems, "political impotence"—the inability to extract forced labor and impose discipline—was among the chief reasons, besides environmental adversity, for the decline in Middle Eastern irrigation systems. Despite repeated attempts to revive them, the "overall picture is of irreversible recession" (21). During the nineteenth century, Europeans introduced the Middle East—as Russians did in Central Asia—to the modern civil engineering technologies they had perfected in Punjab. According to Christensen (1998, 26–27), however, this "Technological optimism, so deeply rooted in the European worldview, has always overruled historical experience . . . Surveyed in the long term, large-scale irrigation systems appear to have limited life-expectancy."

The third irrigation development context was from humid East and Southeast Asia, where paddy-rice civilization had long depended on water control. Nowhere else were water control and statecraft as closely linked as in the deltas of Southeast Asia. The European *mission civilisatrice* left a deep imprint here as well, with the French constructing more than 100 canal projects, mostly of indifferent quality and outcomes, in the Mekong Delta between 1890 and 1930 (Biggs 2001). Yet what we witness here, until the recent past, was an evolutionary continuum of age-old traditions and technologies of water control, with ruthless use of state power to mobilize slave labor for paddy irrigation. An extreme example was the Angkor Empire in Cambodia, which from the eighth to the fourteenth century amassed great wealth from rice irrigation systems built and maintained by slaves. Angkor kings allegedly used water control to achieve annual rice yields approaching three metric tons per ha (compared with 1.2 metric tons per ha in Cambodia today), and successive rulers of Cambodia have believed that achieving Angkorean rice yields is the secret to restoring the splendor the Khmer enjoyed during that era (Himel 2007, 5). Throughout the twentieth century, first the French and then the Sihanouk government gave irrigation construction high priority, and medieval rulers in many parts of the Orient are known to have gone to great lengths in harnessing people power for irrigation-building; however, nothing in the world's irrigation history comes close—in the scale of labor mobilization, ruthless use of state power, and colossal loss of human life—to the irrigation ventures of the infamous Khmer Rouge regime during 1975–1979. For its leader, Pol Pot, Cambodia's "super Great Leap Forward" lay in tripling its rice yield. The Khmer Rouge battle cry was, "If we have water, we can have rice. If we have rice, we can have everything" (Himel 2007), and to get everything, Pol Pot sought to emulate the Angkor kings. He wanted irrigation to increase from 74,000 ha to 1.5 million ha in one year by adopting what he thought was a simple Angkorean[18] program of irrigation construction.[19] The Khmer Rouge emptied all cities and towns, sent merchants, teachers and students, doctors and nurses, officials and clerks off to the villages, created a slave state, and mobilized countless "production groups" to build irrigation canals and dykes, and plant rice. A "person's worth was measured by how many cubic yards of earth he could move" (Short 2004, 322). The Khmer Rouge irrigation strategy employed revolutionary ideas: all land, tools and livestock were collectivized, and thus land acquisition was not a problem; irrigation commands, like a checkerboard, were reparcelized into uniform 1-ha-square plots; thousands of indigenous, locally adapted rice varieties were abandoned in favor of selected high-yielding varieties.

The strategy failed miserably. Pol Pot's irrigation engineers gave short shrift to hydrological or even topographical parameters. Some 20 percent of Cambodia's population, or more than 1.7 million people, died of starvation, exhaustion, execution and diseases while digging canals, yet its rice productivity never reached what it was in the 1960s, let alone the Angkor era. The enormousness of the Khmer Rouge irrigation campaign is evident in the fact that nearly 80 percent of Cambodia's irrigation infrastructure today, such as it is, was built during those three Khmer Rouge years, and all others from earlier eras were modified under Pol Pot (Himel 2007). Irrigation remains a top priority even today; Prime Minister Hun Sen of Cambodia fondly calls his the "irrigation government." Yet the country's challenge is to harness voluntary farmer participation—rather than commandeered slave labor—to sustain a fragile, mostly earthen irrigation infrastructure from the ravages of annual floods that inundate most areas and erode the earthworks.

The fourth irrigation development context was African. The hallmark of European irrigation enterprise in Africa was the combination of civil engineering and large-scale social engineering for an estate mode of production. European irrigation enterprises in Africa imposed a level of uniformity and discipline that uprooted existing social structures and reduced peasants to wage laborers on their own land while transforming irrigation systems into highly productive manufactories. The Gezira irrigation scheme in Sudan, commissioned in 1925, is the best if somewhat unrepresentative example, and the following summary draws largely on Bernal (1997) and Wallach (1988). French philosopher Michel Foucault said that the Gezira scheme must be looked upon as a "disciplinary institution." "Its miles and miles of irrigation canals and uniform fields stretched out in huge grids dominate space, its rigid schedules for agricultural operations command time, and above all its hierarchy of inspectors and bureaucrats supervising, documenting, and disciplining strive to control the people of Gezira" (Bernal 1997, 447). Razing old patterns of land use and social organization, the colonial state used the Gezira plain as a *tabula rasa*, creating a new Sudanese society, a homogeneous one, of hardworking and disciplined people.[20] The 840,000-ha system was constructed, with geometric precision, to produce cotton for the British industry and the world market by compulsorily renting land from its original owners and issuing to them standard irrigated tenancies of 12.6 ha. Within each tenancy, 33 percent was to be planted to cotton, another 33 percent was to be fallow, and the rest was divided between sorghum and fodder in annual rotation. Irrigation, plowing, and other inputs were provided by the scheme, which had a monopoly right to procure cotton and controlled its ginning, grading, and marketing. This was the "estate mode" of farming, with a tripartite arrangement among tenants, government, and the concession companies. The government would receive a 40 percent share in net profits from cotton cultivation for (compulsorily) acquiring land from its official owners, issuing tenancies, and managing the dam. Tenants would absorb cultivation costs and get a 40 percent share. Concession companies would be responsible for cleaning and leveling the land under irrigation, managing the scheme itself, providing field supervisors and inspectors, lending to farmers, and transporting the cotton, for the remaining 20 percent (Ertsen 2003).

Gezira's blend of civil and social engineering left a deep imprint on the way irrigation has evolved in Sudan and elsewhere in Africa. For our purposes, it is useful to note that by the 1980s, 14 years after British rule ended, more than two million Sudanese worked on 2.5 million ha of Gezira-like irrigation schemes spread over Sudan, and cotton contributed half of Sudan's export income; to date, Gezira remains the centerpiece of independent Sudan's development and a part of modern Sudanese identity. The irrigation management regime created by the British has survived Sudan's independence: tenants carry out "their obligations according to an ordinance which allows maximum maneuverability for the highest possible production" (Bernal 1997, 470). The Gezira experiment may be faulted on many grounds, but "it succeeded in the colonial era as a monument to economic modernization, and the values of rationality, discipline, and order, and has continued to function as a potent symbol of progress and state power until today" (Bernal 1997, 448). Gezira also militates against the idea that providing an attractive and secure bundle of private property rights helps nudge users toward more responsible management of water: the colonial government's replacement of existing property rights with much inferior tenancies should have dampened the owners' stakes in farming, yet the Sudanese experience offers little evidence of this.

The fifth irrigation development context is Australia and the United States, which witnessed Anglo-Saxon irrigation enterprise but within a totally different social and institutional dynamic. The state's goal for irrigation in these countries was not maximizing land revenue, as in India, the Middle East, and Africa, but attracting European settlers badly needed to settle vast unpeopled territories. In both the United States and Australia during the nineteenth century, many irrigation systems were constructed privately by settler-farmers, making sizable investments in land and water development—a strategy that Deakin thought inferior to the colonial state's aggressive initiatives in irrigation development in India and Africa. Private investments would not be forthcoming without an assurance of water availability, hence the emergence of doctrines of riparian rights in the eastern United States and many areas of Australia, and prior appropriation in the American West. These rights systems did to water resources what the enclosure movement did to public and common lands in medieval England: early settlers in Australia and the United States had clear and well-developed notions of private property at a time when peasants elsewhere in the world were largely unexposed to the concept. Prior appropriation and riparian rights systems created incentives for settlers to invest in land and water. In much of the United States, the federal government's participation in irrigation remained marginal until the 1930s; as a result, these rights doctrines continued to affect water allocation until growing water scarcity forced change.

In Australia, too, private irrigation development began with riparian rights. However, government leaders in Victoria decided that the state ought to determine water allocation and, led by Deakin, passed the path-setting 1886 Irrigation Act, which was copied by other states over the following 30 years. As the British were promoting farmers' organizations to manage irrigation canals in Indo-Gangetic basin (Stone 1984), they were also lending to irrigation trusts in Victoria—somewhat as the Narmada Corporation is now trying to do in Gujarat, India, by asking farmers to organize into water user associations to build distribution systems. However, Victoria's irrigation trusts met the same fate that water user associations in South Asia regularly meet today: their canals were overcapitalized and underutilized, and their managements could not collect water fees to defray their costs. By 1905, all irrigation trusts were insolvent and abolished, and the government took over their operation and maintenance. The new Water Act of 1905 gave the government a more active construction role and, ironically, issued a *compulsory* "water right" to each farmer, the charge payable regardless of use. Contrary to the colonial strategy in India of promoting extensive, sparsely applied "protective" irrigation to ease moisture stress, Victoria's new law encouraged intensive, "productive" irrigation in closely settled compact family farms of 50 acres each. Twenty years later, these were found "too small to provide sufficient income to support a family" and a consolidation program was initiated. By the 1930s, the ideas of protective irrigation as well as prior appropriation had resurfaced. The idea of closely settled, intensively irrigated areas came, went, and returned several times during the twentieth century. Whereas in the United States, vested rights became central to water allocation, in Australia, licenses issued by the government became the principal instrument for water allocation (Davis 1968). But in both countries, orderly allocation of water among water users was achieved through some form of institutional mediation from the nineteenth century on. In South Asia, except for the *wara bandi* in Indus systems, nowhere else were orderly, institutionally mediated water allocation arrangements evident in canal systems.

By the 1950s and 1960s, when the colonial era was drawing to a close in Asia and Africa, European irrigation initiatives in different parts of the world were in different evolutionary states. In Australia and the United States, a vibrant high-value, export-oriented industrial agriculture based on scalar economies had emerged on the bedrock of secure water rights. In Africa, the disciplinarian organization of Gezira-type schemes in the estate mode of agricultural production had become prevalent. In the Middle East and Central Asia, new, more ambitious irrigation ventures were undertaken with modern technology. Egypt retained a modified version of the estate mode with the central government directing and micromanaging cropping patterns, irrigation schedules, procurement of crops, but also modified its distribution system to force farmers to lift water from *mesqas* (ditches that delivered water from canals) in favor of the basin irrigation they had practiced for ages (Hunt 1986). In Southeast Asia, as population grew, irrigation expansion for rice production continued apace without the benefit of any institutional model for sustainable operation and management. In South Asia, in the Indus irrigation system, *wara bandi* was practiced but it had begun gradually weakening; elsewhere (including in some Southeast Asian systems) *wara bandi* was tried but failed. Other systems of demand-based allocation, such as *osra bandi* (supplying water by rotation based on orders placed by farmers), were tried in western India but without much success. In southern India, localization was the standard irrigation planning and management tool; the crops to be grown in different parts of the system were specified by its managers (Mollinga 2003). But none of these irrigation systems were designed to support differentiated supply (Perry in Prasad 2003, 366), nor were the institutional arrangements suited to the changing socioeconomic reality of agrarian South Asia.

The Halo of Constructive Imperialism, 1948–1970

In British India, colonial irrigation enterprise created a strong civil engineering profession that dominated postcolonial thinking about irrigation. Early irrigation works were designed and executed by military engineers who came from Britain. However, as irrigation engineering became more professional, "the progress in science had outrun the rule of thumb methods," and scientific research and investigation were needed to replace "engineering judgment based on experience" (Central Board of Irrigation and Power 1992, 57). To meet these exacting standards, civil public works departments were established at Delhi and at provincial levels. The government of India became the first to employ civil engineers in large numbers for public works. It was also the first to initiate formal education in civil engineering. A college was established in 1848 in Roorkee (named Thomason College of Civil Engineering in 1854) to train the civil engineers needed to manage massive construction works for the colonial government. In 1871, a new engineering college was established at Coopers Hill in England with funding from the government of India to train British engineers for the irrigation construction boom in India. Punjab also became fertile ground for applied research in irrigation engineering. In 1924, an irrigation research laboratory was established at Lahore University, and in 1930, a full-fledged irrigation research institute began making contributions to the engineering of river works, weirs, barrages, surface water hydraulics, canal hydraulics, distribution, and reclamation of waterlogged and saline soils.

By the time the British left after partition, civil engineering was revered. Arthur Cotton's statues dotted the hinterland in Cauvery and Krishna basins, and Proby Cautley enjoyed demigod status in the Ganga basin. Colonial irrigation ideology—and a distinct "colonial hydrology," considered by many at odds with native water-harvesting practices (D'Souza 2006)—was official doctrine in independent India, Pakistan and Sri Lanka.[21] Engineers trained at Roorkee and Cooper's Hill felt "a new sense of professional mission, and one linked intimately to colonialism." Their mission was ennobled by the "disinterested service to science that empowered the self-image of many engineers as engaged in a moral enterprise" (Gilmartin 2003b, 5058). Leaders of free India, like Pandit Nehru, reinforced this feeling by declaring the Bhakra dam a "temple of modern India." The Gandhian ideas in *Hind Swaraj (Indian Self-Rule)* of self-sufficient villages and the *Swadeshi* ("locally made") movement permeating India's freedom struggle deeply influenced mainstream Indian thinking in many spheres but could not shake the foundations of the colonial irrigation ideology.

Although ancient and medieval India was home to myriad innovations in manipulating water at local scales, and more advanced science and engineering were evident in occasional gigantic structures (Agarwal and Narain 1997), it was during the colonial times that India became a standard-bearer for the world in the application of modern science in design of large and complex irrigation systems. "Among the important technological innovations were masonry headworks, drainage networks, the elimination of erosion and silting by calculating optimal gradients, and of course barrages and weirs making perennial irrigation possible" (Christensen 1998, 22).

The end of British rule in the subcontinent led to the creation of Pakistan, and the bulk of the public irrigation network the British had created ended up in the new nation. India then initiated a string of irrigation projects in quick succession. Indeed, more than 90 percent of public investments in agriculture during the first 40 years after India's independence were devoted to the construction of government dams and canals (Kishore 2002). From 1970 to 1985, irrigation projects in India and Pakistan claimed the lion's share of some US$20 billion lent by the World Bank globally (Briscoe and Malik 2006; Faures et al. 2007).

At the time of independence, a dispute arose between India and Pakistan over the waters of the Indus basin. In a remarkable feat of hydrodiplomacy, the World Bank brokered the Indus Treaty in 1960 that assigned the Ravi, Beas, and Sutlej rivers to India and the Indus, Chenab, and Jhelum rivers to Pakistan. Its survival dependent upon the Indus basin irrigation system, Pakistan took up the challenge of improving its storage in earnest. Both countries embarked on canal construction campaigns, and by 1976, Pakistan had created the largest continuous irrigation system in the world, diverting

105 million acre-feet of water to irrigate 14.6 million ha. Water projects in former East Pakistan (today's Bangladesh) were smaller and focused on flood control.

Even though colonial irrigation ideology continued to hold sway, the relationship between the state and the farming communities began to change. For centuries until the end of the British rule, despite frequent excesses and rent seeking, there had been an unequal but strong economic mutuality in the engagement between the state and the peasantry—in all revenue areas.[22] Since revenue and its administration were central to the affairs of the medieval and colonial state[23] (Gidwani 2002), a sizable apparatus was necessary.[24] Land settlement and revenue assessment before irrigation made these into instruments of "prescription and control" (Mollinga 2003, 68). The hard colonial state ensured that rules were enforced, fees and taxes were collected,[25] and public infrastructure was maintained. Even if only to ensure stable and growing land revenue, resources were found to sustain the productivity and performance of irrigation structures.

Freedom from colonial rule and the rising ethos of a welfare state transformed this relationship of mutuality into a paternalistic one. Farmers—oppressed over the centuries—were now viewed increasingly as "beneficiaries" of development programs rather than sources of revenue. In India as well as Pakistan, land reforms failed to provide land to the landless; however, they also led to the erosion of the apparatus for revenue administration as well as the authority relationships between the state and the peasant. Land taxes and other levies were abolished in many states in India; in others, these retained a token value. Colonial revenue administration and the roles of the collector and district magistrate were also transformed; instead of being revenue administrator-in-chief, the collector became the chief overseer of a development administration. Once a powerful agent of the state, the village-level revenue official was now little more than the record keeper for the village. A large organization to collect land revenue, irrigation charges and other levies was no longer justified: the collection was too small to support the cost of collecting.[26]

In India, traditional authority structures that maintained order and even played quasi-judicial functions were replaced by new, modern *Panchayati Raj* structures of democratic and participatory governance at local levels. These elected councils had constitutional legitimacy but neither resources nor authority to provide effective local governance. In Pakistan, the institution of *lambardar* (a major local landowner who collected government revenues, including irrigation charges) was retained; however, for all other purposes, governance at the village level was a vacuum. This vacuum—in authority and in organization—had myriad implications for the maintenance of public infrastructure as well as land and water resource use. Even as new irrigation projects were being built, the performance of existing systems everywhere in the region began to decline, by every criterion.

Irrigation administration also underwent changes. In Pakistan, the Irrigation Department, which during colonial times had been the fountainhead of all engineering and management innovations, was reduced to operation and maintenance. New legislation created the Water and Power Development Authority, a federal agency responsible for the development of all water and power infrastructure. The Indus irrigation system was so designed that, when water was released, it automatically delivered predetermined volumes of water through *pucca* outlets of differing sizes. This self-acting proportionality concept of Crumps, around which the Indus irrigation system was built, required that the hydraulic configuration of the system, down to the outlet size, be maintained intact—something that the depleted Irrigation Department could not do. Even several donor-assisted modernization projects could not arrest its decline, let alone reverse it (Van Halsema 2002).

Under the colonial irrigation enterprise, building irrigation canals and selling water had been a profitable business for the government, which exacted levies on canal-irrigated lands, the canal water rate, and a "water advantage"—besides of course the regular land revenue. Whitcombe (2005) estimated that returns on the irrigation investments of the government of British India increased from 8.3 percent on productive works and 4.5 percent on all major works in 1912–13 to 12.8 percent on productive works and 7.2 percent on all major works in 1945–46. This calculation, based only on water charges collected, does not include the "water advantage" revenue.[27] By 1960, India and Pakistan had turned this profitable enterprise into a loser. Through the 1960s and 1970s, the World Bank supported construction of numerous irrigation systems, whose regular maintenance and upkeep—and associated resources—implied a systemic discipline that the "soft" welfare states of independent India and Pakistan could not impose. Vote-bank politics took their own toll; irrigation charges remained stagnant and uncollected; and system maintenance was continually deferred (Ebrahim 2004). Constructive imperialism's ethos of "build—manage—generate surpluses—maintain" gave way to a "build—neglect—rebuild" syndrome.

Moreover, the overt justification for investments in public canal irrigation—to stabilize agriculture and improve food security—came under increasing scrutiny during the 1960s and 1970s. Although colonial irrigation investments concentrated in the Indus basin helped West Pakistan to remain food secure at the national level, India and East Pakistan (later Bangladesh) continued to face serious food crises. During the mid-1960s, as its dependence on PL 480 food aid from the United States brought growing international embarrassment, the limits that colonial irrigation ideology imposed on India's capacity to feed its people were becoming evident.

When India finally began her Green Revolution during the late 1960s, it was small boreholes and pumps that helped spread the fruit of the revolution to every corner of the country. B. D. Dhawan, a senior Indian economist, noted that the Green Revolution followed tube well revolution (Dhawan 1982). Some years later, Robert Repetto (1994) was to assert that the Green Revolution, often called a wheat revolution, might also be called a tube well revolution. This tube well revolution, which marks the third, and the most recent, era of evolution of South Asian irrigation, took off only in the late 1960s and by 2000 had swept through South Asia. But it had actually started decades earlier.

Sir William Stamp's Legacy

In the early years of the twentieth century, Punjab witnessed an unusual rivalry among British and Indian engineers employed with the provincial government. Through most of the nineteenth century and early decades of the twentieth century, Punjab was a fertile ground for pathbreaking applied engineering research and experiments in designing canal structures and intersections and minimizing siltation of channels and reservoirs. Above all else, however, the challenge for the Punjab engineers was waterlogged soil and the associated buildup of salinity that all but nullified the gains from canal irrigation development. Waterlogging in Amritsar had forced people from the town, which experienced a decline in population during the first decade of the twentieth century (Randhawa 1983). It was waterlogging that spurred research in the design of tube well strainers.

An efficient, sturdy, durable strainer was the key to making tube wells a cheap and reliable alternative to open wells. In conjunction with the newly available oil engines and electric pumps, tube well technology was a breakthrough comparable to that of the Persian wheel, introduced to northern India in the twelfth century. And a breakthrough was badly needed. After growing rapidly in the closing years of the nineteenth century, the area irrigated by wells in Punjab and United Provinces had stagnated for nearly 40 years. The Royal Commission on Agriculture lamented that well irrigation in British India watered 4.68 million ha in 1902–03 and only 4.73 million ha in 1925–26 (Government of India 1972). Oddly, although the government offered drought-stricken farmers low-interest loans *(taccavi)* and a reduced land tax to those who invested in wells, the use of diesel engines and electricity for lifting water was already growing, even large farmers in Punjab were reluctant to try tube wells.

The breakthrough in northern India's well irrigation economy came not in Punjab but in United Provinces, where during the early 1930s Sir William Stamp established the tremendous power of a simple technology (CBIP 1992). Hydroelectricity from the Ganga canal prompted the government to promote electric pumps for tube wells as well as lift irrigation. From 1931 to 1934, a hundred tube wells were sunk in Meerut, Moradabad, and Bijnor districts, and all were successful. This led Sir William to allocate Rs. 12.6 million for sinking 1,500 tube wells all over United Provinces. Awakened to the potential of the new device, in 1936, Punjab deputed A. M. R. Montague to learn from the tube well experience of United Provinces and subsequently began prospecting for groundwater in Gurudaspur and the upper reaches of Western Yamuna Canal (Government of India 1972). By the end of the 1930s, tube wells numbered some 10,000 in the province (Islam 1997).

Parts of Tamilnadu and central Gujarat were early to adopt mechanized electric and diesel-powered pumps on open wells, especially in response to growing opportunities for marketing valuable commercial crops. In Madras, for instance, "rich peasant middlemen, who gained most from cotton boom, were quick to sink their earnings into wells. Recorded wells multiplied 80 percent between 1850 and 1871 and another spurt occurred after 1890 when they increased 60 percent in one decade. Wells multiplied as commercial conditions favored families who could benefit from well irrigation in different parts of Tamilnadu" (Agarwal and Narain 1997, 285).

However, development of mechanized well irrigation remained sporadic and patchy throughout the 1940s and 1950s. Roy (2007) has recently argued that lagging investment in public irrigation and the slow adoption of well irrigation were prime factors behind the stagnation in Indian agriculture, and indeed the economy as a whole, during the interwar period. From the 1930s onward, following United Provinces, many state governments in India established public corporations to realize this potential of irrigation from tube wells and mechanized pumps. These established large-capacity government tube wells manned by operators employed by the corporations. To serve command areas of 50 to 150 ha, public tube wells in many states were built with buried pipe distribution systems. In Uttar Pradesh, which operated by far the largest public tube well program among Indian states, the World Bank introduced two technological improvements during early 1970s: a dedicated power line to insulate public tube wells from power outages, and an 8-shaped buried distribution system with *pucca* (concrete) outlets for blocks of eight hectares of the command area.

The main objective of the public tube well programs was to encourage the use of tube well and modern mechanical pump technologies. Also important, however, was promoting equitable access to irrigation. Tube well technology was capital intensive, and farms had to be large to make it economically viable; most Indian farms were small. To achieve the aims—and to maintain parity with canal irrigation—public tube well programs everywhere supplied irrigation at heavily subsidized rates. In Pakistan and along Satluj-Jamuna canal in Uttar Pradesh, India, public tube wells were established for a totally different reason—to alleviate the secondary salinization caused by canal irrigation without adequate drainage. Heavy-duty tube wells pumped groundwater into canals, thereby lowering water levels in waterlogged areas and increasing water availability for irrigation in the tail ends of the system. This was the origin of the Salinity Control and Reclamation Project (SCARP) in Pakistan Punjab and Sind during the 1950s and 1960s.

Studies during the 1970s and later began showing that although public tube well programs everywhere met with some initial success, their unreliability and politicization soon turned them into resounding failures (P. Jones 1995; Kolavalli et al. 1989; Pant 1991, 1994). SCARP tube wells in Pakistan too met the same fate (Steenbergen and Oliemans 1997). However, despite all these faults, these programs had served an important if unintended purpose: demonstrating the productive value of modern tube well irrigation. Almost everywhere, the initial success of public tube wells became the reason for their failure, as smaller private tube wells—and the private markets in pump irrigation service that soon emerged in and around their service areas—competed with public tube wells (Shah 1993, 2001). The most telling proof of this came from Uttar Pradesh, where Ballabh (1987), Pant (1984, 1991), Singh and Satish (1988), and other researchers found private tube well owners selling superior irrigation services to their neighbors in and around public tube wells. In Pakistan Punjab and to a lesser extent in Sind, well irrigation was widely practiced throughout the first decades of twentieth century. However, it was after the SCARP program began that tube well technology experienced rapid growth, around 1965.

The Era of Atomistic Irrigation

Just how rapid was the spread of the pump irrigation economy since 1970 is indicated by the growth in the numbers of mechanized pumps and irrigation wells, which we refer to throughout this book as water extraction mechanisms (WEMs). These may include electric or diesel pumps used to lift water from boreholes, open wells, or even rivers and ponds. In India, they numbered fewer than 200,000 around 1960; official estimates for 1994 suggested 14 million (Government of India 2001). An all-India census of small irrigation structures, completed in 2001, counted some 18.5 million (Government of India 2005a). Moench (2003) projected that the number of WEMs in India would be 21 million in 2000 and grow to 27 million by 2007. A 1998 survey carried out by the Government of India's National Sample Survey Organization (NSSO 1999a) sampled 48,649 farm households and found that 25.8 percent owned WEMs. Extrapolating means that the 82 million cultivator households in India owned at least 21.3 million WEMs in 1998, 120 times more than they owned in 1960. The natural corollary is a boom in pump manufacture. Until 1970, Indian pump industry produced only a few thousand units per year; from 1978 to 1982, the industry grew at 15 percent per year, and since then it has grown about 20 percent per year (Prasad and Sarkar 1994). In the early 1990s, India's 500 or so pump manufacturers, large and small, were delivering a million irrigation pumps each year.[28]

In Bangladesh, whose groundwater revolution lagged a decade behind that of India and Pakistan, the number of shallow tube wells soared by a factor of eight in 20 years, from 133,800 in 1985 to 1,182,525 in 2006 (Mandal 2006); in addition, there were more than a million manual water lifting devices (Shah et al. 2000a). In Pakistan, the number of private tube wells grew 28-fold, from 32,585 in 1965 to 627,879 in 2002 (Qureshi et al. 2003) and reached 932,000 in 2004 (Government of Pakistan 2006). Since the average size, in terms of pump horsepower, of a Pakistani WEM is three times that of the WEMs used elsewhere in South Asia (Shah et al. 2006), Pakistan has in effect the equivalent of some 2.7 million WEMs. All in all, WEM numbers in India, Pakistan, Bangladesh, and Nepal Terai went from a few hundred thousand in the 1960s to more than 23 million in 2000. And the trend shows no sign of peaking. A survey of 2,600 WEM owners sampled from India, Pakistan Punjab and Sind, Nepal Terai, and Bangladesh showed that more than half of these WEMs were installed after 1990 (Shah et al. 2006). All available evidence suggests that during the early years of the new millennium, a million new WEMs were being installed in the region every year.

Another indicator of the explosive growth in pump irrigation is the rapid increase in irrigated area dependent on WEMs. Irrigated area can be calculated as *net* or *gross:* 100 ha of land under irrigation yields 100 ha of net irrigated area, but if the land is irrigated for three cropping seasons in a single year, it yields 300 ha of gross irrigated area. And irrigation intensity of 170 percent means that for every 100 ha under irrigation, 100 ha were irrigated for a single season and 70 ha were irrigated for an additional cropping season.

In India, WEM-irrigated area doubled from six million ha in 1950–51 to 11.9 million ha in 1970–71 and further increased to 33.3 million ha in 2000 (Government of India 2005b). The village directory data in the 2001 population census estimated net area irrigated by wells and tube wells at 30.2 million ha. The 2001 minor irrigation census released by the Government of India in 2006 showed the gross area irrigated by WEMs to be 53 million ha, implying an irrigation intensity of more than 170 percent under well irrigation. In Pakistan, with the world's largest continuous surface irrigation system in the lower Indus basin, dependence on lift irrigation from wells has grown by leaps and bounds. According to the Pakistan Economic Survey for 2006–07, between 1990 and 2006, area irrigated by groundwater lifted by WEMs grew by 38 percent, and area irrigated by groundwater in conjunction with flow irrigation rose 32 percent, but area dependent on gravity-flow irrigation from canals fell by 11 percent. By 2006, WEMs were involved in 12 million of Pakistan's 19 million ha of irrigated lands (Ul Hassan et al. 2007). Official data from the Government of Pakistan show that in Punjab, which grows 90 percent of Pakistan's food, 60 percent of the farmers depend on WEMs for delivering irrigation water to their crops, and 40 percent of the crops' water requirements is met by WEMs (Qureshi and Barrett-Lennard 1998). Independent surveys suggest that WEMs likely play a larger role. A 2001 survey of 180 farmers in Rechna Doab in Punjab showed that more than 70 percent received 80 to 100 percent of their irrigation water from WEMs (Qureshi et al. 2003). In Bangladesh, the farming area supplied by groundwater wells increased from a few thousand ha in 1980 to 2.5 million ha in 2000 (Bangladesh Bureau of Statistics 2000). In the 60-year period leading up to 2000, India, Pakistan, and Bangladesh increased the net area irrigated by lift irrigation from wells 10-fold, from 5.3 million ha to 53.6 million ha (Table 1-2).

As Table 1-2 shows, during the 30-year period from 1970 to 2000, the Indian subcontinent added more irrigated area than it had during the previous 170 years of intensive canal building. Of the 46.6 million ha of net irrigated area added, 39.7 million ha, or 85 percent, was created by farmer-built WEMs. Finally, even as the share of "other sources" in irrigated area has stagnated, the irrigation factor—that is, the percentage of net cultivated area under irrigation—has risen fastest during the past 30-year period, from 31.7 to 53.5 percent. After 1970, the irrigation initiative, which the state had controlled throughout the era of constructive imperialism, began slipping into the hands of small farmers.

A third indicator of the change in irrigation is relative shares of groundwater wells to surface irrigation projects, which claimed the lion's share of public irrigation investments. In India, net area irrigated by groundwater WEMs rose from 28 percent in 1950–51 to 61 percent in 2000 (Government of India 2005b). But this government estimate is dwarfed by large-scale surveys. In 2003, India's National Sample Survey Organization asked 51,770 cultivators from 6,770 villages for the source of irrigation they used in *kharif* (rainy season crops) and *rabi* (winter crops); the response was that 69 percent of *kharif* acreage and 76 percent of the *rabi* acreage were irrigated with wells or tube wells (NSSO 2005). In Bangladesh, WEMs—primarily shallow tube wells—accounted for less than four percent of the irrigated areas in 1972 but 70 percent by 2000[29] (Bangladesh Bureau of Statistics 2000). And in Pakistan, where canal irrigation had crowded out wells during the colonial period, in 2001–02, of the gross irrigated area of 18.3 million ha, only 6.8 million ha was served exclusively by canals; 7.5 million ha, or 41 percent, was served by

Table 1-2   Transformation of South Asian irrigation in India, Pakistan, and Bangladesh, 1800–2000: net area (million ha) by irrigation source

	1800	1850	1885–86	1938–39	1970–71	1999–2000
Government canals	<1	~1.0	2.8	9.8	24.2	31.2
Wells	2.0	2.6	3.5	5.3	13.9	53.6
Other sources	4.0	4.4	3.0	6.4	6.8	6.7
All sources	6	7	9.3	21.5	44.9	91.5
Irrigation factor[a]	10	10.3	12.4	25	31.4	53.5

[a] Irrigated area as percentage of net sown area.

Sources: Rosin 1999; Roy 2004; Bangladesh, India, and Pakistan governments

"canal tube wells and wells" and 3.4 million ha, or 18.6 percent, by wells and tube wells outside canal commands (Government of Pakistan 2003). Even though Pakistan has the world's largest continuous flow irrigation system, WEMs are involved in 60 percent of irrigated areas.

As a direct outcome, the volume of groundwater extracted every year is growing commensurately. Information is scarce and numbers speculative, but a reasonable estimate is that until 1960, groundwater extraction for agricultural use in South Asia fluctuated between 12 km^3 in wet years and 25 km^3 in dry years, enough to provide 1,200–2,500 m^3 per ha to around 10 million ha of cropped area supported by supplemental well irrigation. In 2000, however, at 210–230 km^3/year (Planning Commission 2007), groundwater use in Indian irrigation had grown manifold. In Bangladesh, a profusion of shallow tube wells has fueled a *boro* (presummer) rice revolution, and around 20–22 km^3 of groundwater is used to grow this crop on its 3.5 million to 4 million ha of gross area irrigated by wells. Pakistan's gross agricultural groundwater use has soared from less than 10 km^3 in 1970 to more than 55 km^3 in 2000 (Qureshi et al. 2003), and recently the World Bank (2005a) estimated that 75 percent of the value of its gross farm production depended on pumping out canals and natural recharge to the fields. All in all, then, from 1960 to 2000, annual gross groundwater extraction in South Asia increased to about 285–300 km^3, easily 10 times what it likely was in 1960.

Conclusion: Irrigation Management Transformed

Around 1900, R. C. Dutt articulated the prevailing thinking about how irrigation should develop in different parts of India:

> Every province in India has its distinct irrigation requirements. In the alluvial basins of the Ganges and the Indus the most suitable irrigation works are canals from these rivers; while away from the rivers, wells are the most suitable. In Bengal with its copious rainfall, shallow ponds are the most suitable works and these were the numerous in the olden times, sometimes of very large dimensions. In Madras and Southern India, where the soil is undulating and the underlying rock retains the water, the most suitable irrigation works are reservoirs made by putting up large embankments and thus impounding the water descending from hill slopes. Such were the old reservoirs of Madras. (Dutt 1904, vol. II, *119*, n. 1)

For millennia, irrigation in the subcontinent had remained largely faithful to those prescriptions. The adaptive, minimalist, unobtrusive irrigation in Mughal India of 1800 reflected South Asia's hydrogeologic makeup. Constructive imperialism took liberties with the regime, but it was nevertheless endorsed in 1970 by India's second Irrigation Commission.[30] But in the 1970s, a new era of *atomistic irrigation*[31] unfolded. Small-pump irrigation spread everywhere in South Asia: in canal commands and outside their borders, in arid and semiarid and humid areas, upstream and downstream in river basins, in excellent alluvial aquifers as well as in poor, hard-rock peninsular aquifers with limited storage potential. In all those regions of eastern and southern India where Buchanan, Willcox, O'Malley, and Hunter had found little or no trace of well irrigation around 1900, groundwater had become the mainstay of smallholder agriculture. If the engineers of the era of constructive imperialism had tinkered with the hydrology of river basins, farmers in the era of atomistic irrigation went about reconfiguring it totally.

The role of the state and the community in irrigation has undergone a profound transformation. In precolonial India, cooperation at the community level was the dominant irrigation institution. Under colonial rule, collaboration between the state and the engineering profession drove irrigation development. Beginning in the 1970s, government officials and engineers became onlookers in a game whose rules and logic they did not understand, much less dictate. It was the multitude of smallholders—Marx's "millions of disconnected production units"—each with his tiny, captive irrigation system, ostensibly unconnected with the rest, who had become the managers of irrigation.

In the mid-1970s, when Pol Pot and the Khmer Rouge were forcing professors, teachers, doctors, and administrators to dig canals and build dykes to create 1.5 million ha of irrigation by force in Cambodia, smallholders in South Asia, 2,500 km to the west, were adding millions of hectares of irrigation every year of their own free will, and mostly at their own cost.

Tube wells with small pumps transformed irrigation. With surface water irrigation, farmers had to wait for water to be released and flow through a network of canals before reaching their crops; now, water could be scavenged on demand and applied whenever crops needed it. And this technology has redrawn South Asia's irrigation geography, taking it out of command areas of canals and tanks and spreading it to throughout the subcontinent. But it has also transformed the sociology, economics, and politics of irrigation. After 200 years of supply-driven irrigation expansion, South Asia's irrigation development has turned demand driven, giving a whole new meaning to the term irrigation management.

CHAPTER 2

RISE OF THE COLOSSUS

The causes of events are ever more interesting than events themselves.

— *Cicero*

The history of irrigation is the story of farmers' struggle to break free of the hydraulic limits imposed by gravity and open channel flow. The first constraint meant that valleys and lowlands were easier to irrigate than catchments and uplands. The second meant that without siphonage, it was difficult to make water travel across undulating terrain, and although farmers today can make small siphonlike mechanisms using flexible pipes, siphons once required major engineering works. Together, the two limitations defined the irrigation possibilities of reservoirs and channels. During the past 50 years, affordable pumps, boring rigs, and PVC and flexible rubber pipes have overcome these limits and changed the nature of irrigation across the Indian subcontinent. Drilling shallow boreholes and deeper tube wells and using pumps to lift the water, South Asia's smallholders developed three times more gross irrigated land in 30 years than constructive imperialism had in 150 years, and they recaptured the irrigation initiative from the state.

An important yet unresolved question is what drove this change, and why the new technology failed to produce a similar boom in South America or sub-Saharan Africa. The groundwater revolution in South Asia has been attributed to water scarcity in dry regions that were otherwise suitable, in terms of climate and soils, for agriculture.[1] This explains the emergence, during the twentieth century, of intensive agricultural groundwater use in regions like the western United States, Spain, and Mexico, but is South Asia's groundwater boom really a part of the same agroclimatic phenomenon?

In this chapter, I posit that the groundwater boom in South Asia is different, energized by the growing scarcity of farmland more than water. I also show that this boom—which is socioecological more than agroclimatic— is best understood in the wider context of the agrarian transition under way throughout monsoon Asia. Governing Asia's groundwater economies effectively demands a fuller understanding of the socioecological dimensions of this unique phenomenon.

The only other region of the world that has experienced anything comparable to the South Asian groundwater phenomenon is the 350,000-km^2 area of the lower Yellow River basin in the North China Plain. Whereas South Asia's groundwater irrigation history goes back millennia, here it is all of 50 years old. For centuries, farmers here grew three rain-fed crops of maize and cotton in a two-year cycle (Changming et al. 2001). Under Chairman Mao, China built more canals and dams during 1950s and 1960s than the British built in their Indian empire in 200 years, and by the late 1960s, most of China's irrigation depended on surface water from 7,100 reservoirs impounding half of the country's stream flow. Soon, however, the rapidly growing demand for water from industries and growing cities made surface water less available for irrigation in the plain, even as the agrarian population expanded.

Thus began the pump irrigation boom of the North China Plain. It inched forward during the 1970s, surged during droughts, and spread like wildfire during the 1990s. The region's groundwater boom is even less well documented than South Asia's, but the speed and scale of its spread are striking. By 1980, for example, in the Hai and lower Yellow river basins, groundwater wells were already irrigating double the area served by surface irrigation (Ronghan 1988). By the mid-1990s, groundwater accounted for 65, 70, 50, and 50 percent of total agricultural water supply in Beijing, Hebei, Henan, and Shandong provinces, respectively (State Statistical Bureau of PRC 2000).

Estimates of the number of water extraction mechanisms (WEMs) and the area served by them in the North China Plain vary widely. The Food and Agriculture Organization (FAO Aquastat 2003) reported some 8.5 million ha of groundwater irrigation in China. But according to Zhengying (1994), China had more than 11 million ha under groundwater irrigation and 2.48 million WEMs in the early 1990s. In 1997, a Chinese government source counted some 3.3 million WEMs irrigating 14 million ha (Shi 2000). Another government source around the same time put the figures at 3.5 million WEMs and nearly 15 million irrigated ha in just the Hai and Lower Yellow river basins (State Statistical Bureau of PRC 2000). According to yet another source, Zhou Weiping (1997) of the Central Ministry of Water Resources, in 1995 Chinese agriculture used 9.13 million irrigation pumps, diesel and electric, to irrigate 16.7 million ha; 7.32 million pumps were owned by households, 1.69 million by collectives, and 0.12 million by government.[2]

Clearly, the 1990s saw a big surge in WEM irrigation in the North China Plain. According to the 2002 Statistical Year Book of China, nationally, the number of pumps owned per 100 households grew more than fivefold, from 3.86 in 1990 to 19.92 in 2002, with the North China Plain's average much higher than the national figure (State Statistical Bureau of PRC 2000). Around 2000, the plain had a higher density of WEMs than even India, where one of every four farm households owned a WEM (NSSO 1999a).

And yet those WEM figures may be underestimates. Researchers from the Beijing-based Chinese Center for Agricultural Policy surveyed village leaders from 60 counties, 126 townships, and 448 villages in six North China Plain provinces[3] (Wang et al. 2007) and estimated that the actual number of irrigation wells in the plain is two to three times the official estimate of 4.5 million. Furthermore, they estimated that 68 percent of the 34.3 million ha of North China Plain's irrigated areas—that is, some 23 million ha—is served by WEMs, and that, as in South Asia, the region's pump irrigation juggernaut was still accelerating as of 2004 (Wang et al. 2007). The groundwater boom witnessed here during the 1990s was no less dramatic than that in South Asia.

Groundwater irrigation played a critical role in sustaining prosperous agriculture in many areas of the western United States, Mexico, the Mediterranean, and Australia for decades. By the mid-1980s, however, South Asia had surpassed other regions in annual groundwater use and groundwater-irrigated areas. Actual historical use of groundwater for agriculture is speculative, even in industrialized countries. However, Figure 2.1, constructed with information

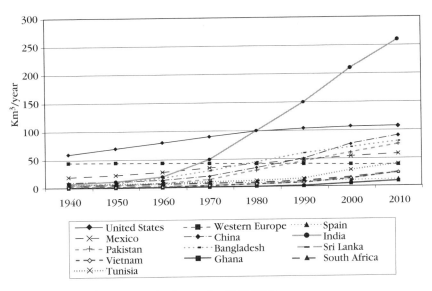

Figure 2.1   Groundwater extraction by country, 1940–2010

available from several independent researchers, indicates the trajectory of growth in annual gross groundwater removals in the major groundwater-irrigating countries of the world (Shah 2005). By the mid-1980s, India had already become the largest groundwater user in the world. And by 2000, South Asia alone had more area under groundwater irrigation than all the rest of the world combined, even according to FAO Aquastat's decidedly conservative figures, some based on outdated data provided by national governments.

Recent government censuses and large-scale surveys in India, China, and Bangladesh show that well irrigation continued to grow during the early years of the new millennium (NSSO 1999a, 2003). All this evidence suggests that instead of FAO's estimate of 69 million ha, more likely some 100 million to 110 million ha of gross cropped area globally was under groundwater irrigation around 2000, most of it in South Asia and the North China Plain. Quantifying the increase is just the prerequisite for improving groundwater governance, however; it is also important to understand why it has occurred.

Drivers of Intensive Groundwater Irrigation

Multiple propositions seek to explain what has driven groundwater usage in South Asia and the North China Plain. There is the technology theory, which considers the small mechanical pump the irrigation technology of the millennium (Sakthivadivel 2007; Shah et al. 2001a). Its easy availability facilitated intensive groundwater irrigation on a scale impossible with the Persian wheel (e.g., Llamas and Custodio 2003). Another proposition gives credit to the virtues of irrigating with groundwater rather than surface water: the generally good quality of groundwater, its greater reliability and availability during droughts, its virtual ubiquity and ease of distribution, and above all, the low capital cost and short payback period of WEMs. A third proposition, based on the Indo-Gangetic experience during the 1960s, is that WEM irrigation is convenient and cost-effective in canal commands and unsustainable outside them; using this logic, proponents see a "complementarity relation between public investments in canal irrigation and private investment" in WEMs (Dhawan 1996a, *538*).[4] Post-1970, however, WEMs spread all over South Asia. According to India's minor irrigation census in 2000–01 (Government of India 2005a), only 12 percent of groundwater wells in the 578 districts covered were in canal commands. Moreover, as we will see in Chapter 3, even within South Asia's canal commands, WEMs are increasingly substituting for canal irrigation rather than complementing it. A fourth proposition credits favorable government policies and equipment subsidies. A fifth emphasizes the spread of rural electrification, especially subsidized electricity, but this overlooks the fact that more than 80 percent of WEM irrigators in the Indo-Gangetic basin—encompassing parts of Pakistan, India, Nepal Terai, and Bangladesh—depend on diesel pumps because they have no access to electricity, subsidized or otherwise. And no other method of irrigation in South Asia is more expensive than lifting groundwater with a diesel pump.

All the above supply-side propositions, however valid, still do not fully explain why pump irrigation spread in South Asia and the North China Plain but not in Africa or South America. Perhaps hydrology can provide better answers. Exploring why only some regions of the world have adopted intensive groundwater use in agriculture yields the following four working rules:

1. Intensive groundwater irrigation would emerge primarily in arid and semiarid areas that satisfy other preconditions for productive agriculture but do not have enough rainfall or surface water (the U.S. Great Plains, Spain, Central Mexico).

2. It would be uncommon in humid areas with abundant soil moisture and surface water because of the absence of a felt need for irrigation (South America, Central Africa).
3. It would be uncommon in regions with poor aquifers that are costly to develop and offer low, uncertain yields often of poor quality water (southern Africa).[5]
4. It would decline on its own in a region as depleted aquifers become prohibitively costly to tap for irrigation or yield poor-quality water (parts of the U.S. West, Saudi Arabia).

Those four working rules of hydrogeology explain much about agricultural groundwater use across the globe—except in South Asia. According to the logic of Rule 2, humid Bangladesh, North Bihar, eastern Uttar Pradesh, North Bengal, Assam and the 20 districts in the Terai areas of Nepal should have no need for well irrigation, and as we noted in Chapter 1. And although northwestern colonial India had known well irrigation for centuries, it was conspicuous by its absence throughout eastern parts of colonial India and Nepal Terai. These regions, within the Ganga-Brahmaputra basin, are as humid as Southeast Asia, Central Africa, or South America: each year more than 1,400 billion cubic meters of floodwater spreads over a territory of 1.1 million km^2. Nevertheless, these regions have experienced growth in WEMs since the early 1980s, in violation of Rule 2 and, by implication, Rule 1.

Rule 3—that intensive groundwater irrigation would not emerge in regions with poor aquifers—has also been violated in South Asia. Peninsular India, which accounts for 65 percent of the country's territory, is underlain mostly by hard-rock formations, primarily Deccan trap basalts and granitic basement complex, yet extensive areas are irrigated with groundwater. And even as these poor aquifers are developed beyond their limit, further groundwater development continues apace in most parts of this region. Rapid growth in well irrigation exploiting karst aquifers in northern and eastern Sri Lanka is also in violation of Rule 3. Many would suggest that energy subsidies in peninsular India have made the farmer immune to the soaring costs of pumping groundwater from hard-rock aquifers. This explanation sounds logical, but I argue later in this book that energy subsidies are now a result, rather than a cause, of the groundwater irrigation expansion.

Finally, as we explore in a later chapter, groundwater depletion and quality deterioration are widespread throughout South Asia. Rule 4 predicts that long before the depleted aquifers themselves constrain development, the economics of overexploitation should do it.[6] In California, Texas, Kansas, Idaho, Nebraska, and New Mexico, large areas formerly irrigated with groundwater went out of irrigation in recent decades as pumping costs became prohibitive (Shah 2006a). During the 1930s and 1940s, farmers growing sorghum and cotton in the high plains of Texas drilled wells to irrigate these crops. Since the benefits of supplemental irrigation were high, full irrigation must be even better, and there ensued a rapid increase in the number of irrigation wells as farmers sought to maximize yields per ha. Later, however, declining water tables and rising energy costs forced farmers to cut back on groundwater use and revert to supplemental irrigation and, eventually, 50 years later, to rain-fed farming (Oweis et al. 1999). Yet there is little evidence that self-regulation, as predicted by Rule 4, has begun to operate on a significant scale anywhere in South Asia or the North China Plain—at least not yet.

The region has bucked a trend that would otherwise explain the global geography of groundwater irrigation. Clearly, forces other than the agroclimatic and hydrogeologic are at work.

Pump Irrigation Revolution Farther East

South Asia's pump irrigation boom represents a confluence of the age-old well irrigation tradition in West Asia and the semiarid Mediterranean and the new wave of pump irrigation expansion arising from the east. Well irrigation is a response to water scarcity, but pump irrigation reflects the quest of monsoon Asia's smallholders to overcome the hydraulic limits imposed by gravity and open channel flow. The mode of field-level water mobilization and delivery—rather than its source, either groundwater or surface water—is transforming irrigation in monsoon Asia. For millennia, induced irrigation development required sustained community cooperation or sustained coercion by overlords or the state. Now, millions of smallholders can have autonomous irrigation. No longer a civil engineering feat, as it was when Sir Arthur Cotton set his sights on the Grand Anicut during 1830s, irrigation in South Asia consists of millions of tiny operations. For understanding this irrigation anarchy, the ascent of pump irrigation over gravity flow as the dominant mode of delivering water has greater significance than the rise of ground over surface water.

For a keen observer, this transformation in the making is becoming apparent throughout monsoon Asia. A striking case is Sri Lanka, known for its traditional tank irrigation of rice paddies. Irrigation pumps were unknown here until the 1980s but numbered some 106,000 by 2000 (Kikuchi et al. 2003).[7] Farmers' intent was to lift water from whatever source was available—wells, tanks, streams—to irrigate dry-season rice and vegetables. Vietnam's story is similar. In 1990, 0.9 million ha of Vietnam's total 5.1 million ha under irrigation was watered by lift irrigation using water wheels and foot pumps (Le Van Hien 1994). But the number of diesel pumps used for irrigation soared from about 20,000 in 1988 to more than 800,000 in 1999. Between 1995 and 1999 alone, Vietnamese farmers purchased 300,000 irrigation pumps (Molle et al. 2003). At this rate, Vietnam likely has 1.5 million to 1.6 million irrigation pumps in use today. In Thailand, irrigation pumps numbered 500,000 in 1985 but more than three million in 1999. Here too the acceleration has been recent; between 1996 and 1999, Thai farmers purchased a million irrigation pumps (Molle et al. 2003).

Observers have been surprised by the spread of pump irrigation in Southeast Asia. In the Chao Phraya delta, 80 percent of farmers may have at least one pump, and in Thailand's Mae Klong project, the World Bank (1991) estimated that in the early 1990s, a million pumps were drawing water from canals, drains, ditches, and ponds to irrigate dry-season crops. Regarding the Makhamtao-Uthong canal system in Chao Phraya, Facon (2002, 23) wrote, "Use of groundwater for irrigation has exploded during the last five years. It is reported that 28,000 tubewells are in use in the region . . . All the farmers interviewed during the field visit reported having individual pumping equipment used to pump from any possible source of water." In the Philippines, Dawe (2004, 2) noted that "approximately 23 percent of rice farms now use pumps to access water, either from sub-soil reservoirs, drainage canals, or natural creeks and rivers. Among these sources, groundwater is the most important." Laos has no recorded history of lift irrigation with mechanized pumps, yet in a 2003 speech, Sanjay Kirloskar, the chairman of Indian pump maker Kirloskar Bros., asserted, perhaps questionably, that the pumps supplied by his firm to Laos had "brought a phenomenal change in the country's economy, with hundreds of thousands of hectares being irrigated. Rice production increased by 25 times. Today Laos can export rice to other countries."[8]

The evidence extends across the region. According to Indonesia's Central Bureau of Statistics (Government of Indonesia 2004), between 1998 and 2002, the number of irrigation pumps increased from 1.17 million to 2.17 million. At 17.5 percent per year, the compound rate of growth in irrigation pumps was higher than that for all other farm machinery. Abi Prabowo et al. (2002) argued that rapid expansion in groundwater irrigation with small pumps in East Java helped small farmers increase cropping intensity, diversify to other crops, and above all shift from protective to productive irrigation. In Myanmar, the number of 5- and 8-hp pumps sold by the government monopoly to farmers increased from 5,126 in 1970 to a cumulative total of 76,888 in 1993. Many of these are installed on boreholes, but they are also used to lift water from channels and waterways—again, to help farmers diversify their wet-season rice-dominated cropping system and grow other crops, such as dry-season rice, wheat, cotton, beans, and pulses (Aung 1994). These trends in pump sales are matched by the rapid ascent of the Chinese diesel pump industry in global markets at the expense of Indian, Japanese, and Korean manufacturers. The Chinese, who have pared the cost as well as the weight of their diesel engines to a fraction of their competitors' products, export some four million diesel pumps annually; at 1 hectare per pump, these are adding around four million ha of pump irrigation every year, mostly in South and Southeast Asia.[9]

In the Indian subcontinent, pump irrigation is no longer confined to open wells and tube wells: pumps are now used in canal and tank commands to supplement gravity irrigation through open channel flow, to lift from surface water bodies, and to recycle seepage water from canals and tanks. In Bangladesh, until the 1970s, gravity flow or manual lift from ditches was the most common practice. Between 1979–80 and 1999–2000, however, the area under mechanized pump irrigation in Bangladesh rose from 15 percent of the total irrigated area to 86 percent: 71 percent from shallow tube wells and 15 percent from surface water (Dawe 2004). From east to west, the share of surface water in pump irrigation is declining, but everywhere in Asia, pump irrigation and pipe conveyance are supplanting gravity irrigation and open channel conveyance. In Pakistan, open wells and tube wells accounted for more than half of the growth in total irrigated area until the early 1980s, and from 1982 to 1995, they accounted for all of the growth, with the area irrigated by gravity flow from canals declining in absolute terms (Dawe 2004). In the Indian Punjab, we know that more than half of the water farmers pump from their wells is recycled canal water (Dharmadhikari 2001;

Dhawan 1993), and this has been the case in many other Indian states as well (Dhawan 1989). In the Mahi Right Bank Irrigation System in central Gujarat, several thousand private pumps are used to lift water to irrigate large areas through elaborate networks of buried pipelines (Choudhury 2006).

Pumps and pipes are rewriting the rules of water distribution in canal commands. In the newly constructed Sardar Sarovar Irrigation Project on River Narmada in Gujarat, the state government has tried hard, without success, to persuade water user associations to build distribution systems below the outlet while the government constructs a lined canal system going up to the outlet serving an area of 400 ha. However, even as irrigation water began flowing into the main and branch canals, tens of thousands of private pumps have begun operating on the banks of minor canals and distributaries. The owners of these pumps are farmers, who besides irrigating their own fields sell pump irrigation services to other farmers, using flexible rubber pipes (Talati and Shah 2004). Something similar is happening in upper reaches of Krishna basin in Maharashtra, where the government is building dams and releasing water in the river at regular intervals. Thousands of pumping stations—owned by private entrepreneurs, lift irrigation cooperatives, sugar cooperatives— have taken over the role of distributing water to farmers (Choudhury and Kher 2006; Padhiari 2006).

Tank irrigation systems are changing, too. Throughout southern India, farmers pump water accumulated in wells from recharge from irrigation tanks instead of using the flow irrigation from those tanks (Sakthivadivel et al. 2004; Shah et al. 2001b; Seenivasan 2003; Rao et al. 2003). Their ability to pump the recharge from tanks is also transforming the socio-ecology of the large irrigation tanks built by kings and overlords in Rajasthan (Shah and Raju 2001) and the famous Chandeli tanks in Bundelkhand in central India (Shah 2003a); as a consequence, the centuries-old norms for managing gravity-flow irrigation have been weakened. Small pumps are also encouraging a wastewater irrigation economy in the peripheries of South Asian cities.[10] Studies in many Asian and African countries show that pump irrigation from wastewater channels accounts for more than 50 percent of urban vegetable supplies (IWMI 2003). In Pakistan, most wastewater irrigators were landless laborers renting land at high rates and practicing intensive vegetable cultivation using pump irrigation from wastewater canals.

Whether irrigation pumps are used to lift water from ground or surface sources, their arrival marks a new water-scavenging irrigation economy.

Having broken free of the hydraulic limits of gravity and open channel flow, Asia's smallholders are scavenging water from whatever source is available at different times of the year to maximize the potential from their land. Hydrogeologic and agroclimatic factors certainly have a role in this drama, but the driver of the water-scavenging irrigation economy is different.

Malthus, Boserup, and Monsoon Asia's Pump Revolution

The pump revolution in South Asia is best viewed as an atomistic response by smallholders to population pressure on farmland. Until the close of the nineteenth century, South Asia had abundant arable land and too few hands available to work it. Even during the 53-year period from 1885 to 1938, net cultivated area in British India increased by 32 percent while the rural population grew by a mere 13 percent. However, by the mid-1950s, arable land was becoming scarce, and farm population per hectare of net cropped area in South Asia, a little over three around 1940, increased to 4.7 in 1975 and 5.6 in 2000. In many parts of the region, especially toward the east, 10 or more people now eke out a living from farming a hectare of land.

Some 200 years ago, British philosopher Thomas Malthus (1798, I.I.5) wrote, "Through the animal and vegetable kingdoms, nature has scattered the seeds of life aboard with the most profuse and liberal hand. [But] she has been comparatively sparing in the room and the nourishment necessary to rear them." Nowhere else did this come truer than in monsoon Asia post-1970, where, for the first time in history, the land-person ratio went seriously awry. But Malthus had left open a small escape route: "The main peculiarity which distinguishes man from other animals, is the means of his support, and the power which he possesses of very greatly increasing these means." The small pump and borehole enabled smallholders in monsoon Asia to increase their means.

In a little 1965 volume, a Danish economist reversed the Malthusian causality by proposing that agricultural productivity growth is the result, and not the cause, of population pressure, as Malthus had theorized. In Esther Boserup's scheme, the "adjustment variable" was the frequency of land use:

> . . . the process of agricultural intensification under population pressure consists in the taking into use of much more effective techniques that come into existence through a gradual change of the environment: a forested landscape

becomes a landscape of fields with shorter and shorter fallow, dry land becomes irrigated, hilly land terraced . . . the increasing population gradually transformed the environment, and this led to a different diet and new techniques of cultivation. (Boserup 1999, *20*)

With mounting population pressure, Boserup argued, societies make a transition from extensive land-use systems to intensive agriculture—that is, from forest-fallow cultivation to bush-fallow cultivation to short-fallow cultivation to annual cropping and finally to multiple cropping. Intensification is driven by the seasonal availability of surplus labor. In seventeenth and eighteenth century Europe, the response to growing population pressure on farmlands was the system of cultivating fodder and hand-feeding cattle, which emerged to absorb idle "off-season" labor. This is happening in twenty-first century South Asia, where agricultural intensification is based on the use of surplus family labor and scavenged water to permit a higher frequency of land use. In 1960, farmland in much of South Asia produced only a single crop per year. The monsoon kept the farmer of rain-fed crops productively occupied for barely five months, but with shrinking land holdings, enforced idleness during the remainder of the year was becoming a life-or-death issue. F. L. Brayne, Punjab's deputy commissioner for agriculture, observed 80 years ago that with a share in a well, "the farmer is busy for three more months" (cited in Roy 2007, *5396*).

Very low population pressure on farmland makes even gravity-flow irrigation uneconomic, but above a population threshold, pump irrigation drives out gravity flow. The rise and decline of tank irrigation in South India illustrates its inverted U-shaped relationship with respect to population density. Von Oppen and Subbarao (1987) showed that, left to itself, tank irrigation in a region becomes feasible and attractive only when population density exceeds 50 to 60 persons per km^2; below that, extensive rain-fed farming is sufficient. However, they also found that tank irrigation declines once population density exceeds 220 persons per km^2. Recent trends in India support this finding because, subject to the hydraulic limits of gravity and open channel flow, tank irrigation fails to support the intensification necessary to keep a larger population fed and employed. Contrary to Boserup's caveat on her own thesis—that investments in further intensification may not be forthcoming at high rates of population growth—South Asian farmers have invested in pumps and boreholes in their struggle to increase land productivity as population pressure grows.

Boserup's caveat has swayed many a researcher. In Bangladesh, Boyce (1988, 11) observed, based on doctoral fieldwork during the early 1980s, "Population pressure may well have played an important role in the development of irrigation in many Asian settings but the low level of irrigation in Bangladesh today, where demographic pressures are exceptionally intense, makes it clear that population pressure alone is not sufficient to ensure irrigation development." But the absence of irrigation in Bangladesh in the early 1980s suggests that population pressure was insufficient for the society to forge voluntary or coercive cooperation to build and manage large-scale reservoirs and canals. Once pumps made irrigation possible without such cooperation, the scenario changed. More than 50 percent of Bangladesh's net sown area today is irrigated, overwhelmingly by small pumps and boreholes.

Hayami and Ruttan's (1971) theory of induced innovation predicts that population growth will drive the direction and pace of technological change in ways that economize on or augment a society's relatively scarce resource endowments. During the nineteenth century, they argued, innovations in Japanese agriculture were predominantly biochemical, and in the United States, they were predominantly labor-saving mechanical improvements. The direction South Asian irrigation has taken is validating Hayami and Ruttan's theory. The prime need here was to raise the productivity of scarce farm land by using all available idle resources, including labor and water. Increasing the frequency of cropping is one approach, and it demands high-frequency, just-in-time watering. Gravity-flow irrigation, which had proved its utility in stabilizing the *kharif* crop raised in most of South Asia during the rainy season or *rabi* or a summer crop in snowmelt-fed canal systems of the Indo-Gangetic basin, was largely insufficient for increasing land-use intensity. Pump irrigation boom could increase land productivity through "land-augmenting" and "labor-absorbing" effects simultaneously.

Tube well technology had been known to South Asia since early years of the twentieth century, and oil engines and electric pumps had been used for irrigation in many parts of India since the 1920s. Subsidies for digging wells, *taccavi* loans and other inducements were offered by the colonial government beginning in the 1880s and on an accelerated basis after 1903, when the first Irrigation Commission began encouraging well irrigation. Governments began promoting groundwater irrigation through public tube well programs in mid-1930s. After Independence, support for groundwater development through subsidies and loans was on the agenda of all state governments. All these helped popularize boreholes and mechanized pumps.

But it was the post-1975 demand at the farm-household level to make better use of land and labor that drove growth in pump irrigation. Public irrigation programs—focused on developing surface water where technically feasible—failed to respond to this urgency. Moreover canal irrigation did not reach even a substantial proportion of the region's smallholders outside command areas. Left to fend for themselves, they turned to the small pump and tube well.

The relation between population pressure and pump irrigation is nowhere more evident than in the Ganga-Brahmaputra-Meghana basin, which has witnessed the fastest spread of pumps and shallow tube wells in South Asia: here, the farmland available per capita fell from 0.35 ha in 1880 to 0.19 ha in 1970 and to 0.15 ha in 1980 (Sikka and Gichuki 2006). By the mid-1990s, when pumps were becoming common, per capita cultivable land was less than 0.1 ha. The pump revolution enabled farmers to stretch their tiny land holdings to provide subsistence for their families.

What groundwater wells offer that tanks and canal systems do not is year-round irrigation on demand and thus the ability to grow multiple crops. A proximate indicator of multiple irrigated crops grown in a year on a representative hectare of irrigated land is irrigation intensity. In India, irrigation intensity grew in step with the increase in the share of groundwater-irrigated area to net irrigated area between 1950 and 2000 (Figure 2.2). In 1950–51, the groundwater share of irrigated areas in India was less than 30 percent, and irrigation intensity was 108 percent. In 2000, the groundwater share increased to 61 percent; in response, irrigation intensity grew to 137.4 percent. For South Asia as a whole, agricultural intensification helped counter population pressure: between 1938–39 and 2000, rural persons per net irrigated hectare increased 83 percent from 3.06 to 5.6, but rural persons per gross irrigated hectare increased only 21 percent, from 3.06 to 3.7. Pump irrigation compensated for the stinginess of nature.

This is also true of other Asian countries. Sri Lanka, Vietnam, Nepal, Laos, Thailand, Cambodia, and China face similarly high population pressure on farmlands,[11] and the increase in pump irrigation is comparable to that in South Asia—or even greater, as in the North China Plain. That pumps are used in these countries more often to scavenge water from surface sources or seepage matters not for our hypothesis—that agrarian societies seeking to intensify land use because of population pressure will move from flow irrigation to lift irrigation. Each of these countries yields compelling evidence to support this hypothesis. Pump irrigation in Vietnam is concentrated in the densely populated south, for example. Pump irrigation in Cambodia

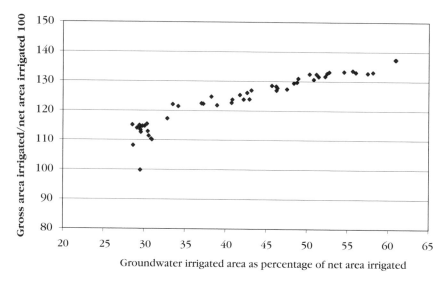

Figure 2.2   Irrigation intensity and growth in groundwater irrigation, India, 1950–2000

is concentrated in its southwest, where tiny rice paddies predominate, while the large land holdings in the northwestern provinces still use Angkor-style gravity-flow irrigation. And the tube well boom in China is concentrated in the densely populated North China Plain. Figure 2.3 illustrates the relationship between pump irrigation and population density for the districts of India and Pakistan. As the rural population per 100 ha of net cropped area increases across districts, the proportion of cropped area under pump irrigation rises.

We find high pump density throughout the Indo-Gangetic plains, where some of the most densely populated areas of the world float over one of the world's largest and best aquifer systems. However, pump density is equally high in many parts of southern and western India; nowhere near as well endowed with groundwater as the Ganga plains, these regions are densely populated and therefore have high WEM density. In contrast, thinly populated central India has relatively low WEM density. Likewise, in Pakistan's Punjab province, the density of WEMs increases as one moves from sparsely to densely peopled districts (Qureshi et al. 2003).

That pump irrigation is driven by land scarcity rather than water scarcity is at odds with a popular hypothesis holding that because tube wells are capital intensive, tube well irrigation is likely to manifest scale bias, with large, capitalist farmers racing ahead of the smallholders to exploit ground-

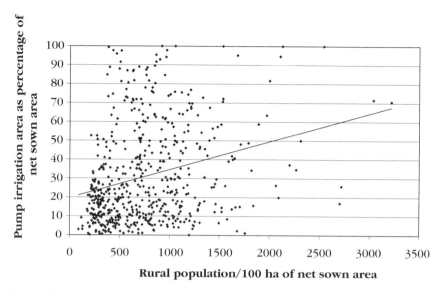

Figure 2.3   Pump density and population density in the districts of India and Pakistan Punjab, c. 2000

water (see, e.g., Ebrahim 2004). At least in South Asia, the opposite is true. Studies in Bangladesh over the past decade have noted that small and marginal farmers dominate ownership of shallow tube wells, and their share has been rising during recent years (Mandal 2000). Evidence from India supports the same thesis. Figure 2.4 traces the pace of expansion in groundwater irrigated areas under different farm-size categories using the Government of India's five-yearly agricultural census from the 25 years since 1970–71. Over this period, marginal and small farmers—who suffer higher levels of "disguised unemployment" with their shrinking rain-fed farm holdings—expanded pump-irrigated areas much faster than medium and large farmers. In India in 1995–96, marginal and small farmers, cultivating only 36 percent of the country's farmlands, accounted for 80 percent of all cultivators but owned nearly half of the wells and pumps, suggesting a *reverse* scale bias in pump irrigation technology. The smaller one's landholding, the greater the need for intensification, and more likely that one owns a WEM.

The linear view—that South Asia's groundwater revolution is a response to growing water scarcity, as in the western United States, Central Mexico, much of the Middle East and North Africa, and Iran—is then incomplete, if not erroneous. On a continuum that begins with land-starved Southeast

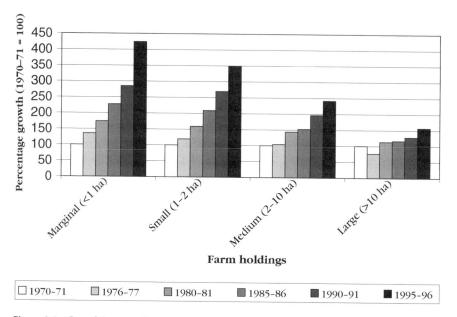

Figure 2.4   Growth in groundwater-irrigated area by farm size, India, 1970–1996

Asia and ends with water-scarce West Asia and the Middle East and North Africa, South Asia lies in the middle, with the worst of both extremes: its pump irrigation is a response to the scarcity of both farmland and water-on-demand.

Intensive Diversification of Farming

Other drivers have served to heighten the Bosrupean response. In many parts of monsoon Asia, the population engaged in farming has begun to decline not only in relative terms but also in absolute terms. Chinese agriculture is already undergoing this agricultural transformation. At the turn of the millennium, Indian agriculture, which had witnessed a relative decline in agricultural population since the 1950s, for the first time registered an absolute decline in farming population. Yet in much of South Asia, it will take decades before population pressure on farmland eases; until then, farmers' husbanding of land, labor, capital, and water resources will continue to be driven by their need to generate more livelihood per unit of land. The intensification of farming based on pump irrigation is evident in the growing popularity of *boro* (presummer) rice in Bangladesh and West Bengal (Bose 1999), dry-season rice in Sri Lanka, Thailand, Laos, and Vietnam, and multiple cropping of land in the rest of South Asia.

Growing differences between urban and rural living standards in many Asian countries, especially China and Thailand, have begun to encourage intensive diversification of agriculture, especially near urban areas. Diversified mixed farming, in which farm households combine field crops, vegetables, orchards, and livestock, has always characterized subsistence agriculture in Asia. With pump irrigation and multiple cropping, farmers acquired further scope for synergies in the mixed farming format to raise land productivity. The 1990s, however, are witnessing a new trend of *intensified* diversification. Growing urban demand for higher-value foods, such as fruits and vegetables, dairy and other livestock products, and plantation crops like rubber and coconut supported further intensification of land use (Rao et al. 2004). Year-round water-on-demand offered by WEMs is encouraging this trend as gravity irrigation by canals and tanks could not.

A good illustration is the rapid expansion in dairy production in India over recent decades. Compared with cereals and pulses (beans), dairy, poultry, and inland fishery production in India has grown at a faster rate throughout the 1981–2000 period (Joshi et al. 2004). Indeed, milk has replaced rice as the biggest "crop" in Indian agriculture. The stimulus was provided by western India's dairy cooperatives, which created strong and stable markets. Farmers responded to the stimulus not by taking up dairy farming as a specialized enterprise but by reorienting their mixed farming systems in favor of intensive dairy production. Doing this required allocating relatively small areas to cultivating green fodder, with weekly irrigation for eight or nine months every year (Kumar et al. 2004b). No flow irrigation system is designed to release water to hundreds of small fodder plots in a village 35 to 40 times a year, but WEM irrigation can meet the need for frequent applications of small quantities of water. Traditional flow irrigation is more commonly associated with irrigation of cereals, mostly rice and wheat.

A similar example is the recent transformation of Kerala agriculture. Kerala invested in surface irrigation projects for paddy irrigation throughout the 1950s and 1960s. However, facing growing labor scarcity, the Kerala farmer has moved away from paddy cultivation and sown plantation crops that thrive with small doses of irrigation, normally provided with small pumps and domestic open wells (Neetha 2003; Viswanathan 1997). So crucial are small doses of on-demand irrigation that the agrarian poor in many areas started manually scavenging for water. In Bangladesh, smallholders bought more than a million treadle pumps during the 1990s, mostly to irrigate vegetables for the market on tiny plots of land, before they began buying cheap Chinese diesel pumps (Shah et al. 2000a).

Expansion of vegetable cultivation, especially near urban centers, and the growing popularity of subsistence dairy and poultry farming are examples of the intensive diversification made possible by water-scavenging irrigation with WEMs. These enterprises yield higher income per unit of land and absorb more family labor but also require more frequent and controlled application of water. Districts that lead in such intensive diversification have smaller average landholdings, higher population density, proximity to urban demand centers, and lower tractor density (Rao et al. 2004). They typically also have a smaller proportion of gross cropped area under irrigation but a higher proportion of irrigated area served by WEMs. Where such intensive diversification expands, pump irrigation, especially with reliable groundwater, becomes a critical adjunct to farmland, slowly reducing the significance of gravity flow.

In 1967, Ishikawa described irrigation as the leading input or the binding constraint for growth of paddy productivity in monsoon Asia. Ishikawa (1967) identified four stages of irrigation-led productivity growth. In the first stage, rain-fed yields remain low and variable, thanks to the vagaries of the monsoon. In the second stage, supplemental irrigation stabilizes paddy yields. In the third stage, irrigation increases land-use intensity through use of fertilizers and high-yielding varieties. In the last stage, when yield per ha as well as land-use intensity reach their limits, irrigation promotes multiple cropping. Today, Ishikawa would likely add a fifth stage—the intensive diversification of farming. Because the productivity dividend of seed-fertilizer technology has plateaued and until 2007 international rice prices had been falling, paddy farming throughout monsoon Asia has been declining in profitability and rice farmers have been diversifying in favor of high-value products.[12] Reliable irrigation-on-demand, supplied by tube wells and pumps, is what enables a transition to this fifth stage. By permitting multiple cropping, pump irrigation in monsoon Asia after 1970 likely added the equivalent of 50 million to 60 million ha of farmland and the equivalent of 70 million to 75 million ha in farm income through higher, more secure yields of traditional and high-value crops.

A Typology of Global Groundwater Socioecologies

We can now revisit our task of considering South Asia's groundwater irrigation socioecology in a broader global context. There are four types of large-
scale groundwater use situations in agriculture and livestock production
around the world (see Table 2-1): arid agrarian systems, industrial agricultural systems, groundwater-supported extensive pastoralism, and smallholder intensive farming systems (Shah et al. 2007). These differ from one
another in their overall climatic, hydrologic, and demographic parameters,
their land-use patterns, their organization of agriculture, and the relative
importance of irrigated and rain-fed farming. Also different are the drivers
of expansion in groundwater irrigation and the nature and level of society's
stake in its groundwater-irrigated agriculture.

Arid agrarian systems. The mostly arid countries in the Middle East and North
Africa have low population pressure on land and a tiny fraction of their geographic area under cultivation. Here, intensive groundwater use in agriculture is a response to water scarcity. Farming is dependent upon irrigation,
mostly from fossil and some renewable groundwater, which is the predom-
inant source for all needs (World Bank and Swiss Agency for Development
Cooperation 2000). However, growing competition for the limited resource
from higher-value uses, especially urban water supply and high-value crops,
has emerged as a resource governance issue in these regions. The "virtual
water thinking"[13] pioneered by Allan and others (Allan 2003; Delgado et al.
2003; Warner 2003) applies best to arid agrarian systems, which can conserve nonrenewable water by importing water-intensive foods instead of
growing them locally. Planning the use of fossil groundwater—even with
large reserves, such as the Nubian aquifer—in agriculture involves different
criteria than those used for managing renewable groundwater. Home to
some of the oldest hydraulic civilizations in the world, most of the region is
long past the limits of irrigation growth. As Allan (2007, 64) has pointed out,
"the most significant feature of [Middle East and North Africa] groundwater
management has been the revelation that groundwater resources are never
sufficient to underpin food self-sufficiency."

Industrial agricultural systems. In industrialized countries—such as Spain,
Italy, the United States, and Australia—groundwater has become increasingly
important for meeting the water needs of large-scale agriculture. Here, too,
intensive groundwater use is a response to water scarcity. Irrigated agriculture
is a small proportion of total agriculture, groundwater irrigation is often a

Table 2-1 Global typology of groundwater use in agriculture and animal husbandry

System	Arid agrarianism	Industrial agriculture	Smallholder intensive farming	Extensive pastoralism
Region	Middle East and North Africa[a]	U.S., Australia, Spain, Italy, Mexico	Monsoon Asia[b]	West and sub-Saharan Africa
Groundwater-irrigated area	<6 million ha	15 million ha	>100 million ha	>500 million ha of grazing land
Climate	Arid	Semiarid	Semiarid to humid; monsoon	Arid to semiarid
Water resources per person	Very small	Good to very good	Moderate to good	Moderate to good
Population pressure on agricultural land	Low to medium	Low to very low	High to very high	Low, with high pressure on grazing areas
Percentage of geographic area under cultivation	1–5%	5–50%	40–60%	5–8%
Percentage of cultivated areas under irrigation	30–90%	2–15%	40–70%	>5%
Percentage of irrigated areas under groundwater irrigation	40–90%	5–20%	10–60%	<1%
Percentage of geographic area under groundwater irrigation	0.12–4.0%	0.001–1.5%	1.6–25.0%	<0.0019%[c]
Organization of agriculture	Medium size, market-based	Industrial, export-oriented farming	Smallholder farming and intensive diversification	Small-scale pastoralism, smallholder farming
Driver of groundwater irrigation	Lack of alternative irrigation	Wealth-creating agriculture	Land-augmenting, labor-absorbing agriculture	Stock watering
Groundwater contribution to national economy	Low: <2–3% of GDP	Low: less than 0.5% of GDP	Moderate: 5–20% of GDP	Moderate: 5–20% of GDP
Groundwater contribution to national welfare	Low to moderate	Low to very low	40–50% of rural population, 40–80% of food supply	High for extensive pastoralism, domestic water supply, and smallholder agriculture
Groundwater contribution to poverty reduction	Moderate	Very low	Very high	Central to pastoral livelihoods
Gross output supported by groundwater (US$)	$6–8 billion	$100–120 billion	$250–300 billion	$2–3 billion

[a]Iran, Iraq, Libya, Tunisia, Morocco, Turkey, Algeria, Egypt

[b]India, Pakistan, Nepal, Bangladesh, North China, Afghanistan

[c]Groundwater-supported grazing areas for stock watering are about 17% of total area (Giordano 2006)

Sources: FAO Global Map of Irrigated Areas (http://www.fao.org/ag/agl/aglw/aquastat/irrigationmap/index.stm, FAO Aquastat 2003)

tiny fraction of irrigated agriculture, and the proportion of the total population tied to groundwater-based agrarian production is minuscule. Groundwater use under the industrial agricultural system has caused severe aquifer depletion and pollution issues but is highly productive and contributes to massive wealth creation. For example, California's US$90 billion agricultural economy depends heavily on groundwater use, as does a large part of Spain's export economy of grapes, olives, citrus, other fruits, and vegetables. Equally, such countries bring to bear vast financial and scientific resources to ameliorate the problems of groundwater abuse arising from intensive irrigation and agriculture. It is here that much of today's scientific and institutional knowledge base for sustainable management of groundwater has evolved and been tested (Burke and Moench 2000).

Groundwater-supported extensive pastoralism. Concentrated in sub-Saharan Africa and, to lesser extent, Latin America, this system draws on a modest groundwater resource, only a very small proportion of which is currently developed, to support the extensive pastoral tradition (Giordano 2006; Sonou 1994). Here, groundwater extraction per hectare is small, used mainly for stock watering. The absolute numbers of poor people dependent on this system may be small compared with those who depend on groundwater-irrigated agriculture in Asia. Yet, as a proportion of African population, pastoralists are a substantial group. In Africa, where improving rural livelihoods is a persistent challenge, relatively small groundwater withdrawals support many poor rural families (Masiyandima and Giordano 2007).

Smallholder intensive farming system. Finally, in much of monsoon Asia, groundwater irrigation—like pump irrigation in general—has been driven by heavy population pressure on farmland, especially since 1975. Smallholder intensive farming differs from the other three systems in that it has, over recent decades, reached the limits of cultivable areas; the only way to increase the carrying capacity of agriculture is by squeezing more from shrinking holdings through intensive diversification—which a farmer can do by scavenging for water with WEMs. Whereas in the other three socioecologies, groundwater is spread on just 0.1 to four percent of the geographic area, in the Indo-Gangetic basin, up to a quarter of the total area is under groundwater irrigation. In terms of groundwater quantity and numbers of people involved, India, Bangladesh, Nepal, Pakistan, and China have experienced the largest growth in groundwater use during the past 35 to 40 years. Of the global annual groundwater diversion of 950 to 1,000 km³ for different uses, 60 percent or more likely supports agriculture in these countries. It is the WEM-based water-scavenging irrigation that defines the resource management challenge here. True, supply-side factors, such as government subsidies for pumps and electricity, helped promote intensive groundwater irrigation, but the primary driver is the rise in population pressure on farmland, which has made intensive diversification a precondition for smallholder subsistence.

Conclusion: Asian Irrigation in Transition

In Dharawi, the Bombay slum considered the largest in Asia, population density in some places can approach a million people per km². Amid its squalor, Dharawi's residents operate a booming informal economy whose productivity is measured in business turnover per m². Daily resource allocation choices here use freely available inputs—labor, garbage, plastic waste—but stringently economize space, the scarcest resource. Similarly, South Asian agriculture during the recent years has evolved into a vast agrarian ghetto in which smallholders struggle to sustain their livelihoods by liberally using underemployed family labor, freely scavengeable water, and such other inputs to make their tiny parcels of land work overtime. That the smallest farming households are capturing growing shares in quality milk animals and irrigation wells is symptomatic of this ghettoization of agriculture.

Intensive groundwater use in agriculture may mean different things at different levels[14]: at the level of a field, it may mean high application of groundwater per hectare; at the level of a village or a district, it may mean a large proportion of cropped area under groundwater irrigation; at the level of an aquifer, it may mean groundwater extraction as a high proportion of sustainable yield; and at the level of a region or a country, it may mean large proportion of the total farming area and population dependent on groundwater irrigation. South Asia has intensive groundwater use in agriculture under all these different definitions, except perhaps the first. Unlike the arid and industrial agricultural socioecologies, much of the smallholder system of South Asia uses groundwater irrigation to supplement either rainfall or flow irrigation.

Pump irrigation in South Asia is a phenomenon that cannot be fully explained by the historical experience of arid and semiarid countries. The driver is as much the scarcity of farmland as it is the need for year-round, on-farm water control, which permits intensive diversification of subsistence farming. Water extraction mechanisms have helped monsoon Asia's small-holders make their tiny landholdings work harder for them. In the western United States, with precisely the opposite land-person ratio to South Asia's, groundwater irrigation was catalyzed by center-pivot irrigation technology, which made it possible for a single laborer to irrigate as much as 2,000 acres and popularized groundwater irrigation across the U.S. West (Ashley and Smith 2001; Nagaraj et al. 2000).

Africa and Latin America, despite their lower population density, have also seen the emergence of intensive pump irrigation pockets, but in grow-ing periurban areas where people find profitable opportunities for intensive diversification of subsistence farming—in this case, market-oriented veg-etable cultivation. However, these are unlikely ever to experience the inten-sive groundwater irrigation of the South Asian kind. This is not "because the hydro-geologic formations underlying most of sub-Saharan Africa are not of the type necessary to supply large-scale water resources development" (Masiyandima and Giordano 2007, 79) but because this region will not face South Asia's population pressure.

Many analysts of irrigation in South Asia have focused on the *source* of water—that is, groundwater versus surface water. More important for future resource management is the *mode* of farm-level water mobilization and deliv-ery and its sociotechnical and resource governance ramifications. As pump irrigation replaces gravity-flow irrigation, age-old notions of managing irriga-tion and irrigation agriculture are losing their relevance.

The greatest challenge to South Asia's irrigation business model comes from the ascent of this atomistic irrigation. Induced irrigation development, with the state or the community as the initiator, investor, architect, builder, and manager, has given way *to autonomous* irrigation, with millions of small-holders undertaking individual entrepreneurial initiatives. When irrigation development was supply led, irrigation water was available only when pro-vided, and farmers adapted. Now, irrigation expansion follows a demand pull: water is scavenged at will by farmers from the nearest source when it is needed, and the old command areas determined by the hydraulic limits of gravity and open channel flow, are increasingly irrelevant. Pump irriga-tion has spread upstream and downstream of river basins, unconstrained by topographic constraints. In the gravity-flow irrigation regime, farmers' fortunes were determined by the effectiveness of centralized management of large irrigation works and the quality of community cooperation in tank irrigation; the pump has reduced their vulnerability to the vagaries of centralized management and defunct water user associations. Millions of pump irrigators have become proactive, empowered irrigation players, exercising far greater control on their tiny irrigation economies than they ever enjoyed before. This irrigation has eroded the capacity of the state to maintain order in the appropriation and allocation of water, but it has enabled smallholders to meet an epochal demographic challenge.

CHAPTER 3

THE FUTURE OF
FLOW IRRIGATION

The development of irrigation has outrun its administration . . .
— *Col. W. Greathed, Chief Engineer, Upper Ganga Canal, 1869*

Gravity-flow irrigation has dominated irrigated agriculture around the world for millennia. As with all complex sociotechnical systems (Trist 1991; Uphoff 1986; Vincent 2001), to work well, gravity-flow irrigation has required, generated, and nurtured a "culture of irrigation" among irrigators. Social order and patterns of cooperative behavior have determined crop choice, irrigation scheduling, maintenance work, sharing of costs and responsibilities, distribution and allocation of water in abundance and scarcity, and compliance with rules, norms, and authority. The irrigation regimen was so central to shaping the social lives of irrigators sharing the same source that anthropologist Robert Hunt (1989) called such groups irrigation communities. With large gravity-flow systems constructed by the state, system design and centralized operation acquired greater significance. Nevertheless, catalyzing and nurturing irrigation communities among diverse irrigation groups over the command area remain important around the world.

But as a sociotechnical system, gravity flow as a mode of irrigation is in decline in South Asia. For decades, groundwater and surface irrigation here grew in tandem. Surface irrigation systems were always underutilized, and typically only a fraction of the designed command was actually irrigated soon after the completion (Daines and Pawar 1987). Repetto (1986, 4) foresaw the problem when he wrote that "public irrigation systems themselves are sinking under their managerial, economic and environmental problems." However, even the skeptics did not foresee the new threat to public irrigation systems from the rise of atomistic irrigation. After 1975, even as surface systems continued claiming a large share of public investment in irrigation, their relative share in the area irrigated began to fall, and by the 1990s, the area irrigated by gravity-flow works began to show an absolute decline. Small surface irrigation structures, notably tanks in southern India and Rajasthan and *ahar-pyne* systems in southern Bihar, had been losing irrigated area since the 1950s. Now, the loss of area served by large irrigation systems marked the onset of a fundamental change.

A chapter on gravity-flow irrigation may appear to deviate from the main story of this book, but the apparent deviation is very much a part of my story. The performance of surface irrigation—and the agencies in charge of its management—has been a matter of much concern in the region. This is not a recent concern; David Seckler issued a warning 25 years ago: "As the rug of irrigation development is rolled out ahead through construction of new facilities, it will roll up behind through poor maintenance and management of existing facilities" (cited in Wade 1984, 286). The answer, analysts and policymakers aver, is infusion of fresh capital in modernizing irrigation systems—such as the Accelerated Irrigation Benefit Program initiated in India and the major new investments Pakistan has planned in lining watercourses in the Indus basin.

This chapter suggests that bolder thinking is in order. It argues for rethinking the role of surface water structures in the rapidly changing irrigation context of South Asia. As a sociotechnical system, flow irrigation is facing two challenges: the narrow set of conditions under which it performs best, some of which were present in Mughal and colonial India, are fast disappearing in South Asia; and it is proving unequal to the new pressures and opportunities of the region's smallholder agrarian economy. The era of constructive imperialism—of the supremacy of command and duty in irrigation creation (Gilmartin 2003b)—seems finally passé.

Rivalry Between Flow and Lift Irrigation

Historically, surface irrigation has always driven out well irrigation in South Asia. Beginning in the late nineteenth century, canals were replacing wells in northern and northwestern India. The reasons were not far to seek. Elizabeth Whitcombe (1971, *80*) cites a colonial official's observation:

> . . . the great relief from labor given by the canal probably goes as far as anything else with an ordinary peasant in directing his choice when it is possible for him to choose [between canal and well]. When a man has no sons or male relatives to help him, or when he has to keep more bullocks for irrigation than he wants for his plough, he may realize that he actually saves money by employing canal.

In undivided Punjab, during the era of constructive imperialism, the area irrigated by wells declined from 1.86 million ha in 1868–69 to 1.54 million ha in 1918–19 to about 1.42 million ha in 1926–27 (Randhawa 1983).[1] Whitcombe (1971) estimated that in 1860, some three million to four million acres—one-seventh of the cultivated land in Oudh (present western Uttar Pradesh)—was irrigated by shallow earthen wells. But with the onset of the Ganga canal, W. A. Forbes in 1866 lamented that the inroad of canals had left most wells in disuse and that well sinking was "now almost entirely abandoned" (Whitcombe 1971, *70*). This trend continued even as independent India and Pakistan began building new dams and canal systems after 1947.[2]

The rise of surface irrigation has been interlocked with the decline in groundwater irrigation in a seesaw fashion. Farmer preference for gravity-flow over lift irrigation from wells may also perhaps explain why we seldom find extensive groundwater irrigation in well-managed canal commands elsewhere in the world. In a recent study of 16 irrigation systems around the world, Burt and Styles (1999) noted that in 13, gravity flow was the only source of irrigation water. In Gezira system in Sudan (Plusquellec 1990) or in the Nile basin irrigation in Egypt (Depeweg and Bekheit 1997; Mehanna et al. 1984), where crop production is entirely irrigated, there is little or no irrigation with groundwater.

In a phenomenon that appears unique to monsoon Asia, the adoption of surface irrigation at the expense of wells has been reversed since 1970, with the spread of pump irrigation. During the 1960s and 1970s, canal managers actively discouraged wells in canal commands, but as Vaidyanathan (1996,

187) showed for the Lower Bhavani project in Tamilnadu, "the enforcement was practically abandoned." Well irrigation is widespread in South Asian canal commands but uncommon in many other parts of the world. In the Burt and Styles study (1999), of the 16 surface irrigation systems studied around the world, the only three that had substantial groundwater irrigation in the command area were all Indian systems. For a period, this reversal appeared to foster the conjunctive use of groundwater and surface water that scientists advocate. Researchers like Dhawan (Dhawan and Satya Sai 1988) considered the high productivity of well irrigation in command areas a major benefit of canal projects, and Palanisami and Ranganathan (2004) showed the same benefits in the tank commands of Tamilnadu.

However, throughout South Asia, pump irrigation continues to replace flow irrigation leaving surface irrigation systems reconfigured and their command areas curtailed.[3] In Baluchistan, expansion of dug wells after 1960, and later of deep tube wells, hastened the decline of the ancient system of flow irrigation with *karezes* (also known as *qanats*, tunnels that convey groundwater from a well to a series of surface outlets[4]) (Steenbergen and Oliemans 1997). Flow irrigation from tanks, used for centuries to grow rice, especially in southern India, is declining because of the increased number of wells in tank commands. In Tamilnadu, the heartland of tank irrigation, between 1960 and 2000, flow-irrigated area from tanks fell by a third, from 940,000 to 601,000 ha (Palanisami and Ranganathan 2004).[5] Palanisami and Ranganathan (2004) have determined the optimal level of well density in a tank command, beyond which additional wells curtail overall benefits, reducing irrigation tanks to percolation tanks. Janakarajan and Moench (2006) note the positive correlation between the rapid growth of well irrigation and the decay of tanks.[6] According to Selvarajan (2002), Andhra Pradesh, Tamilnadu, Karnataka, and Orissa, which together accounted for 60 percent of India's tank-irrigated area, lost about 37 percent of their tank-irrigated area from 1965 to 2000.

Now, large canal systems are going the way of the tank. In many canal commands, areas irrigated by gravity flow are shrinking. In Pakistan's Indus Basin Irrigation System, between 1990 and 2006, area irrigated with tube wells increased by 38 percent while that under flow irrigation declined by 11 percent (Ul Hassan et al. 2007). In the Bhakra command on the Indian side, canal irrigation at first drove out wells; however, especially since 1990, the trend has been reversed (Dharmadhikari 2005), and now, 75 percent of all irrigated areas in Indian Punjab depend upon well and tube well irrigation

(Singh 2006 citing a Government of Punjab 2005 document). Between 1990 and 2002, gross sown area in Punjab increased by 440,000 ha, but the area served by flow irrigation from canals fell by 589,000 while that served by tube wells soared by 837,000 (Down to Earth 2005). Even the Punjab government's 2005 State of the Environment Report lamented a reduction of 36 percent in the canal irrigation area since 1990. Canals irrigated 1.3 million ha in 1970–71 and more than 1.6 million ha in 1990–91, but in 1999–2000, canal-irrigated area in Indian Punjab fell to one million ha (PSCST 2005). In Uttar Pradesh, whose western parts have a long history of canal irrigation, area irrigated by canals declined 40 percent and from "other sources" by 60 percent, while the area irrigated by tube wells increased 37 percent (Pant 2005, Table 1). In eastern Uttar Pradesh, still in the early stages of irrigation development, canal-irrigated areas increased at the expense of "other sources" but tube well irrigation increased 13 times since 1964–65. Even as tube well–irrigated areas expanded, canal-irrigated areas fell. According to Selvarajan (2002), around 2000, canals were irrigating 3.06 million ha in Uttar Pradesh, compared with 3.33 million ha in 1985. In Andhra Pradesh, they were irrigating 11 percent less than 15 years ago. Uttar Pradesh, Andhra Pradesh, Bihar, Orissa, and Tamilnadu—which account for 45 percent of India's net irrigated area—all witnessed an absolute decline in canal-irrigated areas but large increases in pump irrigation from wells (Selvarajan 2002). During the five-year period from 1997–98 to 2002–03, canal-irrigated area in Gujarat fell 46 percent, from 0.78 million ha to 0.42 million ha.[7] Many say that tube wells are pumping canal seepage. That may be; the point is that the *mode* of delivering water to crops—and the regime tied to it—is changing from flow to lift, collective to individual, public to private, formal to informal.

The Punjab trend is reflected in national figures, too. In India, this is evident from the figures compiled by the central Ministry of Agriculture, and in Pakistan, by the Pakistan Statistical Bulletin of recent years.[8] In India, area irrigated by major and medium irrigation projects declined by 1.3 million ha—eight percent—between 1990 and 2000. In Pakistan, areas irrigated with gravity flow from canals fell by more than 1 million ha—13.3 percent—between 1980–81 and 2002–03.[9] Bangladesh never had much public irrigation infrastructure; nevertheless, agriculture depended on flow- and low-lift irrigation from surface water until the 1980s. Pumping groundwater from shallow tube wells is now the norm on 90 percent of Bangladesh's irrigated areas (Ministry of Water Resources Bangladesh 2005).

Comparing land-use statistics for India, Janakarajan and Moench (2006) note that between 1996–97 and 2002–03, the area under canal irrigation declined by 2.4 million ha (13.8 percent), the area under tank irrigation fell by 1.4 million ha (42.4 percent), and the area irrigated by all other sources declined by one million ha (28 percent). The only irrigation source that increased was groundwater wells, by 2.8 million ha (more than nine percent). In India, land-use statistics are considered suspect, especially since the revenue administration for which these were critical no longer enjoys the significance it did during colonial times. However, the recently released minor irrigation census data for 1993–94 and 2000–01 indicate the changes that have been taking place in the seven intervening years. Table 3-1 presents irrigated areas under surface irrigation and groundwater irrigation in Pakistan, Bangladesh, and all those Indian states that were common to the two censuses. In seven years, South Asia's surface irrigation systems lost 5.5 million ha from their command, roughly at a rate of 0.8 million ha per year. Groundwater-irrigated areas have grown by 7.4 million ha, roughly 1.1 million ha per year. In net terms, however, irrigation expansion has more or less stagnated during the most recent years. And the reason is shrinking of surface irrigation command areas.

One long-held argument in India is that stagnation in public irrigation command areas is caused by diminished public investment in irrigation. To

Table 3-1   Decline in canal irrigation in South Asia, 1993–2001

	Net irrigated area under surface irrigation (thousand ha)[a]			Net irrigated area served by groundwater (thousand ha)[b]		
	1993–94	2000–01	Percentage change	1993–94	2000–01	Percentage change
India: major states[c]	15,633	11,035	−29.4	17,413	21,760	+25
Pakistan Punjab	4,240	3,740	−11.8	8,760	10,340	+18
Sind	2,300	1,960	−14.8	140	200	+42.9
Bangladesh	537	480	−10.7	2,124	3,462	+63
All areas	22,709	17,215	−24.2	28,437	35,762	+25.8

[a] Area under surface irrigation in India includes area irrigated by major and medium projects as well as other sources, which include surface flow and lift schemes.
[b] Area served by groundwater in Pakistan includes area under canal wells and tube wells as well as other wells. Area served by groundwater in Bangladesh includes area served by deep and shallow tube wells and low-lift pumps.
[c] Andhra Pradesh, Arunachal, Assam, Bihar and Jharkhand, Goa, Himachal Pradesh, Madhya Pradesh and Chattisgarh, Orissa, Punja, Rajasthan, Uttar Pradesh and Uttaranchal, West Bengal, Gujarat, Maharashtra, Tamilnadu, Karnataka, Haryana are excluded. Also excluded are smaller states and Union Territories, where irrigated areas are small.
Sources: Government of India 2001, 2005; Pakistan Statistical Bulletins, various years; Bangladesh Bureau of Statistics (http://www.moa.gov.bd/statistics)

correct the problem, the government of India has instituted the Accelerated Irrigation Benefits Program, to step up the investment in the so-called last-mile projects. More than US$7.5 billion has been invested in these projects since 1997. However, the effort has not arrested the deceleration in India's surface irrigation (Figure 3.1); governments have to invest twice as much in canal irrigation projects just to keep their command areas from shrinking. Are these trends reflected in microlevel studies?

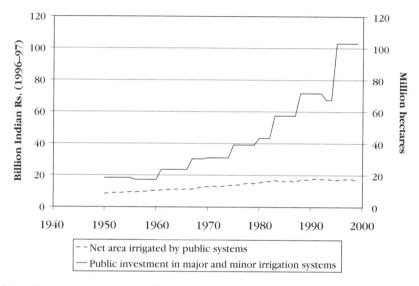

Figure 3.1 Increasing investment in and decreasing use of public irrigation systems, India, 1940–2000

Surface Irrigation Under Siege

The merits and demerits of dams are often debated, but the real problem besetting surface irrigation is downstream of the dam, at the periphery of the main system where water begins flowing into the fields. Students of surface irrigation like Robert Chambers, B. D. Dhawan, A. Vaidyanathan, Robert Wade, Peter Mollinga, Walter Coward, Norman Uphoff, Robert Hunt, and others—whose writings since the 1980s have shaped our understanding of canal irrigation and its complexities today—could not have imagined canal commands competing with intense private pump irrigation.[10] Literature on the subject lists the ills of canal irrigation systems (e.g., Chambers 1988). But nobody foresaw the most striking result: the shrinking of command areas. Systems meant for protective irrigation are collapsing into intensively irrigated small paddy-rice wetlands in upper commands.[11] As pump irrigation moves in from all sides, flow irrigation is receding.

Early in the new millennium, while studying the performance of public irrigation systems in Gujarat, the late Anil Shah found that 59 percent of the designated command area, mostly on the periphery of the Dharoi system on the Sabarmati River, was deprived of gravity-flow irrigation, which Shah considered was the right of their local owners (A. Shah 2003). Curious, he surveyed farmers in 31 villages in the Mahi Right Bank System in central Gujarat, considered one of India's best-managed irrigation systems, having surplus water to drain into the sea. Here, he found only 27 percent of the command area farmers totally "flow irrigation deprived." And of the remaining, only half received two or more irrigations during the entire season, and less than 10 percent received the five or six irrigations usually expected by farmers in canal commands (A. Shah 2003). Gidwani (2002, 23) noted that this problem in the Mahi system was old and persistent; even in 1992–93, its best year ever, the system's performance was "well short of its designated irrigation potential."

In the course of the following year, Shah collaborated with several NGOs to assess levels of flow irrigation deprivation in command areas of large and small, old and new surface irrigation systems in six Indian states. Everywhere, researchers found the deprivation level to be minimal or even negative in the head reach but noted high levels in the peripheries of the system, as summarized by Shah for the Planning Commission of India (see Table 3-2).

Everywhere, the problem was overappropriation of water by head-reach farmers for growing crops that irrigation planners had never expected them to grow. In Karnataka's Tungabhadra canal, the area under rice during the previous decade had risen from 18,000 to 50,000, which was 20 times the area originally "authorized," in a system designed to irrigate "dry" irrigated crops, such as sorghum, millet, and local varieties of cotton.[12] The original goal of providing protective irrigation over large areas was uniformly defeated (Mollinga 2003). In the northwestern systems, as in Haryana, researchers found the much-celebrated *wara bandi* (rotational water supply) system—designed to minimize head-tail inequity—eroded; the same has been found for the Indus system in Pakistan (Jurriens et al. 1996; van Halsema 2002) and elsewhere in monsoon Asia where it has been tried

Table 3-1   Flow-irrigation deprivation levels of tail-enders in selected gravity-flow irrigation projects in India

State	System	Extent of deprivation (percent)
Gujarat	Dharoi (major), Mahi right bank (major)	7–37
Haryana	Western Yamuna (major), Bhakra (major)	56–84
Karnataka	Tungabhadra (major), Vanivilas (medium), two tanks (minor)	40–91
Maharashtra	Mule (major), Walen tank (minor)	29–70
Orissa	Hirakud (major)	35–72
Tamilnadu	Parambikulam Aliyar (major), two rain-fed tanks (minor)	24–55

Source: Shah, A. 2006. Issues in management of canal irrigation projects. Presentation to Planning Commission of India subgroup, New Delhi, 6 April.

(Rice 1996). Under the *wara bandi*, every farmer is supposed to get an equal number of water turns, for equal time, per unit of land. But the study by the late Anil Shah (2003) found high levels of flow irrigation deprivation at the tail ends during monsoon as well as winter seasons.[13]

Other studies by independent researchers convey the same picture. Choudhury (2006) sampled irrigators in eight canal systems around India and found that, thanks to unreliable and unpredictable canal supplies, the only farmers who did not suffer crop losses were owners of pumps and wells, most of whom were concentrated in head reaches. An investigation by Neetha (2003) in the command area of the Chalakkudy River Diversion Scheme in Kerala found that only 15 percent of the plots studied were able to depend solely on public provision of flow irrigation. The rest scavenged water from channels or groundwater through a wide array of informal institutions for sharing irrigation assets.

All this suggests that even as the governments of India and Pakistan spend large sums to accelerate irrigation, public irrigation is decelerating. It also suggests that the pump irrigation economy is getting progressively larger at the expense of the flow irrigation economy. In Pakistan Punjab, local observers think gravity-flow irrigation generally extends a maximum of 2 km on either side of the distributary canal; beyond that, farmers mostly pump groundwater for irrigation. The official position in India is that around 60 percent of the irrigated area is served by wells and tube wells. However, recent large-scale surveys by the government-managed National Sample Survey Organization suggest otherwise. An all-India survey of 78,990 farm households in 1998 compared its findings with 1991–92 data and noted that "the difference between the estimates of the two rounds indicates a marked rise in privately owned irrigation facilities during the period of six years . . . [and a] large part of the cultivated land today is irrigated by hiring pumpsets" (NSSO 1999a, Report *451, 39*). Being in the command area of a canal makes little difference today. The same survey showed hardly any difference in average gross area irrigated per sample households in villages with government canals (1.8 ha) and those without government canals (1.69 ha). A 2002–03 survey of 51,770 farm households from 6,638 villages around India showed that 69 percent of the sample area irrigated in *kharif* and 76.5 percent in *rabi* were served by wells and tube wells (NSSO 2005). Yet another NSSO (2003) survey found that in 2002, 76 percent of the 4,646 villages surveyed had irrigation facilities, but mostly in the form of tube wells. Per 1,000 villages surveyed, only 173 had water from a government canal, but wells and tube wells abounded in 762 villages per 1,000 that reported having an "irrigation facility."

A smaller survey, of 2,600 WEM owners from 278 villages from India, Pakistan, Bangladesh and Nepal Terai in 2002, confirmed the trend (Shah et al. 2006). It found that pumped groundwater irrigated more than 75 percent of the irrigated areas in the sample villages. It found hardly any purely rain-fed regions or villages, although rain-fed plots within villages abound. Groundwater is used essentially for supplemental irrigation to provide 30 to 50 percent of the consumptive requirements of crops. Despite government subsidies for electricity and canal irrigation, at the aggregate level, it was the diesel pump that according to this survey was the basis of the subcontinent's irrigation economy. Regression models showed that, in explaining variations in net irrigated areas across sample villages, electric and diesel tube wells together are five times more important than the presence of a canal in a village, and 15 times more important than the presence of a tank or river or stream (Shah et al. 2006). The dynamic that explains the rapid decline in canal and tank irrigation is complex, but deteriorating performance is undoubtedly the main culprit.

Build-Neglect-Rebuild

From the viewpoint of irrigators, the performance of an irrigation system is judged by the level of water control it offers (Boyce 1988). After Freeman et al. (1989), water control can be defined as the capacity to apply the proper quantity and quality of water at the optimum time to the crop root zone to meet crop consumptive needs and soil leaching requirements. The performance gap between the level of water control that command area farmers expect and the one they actually receive is explained by three systemic infirmities: anarchy, chaos, and noise.

Anarchy includes acts of omission and commission that subvert the objectives of system management. Acts of commission include water thefts, vandalism, violation of water distribution norms, and unauthorized diversion or lifting of water from canals by head-reach farmers. Acts of omission include farmers' own failure to cooperate in maintenance and repair, to pay irrigation charges, and so forth (Burt and Styles 1999).[14] *Chaos* is the gap between promised and actual level of water control offered at a point in time because of inept system management as well as physical deterioration of the system and reengineering by farmers (Oorthuizen 2003). *Noise* is the gap between the level of water control the system was originally designed to provide and the level of water control the users expect in the today's changed context.

For long, poor performance was blamed on the physical deterioration of systems and poor maintenance, and numerous programs were launched to "rehabilitate" surface irrigation systems. But as Boyce (1988, A-9) pointed out, "The social difficulties of achieving joint water use among many irrigators may exceed the technical difficulties of constructing large-scale systems." As a result, evaluations repeatedly found that physical rehabilitation was not a silver bullet. Typically, a visible performance jump in the immediate aftermath of physical rehabilitation enlarged the command area and improved fee collection, water flowed unimpeded to the tail end, and users expressed satisfaction. A few years later, however, water fee collection would languish, and anarchy levels rise. Maintenance would be deferred; degradation of the system would begin slowly and then accelerate, causing head-tail imbalance and prompting another round of rehabilitation. In Sri Lankan tanks, the cycle has been so short that new rehabilitation plans are afoot even before the last plan is fully implemented. Mohanty (2005), an Indian infrastructure expert, calls this the *build-neglect-rebuild* syndrome. Recent thinking about improving performance of surface systems therefore favors modernization, defined as the "process of technical and managerial upgrading . . . of irrigation schemes combined with institutional reforms, with the objective to improve resource utilization . . . and water delivery service to farms" (Renault 1998, 8). Modernization thus aims at reducing anarchy, chaos, and noise all at once, but it cannot eliminate them.

Participatory irrigation management (PIM)—and its sibling, irrigation management transfer (IMT)—have proved surprisingly sterile for revitalizing canal and tank systems. The validity of transforming traditional "irrigation communities" into PIM through water users' associations in a government-run irrigation system itself has been questioned (Hunt 1989; Narain 2004). More than two decades ago, Coward (1983) put his finger on the problem:

> The basic point is to understand that the fundamental processes of investment now being made by the State [in large irrigation projects] fail to create property relationships among the water users, and thus are unable to support the creation of a social basis for action among local people.

What is extraordinary about PIM (and IMT, which is as yet untried in South Asia) is the sway it has continued to hold on the irrigation management discourse despite virtually no evidence of its having succeeded in the developing world except on an experimental basis, and only with facilitation of irreplicable quality and scale.[15] That system managers want farmers to manage irrigation canals is not new; the British tried hard in the late nineteenth century to get farmers from the Indo-Gangetic basin to participate in irrigation management but without much success, except in *wara bandi* in the Indus canals (Whitcombe 2005). Since Independence, farmers' organizations for irrigation management have been regularly tried, with uniformly disappointing results. In the early 1960s, Uttar Pradesh tried *Sinchai Samitis* (irrigation committees) on irrigation tanks and reservoirs; later, Madhya Pradesh tried it on thousands of its minor irrigation tanks. Other states have been struggling to make *Pani Panchayats* (water assemblies) work. But the *Sinchai Samitis* of Madhya Pradesh and Uttar Pradesh have disappeared, and so have *Pani Panchayats* in Gujarat and elsewhere. Gujarat introduced its Joint Irrigation Management Program in 1983, but the 17 irrigation cooperatives lost money and disbanded. In 1991, it made another attempt, this time with assistance from local nongovernmental organizations, and 144 irrigation cooperatives were formed to cover 45,000 ha of irrigated area (Shukla 2004). However, these cooperatives never functioned well.

Nevertheless, fascination with participatory irrigation management continues as governments and donors seek to rejuvenate irrigation systems. Orissa recently passed a law that transferred all its minor irrigation systems to new *Pani Panchayats*. And Andhra Pradesh created some 10,000 water users' associations by a stroke of its chief minister's pen. The Andhra Pradesh reform is considered by some observers a great example, even though dozens of such efforts have faltered. And if the 250,000-ha decline in surface irrigated area in Andhra Pradesh between the 1993–94 and 2000–01 minor irrigation censuses is any indication, Andhra Pradesh's reforms are already failing. The World Bank loan spent, field researchers in Andhra Pradesh too are beginning to wonder whether water users' associations are making a difference (Jairath 2001; Madhav 2007; Reddy 2003).

Indeed, a primary purpose of the command area development agencies (CADAs) formed by the Government of India in early 1980s was to involve farmers' organizations in the management of irrigation projects. But we see no trace of CADAs or their "beneficiary farmers' associations." In Kerala, thousands of such organizations were formed during 1986. An assessment by Joseph (2001) in late 1990s suggested that, even in this land of strong traditions of local governance, high education, and high levels of participation in public affairs, the beneficiary farmers' associations were damp squib.

For some researchers, PIM interventions are laboratories in democratic governance. Indeed, PIM action the world over is driven by the idea that water users' associations can manage irrigation systems better than remote bureaucracies and would be better at controlling anarchy, improving water service, collecting fees, and maintaining the system. That would raise water and land productivity and improve the fortunes of the farmers. Democratic governance aside, PIM programs have belied many of these lesser expectations even where they are widely considered successful, in Turkey, Mexico (Kloezen 2002; Rap 2004), and the Philippines (Oorthuizen 2003). As a result, expectations have been increasingly moderated, and participatory management is now considered successful if it just "saves the government money, improves cost effectiveness of operation and maintenance while improving, or at least not weakening, the productivity of irrigated agriculture" (Vermillion 1996, 153).[16] The discussion, in recent times, has been more about shifting responsibility away from governments than about improving the lot of farmers—the original goal to which much public irrigation investment has been directed over the past 50 years.

The lesson is that the benefits of rehabilitation and upgrades are transitory without the capacity to control anarchy. And when it comes to controlling anarchy, the idea of gravity-flow irrigation itself faces challenges in South Asia.

Fertile Ground for Flow Irrigation

PIM is based on the experience of traditional irrigation systems—tanks in southern India, the *ahar-pyne* systems of South Bihar, the hill-irrigation systems in Nepal (Pradhan 1989) and Indian Himalayas, *subaks* (farmer cooperatives that manage paddy irrigation systems[17]) in Bali, Indonesia. As Hunt (1989, 79) suggested 25 years ago,

> To some degree the idea of [water users' associations] has been derived by analogy from what are perceived to be the organizations of small indigenous and traditional irrigation systems . . . Farmers are clearly capable of building, operating and maintaining complicated irrigation systems . . . [and] if indigenous systems are so capable, then the farmers at the tail end of the large bureaucratic irrigation projects should also be capable of doing the same things. There are serious problems with this analogy however . . .

And as a result, the user association model has not proved an effective mechanism to control the anarchy levels in large gravity-flow irrigation systems except when conditions are ideal for gravity-flow irrigation itself—that is, when the number of farm units served by a system is relatively small; when the farming systems in the command show high levels of homogeneity in crops grown and irrigation schedules; when effective authority structures make and enforce rules and norms; and when irrigators are captive to the system because alternatives to it are absent, inferior, or costly.

The presence of those four conditions—fewness, homogeneity, authority, and captivity—appear to help create what North (1990) called institutional lock-ins that mandated and facilitated collective action. Their presence helps reduce anarchy and make gravity-flow irrigation sustainable and farmer participation in irrigation management an attractive proposition. In contrast, as some or all of the anarchy controllers become remote or absent from an irrigation system, as is happening in South Asia, surface irrigation systems have a tendency to atrophy that PIM seems unable to arrest, much less reverse.

Fewness

In a surface irrigation system with few, large farmers, anarchic behavior would be easily noticed and curbed. Cooperation among farmers would be easier to forge, irrigation charges would be easier to assess and collect, and volumetric water delivery on demand would be easier to operationalize than with a large number of smallholders in a command of the same size. Boyce (1988, A-9) noted that "for some purposes . . . the number of cultivators involved may be a more meaningful measure of scale than the number of acres irrigated;" this is particularly the case for the purpose of improving the performance of flow irrigation systems. Burt and Styles (1999, 93) conclude, "The quality of water delivery service to individual farmers is inversely related to the number of farmers who must cooperate in the final distribution of water." In a game of rotating irrigators with self-enforced rules, Weissing and Ostrom (1991) found levels of anarchy rising with an increase in numbers of irrigators.

Institutional economists distinguish between two types of costs involved in running an economic enterprise: *transformation costs,* for converting inputs into outputs, and *transaction costs,* incurred by economic agents in making, negotiating, and enforcing contracts, norms, and rules and tracking and penalizing violators.[18] In a surface irrigation system, transaction costs arise from controlling the anarchy ensuing from water distribution to numerous and disparate users. Imagine a 10,000-ha estate with a captive reservoir and a distribution system that delivers water to different plots—such as Cubbie Station in Queensland, Australia.[19] If the estate were owned by a single farmer, he would not have to deal with other participants in the irrigation system and therefore face no anarchy; his irrigation cost would consist of only transformation cost.[20] But if the estate were broken up into 10,000 small parcels and given away to independent smallholders competing with and scheming against each other to get water when they needed it, transaction costs come into play, and because the control of anarchy in an irrigation system is a public good,[21] irrigators are not willing to absorb these transaction costs unless compelled to do so (Olson 1965). If the estate were divided in to three holdings of, say, 1,000 ha each and 7,000 parcels of one ha each, there is a good chance that the large landholders would absorb the transaction costs on behalf of all farmers because each may find his gain from anarchy control larger than one-third of the total transaction of achieving it (Shah et al. 2000b). In Baluchistan, for example, the highly unequal land holdings likely helped *kareze* irrigation survive into the 1960s.

Worldwide, surface irrigation systems are easier to manage—and their transfer to farmer associations is smooth and trouble free—where they serve a few, large farmers engaged in highly productive commercial agriculture

(Turral 1998).[22] A World Bank study of two irrigation systems in Colombia found one of them, Coello district, managed well by its water users' association and attributed its success, *inter alia*, to the "relatively large size of farm holdings" (Plusquellec 1989, 5) of 100 ha each (Burt and Styles 1999). The authors wondered whether "the same approach . . . would work with the very small holdings found in most developing countries."[23] Small numbers of users can easily come together, negotiate rules, and evolve and enforce cooperative solutions. It is not surprising that we find more examples of success in anarchy control through participatory irrigation management in Colombia, Chile, Mexico, and Turkey, where farming units served per system are relatively few. In the United States, farmers could forge binding contracts even to construct irrigation systems, often with their own resources, and in South Africa, irrigation boards (now called water boards) consisting of few large commercial farmers with their own irrigation system informally undertook PIM long before the term was coined (Shah et al. 2002). Extreme inequality in land holdings seems to have helped rather than hindered anarchy control[24] (see also Boyce 1988).

The key is fewness not of plots but of independent agents served by the system. A South Asian *zamindar* of the colonial era lording over numerous tenant farmers found controlling anarchy simpler than a water users' association would find today. The *ahar-pyne* systems of South Bihar, some of them serving several thousand acres, emerged and survived because they were captive systems serving *zamindari* estates (Pant 1998). Captive canals owned by large landowners who could irrigate sizable commands might help explain why surface irrigation worked better in medieval and colonial times than today.[25] Similarly, the British policy of land allocation in large chunks in canal colonies of the Punjab reduced the numbers of users and, thereby, the potential for anarchy.[26] In the Ganga canal, for some years, outlets were auctioned to the highest bidder, who then established a property right on water, constructed the distribution system below the outlet, and sold water to cultivators (Stone 1984). Command areas in the Punjab of nineteenth century were more like systems in United States or Australia than those in Tamilnadu or Maharashtra, where it would be difficult today to find many farmers with 50-acre plots.

In the Punjab of the nineteenth century, the construction and maintenance of watercourses, each serving 750 to 1,750 acres—and field channels farther down—were the responsibility of farmers (Islam 1997). In modern-day Gujarat, the government incorporated the same concept in the new Sardar

Sarovar Irrigation Project. Its planners assumed that water users' associations of 200 to 500 smallholders in a village service area served by an outlet, mimicking the Punjab's large landowners in the nineteenth century, would mobilize resources and build watercourses below the outlet. However, the assumption proved naïve, and five years after water began flowing down the system, not even one of the 1,100 service areas in the command had watercourses or field channels constructed by the users' association. Instead, pump irrigation emerged in each area, with private farmers lifting water from the distributary to irrigate their own fields and selling pump irrigation service to others (Talati and Shah 2004). The Narmada irrigation system is beginning to resemble that of Egypt, where canals deliver water into *mesqas* (ditches) dug 45 cm below ground level from which farmers lift irrigation water using animal power and diesel pumps (Hunt 1986; Mehanna et al. 1984). The Narmada irrigation experience, like many others, suggests that PIM does not reduce total transaction costs of anarchy control; it merely transfers bits of anarchy from the system to the water users' associations which, expectedly, are reluctant to absorb the transaction costs of controlling it. As a result, associations seldom form on their own and have to be constantly propped up.

Homogeneity

Another factor that simplifies the management of gravity-flow irrigation— and the containment of anarchy as well as chaos—is uniformity in the farming systems (but not necessarily in farmers or land holdings) used within the command area. Institutional economists aver that the transaction costs of managing a human system increase in proportion to not only the number but also the diversity of parties involved (Williamson 1993). When all water users in the command grow the same crop at the same time, the tasks of scheduling water distribution and drainage become simpler than when users grow different crops with varying scales and schedules of water demand. That most flow irrigation systems in Southeast Asia irrigate only paddy is their only advantage over South Asian systems. A World Bank review team studying the state of paddy irrigation systems in Thailand, Myanmar, and Vietnam found the systems performing better than expected. The primary reason was the homogeneous paddy-rice farming system that simplified scheduling and distribution (Rice 1996). Traditional irrigation communities imposed such homogeneity and thus kept anarchy in check. It is no accident that tanks in southern India and Sri

Lanka *always* irrigated paddies, and so did the *Ahar-Pyne* systems in South Bihar (Pant 1998) and the hill irrigation systems in Nepal (Pradhan 1989) and elsewhere in the Himalayas. Design of protective canal irrigation systems in South Asia generally abstained from specifying crops farmers could grow, except in some southern Indian systems; however, they were designed to spread water thinly over a large area. The implicit assumption was that if this protective character were preserved through design and management, it would overcome the problems of heterogeneity in cropping patterns (Jurriens et al. 1996). But this assumption has proved unrealistic, especially during recent decades.

Imposing farming system homogeneity to contain anarchy and chaos has been central to many small and large irrigation systems[27] throughout Africa. The 840,000-ha Gezira irrigation scheme in Sudan—whose history we briefly reviewed in Chapter 1—and several others that mimicked its design throughout British and French Africa as well as the Netherlands East Indies are good examples. Around 1990, the Gezira scheme was believed to have an efficiency of 70 percent, the highest found in surface irrigation projects. Fewness of farmers helped. Each tenant was assigned an eight-ha plot, leading to an "absence of constraints imposed by small, fragmented, field plots found in many developing countries" (Plusquellec 1990, 3). However, farming system homogeneity imposed by its design helped, too. Ever since it was commissioned in 1920s, cotton, wheat, groundnuts, and sorghum are grown in a strict four-course rotation, including fallow. The Gezira scheme created a vast, state-controlled cotton estate by dispossessing native Sudanese of their lands and giving them tenancies instead. According to Bernal (1997, 449), it is "a technology of power that above all established relations of authority over rural populations." The bureaucratic management structure created by the colonial administration was one of "absolute despotism" having "much more to do with control over Sudanese farmers than with control over water" (451). The "farmers' official role was to supply labor for cotton production" (452). "The degree of regimentation led some observers to liken Gezira farmers to workers on assembly lines" (452). Though the enterprise purported to lead the Sudanese to scientific farming, the head of the colonial government's department of agriculture was not an agriculture specialist. Independent Sudan has retained this regimentation pretty much intact. "The Gezira scheme is as much about discipline as about development" (449).

Elsewhere in Africa, canal irrigation projects begun during the apartheid era for smallholder farmers have been associated with the estate mode of farming, in which farmers pooled their holdings into large estates managed in a centralized manner through a top-down, command-and-control system. The Mwea scheme in Kenya, Kano in Nigeria, and the French Office du Niger scheme (Mali) are other examples of the Gezira design of social and civil engineering, its salient elements being factory-like organization, geometric precision in canal design, uniform cropping patterns, farmers as tenant-share-croppers, and a management regime of command-and-control. Under a variation of contract farming, one or two crops are grown, and government agencies organize mechanized cultivation, planting, irrigation, and fertilizer application centrally. In this arrangement, all that the plot holders do is weed, harvest, and move irrigation pipes. The managing agency also organizes the marketing of pooled produce and deducts all its expenses before giving the residual sum to the farmers. In this regime, Africa's smallholders became neither farmers nor wage laborers. They made no entrepreneurial or managerial decisions, only collected wages for weeding, harvesting, and managing field irrigation, but because they absorbed the risk of crop yield variability, they were not pure wage earners, either. Though it impoverished some African smallholders, the estate mode of farming did impose total homogeneity in farming systems within the command areas and minimized anarchy (Shah et al. 2002).

In Egyptian canal irrigation, with the problem of numerous small-holdings as severe as in South Asia, strong government control over cropping patterns was the hallmark of tight irrigation management aimed at producing homogeneity. In the mid-1980s, Hunt (1986, *200*) wrote,

> Irrigators must submit to cropping discipline by mutually coordinating plant-growth cycles . . . Crop discipline . . . is officially imposed by the national government, and there should be a good fit between the timing and distribution of the plants in the fields and the timing and distribution of the irrigation water . . .

In some systems in peninsular India, cropping plans were made when the irrigation systems were designed, but there is no known case of a canal irrigation project where farmers' actual cropping pattern followed the original plan—even in localization schemes of southern India, where doing this was a precondition to effective system operation. Once the system gets commissioned, head-reach farmers take to paddy, sugarcane, and banana without hindrance, leaving the outer periphery of the command to fend for itself, implying a complete erosion of authority of system management.

Authority

Even though widely challenged and discredited, Wittfogel's (1957) seminal work highlights the role of authority structures in containing the anarchy endemic in flow irrigation systems serving large numbers of smallholders. Wittfogel's thesis was that construction and maintenance of large irrigation systems necessitated a political and social structure capable of forceful extraction of labor, leading to despotism[28] and a different social and political organization of society in the Orient than in medieval Europe. Hydraulic management caused internal pressures for a structured bureaucratic organization under centralized control and forced people into inequality: "Those who control the hydraulic network are uniquely prepared to wield supreme power" (45). As systems grew, leadership was required to build new canals, maintain existing ones, and ensure efficient distribution of water.

The leap Wittfogel made from compulsions of orderly management of irrigation systems to the inevitability of despotism and absolutism in medieval arid societies is perhaps the most discredited aspect of Wittfogel's work. Critics say Wittfogel overstretched a valid argument too far by contending, "If one source of power is so much more important than all others, a monopoly could develop within a society, and a single-centered government arose from such 'oriental despotism.' "

However, a weaker version of Wittfogel's hypothesis—that strong political authority is the cause and not the result of successful large-scale irrigation works—would have credibility even in today's context. Few would gainsay his contention that "irrigation itself had an organizing effect: scheduling of water use, maintenance of canals, and defense of canals from hostile neighbors all were forces at work within 'hydraulic societies.' " All evidence in the history of irrigation highlights the critical role played by authority in countering anarchy in surface irrigation, so much so that Hunt (1989) considered an "authority charter" the first element of an irrigation community as a going concern. True, it would be farfetched to argue that despotism in Myanmar is rooted in the imperatives of its paddy-rice irrigation system. But that the authorities in Myanmar can even today "gather large numbers of irrigator and nonirrigating farmers to clean canals" does help cope with anarchy in its rice irrigation systems (Rice 1996, 5). Bernal (1997, 455) found Barnett's description of the Gezira scheme in the 1970s compelling for "the sense it conveys of man-made order so totalizing that it becomes natural." In the million-acre Menagil extension on the Nile opposite Gezira, the Gezira board issued smaller tenancies but promoted much higher cropping intensity. Fifteen years later, the board concluded that the high cropping intensity was the cause of low and declining cotton yields and,

> in an amazing demonstration of its power over tenants who had been settled for thirty or more years, the board induced all tenants to give up their tenancies and shift from three plots of five feddans each to four plots each of 3.75 feddans, one of which was to be fallowed each year. Most tenants found themselves cropping entirely new plots, in some cases at considerable distance from the lands they formerly worked . . . yet the change was accepted, seemingly without protest. (Wallach 1988, 432)

Lipton (1985) argued that discipline backed by the authority of a despotic state, more than any spontaneous spirit of cooperation, was behind numerous flow irrigation systems in Sri Lanka and southern India going back millennia. "Under the Kandyan kings, strict discipline was enforced. The rare farmer who took water before the scheduled time was punished. The very rare sluice-cutter might even, on some accounts, have a hand cut-off in return" (83). Lipton suggests this exercise of authority in imposing an irrigation discipline had "general consent" because there was a sufficiently large core of gainers who endorsed it. During most of the British rule, this discipline was maintained, though with less extreme punishments, because, Lipton suggests, it had the backing of gainers and "was ultimately supported by State power" (84). In tracing how the system of localization emerged in southern India's protective irrigation systems during colonial times, a retired engineer whom Mollinga (2003, 68) interviewed "characterized localization as a regimental, magisterial form of governance, conceived by a government that could not imagine that its subjects would not do as told." Many consider poor performance of surface irrigation a case of market failure; others consider it a participation failure. In truth, it is a case of authority failure.

The role of authority in flow-irrigation management arises from what Oliver Williamson (1981) would call the high "asset specificity" of canal infrastructure. A flow irrigation system designed to irrigate a particular area, once completed, has few alternative uses. Indeed, system managers are under great pressure to release water for irrigation to ready the dam and reservoir for the next rainy season. Between irrigation managers and command area farmers of a completed system, then, the balance of power must stand tilted in favor of the latter. High asset specificity of flow irrigation systems requires that the system manager enter into strong prior contracts with irrigators, effectively enforced, to counter the threat of their opportunism; failing to do this leads to "holdup" by irrigators. Untrammeled by rules backed by the sustained presence of authority, irrigators' opportunism readily translates into anarchy, evident in poor recovery of water charges, breakdown in distribution rules, and widespread vandalism.

In Pakistan's Indus irrigation system, over decades of weakening of irrigation management structures, powerful landlords have been carrying out unauthorized enlargements of the outlets that deliver irrigation to their fields. This distorted the system's capacity to deliver water according to the original water rights and made a mockery of the *warabandi* system (Jurriens et al. 1996). The problem was long recognized, and yet competitive politics and compliant bureaucracy conspired not only to maintain the status quo but even to allow this power play to spread to new areas. No elected government offered to intervene. It took General Musharraf to send the army to implement a *moga* (outlet) restoration program to return the outlets to their original size (Shah et al. 2000b).

That burst of display of state authority, however, had only short-lived impact. The *moga* restoration program was implemented during 1999–2000. Recent reports suggest that as soon as the army turned its back, many *mogas* were enlarged to the size that reflected the clout of the landlords they served (Hassan 2006, pers. comm.). This highlights an important point: an intervention of authority is seldom sufficient to create order; sustained presence of authority is the key to anarchy control.[29]

Even while rejecting the Wittfogel thesis, Niranjan Pant (1998) argues that the abolition of the *zamindari* explains the decline in the *ahar-pyne* systems in South Bihar. The *zamindars* used to maintain these systems because "they had the capital resources and a vested interest in doing so" and could earn quick returns on their investments through *Gilandazi* (the irrigation improvement tax). Pant quotes a 1919 district gazetteer:

> Gilandazi is an excellent form of investment as the capital spent on it returns a dividend of 40 to 50 percent in the first year itself, in some cases 100 percent. Even if the landlord received only half of the produce of the land irrigated by these works they would get a very good return on their capital outlay. (O'Malley 1919 cited by Pant 1998, *3133*).

Paraphrasing O'Malley's description, Pant notes, "Writing even in the early part of this century, O'Malley noted that no new *Pynes* of any considerable size were being constructed in his times. According to him, large *Pynes* were constructed several years ago when *larger areas were under the control of single zamindar (land-lord)* and *their authority to enforce their orders and wishes was more absolute than during O'Malley's times."* (Pant 1998, *3135*, italics added) Stone's (1984) analysis of the management of the Ganga canal highlights the support *zamindars* provided to the canal department in securing forced labor for maintenance.

Even in the small irrigation communities studied by Coward (1985), Hunt (1989), and others, though there was no role for exogenous authority structures like that the *zamindars* played in the *ahar-pyne* systems, we invariably find that endogenous authority structures created by the communities themselves played a critical role in containing anarchy. In canal-irrigated villages in southern India, Wade (1986, 253) found anarchic behavior contained through "mutual cooperation via mutual coercion (with some individuals more coerced than others)." Gupta and Tiwari (2002, 13), who analyzed traditional irrigation systems in Ladakh, highlight the "integral and indispensable" role of the institution of *chud-pon*, the water appropriator who has the "responsibility for overseeing that the entire system works smoothly and efficiently as laid down in the rules." *Chud-pon* is a respected man whose "appointment is based on a collective decision." The central role of the institution of *chud-pon* is reining in the anarchy inherent in community surface irrigation.

Creating and sustaining endogenous authority was the role of village elders and the *neerkatti* (water manager) for tanks under community management in southern India, as can be observed from occasional tank communities whose age-old management institutions are intact (Sakthivadivel et al. 2004). This is put into bold relief in a case study of community management institutions in a system of 10 tanks in the Uthanur watershed in Kolar district in Karnataka (Intercooperation in India 2005). Despite sweeping socioeconomic changes during recent decades, as if stuck in a time warp, management of the 1,200-year-old Mudiyanur tank retains many of its traditional features. The most striking of these is the absolute authority, for orderly management of tank affairs, vested by the irrigation community in the institution of a council of elders, the *neerkattis* and *thootis* (village guards). Shaktivadivel et al. (2004) describe variations of such arrangements for the orderly management of tank irrigation in several villages of southern India.

Captivity

Why would irrigators subject themselves to such authority and imposed homogeneity and accept command-and-control irrigation institutions? There are, no doubt, many explanations. But my hypothesis is that, in some ways, successful gravity-flow systems held irrigators captive to an "irrigation culture" that in time came to grow upon them. Irrigation communities spawned institutional arrangements that minimized anarchy when alternatives were absent, inferior, or prohibitively costly. Irrigation institutions—rules, norms, conventions, in short, an entire culture of irrigation—for the orderly management of irrigated agriculture emerged and survived because of both their *instrumental* value and the *intrinsic* value the communities associated with them.[30] Agrarian life would have been far less gainful and far more risky without them. Members subject themselves to rules and authority they would normally disdain because it benefits themselves as well as the community and creates security for all to share (see, e.g., Pradhan 1989). This rather negative way of explaining the instrumental value of irrigation institutions heightens the point: it is only natural that the arrangements would begin to weaken as alternatives emerged for members to improve their well-being without being captive to institutional discipline and coercion. What raises questions about the future of flow irrigation in South Asia today is that new alternatives—pump irrigation being the most prominent of them—are rendering the culture of irrigation irrelevant.

Irrigation cultures, built and sustained over centuries, are suddenly appearing fragile with the onslaught of pump irrigation. The best example is the impact of the expansion of well irrigation on the centuries-old system of *kareze* irrigation in Baluchistan (Steenbergen 1995) and farther west. Iran had an estimated 32,164 *karezes* whose galleries extended 3.1 million km. Fifty years ago, these delivered 18 km³ of water annually by gravity flow; in recent years, because of well irrigation, the water output of Iran's *karezes* has been halved. And if well irrigation expands further, before long, Iran's *karezes* will lose their relevance (Khaneiki 2007).[31] The parallel in India is the gradual atrophy of tanks and *ahar-pyne* systems, and along with them, a whole culture in which they thrived. In the Indian Punjab, collective maintenance of surface water distributaries was better in a district with a low density of tube wells than in a district with a high density (Jairath 1985). In Kerala, as labor becomes scarce and paddy cultivation unprofitable, the centuries-old tradition of rice cultivation itself is in decline, with paddy areas reduced by some 65 percent and replaced by pump-irrigated plantation crops (Kumar et al. 2007). Substitution of paddy by plantation crops that need frequent waterings for five or six months in a year has raised questions about precisely what purpose flow irrigation systems serve.

Concluding a study of farmer-management in irrigation systems based on case studies from around the world during the early 1960s, Hunt (1988, *349*) noted, "No canal irrigation system ought to be able to exist without constituted authority. Yet they do. And no large canal irrigation system ought to be able to function if managed only by farmers. Yet they do and very successfully." In South Asia, increasingly, they do not.

Exit or Voice and Loyalty?

All the factors that sustain gravity-flow irrigation—fewness, homogeneity, authority, and captivity—are at their nadir in South Asia today, making it increasingly unfit as an irrigation technology for this region. The number of farmers in command areas of the region's surface irrigation system, which was never small, is at an all-time peak, and it will take some decades for the present demographic momentum to work itself out before these numbers begin to decline. Moreover, canal commands in many South Asian systems have acted as magnets that attract poverty from surrounding dry areas, leading to further fragmentation of "operated holdings" (Shah and Singh 2004). In the Punjab and Haryana of the Green Revolution years, owner-cultivators depended on migrant labor from Bihar for farming operations. Today, as younger Punjabi farmers seek greener pastures outside agriculture, farms are parceled out to Bihari migrants working as crop-sharing tenants. Nowhere else in the world, not even in Egypt, do surface irrigation systems have to contend with as many independent customers as in South Asia.

The growing diversification of farming systems in command areas is making matters worse. In Southeast Asia, the rice irrigation systems at least have the advantage of homogeneous farming systems to help to control anarchy and chaos.[32] Many South Asian systems designed for extensive irrigation and less thirsty crops, such as millets and pulses (beans), have been subverted by head-reach farmers who grow water-intensive crops, as shown by the numerous studies cited earlier. Away from the main and branch canals, many South Asian irrigation systems are experiencing a growing diversity of crops, cropping seasons, and irrigation requirements. Wade (1986), for example, reported that in Andhra Pradesh, irrigators invariably hired and shared the cost of canal water managers for the rainy season, when everyone used canal irrigation for paddy, but managers were not hired in the dry season, when a wide variety of crops were grown. Differentiated irrigation needs are being increasingly met by the atomistic pump irrigation economy rather than by gravity flow from canals. Even in rice irrigation systems, the homogeneity of farming systems is rapidly eroding. In a central Kerala irrigation system, Kumar et al. (2007) counted 71 varieties of rice planted by farmers, with transplant dates varying by 50 days or more. No flow irrigation system is designed to meet such variety, so system managers simply empty the reservoir at the beginning of the monsoon to keep the command area flooded, allowing farmers to choose their transplant dates.

We saw in Chapter 1 that at no time in history has a South Asian village experienced a weaker authority structure than now. Alfred Deakin, the canny Australian politician, observed that the autocratic character of the colonial state in India allowed the irrigation engineer to play a role more powerful than he could expect in most other societies. The engineer in India, he noted, was often not only a man of science but also a ruler of men, who could take advantage of India's "despotic" system of colonial rule to plan irrigation works (in ways that would be impossible in Australia) without much bother for "the individual wishes or interests of their constituents" (Gilmartin 2003a, 2). Hardiman (2002, 119) suggests that throughout India, except perhaps in the Punjab, from which soldiers were recruited in large numbers, "local authorities routinely crushed protests by peasants without any intervention by the central government." Stone (1984, 231) pointed out that "Concern over the pervasive and unaccountable exercise of powers by the canal bureaucracy lay behind the attempts in the 1860s and 70s to regulate the activities of the canal service . . ." Ebrahim (2004, 223) notes that the colonial "government's authority over water resources at this time was absolute." For centuries until Independence, when the state as well as the people lived off the land, the unequal but strong economic mutuality in the deeply self-interested engagement between the state and the peasantry prevented anarchy. Even if to just provide stable and growing land revenue, the authoritarian colonial state ensured—better than the populist state does today—that resources would be spent on sustaining the productivity and performance of irrigation structures.

Creating and maintaining authority in irrigation systems are proving hard work for the welfare state, thanks to the rise of populist politics and a wide gulf between the state and the peasantry. The old order has crumbled, replaced by new governance structures driven by the pressures of competitive populism (Mollinga 2003). In small and large surface irrigation systems, this has meant erosion of authority, and the encroachment of the welfare state in affairs of small local irrigation systems has further weakened traditional mechanisms of controlling anarchy (Pradhan 1989; Shah 2004).[33] Devolving the irrigation management to farmers is often held out as a panacea for improving service, as if the management agency is the central player in a canal system. However, in his study of allegedly successful irrigation management transfer in the Philippines, Oorthuizen (2003, *14*) wondered whether "these agencies have the necessary room for maneuver to exert sufficient control over their clientele." This is even more of a problem for South Asia.

The last straw has been the rise of liberating alternatives. The power of irrigation communities to hold their members captive in a regime of "mutual co-operation through mutual coercion" (Wade 1986, *253*) has rapidly eroded because of three changes: new opportunities for off-farm livelihoods, pressures and temptations to diversify cropping, and pump irrigation. Intensification and intensive diversification of farming—a combined result of population pressure on farmland and the growing market orientation of agriculture—are eroding the community-managed flow irrigation that required and enforced a high level of homogeneity in farming systems.

Community institutions that sustained surface irrigation from tanks and small-scale diversions have been the first to succumb. Hill irrigation systems in Ladakh, described by Gupta and Tiwari (2002), are weakening as alternative options—jobs in the military, government, and tourism—are changing age-old values and livelihood patterns. Cultures of rice irrigation are declining in many areas, as in Kerala and parts of Tamilnadu, where farmers have over the past three decades abandoned rice in favor of plantation crops, making much surface irrigation infrastructure redundant (Vishwanathan 1997). Throughout southern India, the institution of *neerkattis* and the tanks they once managed have suffered in the wake of the groundwater boom (Seenivasan 2003). The decline in *karezes* of Baluchistan is much bemoaned, but maintaining them was expensive, necessitating collective action and annual contributions managed by a *mirab* (the equivalent of a *neerkatti*, or water manager). Steenbergen (1995, *57*) provides an eloquent account of the demise of *karezes* in Baluchistan:

Soon after the large-scale introduction of dugwells in the 1960s, the flow of many nearby *karezes* was affected. This process had a social as well as a hydrological component . . . [As *karezes* became less viable,] often the first to release their share in the communal systems were the larger farmers, who had the resources to develop a private well. The heavy burden for maintaining the drying *karezes* then fell increasingly upon the smaller farmers. The final outcome often was the collapse of the traditional system.

Above all else, however, gravity-flow irrigation is threatened by pump and tube well technology, on both the demand and the supply side. In tank irrigation commands, much as with the *kareze* irrigators of Baluchistan, owners of pumps and wells no longer have obligations to the irrigation community. And since early adopters are typically the elite, their withdrawal from the tank community, with its maintenance tasks and protocols for water distribution and sharing of water scarcity, is often devastating (Raj and Sundaresan 2005). In the study of 48 villages in Tamilnadu mentioned earlier, Bardhan (1999) found poor maintenance of supply channels in villages where more farmers had pumps and wells compared with villages that depended on tanks; the former villages also had greater inequality in landholdings, with larger farmers owning most pumps and wells. When in early 1980s Walter Coward (1983, 4) observed, "Developing irrigated agriculture is a property-creating process," the full import of pump irrigation in monsoon Asia was not visible. Today, privately owned small pumps and wells disrupt the "social basis" for "collective action in performing various irrigation tasks" (Coward 1983, 4). The new water-scavenging irrigation economy of South Asia has broken free of the hydraulic limits imposed by gravity and open-channel flow and has no need for the associated irrigation culture.

On the supply side, as pump irrigators have begun scavenging water, even from tank catchments and supply channels, water availability in tanks and small reservoirs too has declined. It is a combination of factors, rather than any one of them, that is making gravity-flow irrigation irrelevant in South Asia's agrarian economy. *Ahar-pyne* systems are declining not only because *zamindari* is abolished but also because shallow tube wells are better able to meet irrigation needs for multiple cropping and diversified cropping patterns. The same holds true with tanks in southern India and *karezes* in Baluchistan.

So, too, with large reservoirs. Within canal commands of Pakistan's Indus Irrigation System, the proliferation of tube wells has helped mask the poor performance of irrigation bureaucracies (Steenbergen and Oliemans 1997) and weakened accountability mechanisms in public irrigation systems (Halsema 2002). Ineptitude and malfeasance combined with the politics of populism are certainly a major cause of the declining performance of large irrigation systems, but it is not the only one. Reductions in reservoir storage caused by intensive groundwater development in catchment areas is compounded by siltation, as Ranade (2005) showed for the Narmada project.[34] Head-reach farmers with pumps, who can take surface water as well as groundwater recharge from irrigation return flows, are in effect shrinking the effective command—and they become energetic opponents and saboteurs of institutional reform.

Proliferation of pump irrigation in outer command areas has weakened irrigators' stake in flow irrigation. In India, energy subsidies for pumping water in most states have inspired apathy toward orderly gravity-flow irrigation. In Baluchistan, electricity subsidies have made *karezes* more dispensable. Intensification and intensive diversification of farming are hastening the ascent of pump irrigation and decline of gravity flow, both at once. Ironically, the growing irrelevance of canal managers within the command areas is evident in the recent lessening of corruption in most Indian surface irrigation systems. During the 1970s, when Robert Wade (1975) created a sensation by writing about large-scale corruption in irrigation bureaucracies, nontrivial rents for favored allocations were extracted from farmers. This was before the rise of pump irrigation, a time when irrigation managers enjoyed a monopoly control over a resource for which there was no substitute. Their monopoly power—and their power to extract rents—has rapidly declined with the rise of well irrigation in canal commands. Stone (1984) noted that even during the nineteenth century, illegal rents extracted by canal bureaucracy in the Ganga canal were inversely related to the number of wells in a village. Now, with the easy availability of pumps and subsidies for electricity, irrigation managers have lost their power. Coveted postings for engineers are only in construction; managing the system is a punishment posting. The service the system provides is recharging the aquifers, a service that has a strong public goods characteristic of nonexcludability even though it does not satisfy the other characteristic of a public good—nonrivalry in consumption. Since irrigation managers have no mechanism to exclude particular farmers from using the recharge, their power to extract rents has dissipated.

Large dams and gravity irrigation systems inspired widespread disillusionment even in early decades after the end of the Empire. Nehru, who extolled the Bhakra dam as a "temple of modern India" at the dawn of Independence lamented a few years later, "We are suffering from . . . the disease of gigantism . . . It is the small irrigation projects which will change the face of the country far more than half a dozen big projects" (Sharma 1989, 43). And change the face of the country they did—not minor government irrigation projects but 20-odd million groundwater wells and tube wells.

In many ways, then, the emergence of the booming pump irrigation economy in South Asia is both a cause and a result of the erosion of anarchy controllers in gravity-flow irrigation. Reinstalling effective anarchy controllers will help arrest the decline in flow irrigation, but only to a limited extent. As I argued in Chapter 2, the decline in flow irrigation and ascent of pump irrigation are the result of enduring changes under way in the human geography of rural South Asia. Back in the 1980s, von Oppen and Subba Rao (1980; 1987, 36)[35] showed that the rise and decline of tanks in India had a great deal to do with population pressure on farmlands, among many other factors. Until population density in a region rises to 60/km², farming communities have neither enough labor supply nor strong incentive to build and maintain tanks for irrigation because they can depend on extensive, mixed rain-fed farming. At the other extreme, once the population density crosses 220, tanks become an inefficient technology for capturing and storing rainwater, especially after small pumps and bore holes make aquifers easier to tap and use. Deforested catchments, encroached supply channels, and tank-bed cultivation reduce storage and command areas, and crop diversification away from paddy and the rise of well irrigation hasten the decline. This logic works much the same way for large flow irrigation systems as well: with population pressure mounting in much of South Asia, the same agroecological and demographic dynamic that explains the decline of tank irrigation also drives the shrinking of command areas.

Several implications follow. First, expectations that improved management of surface irrigation systems can reverse these trends—through institutional reforms, participatory management, more accountable bureaucracy, volumetric water pricing—need to be tempered because these efforts do not affect the agroecological and demographic fundamentals of a region. Second, over a 30- to 50-year time horizon, as population pressure on South Asian agriculture declines, the current pressure for land-augmenting irrigation technologies will ease; this, combined with rising energy costs and better irrigation system management, may pave the way for the return of gravity flow. On that time scale, however, much else in South Asia will change too, including the nature of farming itself. Third, Africa and Latin America— which are unlikely to encounter the kind of population pressure on farmland that parts of Asia face today—are unlikely ever to experience comparable pressure on groundwater aquifers, except in urban areas and pockets of high-value intensive farming, as in southern Africa, Namibia, and West and North Africa. Fourth, and relatedly, in most of these latter areas, the irrigation challenge for long will be to grow the population in irrigation commands so that canal systems become viable for smallholder African farmers to build and maintain.

Conclusion: Cosmic Disconnect

In *Exit, Voice and Loyalty*, Albert Hirschman (1965) showed that as users, members, or customers, people react to a decline in the performance of sociotechnical systems either by exiting them or by using their voice to generate internal pressure for performance improvement. When sufficient members press the exit button, they hasten the system on its downward spin, which could be prevented if more members used their voice instead. Hirschman pled for the latter but bemoaned that exit was often people's option. Gravity-flow irrigation in South Asia is confronted with the Hirschman dilemma. And all the evidence we have is suggesting that farmers of South Asia are choosing exit in large numbers. This means not that tanks and surface irrigation systems will disappear from South Asia, but that their role will continue to decline.

Sociologists of surface irrigation systems have long lamented that public irrigation systems perform poorly because farmers' preferences are not included in their design and operation.[36] The era in which this was likely true is coming to a close in South Asia. No matter how inclusive public irrigation management, it will be unable to check the expansion of the water-scavenging economy, which gives smallholders greater degrees of freedom to squeeze more livelihood from their postage-stamp landholdings. Canals and tanks cannot compete with individually owned pumps, pipes, and boreholes for watering whatever crops small farmers choose to grow. Ostrichlike, much public irrigation planning and management (and even canal irrigation research) in South Asia carries on with business-as-usual, overlooking the groundswell of pump irrigation all around.

Massive new infusion of capital in surface water infrastructure is promised, implying more of the same. In India, between 1996 and 2005, the central government invested more than US$4.5 billion (Rs. 19.4 billion) on the Accelerated Irrigation Benefits Program, with the objective of completing the "last-mile projects." The result, according to an NGO: "No acceleration, little irrigation, minuscule benefit" (SANDRP 2006). Yet government reports insist that 57 to 61 percent of the increase in agricultural demand and 78 percent of the increase in demand from other sectors by 2025 will be met by existing and new surface systems (Ministry of Water Resources 1999). Ominously, the World Bank (2005a, b) has offered substantial assistance. Even aside from their environmental and displacement impacts, large surface irrigation systems have been shown to be economic disasters and would be difficult to justify by any cost-benefit rule. As Repetto (1986, 1) lamented 20 years ago, "The fundamental problem is the financing system . . ."

What prompts governments' and lenders' continuing obsession with irrigation systems? Researchers like Nijman (1993) advance the "spoils system" theory, suggesting that the impetus comes less from the promise of improved welfare and more from a political economy run by a minority—lenders, politicians, technocrats, and contractors—and tolerated by an apathetic majority of farmers uncertain about their gains from a debt they will not be called upon to redeem. Although South Asia also has influential thinkers who feel passionately about large irrigation projects, such as those Arthur Cotton built, and their capacity to generate welfare, the pump irrigation economy will only grow as the region's agriculture diversifies. The tail has begun to wag the dog.

CHAPTER 4

WELLS AND WELFARE

All that is wanted is water and this want supplied, everything else will almost follow of course . . .

— *Sir Arthur Cotton*

When the late Professor V. M. Dandekar called Indian agriculture the parking lot for the poor, he was describing contemporary agrarian conditions in all of South Asia as well as the North China Plain. A millennium survey of Indian agriculture—aptly called the Situation Assessment Survey—sponsored in 2003 by the Government of India asked 51,770 farming households around India, "Are you happy being in farming?" (NSSO 2005, Table 7). Many readers of the survey were surprised that only 40 percent said they wanted to get out of agriculture; the same survey showed that the average net income per farm household reported was just US$577[1] (Narayanamoorthy 2006, 471), less than the poverty-line income of US$1 per person per day, assuming an average family of five. Barring a small class of large landowners mostly in Pakistan, who manage a standard of living comparable to that of urban middle classes, for a majority of farmers in rural South Asia, being in farming is synonymous with a life of abject poverty. Even larger farmers in South Asia are vulnerable to poverty during a drought.

Montek Singh Ahluwalia's (1978) seminal work showed that the fortunes of Indian farmers fluctuate from year to year, in keeping with the performance of agriculture; in years with good crops, poverty levels of farm households drop, and in years of poor crops, they rise.

Nothing comes as an unmixed blessing, and South Asia's pump irrigation revolution is no exception, having had its critics (see, e.g., Brown 2003; Dhawan 1995; Postel 1999; Seckler et al. 1999). I deal with the negatives in Chapter 5; in this chapter, I discuss the benefits that pump irrigation has brought for South Asia's subsistence farmers. As the world's largest non-government irrigation initiative, complete with its own specialized economic institutions, South Asia's pump irrigation economy has been a boon that for long dwarfed the collateral damage it produced. Rapid expansion in this form of irrigation has had a powerful equalizing, stabilizing, and income-enhancing impact on a subcontinental scale, giving succor to small holders in regions where public irrigation programs would never reach and few development interventions offered help.

The benefits of pump irrigation can be summarized in a short list:

- *Some for all rather than all for some.* It offered some irrigation access to an overwhelming majority, rather than concentrating all irrigation benefits on a privileged class of farmers in canal commands.
- *Diffusion of social tensions.* It helped soften farmer unrest in dry-land areas, which would have otherwise destabilized social and political structures.
- *Some regional balance in irrigation.* It has "democratized" irrigation and now accounts for more than 60 percent of irrigated areas and 80 percent of irrigated farm output and farm incomes;
- *Drought-proof monsoon agriculture.* It insured the region's agriculture against at least one monsoon failure and appears to have ended large-scale famines.
- *Benefits for landless.* It has improved farm wages and increased the demand for farm labor year-round.
- *Relief to the poor.* The technology for pump irrigation proved ideal for marginal farmers short on land but long on family labor; whereas large public irrigation projects were scale-neutral in their benefits, pump irrigation has a strong bias toward the poor with its land-augmenting and labor-absorbing impact.
- *Intensive diversification.* It catalyzed and sustained the production of high-value milk, fruits, and vegetables, especially by smallholders in dry-land areas.

Those effects have benefited—directly and indirectly, to lesser or greater extent—more than half a billion rural people in South Asia. It would be an exaggeration to say that, as a result, the South Asian smallholder is much better off in 2000 than in 1975. But it is no exaggeration to say ceteris paribus, that, he[2] would have been immensely worse off but for pump irrigation.

People's Irrigation Initiative

If participatory irrigation management is about "the involvement of irrigation users in all aspects and all levels of irrigation management,"[3] the South Asian context in which it has worked best is the groundwater economy. It represents a people's irrigation economy in which the initiative, investment, and management have come primarily from farmers. Public agencies and NGOs played a catalytic role during the 1930s through to the 1960s, as we reviewed in Chapter 1, but public tube well programs are now dying in India as well as Pakistan, and deep tube wells established by NGOs in Bangladesh and donors in Nepal Terai, too, have lost out to the boom in shallow tube wells and pump irrigation service markets.

Governments sometimes helped by getting out of the way, as in Bangladesh, where the government remained for long a monopoly seller of imported irrigation equipment. Together with unwarranted siting norms strictly enforced, this government monopoly kept Bangladesh's pump irrigation revolution bottled up until the mid-1980s. Without spending a farthing, international donors did a big turn for Bangladesh's poor merely by making the government see the irrationality of its controls. Once imports and trade in irrigation equipment were liberalized, shallow tube well engines were destandardized, and institutional credit expanded, Bangladesh's shallow tube well boom—as well as its small-holder agriculture—took off beginning around 1985 (Fujita and Hossain 1995; Palmer-Jones 1999).

In Nepal Terai, too, a deep tube well program supported by donor funds began driving out traditional surface irrigation systems, called *kulos and jharan*. But deep tube wells are expensive to operate and maintain and require collective action and were themselves crowded out by private shallow tube wells (Gautam 2006). In Pakistan, government policy has left pump irrigation expansion pretty much alone, with neither restrictions imposed nor stimuli offered. In India, different states have adopted different approaches to siting and licensing norms, based often on guidelines issued by the National

Bank for Agriculture and Rural Development, which is the central refinancing institution influencing the flow of institutional credit to agriculture, including support for pump irrigation. Although spacing and licensing norms are seldom enforced strictly by local government agencies, the flow of institutional credit has played a role in stimulating or impeding the development of pump irrigation in different regions. However, available evidence suggests that well over half of the pump capital created in South Asia until the early 1990s was wholly self-financed by individual owners.[4] Government's role has declined further. According to the 2000–01 minor irrigation census in India, more than 80 percent of dug wells, 66 percent of shallow tube wells, 54 percent of deep tube wells, and 62 percent of surface lift schemes were farmer financed, with neither subsidy nor loan inputs from government. Especially in India, government support for pump irrigation is essentially through electricity subsidies, which we analyze in Chapter 5.

In assessing impact on rural poverty in India, Fan et al. (1999) found that a million rupees (US$25,000 in 2007) of government expenditure on irrigation would raise 7.4 poor people out of poverty, compared with 165 people by an equivalent investment in roads, 91.4 by investments in agricultural research and extension, 31.7 by investments in education, and 27.8 by investments in rural development. This is not surprising, since as we saw in Chapter 3, the funds spent on public irrigation projects are irrigating less and less land. But government expenditures are for public works, not the pump irrigation that sustains India's agrarian poor. A million rupees would enable small farmers in the Ganga basin to create 40 shallow tube wells that would irrigate 100–120 ha and likely lift more poor people above the poverty line than a million rupees of government investment in virtually anything.

The idea of self-governing "irrigation communities"—once central to the discourse in tank and canal irrigation—influenced early public tube well programs, too. The communitarian ideal, in which a tube well owned by a farmer cooperative provides equitable irrigation access to large and small farmers, rich and poor, has for long appealed to governments as well as NGOs. Seeds of this idea were seen in NGO programs in Bangladesh (Mandal and Palmer-Jones 1987), eastern Uttar Pradesh (Ballabh 1987; Pant 1984), North Bihar (Pant and Rai 1985), Nepal Terai (Gautam 2006), and Gujarat (Shah 1996). Indeed, as the performance of bureaucratically managed public tube well programs deteriorated during the 1970s and 1980s, some governments began imposing irrigation management transfer schemes on them, with success rates as poor as in surface irrigation projects. Commonly, the tube wells were so expensive to operate and maintain that farmers were willing to use them under government management but loath to take them over.[5]

For decades in South Asia, debates about the appropriate institutions for local irrigation management have pitted participatory against bureaucratic models of management. Although both approaches have remained on the margins, the region has witnessed the spontaneous emergence and spread of informal, decentralized irrigation service markets with powerful productivity and equity effects in improving irrigation access for smallholders. Hybrid forms of user organizations—combining features of water user associations and irrigation service markets—have also emerged, including the tube well companies of North Gujarat (Shah and Bhattacharya 1993), tube well partnerships in Punjab, and informal user organizations to which public tube wells have been transferred with great success in Gujarat (Mukherji and Kishore 2003). These spontaneous institutions in groundwater irrigation are highly influential, unlike surface irrigation institutions, which are researched far more extensively than their influence warrants.

Pump Irrigation Service Markets

There are various ways to assess the significance of the pump irrigation boom to South Asia's agrarian economy. One is to ask, as marketers would, about its market penetration[6]: has pump irrigation benefited a privileged few or a large majority of the region's farmers? The straightforward answer is the proportion of cultivating households who own water extraction mechanisms (WEMs). Considered thus, the results are not impressive: in 2000, WEM ownership was confined to approximately one of every 21 farm holdings in Bangladesh, one of 26 in Nepal Terai, one of 12 in Pakistan, and one of six in India.

However, in South Asia, WEM ownership is no indicator of the pump irrigation penetration, thanks to vibrant and pervasive water markets that have emerged as a growth industry. In Chapter 1, we saw the nineteenth century practices for sharing irrigation turns from large, jointly owned wells in northwestern India. The irrigation service markets that emerged in Gujarat around 1910 began as a variation of these shared wells but quickly became sophisticated economic institutions that encouraged a class of pump irrigation "entrepreneurs," who invested in heavy-duty WEMs and extensive buried pipeline networks, expressly to sell pump irrigation to a client base for profit. As more entrepreneurs entered the business, competition among them created an economic dynamic amenable to generalized market analytics (Shah 1993). As they spread across regions, pump irrigation markets became a common decentralized institutional arrangement, unique to South Asia (Fujita and Hossain 1995; Meinzen-Dick 1996; Meinzen-Dick and Sullins 1994; Shah 1993). How best to label this institution has been a matter of some debate.[7] The substantive discussion has, however, focused on its internal dynamic and its effects as a pervasive and powerful agrarian institution in imparting leverage to private WEM capital.

What drives WEM owners to sell irrigation services is the microeconomics of owning and operating a WEM. Even small WEMs—those with a 5 hp pump—are too large for the 100 million-plus family farms that work less than a hectare. The household that buys one has spare capacity to pump water, and there are willing buyers in the neighborhood. This double coincidence of wants produces a powerful incentive for WEM owners to spread the overhead of their irrigation asset over a larger farming area than they own. In India, for instance, 71 million cultivator households operate holdings of one acre (0.4 ha) or less. A holding of this size cannot use even the smallest available WEM for more than 200 or 250 hours in a year, yet it can run 10 to 15 times as long. As a result, WEM owners share the services of their pumps with neighbors who are willing to cover the variable costs of electricity or fuel and make some contribution to the overhead.

In India, state-owned electricity utilities unwittingly gave a powerful stimulus to these markets when instead of charging electric WEM owners for power actually consumed, they began levying a flat power charge per month per horsepower rating of the pump assembly to save on the costs of metering and metered billing (Shah 1993; Shah et al. 2004c). This turned energy costs, normally part of the variable costs of pumping, into overhead. Once having paid the monthly flat electricity charges, the WEM owner now had an even stronger incentive to sell pump irrigation service to neighbors who often were poorer and had too little land to justify a WEM. The change in electricity pricing unleashed a powerful energy-irrigation nexus in Indian agriculture, to be discussed in Chapter 5. The nexus opened up irrigation access to many millions of marginal and smallholders in rural India who would have had access neither to public canals nor to their own WEMs to irrigate their fields (Chambers et al. 1989; Pant 1992; Shah 1993). This is an important gain because reaching out to the agrarian poor has not proved easy, even when governments earmarked large sums to benefit them. Indian Prime Minister Rajiv Gandhi once conceded that for every 100 rupees his government allocated to antipoverty programs, only 15 reached targeted families, the rest lost to "leakage" on the way. Here was a subsidy that appeared to go to well-off WEM owners but in fact provided irrigation service to the poor.

Many observers consider flat electricity tariffs antipoor because smallholders cannot make full use of their WEMs and yet have to pay the full flat charge. In reality, for every owner of a WEM in South Asia, there are six to 15 potential customers of pump irrigation service.[8] This gives rise to a seller's market for irrigation service, and with their bargaining power, WEM owners can extract a monopoly premium (Shah 1993). Moreover, in many situations, well owners can coerce the desperate buyers of their irrigation services to enter into disadvantageous transactions (Boyce 1988; Bhatia 1992; Dubash 2002; Janakarajan 1994; Prakash 2005).[9] At first, these possibilities raised fears about a rising class of "water lords" who might capture groundwater, the last resource, and use it as an instrument of exploitation of the poor and the weak. Subsequent research, however, has found that with occasional exceptions, the spread of pump irrigation markets had large-scale and beneficial equity effects by spreading irrigation among smallholders (Chambers et al. 1989; Meinzen-Dick 1996; Shah 1993; Shah and Raju 1988).

Recent national surveys in India lend ample support to the thesis that a substantial segment of marginal farmers depend on pump irrigation service markets for surviving on their tiny land holdings. However, nowhere are these impacts put into bolder relief than in personal accounts of field researchers deeply interested in understanding the conditions of the rural poor. I will cite just five. In a village in northern Bangladesh, Fujita and Hossain (1995, 459–60) found that thanks to pump irrigation markets, "the economic value of land . . . has decreased in a relative sense" in farm income generation and "opportunities for the landless and near-landless to climb the social ladder [have] expanded greatly." In a similar field study in Uttar Pradesh, Niranjan Pant (2005, *2680*) writes, ". . . the smallest farmers with land-holdings up to 0.4 ha are the largest beneficiaries of the groundwater markets as 60 percent of the farmers of this category irrigated their wheat crop by water purchased from the owners of private Water Extraction Devices . . ." Studying the plight of marginal farmers in accessing irrigation in Chandkura block in central Bihar, Wilson (2002, *1232*), otherwise critical of profiteering by water sellers, highlights the role of pump irrigation markets: the "extension of irrigation through hiring out [mobile diesel pump sets] to small and marginal holdings is in fact the major factor accounting for the further increase since 1981–82 in cultivated area irrigated at least once to approximately 73 percent in 1995–96. Those hiring in pump sets are overwhelmingly small and marginal cultivators; they cultivate an average of 1.35 acres (compared with an average of 3.89 acres cultivated by pump set owners) . . ."[10] In a 2005 survey of 580 buyers and sellers of pump irrigation service in West Bengal, Mukherji (2007) found that smallholders dominate not only as buyers in pump irrigation markets but also as sellers. In the early years of the pump irrigation economy, medium farmers often dominated water selling. Over time, however, marginal farmers have come to own the bulk of the pump irrigation assets in West Bengal and dominate the water markets as buyers as well as sellers (Mukherji 2007). Finally, in a survey of 180 households from Meerut district in Western Uttar Pradesh, Singh and Singh (2003) found that 82 percent participated in water markets as buyers or sellers or both. Marginal, small, medium, and large—farmers at all levels were engaged in buying and selling pump irrigation service; only the proportions differed. The larger the farmer, the more likely that he is self-sufficient; even so, more than half of large farmers purchased pump irrigation service, and 22 percent of marginal farmers and 30 percent of small farmers were water sellers. Buying and selling were more important for marginal and small farmers than for large landholders who were self-sufficient in water and had little surplus pumping capacity. Cropping intensity (the number of crops grown on a piece of land during a year) was highest for buyers, and irrigation intensity (the number of waterings given to a piece of land in a year) was highest for WEM owners.[11]

In describing the nature and working of the irrigation markets, a very considerable volume of empirical and theoretical literature has deployed models and conceptual ideas from neoclassical economics, political economy, institutional economics, game theory, theory of imperfect information, and so on. Synthesizing this formidable literature is an ambitious task that I do not attempt here, but it is perhaps relevant to note the wide variety of transaction types that are found across the subcontinent. In the simplest, a WEM owner retails pump irrigation on demand, levying an hourly charge; this model obtains in much of South Asia, as illustrated by several studies from Pakistan (Meinzen-Dick 1996), Gujarat (Shah 1993), Uttar Pradesh (Pant 1992; Shankar 1987), North Bihar (Kishore and Mishra 2005; Pant 1992; Shah and Ballabh 1997), Rajasthan (Singh and Singh 2003), and Karnataka (Deepak et al. 2005, Nagaraj et al. 2005).

In central Gujarat, farmers often invest in laying buried pipeline networks with outlets opening into the fields of all neighboring farmers who want to use his service. But the buyers are by no means tied to the WEM owner; they still have the option to buy irrigation service from other WEM owners, several of whom have opened outlets from the buried pipe network into their fields.[12] When the construction of WEMs becomes too capital intensive as well as risky for individual farmers, as in North Gujarat (Prakash 2005; Shah and Bhattacharya 1993; Shaheen and Shiyani 2005), farmers owning land around a potential tube well site come together to share the capital costs, risks, irrigation benefits, and profits or losses in proportion to their area served by the new WEM. These are similar to the professional pump irrigation sellers in central Gujarat but are organized more like a joint-stock company and are therefore called tube well companies; they come closest to Robert Hunt's flow "irrigation communities" applied to pump irrigation.

Throughout South Asia, the focus of transaction is pump irrigation service itself. Sellers seldom try to influence or dictate what crops buyers will grow and how they will allocate their labor and other inputs. In early stages, WEM owners' monopoly power tends to be manifest in "concentric circles of moral proximity" (Wood 1999, 787), in which kith and kin get preferential treatment, but as WEM density increases, transactions tend toward the impersonal. In a study of six villages in Hoshangabad and Narsingpur in Madhya Pradesh, Kei and Takeshi (1999) found that more than 60 percent of pump irrigation sales were cross-caste transactions. Terms of payment may vary; some sellers may accept payment at the harvest time; others may accept a share in the produce. However, the implicit price of pump irrigation service in a given region and for a given technology shows a level of uniformity that hints at an equilibrium tendency (Ballabh et al. 2003; Deepak et al. 2005; Kishore and Mishra 2005; Shah and Ballabh 1997; Sharma and Sharma 2004; Singh and Singh 2003). Where production risks as well as incremental pumping costs are low, seasonal contracts are popular. In West Bengal as well as Bangladesh, trade in pump irrigation for the early summer rice crop— popularly known as *boro* rice—is a case in point (Kolavalli and Atheeq 1990; Mukherji 2007; Palmer-Jones 1994). In some situations, however, pump irrigation service transactions are interlocked with transactions in other inputs as well; here, sale of pump irrigation becomes part of a larger deal that involves sharing of costs, benefits, production and even market risks between pump irrigation buyer and seller.[13] In the early stages of the pump irrigation markets in Bangladesh, Palmer-Jones (1987) found sharecropping with water a common transaction. The rise of crop-sharing contracts against water provision for cultivation of high-risk crops, such as cumin in North Gujarat, is a case in point (Bhatia 1992; Dubash 2002; Shah 1993; Shah and Ballabh 1995). The cost-benefit calculus involved for both buyer and seller is complex because such a transaction involves much more than just the sale of pump irrigation service, but it is not always unfair to buyers, as commonly believed (Fujita and Hossain 1995).

In general, then, where the risks and costs of pump-irrigated farming are low, as in much of eastern India, service markets boom and are highly beneficial to buyers. As the risks and costs of pump-irrigated farming increase, as with cumin crops in North Gujarat, pump irrigation service exchange contracts tend to involve sharing of risks between water buyers and sellers and become increasingly unfavorable to buyers. In contrast, as the risks and costs of tube well installation and operation increase, irrigators tend to look for ways to share these by organizing into institutions akin to tube well companies. But in much of hard-rock peninsular India, pump irrigation markets have become thin and shallow, with owners of successful wells barely managing to meet their own supplemental irrigation needs.

Despite controversies around the structure, conduct and performance of pump irrigation markets (Bhatia 1992; Copestake 1986; Dubash 2002; Janakarajan 2002; Mandal 1989; Meinzen-Dick 1996; Palmer-Jones 1994; Shah 1993), there is broad agreement around four effects: they have helped well owners improve the operating factors (utilization rates) of their wells and pumps; helped irrigate marginal land otherwise dependent on rain and thus assisted small farmers too poor to invest in the technology; created pressures to move water to high-value uses, *ceteris paribus;* and leveraged the existing stock of pump capital to produce a large pump irrigation economy and spread irrigation benefits. The scale of this leverage effect of pump irrigation markets depends on their breadth and depth—how widespread and common are the buying and selling of pump irrigation services, and how significant are these transactions in the household economies of buyers and sellers.

Indicators of breadth can be found in the studies by Mukherji, Pant, Singh and Singh, and Wilson cited earlier. In Pakistan, for example, a 2001 report for the Ministry of Water and Power (Government of Pakistan 2001, 1) asserted that although the number of WEMs in use soared from 3,000 in 1950 to 560,000 in 2000, "the number of users [of groundwater] are over 2.5 million farmers, who exploit groundwater through their own tubewells or hire the services of tubewells from their neighbors." Using Pakistan's agricultural machinery census of 2004, one can estimate that some 300,000 WEM owners sold around 180 million hours of irrigation service, mostly to supplement unreliable canal irrigation, on around three million ha of buyers' land (Government of Pakistan 2006).

In Bangladesh, in a survey of 245 well owners in 40 villages scattered around the country, Roy and Mainuddin (2003) found that 87 percent of WEM owners sold water to, on average, 12.5 neighbors irrigating, on average, a gross cropped area of 2.5 ha plus a little over 1 ha of their own land. This is perhaps how the 0.9 million shallow tube wells in Bangladesh irrigate over 2.5 million ha of net cropped area. In West Bengal, India, the survey by Mukherji (2007) of 580 pump irrigators found that the average WEM owner served more than 27 buyers of pump irrigation service. She also found that 77 percent of all water pumped, and 69 percent of the area irrigated by a typical WEM, was for the benefit of buyers, and that 70.5 percent of farmers surveyed purchased pump irrigation service. In fact, so broad are the pump irrigation markets in West Bengal that only nine percent of her sample farmers were not either buyer or seller or both. As a result, not owning a WEM puts a small farmer at no disadvantage compared with WEM owners. Owners irrigated 84 percent of their gross cropped area; buyers irrigated 80 percent.

The 2002 IWMI survey, mentioned earlier, of 2,600 well owners and village leaders from India, Pakistan, Bangladesh and Nepal Terai (Shah et al. 2006) found that pump irrigation service markets had less depth as well as breadth in central and peninsular India than in northern parts of the subcontinent, where the institution was omnipresent. All villages in Bangladesh, 90 percent in Pakistan Punjab and Sind as well as lower Nepal, 80 percent in eastern India, and 75 percent in northwestern India had "deep" and "broad" markets in pump irrigation service. In eastern India, Bangladesh and Nepal Terai, at least two-thirds of the WEM owners interviewed sold irrigation services to neighbors.

How large is the irrigated area served by pump irrigation markets in South Asia? Based on their subcontinental survey, Shah et al. (2006) estimated that a modest 4.94 million ha of land is irrigated through purchased pump irrigation. Saleth (1998) had earlier placed the figure for India alone higher, at six million ha. A 1998 National Sample Survey covering 78,990 rural households in India, however, dwarfed all other estimates of the area served by pump irrigation markets in India (NSSO 1999a, A-44). The survey concluded that "for 46 percent of the irrigated area under five major crops in the country, irrigation was hired from other sources" (NSSO 1999a, 42). Comparing NSSO survey rounds 31, 48, and 54, Mukherji (2005) concluded that the area irrigated through pump irrigation markets in India grew from one million ha in 1976–77 to 20 million ha in 1997–98, more than the area *actually* served by all public irrigation systems together. This would suggest a much higher dependence of Indian agriculture on pump irrigation service markets than believed by most researchers. The point remains that many of South Asia's marginal holdings of less than 1 ha depend on pump irrigation markets for improved productivity and livelihoods; as a result, their operation is of great welfare significance.

Fifteen years ago, Bhatia (1992, A142), concerned about a few "haves" monopolizing groundwater, asked, "Who owns groundwater resources? Who benefits from their use? Who causes and who suffers from their overexploitation? How can we make sure these resources are utilized to meet real needs rather than to enrich a privileged minority?" Most of these questions are valid still. However, there is enough evidence to suggest that thanks to pump irrigation markets, the benefits of WEM irrigation, which would have remained confined to the 25 million WEM owners in South Asia today, have been available to additional 50 million to 70 million smallholder farmers, who are often too poor to invest in their own WEMs. In a study of pump irrigation markets in Faizabad and Bahraich districts of Uttar Pradesh, Pant (1992, 106) arrived at two conclusions:

> The first one is that canals and [public] tubewells do not work in the interest of farmers who belong to land holding categories up to 1 ha and [who] are from the lowest castes. The second one is that water markets make groundwater accessible to the very small and sub-marginal farmers.

Despite occasional dismal stories of water lords exploiting water buyers, Pant's conclusion still reflects the more general reality of the powerful welfare effect of pump irrigation markets in much of South Asia. The pump irrigation economy thus likely touches the lives of some half a billion rural people in India, Pakistan, Bangladesh, and Nepal Terai.

And neither that estimate nor any of the studies I have cited above include the benefits to an underclass of rural South Asia—those who work as tube well operators. In eastern parts, where WEM owners themselves are underemployed marginal farmers, operating the tube well is a part-time job for a family member. But as we move west, tube well operation and serving the water market is a full-time job. In Pakistan, land as well as WEMs are owned mostly by a minority of large farmers, and Pakistan's large WEMs operate for 15 to 18 hours a day. For Pakistan's poor youth, the pump irrigation economy has been a source of employment; an estimated 1.28 million rural youth are employed as tube well operators and in tube well water distribution work (Ul Hassan et al. 2007).

Effects of the Pump Irrigation Boom

The microeconomic impacts of pump irrigation at the level of the farm or even the village are many and diverse; I will briefly consider six and cite some references without engaging in a detailed discussion because there is wide agreement on these benefits. Note, once again, that we are concerned not so much with groundwater or surface water but with pump irrigation versus flow irrigation, the categorization used in Chapter 3. The benefits of pump irrigation have to do with the high degree of water control it offers: the farmer can scavenge water on demand, rather than have to adapt his farming system to an irrigation regimen not tailored to his needs, as with flow irrigation from tanks and canals. Because it is on-demand, ceteris paribus, WEM irrigation enhances productivity, allows higher cropping intensity, permits diversification, provides stability, encourages efficiency in water use, and alleviates rural poverty.

Productivity. With pump irrigation, a farmer can secure higher crop yields by meeting moisture stress better and by making more intensive use of other yield-enhancing inputs, such as chemicals and labor. WEM irrigation, especially when purchased, is often eight to 15 times costlier than flow irrigation, but it promises on-demand and just-in-time irrigation service and therefore helps the farmer achieve higher production per unit of land as well as unit of water applied (Kahnert and Levine 1993). Dhawan (1989) found that the rice-equivalent output per hectare of net cropped area for groundwater-irrigated areas in Punjab and Tamilnadu was 50 to 100 percent higher than canal-irrigated areas in comparisons at three different points in time. Similar evidence was documented in early studies in Pakistan (Lowdermilk et al. 1978; Meinzen-Dick 1996) and in Gujarat and eastern Uttar Pradesh in India (Shah 1993). These microlevel consequences are reflected in macrolevel studies as well.

Intensification. Pump irrigation enables small farmers to use land more intensively through multiple cropping. Land-use intensity through multiple cropping in India increased post-1975 in response to the spread of groundwater irrigation (Chapter 2). A 2003 survey of 51,770 farm households in 6,760 villages around India asked respondents the means of irrigation used by them for their monsoon and winter crops. Expectedly, of those who used irrigation, the proportion that depended on flow irrigation declined from 31 percent during the monsoon to 23.5 percent during winter, while the proportion dependent on WEMs increased from 69 percent during the monsoon to 76.5 percent during winter (NSSO 2005). India's 2000–01 minor irrigation census (Government of India 2005a) showed that under pump irrigation (from groundwater and surface water), only a third of the irrigated area was served during the monsoon and the rest was planted to winter, summer, or perennial crops. In the case of flow-irrigation schemes, in contrast, two-thirds of the area served was during the rainy season, mostly supplementing rainfall.

Diversification. Pump irrigation helps marginal and small farmers enhance income, employment, and food supply per unit of land; it helps them choose profitable farming systems (field crops, vegetables, orchards, plantations, livestock, and dairying) that are sensitive to moisture stress and thrive with more frequent watering year-round (instead of a large volume of water released in one or few spells). Fruit and vegetable crops require frequent watering, as do fodder crops that support intensive dairy production in many parts of South Asia. NSSO (2005) shows that farmers tend to rely on WEM irrigation more than on flow irrigation in raising high-value market crops—fruit and vegetables, orchards, plantations—which offer a higher economic return to on-demand irrigation. Surface water bodies, especially small ones like tanks, generally dry up soon after the departure of the monsoon and cannot always supply the final irrigation needed by winter crops. Similarly, many run-of-the-river irrigation systems in South Asia also suffer from drastic reductions in available water after the monsoon months. In contrast, groundwater is available continually in regions with abundant recharge, such as the Ganga basin, but even in hard-rock aquifers of the southern peninsula, WEMs manage to produce some water for winter and even small summer crops, and farmers therefore rely more heavily on WEMs for irrigating high-value crops. In dry regions of Gujarat and Rajasthan, crop production has been replaced by dairying as the main source of household income, since a milk cow can produce more net income in a year than a double-cropped hectare of land, according to a study of four villages in Banaskantha district of North Gujarat (Kumar et al. 2004b). As a result dairying is dominating village economies, accounting for 45 to 75 percent of the total value of output generated. Behind the increase in dairy production in dry regions of western India lie two drivers: stable markets for milk provided by dairy cooperatives, and tiny plots of alfalfa and other green fodders irrigated every week with tube well water.

Stabilization. WEMs are insurance against the frequent meteorological and hydrological droughts that visit large regions of South Asia.[14] Long after the surface water reservoirs turn dry, even limited groundwater aquifers can often be tapped to save the crops. For centuries, well digging has tended to peak during drought years. More recently, this has also been the experience in the North China Plain (Changming et al. 2001). The power of pump irrigation to provide insurance against both long and short periods of moisture stress has been studied by Burke and Moench (2000), Palanisami and Ranganathan (2004), Tsur (1990) and is called its stabilization value, as distinct from productivity value. In 1965–66, when rainfall was 20 percent below normal, India suffered a 19 percent fall in food grain production over the previous year; that was before the pump irrigation boom. In 1987–88, rainfall was 17.5 percent below normal, but thanks to groundwater pumping, food grain production was down by just over two percent (Gandhi and Namboodiri 2007).

Efficiency. When water supply is unreliable, as gravity flow often is, farmers tend to overirrigate their crops when they have water. This tendency is reinforced by the low marginal cost of surface irrigation, which nowhere in South Asia is charged on volumetric basis. Wells, in contrast, offer just-in-time irrigation. Well irrigation is less uncertain, and buyers, diesel pump owners, and electric pump owners subject to metered electricity tariff face steep marginal costs, forcing them to use pump irrigation efficiently. This produces two results: farmers using WEM irrigation tend to apply less water per hectare of the same crop than farmers dependent on flow irrigation; and farmers dependent on flow irrigation tend to plant crops that thrive on abundant but unreliable irrigation, typically cereals and oilseeds, rather than the higher-value crops that require reliable irrigation. At the macro level, this has a profound impact on productivity of flow and pump irrigation. Around 380 to 400 km^3 of the water actually stored in South Asia's surface reservoirs supports a fifth of the value of the region's farm and livestock output in command areas that constitute less than one-eighth of its farmland; in contrast, 285 to 300 km^3 of pump irrigation—more than 90 percent of it from wells—supports three-fifths of the value of farm output, benefiting two-fifths of farmland and the overwhelming majority of farmers.

Poverty alleviation. Finally, pump irrigation is easing the stress on the agrarian poor of South Asia. The strong positive relationship between the spread of irrigation and demand and real wages for labor has been postulated and explored (Bardhan 1973; Kumar 1974; Narayanamoorthy and Deshpande 2003). However, many researchers have argued that because groundwater irrigation, compared with irrigation in general, has stronger impact on intensification and intensive diversification of agriculture, it also has a stronger positive effect on labor demand and wage rates (Chambers et al. 1989; Shah 1993). Narayanamoorthy (2007), who used Indian population census data to analyze drivers of nonfarm rural employment in 256 districts in 1971, 1981, and 1991, found that besides rural roads and literacy levels, irrigation access had a significant impact on nonfarm job generation. It is not surprising, then, that when the same researchers (Narayanamoorthy 2007, 349–350) analyzed state panel data on rural poverty ratios in India for 1973–74, 1977–78, 1983, 1987–88, and 1993–94, they found a "significant inverse relationship between availability of groundwater irrigation and the percentage of rural poverty at all five time points." Furthermore, they were puzzled: "Despite the fact that groundwater irrigation helps to reduce rural poverty through increased production and wage rates as well as employment . . . ," researchers have largely missed this benefit. Moench (2003) echoed the same sentiment.

All those effects at the level of household farming systems translate into regional and national level socioeconomic consequences for South Asia's farm economy and farmers. In the next section, I offer a selective overview of the macrolevel effects.

Significance in Agrarian Economy

How significant is the pump irrigation economy of South Asia—in absolute terms, and in relation to the national agrarian and overall economies? Researchers have estimated that during the late 1980s and early 1990s, groundwater-supported agriculture accounted for nine to 10 percent of India's GDP (Daines and Pawar 1987; World Bank and Government of India 1998). In Pakistan, the World Bank (2005b) estimated in 2005 that some 60 percent of irrigation water was delivered by tube wells, and this accounted for

75 percent of the value of farm output in the Indus basin. Though rough estimates, these figures provide a useful indication. Another computation of the
economic value of groundwater use in agriculture—the weighted average
price of pump irrigation service transactions—was carried out by Debroy and
Shah (2003), a revised and updated version of which is shown in Table 4-1.
This calculus suggests the economic value of groundwater use in South Asian
agriculture was around US$12 billion per year in 2003–04.

The value productivity of groundwater irrigation is of course several times
larger; a small farmer would buy pump irrigation only if it helped him make
many times more than the cost. Moreover, this calculus does not account for
the indirect but substantial impact of pump irrigation on the expansion of
dairying, meat, silk, and other high-value products, which now likely constitute 60 percent of the value of aggregate farm sector output. All in all, in 2000
the gross value of output of farm, livestock, and related produce grown with
groundwater irrigation in South Asia was probably on the order of US$180
billion to $200 billion.

The figures tell only a small part of the groundwater irrigation story. In the
Indian state of West Bengal, governed by the Communist Party of India
(Marxists), and its neighbor, Bangladesh, agricultural productivity stagnated

Table 4-1   Proximate size of agricultural groundwater economy in South Asia, 2003–04

	India	Pakistan[a]	Bangladesh	Nepal Terai
A Total groundwater structures (million)	17.5	0.96	1.2	0.06
B Average output of groundwater structures (m³/hr)[b]	30	60	30	30
C Average hours of operation/well/year	360	1090	1300	205
D Price of pump irrigation from standard-size pump (US$/hr)	1	2.5	1.5	1.5
E Estimated groundwater used (km³) {(A*B*C)/1,000,000,000}	210	62.8	31.2	0.37
F Imputed value of groundwater used/year in US$billion (E/B*D) or {(D*C*A)/1000}	8.4	2.6	1.6	0.02

[a] Estimate for Pakistan includes only Pakistan Punjab, which has almost 90 percent of country's groundwater structures.
[b] Average output of groundwater structures (m³/hr) depends, among other things, on average horsepower (hp) of
pumps and depth to water table. In Pakistan, average hp is almost three times that of India, and Pakistan Punjab has
high water tables. In Bangladesh, pump hp is comparable to that of India, water tables are high, and WEMs pump
water from average depth of five to eight meters. Average output in Bangladesh is therefore assumed to be margin-
ally higher than that of India, and that of Pakistan, two times that of India.
Sources for groundwater structure figures: India Minor Irrigation Census 2001; Bangladesh Minor Irrigation Census
1996–97; Pakistan Agricultural Machinery Census of 2004 (Government of Pakistan 2004).
Source for hours of operation and price of water: (Deb Roy and Shah 2003)

during the 1947–1985 period but experienced large and rapid increases during 1985–1995. The causes of both the stagnation and its reversal have been the subject of debate. Although researchers have identified poor water control as one of the 'built in depressants' (Thorner 1956) of productivity growth in eastern Ganga basin before 1985, what triggered the rapid growth afterward remained obscure, though "there was no shortage of claims to credit for the achievement" (Rogaly et al. 1999, 11). In particular, Communist ideologues in West Bengal said that the feudal agrarian structure of Bengal, a legacy of the colonial *Zamindari* system, was at the root of the stagnation, and that Marxists' agrarian reforms had a transformational impact, spurring agricultural productivity growth that made Bengal the envy of all its neighbors.

However, others argued that the primary driver of productivity growth was intensification of agriculture through large-scale expansion in the cultivation of *boro* (presummer) rice as well as winter potato crops, and high, stable yields of the main crop of *aman (kharif)* rice. New varieties of rice and other inputs were certainly factors, but the growth spiral was "enabled by the rapid spread of groundwater irrigation, mainly in the form of privately owned shallow tubewells . . . , but later, as the water tables dropped, through mini-submersible tubewells" (Rogaly et al. 1999, 20). In Bangladesh, too, productivity growth was led by expansion in *boro* rice, which in turn was made possible by the improved water control offered by tube wells and WEMs (Adnan 1999; Palmer-Jones 1999). Indeed, Bangladesh, unlike Marxist West Bengal, made no attempt to change the agrarian structure at all—merely liberalized prices of irrigation equipment and deregulated its sale and purchase by allowing private agencies to import pumps and removing spacing restrictions—yet its agrarian growth was no less dramatic than West Bengal's (Rogaly et al. 1999). And during the early 1990s, the productivity expansion in both West Bengal and Bangladesh began to slow, WEM purchases and the area irrigated by tube wells (especially of *boro* rice and winter potatoes) having run their course.

The experience of West Bengal and Bangladesh was repeated in other parts of the Ganga-Brahmaputra basin of South Asia. During the 1970s, the Green Revolution spread from Punjab eastward, closely following the spread of tube well technology, and researchers like Dhawan noted that this march halted at Lucknow in central Uttar Pradesh around 1975. In the 1980s, shallow tube wells spread through eastern Uttar Pradesh (Pant 2004; Shah 2001), North Bihar (Ballabh et al. 2003; Shah and Ballabh 1997; Wilson 2002;

Wood 1999), and North Bengal (Shah 1998), bringing a rapid productivity surge in regional agrarian economies.

Tube wells have had a strangely equalizing effect that has dissolved, to some extent, age-old inequalities rooted in the complex calculus of caste, class, and power relations in a typical South Asian village. In the early years of tube well irrigation, kinship and power relations did mediate irrigation transactions between pump haves and have-nots, and researchers like Wood wrote about "concentric circles of moral proximity," in which sharing of pumps by tube well owners was determined by complex relations of caste, class, and kinship. However, it was much easier for disadvantaged farmers to make a borehole and obtain a diesel pump than for the welfare state to implement land reforms and transform the agrarian structure. And as more and more farmers without pumps became pump owners, the power that the agrarian structure held over the lives of smallholders weakened in many areas, as Shah and Ballabh (1997) discovered in a study of pump irrigation markets in six villages of North Bihar, and as Pant (2005) noted for Uttar Pradesh.

Wells and Welfare in Dry-land Agriculture

In humid parts of South Asia, the impact of tube wells and WEMs went considerably beyond creating the "stabilization value" that Tsur (1990) has analyzed; indeed, here it encouraged new crops like *boro* rice and winter potatoes and supported high-yielding varieties and intensive use of fertilizers. In dry-land agriculture, too, WEMs promised dramatic improvements in the productivity of rain-fed agriculture by making possible crop saving irrigation during the period of peak moisture stress. The yield impacts of such just-in-time irrigation are not well quantified; however, Umrani (1999) reports results of field trials by agricultural scientists on various crops at different centers in India over several seasons. These results suggest that in a drought, a single irrigation can raise productivity of rain-fed crops like wheat, barley, sorghum, and upland rice by 30 to 230 percent. Sharma et al. (2007) have recently shown that the livelihoods and food security of farmers cultivating 86 million ha of India's rain-fed areas are seriously impaired because of frequent midseason or terminal droughts lasting one to three weeks during *kharif*—their dominant cropping season. A single supplemental irrigation of 100 mm may not only stabilize rain-fed farming in these areas but also increase production by 50 percent or more. In dry-land areas, tube wells and pumps have also helped farmers experiment with Green Revolution technologies—high-yielding varieties, chemical fertilizers—because WEMs reduce the risks of drought.

In some ways, the expansion of pump irrigation in South Asia's dry-land areas is an outcome of the colonial and postcolonial strategy of "unbalanced irrigation development," which invested in irrigation around hydraulically opportune sites and created a class structure of irrigation haves and have-nots, concentrating more than half of India's canal irrigation in less than 10 percent of the country's farmlands. India's 2001 minor irrigation census shows the Ginny coefficient[15]—which increases with the level of inequality—for surface irrigation is 0.79 but that for pump irrigation is 0.55. Fifty privileged districts of India—8.5 percent of the 592 covered by the Indian minor irrigation census of 2000–01—have 59 percent of the area irrigated by major and medium public irrigation projects. The canal-induced recharge enables these districts to put another 3.7 million ha under WEM irrigation, thus raising irrigated area to 55 percent of their net cropped area. In the remaining 531 districts, only 3.7 percent of net cropped area is irrigated by major and medium systems; these districts depend on pump irrigation for 89 percent of the irrigated areas and 32 percent of the net cropped area. The fallacy that the bulk of India's groundwater irrigation is concentrated in command areas is also exposed by the census, which shows that 88 percent of groundwater WEMs are outside the command areas.

As long as irrigation played a stabilizing role, as was largely the case before the onset of the Green Revolution, differences in farming productivity and profitability between irrigation commands and dry-land areas were less sharp than afterward. As the perceived deprivation of dry-land areas increased, the doctrine of "unbalanced irrigation development" began to polarize farmers and mobilize vote banks. Persistent and growing subsidies for canal irrigation made matters worse—command-area farmers vastly benefited from state munificence already—and heightened the dry-land areas' sense of deprivation. Economist Ashok Gulati called canal irrigation subsidies "a massive fraud on dry-land agriculture" (Gulati and Narayanan 2003). Being at the short end of "unbalanced irrigation development" became an important point around which demand for separate states arose, as in Telangana in Andhra Pradesh, Vidarbha and Marathawada in Maharashtra, and Saurashtra and Kutch in Gujarat. Victimhood is also at the center of the political economy of electricity and other subsidies that have helped energize and sustain the pump irrigation boom in dry-land areas of India and regions like Baluchistan and Northwest Frontier Province in Pakistan.

WEMs have come to the rescue of governments unable to alleviate social and economic inequities. The rapid spread of groundwater irrigation throughout the dry-land areas has been gradually increasing the density of green specks in this otherwise brown terrain. True, dry-land farms will never be as productive and profitable as farms in command areas; however, groundwater irrigation has helped reduce dry-land farmers' sense of state-inflicted deprivation. A classic example is Telanagana in the Deccan plateau:

> Despite the fact that Telangana has been neglected by the state government in the development of canal irrigation area . . . [W]ith rapid spread of groundwater irrigation, Telangana districts have been witnessing high agricultural growth. (Vakulabharanam 2004, *1421*)

Vakulabharanam's study began by focusing on the vast gulf in agricultural production and productivity between coastal Andhra Pradesh, the state's irrigation have, and Telangana (and Rayalaseema), its irrigation have-not. The former region had always had some 55 percent of its net sown area under irrigation, and the latter, less than 10. But by 2001, Telangana had increased its irrigated area to 38 percent of the net sown area, and its agriculture was booming, thanks entirely to spread of WEMs. By providing seven hours daily of free electricity to 2.7 million WEM owners—of these, 2 million in the dry regions of Telangana and Rayalaseema—Andhra Pradesh Chief Minister Y. S. R. Reddy has built himself an unassailable votebank, and by promising free electric power until 2017, he has not only entrenched his power base but may have effectively quelled Telangana farmers' demand for a separate state (Tata 2007).

The same is true of most other dry-land areas of western and peninsular India, including much of Rajasthan, Saurashtra and Kutch in Gujarat, dry-land areas of Karnataka and Tamilnadu, and Balochistan in Pakistan. The exceptions are tribal areas, such as in Jharkhand, Chattisgarh, western Orissa and parts of Vidarbha, where the spread of WEM irrigation has been recent and slow. However, if one considers the rates of change in the number of WEMs between the 1993–94 and 2000–01 minor irrigation censuses in these districts, there is little doubt that groundwater-fired productivity growth in agriculture in these regions too is round the corner. In Pakistan's Northwest Frontier Province, much like the tribal highlands of central India, farmers have only recently realized the benefits of WEM irrigation (Steenbergen and Oliemans 2002).

All in all, purely rain-fed districts and villages are dwindling in South Asia's dry-land areas. In an increasingly common situation here, farmers focus their labor and inputs on the best one or two of their several parcels, using their own or purchased pump irrigation, and derive most of their livelihood from the WEM-irrigated land. Selective application of labor and inputs to the WEM-irrigated area and neglect of the rest of the land may be an optimal strategy for farmers but may not augur well for the stewardship of dry lands more generally. Nor does it augur well for the culture of dry-land farming, with its indigenous practical knowledge about husbanding abundant land with scarce water resources (M. Shah et al. 1998).

Table 4-2 combines estimates of the average value of field crop output per ha from the Centre for Monitoring Indian Economy with irrigated area data from the 1993–94 minor irrigation census. The conclusions that follow are several:

- Districts with substantial area under irrigation do better than those with little irrigation.
- Districts with high farm productivity are not necessarily the most irrigated.
- Districts heavily dependent on groundwater irrigation have higher productivity than those irrigated predominantly by gravity-flow systems.

Table 4-2   Irrigation impact on farm productivity in 323 Indian districts

		Percentage of net sown area under irrigation, 1995			
	Value of gross farm output/ha, 1995	Major and medium systems	Ground-water	Minor surface systems	Total
323 districts for which data are available	9,093	7.8	24.2	3.9	35.8
Top 30 growth districts (excluding plantation districts)	19,117	17.1	39.4	5.3	61.8
Bottom 30 growth districts	2,727	2.2	15.3	1.8	19.4
Top 30 major and medium irrigation districts	10,830	38.3	25	5.3	68.6
Top 30 groundwater irrigation districts	11,630	5.65	77	0.5	83.2
Bottom 30 irrigated-area districts	5,471	0.7	4.5	1.3	6.5
Top 30 irrigated-area districts	12,295	26	62	1.33	89.4

- If only field crops are counted, irrigation adds just about Rs. 7,000 (US$155) to the gross value of output per ha.

The real productivity impact of pump irrigation, however, lies not in traditional field crops but in diversification and high-value agriculture.

Pump Irrigation and Agricultural Diversification

The South Asian agrarian economy is in transition. The old agrarian economy—irrigated or rain-fed cultivation of grains, pulses, oilseeds, and fiber for subsistence or market—still occupies a large part of the region's area and farm labor. However, in 2000–01, a new agrarian economy—fruits and vegetables, milk and other livestock produce, culture fishery, all for the market—accounted for 54 percent of India's farm sector output (Figure 4.1). The situation in Pakistan and Bangladesh is similar.

Expansion of pump irrigation is supporting, and sometimes driving, massive changes in the agricultural economy. Diversification involves a shift in resources from farm to nonfarm activities, toward a larger mix of diverse and complementary activities within agriculture, and from low- to high-value

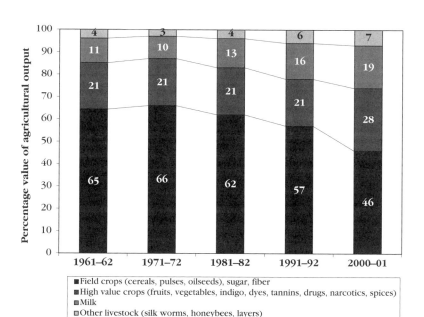

Figure 4.1   Change in India's agrarian economy, 1961–2001

crops, animal husbandry, and fisheries—all of which lead to higher net income per net cropped ha (Joshi et al. 2004).

Although diversification is energized by demand-pull from urbanization and economic growth, it is supported by pump irrigation—a necessary condition for intensive diversification. Areas served by surface irrigation systems, large and small, still use wheat-rice or rice-rice cropping cycles. Intensive diversification is more robust in dry-land areas (Joshi et al. 2004), where small pockets of mostly WEM-irrigated fields account for a small proportion of the net cropped area but a large and growing share of dry-land farming incomes.

Rice was always the biggest crop in India; now, however, milk has overtaken rice in gross value of output. Major increases in dairy production in India have occurred largely in dry-land areas such as Gujarat, Rajasthan, Karnataka, and Andhra Pradesh. Dry-land farmers, looking for opportunities to maximize income per drop of water have adopted breed improvement of their cattle and buffalos, and they raise alfalfa or other green fodders on small plots. These fodder plots need relatively small amount of water throughout the year except in the monsoon months, if rains are good. Pump irrigation from wells is better suited to such year-round irrigation than tanks or even canal systems. In dry districts of North Gujarat, such as Mehsana, Banaskantha, Sabarkantha, and Panchmahals a five- to 10-fold expansion in dairy production over the 1980–2000 period was catalyzed by the rise of dairy co-operatives but has been supported by pump-irrigated fodder plots for cross-bred cattle and genetically improved buffalos. In a study of four villages in Banaskantha district, Kumar (2007) calculated the productive value of groundwater used at US$72,000, nearly 60 percent of which came from dairy production. Local newspapers report on the dozens of women dairy farmers who sell to their cooperatives' milk valued at US$50,000 a year, and hundreds who supply milk worth US$20,000 to $25,000; these farmers typically have just an acre or two of farmland but access to a WEM and good cattle or water buffaloes. Intensification of smallholder dairy production based on pump-irrigated green fodder cultivation has emerged as one of the biggest livelihood improvement options in many of India's dry-areas.

Rapid expansion in the cultivation of fruits and vegetables is a trend in hilly areas of Himachal Pradesh and in arid lands of Baluchistan (Steenbergen 1995), especially near urban centers. Fruits and vegetables are considered water-intensive crops. However, common experience as well as agronomic research show that yields manifest dramatic response to a few just-in-time irrigations. Experimental farm results reported by scientists of India's Dryland Research Institute (CRIDA) showed that five or six well-timed waterings can raise yields of chilies, *brinjal* (eggplants), tomatoes, bottle gourds, and sword beans by 15 to 175 percent (Vijayalaxmi 1987, cited in Umrani 1999). Pump irrigation, often from wastewater channels or wastewater-recharged wells in urban peripheries, is commonly the mainstay of periurban vegetable and fruit cultivators. WEMs support such intensive diversification. In Andhra Pradesh, WEM irrigation was at the center of recent moves to promote contract farming of gherkin and oil palm by small farmers, and participating farmers demanded additional and more reliable electricity for operating pumps (Mahendra Dev and Rao 2005).

Pump irrigation also explains the growth in apple and other fruit orchards in Baluchistan and Northwest Frontier Province in Pakistan. The role of WEMs in high-value farming is also best illustrated by the rapid spread during the 1990s of treadle pumps—a low-cost but laborious manual device for lifting water from shallow depths or surface water sources in high water table areas of eastern India, Nepal Terai, and Bangladesh. Millions of farmers in these regions were too poor to buy diesel pumps, but high water tables in the Ganga, Brahmaputra, and Meghana basins made manual irrigation of small plots possible, given a convenient and affordable device. The treadle pump answered this need, and its use in small-scale vegetable gardens proved so profitable that at the end of the 1990s, about a million were in use in Bangladesh. A study on the apparent success of this technology explained why: by irrigating vegetables and some *boro* rice, its adopters could increase their incomes by around US$100 per year; the implicit wage rate in peddling the treadle pump was 1.5 to 2.5 times the market wage rate, and the investment of $12 to $15 in a treadle pump gave its owner an internal rate of return of around 100 percent because it enabled him or her to diversify with high-value crops (Shah et al. 2000a).

In India, the spread of treadle pumps was never as widespread as in Bangladesh. However, Pant (2005), who began a field investigation by questioning the widespread use of treadle pumps in Uttar Pradesh, confirmed its benefits in a survey of 90 treadle pump owners. Three-fourths of Pant's sample treadle pumps were owned by low-caste farmers with large families and small landholdings, and 60 percent of the adopters of treadle pumps generated an additional income of Rs. 1,200 (US$27) a year from the sale of vegetables; of these, more than a quarter earned Rs. 3,000 (US$67) a year by using this simple manual device.

In Bangladesh, treadle pumps have gone as fast as they came. With the liberalization of irrigation equipment trade and import, inexpensive Chinese diesel pumps have crowded out treadle pumps; many smallholders used treadle pump irrigation to generate the capital they needed to buy mechanized WEMs. In eastern India, easy access to pump irrigation through vibrant pump irrigation markets made the treadle pump technology obsolete.

Other Macro-impacts

Pump irrigation has had several other significant macrolevel impacts. First, it has worked for as well as against canal irrigation. Although expansion in WEM irrigation in canal commands hastened the decline in gravity-flow irrigation and dampened enthusiasm for participatory irrigation management, it also ensured that overall economic benefits of canal projects were much higher than they would have been without private investment in pumps.[16]

Second, for the region as a whole, groundwater-irrigated area also supported by canal irrigation is small, around 12 to 15 percent. In India, the 2000–01 minor irrigation census showed that only six percent of dug wells and 18 percent of shallow tube wells were located in the commands of major and medium projects (Government of India 2005a). The IWMI survey of 2,600 farmers in India, Pakistan, Bangladesh, and Nepal Terai also found that pure canal irrigation benefited only 14.5 percent of the irrigated areas covered by the survey; in contrast, 56 percent was accounted for by purely groundwater irrigation, and counting conjunctive use, WEM irrigation's contribution rose above 75 percent of net irrigated area in the subcontinental sample (Shah et al. 2006).

Third, the spread of pump irrigation in semiarid and arid areas has played an important role in drought-proofing agriculture and farm livelihoods. I mentioned earlier that a single drought has much less effect on farm production today than during the 1960s. Of even greater importance now is the intensification of the livestock economy, which with the help of supplemental pump irrigation is less affected by the vagaries of the monsoon. For example, S. P. Tucker (2005), Andhra Pradesh's secretary of water resources, has shown that although agricultural production fluctuates with rainfall, livestock production in his state shows hardly any fluctuations and has steadily risen to approach the value of crop production. In Gujarat's dryland areas, dairy cooperatives now procure more milk in a drought year than in a good year.

Fourth, by far the largest and most beneficial impact of South Asia's pump irrigation boom is that it draws from a massive reservoir at almost no cost to the public exchequer. Unlike in the Middle East, where the groundwater used in agriculture is mostly nonrenewable fossil water, South Asian groundwater economy is based largely on shallow circulating groundwater recharged during years of normal or above normal monsoons. This vast reservoir lay dormant for millennia, rejecting most monsoonal natural recharge for lack of space because it was only sparingly used between two monsoons. After 1970, South Asian farmers began creating space to store 285 to 300 km³ of water by emptying this reservoir after the monsoon so that it could fill up again during the monsoon.

No reservoir comes without problems. Surface reservoirs displace poor people, they cost a lot, they begin silting up after a few years, and in arid and semiarid South Asia, they work as evaporation pans. Shallow aquifer storage has its own problems, chiefly the slow and highly variable rate at which it recharges from natural and artificial sources. However, unlike surface reservoirs, aquifers evaporate little, can be accessed at the point of use, have unlimited life (with good management), and do not silt up (although they can be degraded). Since 1970, South Asian farmers have probably withdrawn a total of three trillion m³ of water from this reservoir to irrigate an average of 30 million ha per year. Without any recharge, water tables in South Asia's groundwater irrigation pockets would have dropped to an average of 100 meters, assuming a storage coefficient of 10 percent (and 200 meters if we assume a storage coefficient of five percent). However, the 2001 minor irrigation census recorded that fewer than 0.3 percent of India's villages had groundwater levels over 70 meters, and in 89 percent the level was less than 20 meters. This suggests that South Asia's aquifer storage could be a fairly robust and dependable reservoir for pump irrigators. If this reservoir is managed well, there is potential to multiply its storage and its manifold benefits.

Conclusion: The Unorthodox Route to Water Security

In a recent World Bank paper, Grey and Sadoff (2005) postulate an S-curve relationship between the level of water security a country enjoys and the scale of public investments in water infrastructure and institutions (Figure 4.2). The Grey-Sadoff thesis has two interesting propositions: first, that water investments drive economic growth (rather than the other way round), and second, that investments offer different payoffs at different stages of economic evolu-

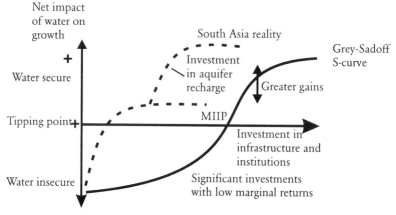

MIIP: Minimum Infrastructure and Institutional Platform

Figure 4.2   Level of water security and public investment in water infrastructure and institutions

tion. For societies in the early stages of development and facing adverse hydrologic conditions—in terms of rainfall variability and seasonality—the water economy is a bottomless pit. Large infrastructure projects, which in countries like Ethiopia "may require investment of many times annual GDP" (World Bank 2006, 2), keep devouring precious capital without offering any return in either economic benefits or water security. Only after they achieve a minimum infrastructure and institutional "platform"—a kind of water security tipping point—do returns to investments zoom. And the benefits begin tapering off as the country approaches European levels of water security.

According to Grey and Sadoff, S-curves for countries with favorable hydrology are different than for those with adverse hydrology. However, they presume a uniform technical path to achieving water security—the one that today's rich countries know best: via the public sector and institutions. The pump irrigation boom in South Asia does not conform to the Grey-Sadoff thesis. South Asia has a hydrology as variable and seasonal as Ethiopia's, and giving vast agricultural areas water security through a traditional strategy of irrigation reservoirs and canal networks would cost the region at least 10 times more in public investments than it has cost individual farmers participating in the pump irrigation boom.

The path South Asian agriculture has followed since 1970s is substituting private capital and institutions for public capital. This has created an altogether new curve—indicated by the broken lines to the left of the S-curve—that lowers the water security tipping point and yields immediately high rates of return in economic benefits and water security but demands an unorthodox strategy—public investment and institutions that support and sustain the private investments. The Grey-Sadoff thesis overlooks this alternative path to water security simply because none of today's rich countries have taken it.

Although supporting information is difficult to come by, Table 4-3 presents my guesstimates of the quantitative significance of public and private sectors in South Asia's irrigation economy. At the level of the subcontinent, surface irrigation—predominantly under government and community management—mobilizes, applies, and makes consumptive use of a large

Table 4-3   Irrigation socioecology of South Asia: rough balance sheet, 2000

	Pump irrigation[a]	Flow irrigation[b]	Rain-fed[c]
Percentage of gross cropped area (240 million ha)	50–55	10–13	27–40
Percentage of districts benefited	75	10–12	13–15
Percentage of farm households dependent on irrigation (140 million)	55–60	10–13	27–35
Percentage contribution to value of farm output (US$180–200 billion, 2000)	70–72	18–20	10–12
Percentage of "blue" water mobilized and applied (750–800 km³)	35–40	60–65	0
Percentage of "blue" water consumptively used for crop production[d] (500–550 km³)	40–45	50–55	0
Capital cost per irrigated ha for 50-year economic life (US$/ha)[e]	1,500	6,000–7,500	50
Energy subsidy of electric pump–irrigated area (US$/ha/year)	120	0	0
Operation and maintenance subsidies for flow-irrigated areas (US$/ha/year)	0	35–50	0

[a] Surface water bodies in conjunctive use in canal commands and groundwater use in regions dependent on natural recharge; "pump irrigation" therefore includes more than groundwater irrigation, as normally understood.
[b] Gravity-flow irrigation from canals, tanks, and other surface water bodies.
[c] No artificial application of water except in situ water conservation through field bunds.
[d] The difference between "blue water mobilized and applied" and "blue water consumptively used for crop production" includes, besides irrigation return flows, nonbeneficial evaporation, which is significantly lower for pump irrigation. Thus, pump irrigation accounts for a larger share of consumptive use of blue water applied than of blue water mobilized.
[e] Unit capital cost for pump irrigation potential has been adjusted upward for an economic life of 50 years; that for flow irrigation has been adjusted upward to reflect the fact that area actually irrigated is a fraction of the designed command.

portion of "blue" water[17] in South Asian agriculture, but its contribution to agrarian value creation and its reach into farming populations are modest in comparison. In contrast, pump irrigation is supported predominantly by farmers' investments, waters more than half the subcontinent's gross cropped area, and supports nearly three-fourths of the total value of output but accounts for just two-fifths of the total blue water applied and an even smaller proportion of consumptive use of water in agriculture. Because aquifers offer more efficient storage of water (Keller et al. 2000) and because WEMs deliver water at the point of use and on demand, pump irrigation accounts for a small portion of the consumptive fraction of blue water use.

The S-curve for achieving this level of agricultural water security by South Asian farmers is lower than that implied by Grey-Sadoff thesis, but several confounding factors must be taken into account:

- *Capital cost.* At around US$600 per ha, pump irrigation costs only about an eighth as much to create as large canal irrigation, at US$4,500.
- *Longevity.* Major and medium systems are supposed to last for 50 to 60 years, whereas wells and pumps generally have an average economic life of 15 to 18 years—shorter in peninsular India than in the Ganga basin.
- *Reach.* South Asia's past experience has been that surface irrigation systems end up irrigating only a fraction of their design command,[18] and thus capital cost per ha actually irrigated may be 1.5 to 1.8 times the estimated cost of the potential created (Daines and Pawar 1987). A typical WEM, on the other hand, often ends up irrigating more than it was planned to.
- *Subsidization.* In many parts of the subcontinent, pump irrigation depends on energy subsidies. Some two-fifths of the pump-irrigated areas, mostly in India, enjoy annual electricity subsidies of about US$120 per ha. Most flow-irrigated areas everywhere in South Asia enjoy an effective annual subsidy of about US$35 to $50 per ha, which is roughly the difference between the operations and maintenance costs of major and medium irrigation systems and the small water charges recovered from farmers.

If we take into account all those factors, the adjusted capital cost of irrigation potential actually achieved by pump irrigation may be one-quarter or one-fifth of the cost for major and medium systems. In balance, then, the pump irrigation boom in South Asia has many things going for it, while flow irrigation, which has been shrinking, will in all likelihood continue to shrink further.

Many hydrologists believe that pump irrigation on such a vast scale cannot be sustained except in a conjunctive use mode with surface water. If this is true, the shrinking of flow irrigation is bad news for the pump irrigation economy of South Asia and all its socioeconomic benefits. Signs of a coming crisis of groundwater sustainability are visible all over South Asia. If the region fails to respond, the boom will go bust—sooner rather than later, and spreading misery and pain far and wide.

CHAPTER 5

DIMINISHING RETURNS?

There's no such thing as a free lunch.

Using a renewable resource intensively requires that the resource and its economy be *managed* intensively, too. Here, South Asia's public systems are wanting. Even as groundwater development and use have experienced runaway growth, no strategy to sustain this *laissez-faire* economy is apparent. This is a threat to the resource, as well as to the agrarian economy and livelihoods tied to it. In this chapter, I briefly describe groundwater depletion and abuse in South Asia before moving on to what might be best described as the hydropolitics of the pump irrigation revolution.

First, I explore the pathology of rise and decline in a groundwater irrigation economy, and then assess the scale and seriousness of this threat to the resource. Accounts of groundwater depletion on subcontinental scale are the subject of international reports on South Asia's agriculture. This grim scenario certainly deserves highlighting, but an agenda for practical action needs to explain the underlying hydropolitical dynamic. I argue that the pump irrigation boom is reconfiguring river basins in ways that make it extremely difficult to systematically plan and manage large irrigation infrastructure projects. I then consider the impact of pump irrigation boom on the organization of South Asian water economies and its implications for water governance. I also explore the invidious political economy of energy use in pump irrigation in South Asia and show how electricity subsidies began as a cause of groundwater depletion but have now ended up as its result. Finally, I examine groundwater policies in South Asia in the framework of positive political theory.

Threatened Sustainability?

Groundwater depletion, and all that goes with it, has become the most vivid indicator of water scarcity facing South Asia. There are urgent calls for regulation of groundwater draft, even as demand for more water extraction mechanisms (WEMs) continues. Hydrogeologists like Ramon Llamas and Emilio Custodio (2003) are among the minority who would like the "regulatory zeal" to be tempered. They believe that the livelihood impacts of pump revolution in South Asia are great—and the large-scale environmental threat remote. At the other extreme are Lester Brown (2003), Sandra Postel (1999), David Seckler (1999), and others. Seckler warned that a quarter of India's food harvest was at risk if the country failed to manage its groundwater properly. Postel (1999) has suggested that some 10 percent of the world's food production depends on annual overdraft of groundwater to the extent of 200 km^3, and two-thirds of this may be occurring in western and peninsular India. In the lower Indus basin in Pakistan and the Bhakra system in northern India, groundwater depletion is a fast-emerging problem, but soil and groundwater salinization is apparent everywhere.

Research to understand the dynamics of groundwater socioecologies in South Asia suggests that their rise and fall follow a four-stage progression, outlined in Figure 5.1. The typical progression begins when farmers tap a previously unutilized groundwater resource and create an agrarian boom but then deplete the aquifer and go bust. Institutions and policies too suggest a predictable regularity: for instance, policies designed to support further development of the resource remain entrenched far beyond stage 3, when effective "resource management" policies are indicated. Similarly, pump irrigation service markets boom in stage 2, stagnate in stage 3, and decline or disappear in stage 4.

	Stage 1	Stage 2	Stage 3	Stage 4
Stages	Rise of Green Revolution and tube well technology	Groundwater-based agrarian boom	Early symptoms of groundwater overdraft	Decline of the groundwater socio-ecology with immiserising impacts.
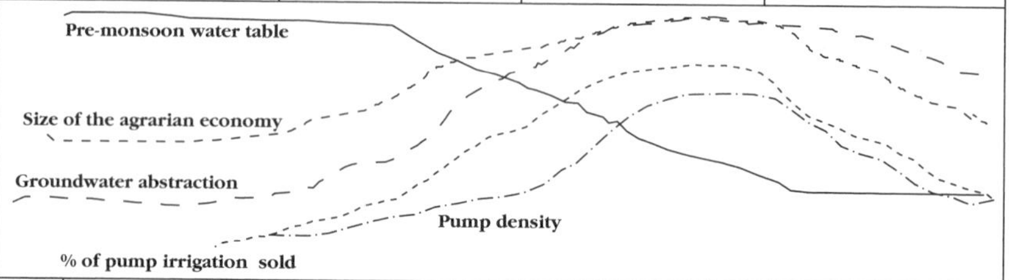	Pre-monsoon water table / Size of the agrarian economy / Groundwater abstraction / Pump density / % of pump irrigation sold			
Examples	North Bengal and North Bihar, Nepal Terai, Orissa	Eastern Uttar Pradesh western Godavari central and South Gujarat	Haryana, Punjab, western Uttar Pradesh, Combatore and Madurai, Tamilnadu	North Gujarat, coastal Tamilnadu, coastal Saurashtra, South West Bengal
Characteristics	Subsistence agriculture and concentrated rural poverty; traditional water lifting devices using human and animal power	Skewed ownership of wells; access to pump irrigation prized; rise of 'exchange' institutions in irrigation service. Rapid growth in agrarian income and employment	Crop diversification and falling water tables. The groundwater-based 'bubble' economy continues booming but tensions surface as pumping costs soar and private and social costs of groundwater use diverge.	The 'bubble' bursts; agrarian growth slows leading to migration and pauperization. Water quality becomes a serious issue; the 'smart' make a planned transition; the poor suffer decline.
Interventions	Targeted subsidy on pump capital; public tube well programms; electricity subsidies and flat tariff to stimulate tube well irrigation by the poor	Subsidies and credit continue for WEMs. Donors augment resources for pump capital formation; NGOs promote small farmer irrigation as a livelihood program.	Subsidies, credit, donor and NGO support continue apace; laws are made but not enforced. WEM owners emerge as a powerful vote-bank that politicians cannot ignore.	Policy support to WEMs reluctantly ebb as NGOs, donors adopt a conservation posture. Regulations begin to get enforced but with pre-election relaxations; ameliorative action starts but demand-management remains neglected.

Figure 5.1   Rise and fall of groundwater socioecologies

The four-stage framework illustrates the transition that South Asian policymakers and managers need to make—from resource *development* to resource *management*. Forty years of Green Revolution and mechanized tube well technology have nudged many regions of South Asia into stages 2, 3, and 4. There are places—such as Nepal Terai, North Bengal, North Bihar, Orissa, and Northwest Frontier Province of Pakistan—that exhibit character-istics of stage 1, but such areas are shrinking by the day. Many parts of west-ern India were in this first stage in the 1950s or earlier but have advanced into stage 3 or 4. An oft-cited case is North Gujarat, where groundwater depletion has set off a long-term decline in the once-booming agrarian econ-omy; here, well-off farmers who saw it coming made a planned transition to a nonfarm, urban livelihood (Prakash 2005), leaving the resource-poor behind. This drama is being reenacted with frightening regularity (Barry and Issoufaly 2002; Moench 1992; Shah 1993).

In stage 1 and the beginning of stage 2, the prime concern is to promote profitable use of a valuable, renewable resource for generating wealth and economic surplus for poverty reduction; however, in stage 2 itself, the thinking needs to change toward careful management of the resource. Yet the policy regime of promoting rapid development of the resource—appropriate for stages 1 and 2—tends to become "sticky" and persists long after an area moves into stage 3 or even 4, as for example in Baluchistan (Steenbergen 1995). Recent studies in the North China Plain suggest that the story is much the same there as well (Kendy et al. 2003). The critical questions are several. Must stage 4 always play out the way it has in the past, or are there adaptive policy and management responses in stage 2 that can generate a steady-state equilibrium that sustains the groundwater-induced agrarian boom without degrading the resource itself? And what is the future for regions already in stage 4? Are there intervention strategies that can stabilize groundwater irrigation economies and chart a socio-ecologically sustainable path, creating a new, fifth stage?

Diversity in South Asia's Groundwater Management Challenges

In popular perception, resource depletion and falling groundwater levels are at the heart of South Asia's water crisis, and irrigation is the culprit. However, the challenge of governing management varies with the hydrogeological con-ditions in different regions, as outlined in Table 5-1.

Table 5-1   Scale and severity of groundwater management challenges in South Asia

	Socioeconomic and management challenges			
Hydrogeological setting	Resource depletion	Optimization of conjunctive use	Secondary salinization	Natural groundwater quality concerns
Major alluvial plains Arid	++	++	+++	+
Humid	+	+++		++
Coastal plains	++	+	+++	+
Intermontane valleys	+	++	+	+
Hard-rock areas	+++	+	+	+++

In vast areas of South Asia, even today, pump irrigation expansion generates a large socioecological dividend. In the eastern Ganga basin, endowed with alluvium to the depth of 600 meters and annual flood discharges of more than 500 billion cubic meters, intensive groundwater irrigation has not only delivered livelihood benefits but also eased acute waterlogging and flooding (Shah 2001). By all accounts, there is enormous scope for expanding these benefits with little threat of resource depletion for a long time to come. Valid concerns about the effects of groundwater development in eastern India on lean-season flows in Bangladesh need to be addressed by both countries. Arsenic contamination of groundwater, a serious public health issue in Bangladesh, West Bengal, Nepal Terai, and parts of Bihar and eastern Uttar Pradesh, also needs a major response; but restricting pump irrigation will likely not eliminate the arsenic, which is geogenic. Despite such problems, the vast, humid Ganga-Brahmaputra-Meghna basin cannot be labeled a pump irrigation "hotspot."[1] If anything, these regions offer a major opportunity for jointly managing surface and groundwater resources to improve the livelihoods for several hundred million poor people.

The Indus basin too has earned socioecological dividends from pump irrigation, although returns are diminishing. Fifty years ago, many areas of Pakistan and Indian Punjab, Haryana, western Uttar Pradesh, North Rajasthan, and Sind faced acute problems of waterlogging. Pakistan and the World Bank invested in building tube wells to pump groundwater into canals with the twin objectives of reducing waterlogging in head reaches and improving canal deliveries at tail ends. The tube well program of the Salinity Control and Reclamation Project failed, but private pump irrigation performed better than SCARP, and on a much larger scale and with large socioecological dividends. The increasing salinity in groundwater is now forcing farmers here to better husband their freshwater supplies from surface irrigation and saline groundwater to improve salt balances in their irrigation agriculture.

Groundwater problems in South Asia are mostly in arid alluvial and hard-rock aquifers that fall outside the command areas of surface irrigation systems. In some coastal plains and arid alluvial plains, the governance challenge is coping with chronic salinization and depletion, which may preclude agriculture and even human settlement. Then, in hard-rock areas of peninsular India, where WEM irrigation expansion is out of proportion to the limited storage offered by aquifers, resource depletion is a serious issue in itself but has also contributed to the growing concentration of fluoride and other salts in groundwater, the main source of drinking water for rural as well as urban populations. Problems of geogenic contamination of groundwater—such as with arsenic in the eastern Ganga basin and fluoride in much of western and peninsular India—are large and serious. The causal role of pump irrigation in mobilizing fluoride and other salts in groundwater is clearer than for arsenic contamination, whose chemistry is not fully understood.

Aggregate data give no indication of such water quality and depletion problems. In India, annual groundwater use, estimated by the Central Ground Water Board at 231 km^3, is just over 50 percent of the utilizable groundwater resource, estimated at 433 km^3 per year (Planning Commission 2007). If this resource were uniformly distributed, India would have less to worry about. Most of the potential, however, is in the Ganga-Brahmaputra basin, and much groundwater development occurs outside it. India's irrigation potential from groundwater is estimated at 64.05 million ha, but according to the 2000–01 minor irrigation census, in many states, farmers have already installed far more pumping capacity than their groundwater potential justifies.[2] The implication is widespread exploitation of the resource beyond dynamic resource availability (Planning Commission 2007). In Pakistan, groundwater depletion is a reality in Baluchistan, where extraction is far in excess of the recharge. In India, semiarid North Gujarat withdraws 17 percent more groundwater every year than the recharge (Kumar 2007). In Mehsana district, Kumar (2007) found water tables falling by two to six meters per year. As a result, fluoride contamination of groundwater—the main source of drinking water—is leading to widespread incidence of dental and skeletal fluorosis, especially among the poor, whose diets are deficient in calcium.

India's Central Groundwater Board, which monitors groundwater fluctuations in more than 50,000 observation wells throughout the country in a scientific and methodical manner, paints a worrying picture that justifies fears expressed by authors like Brown (2003), Seckler et al. (1999), and Postel (1999). The board classifies areas as white, gray, dark and overexploited in ascending order of level of groundwater development, with "white" being safe for further resource development and "overexploited" being in urgent need of stringent regulation.[3] This manner of classifying administrative areas—and the methodology used by the groundwater board to determine the level of exploitation of the resource—is a subject of much discussion and criticism (Vaidyanathan 1996, 185). Given the absence of a better methodology, however, we will use it.

The results of the Central Groundwater Board's crude method show that of India's 5,723 blocks (subdistricts) where the board has done its assessments, 71 percent (or 4,078) are still considered safe for further development. But 15 percent (or 839) are already in the overexploited category; moreover, 550 gray and 226 dark blocks will soon enter the overexploited category. The rate at which blocks are crossing from lighter to darker color bars is worrisome; in Rajasthan, overexploited blocks rose from 17 to 60 percent in just seven years of intensified well drilling by farmers (Briscoe and Mallik 2006). Under the worst scenario, India is expected to have 60 percent of blocks declared overexploited in 25 years (Planning Commission 2007). In 1967, the Indian Punjab had 55,000 mechanized tube wells; today, it has more than one million. In seven of Punjab's 17 districts, annual groundwater draft exceeds recharge. In Sangrur, Moga, Jalandhar, Kapurthala and Fatehgarh districts, all blocks are in the so-called dark zone. In Amritsar, Patiala and Ludhiana districts, most blocks are dark. The only districts where groundwater is not overexploited—Bhatinda, Mansa, Mukatsar, Hoshiarpur, Nawanshahar—are those where the water is saline or contaminated with chloride (Dutt 2004).

Local studies are often more revealing of the consequences of WEM excesses. Groundwater is vital for rural and urban settlements for much else besides irrigating crops. Unmanaged, however, pump irrigation expansion has caused collateral damage. The most important is loss of resilience. Aquifers are the only sources of fresh drinking water for humans and animals and for critical irrigation during droughts. Depleted aquifers cut into groundwater's life-support and drought-proofing role, as shown by Bhatia (1992).

Intensive development has meant a decline in water levels in most parts of Gujarat, salinity ingress in parts of the 1,400-km-long coastline of the state, and rising fluoride concentration in groundwater in many areas. Between 1979 and 1987, the groundwater level in most parts of Gujarat fell by two meters; in some places, it fell by four meters or more. According to Bhatia (1992, A152), "inequity and overexploitation are the two ugly heads of the monster of groundwater misutilization in Gujarat."

The dry alluvial plains of the Indus and western Ganga basin are now witnessing the advance of the fresh-saline water interface. Irrigation with marginal to poor-quality groundwater has worsened soil salinization and sodification (Qureshi and Masih 2002; Steenbergen and Oliemans 1997).[4] In the dry alluvial plains of South Asia, the native groundwater is deep and saline because of the marine origin of the hydrogeologic formation. Percolation of freshwater has formed a fresh groundwater lens up to 150 meters thick above the saline layer. Usually, the fresh groundwater areas are adjacent to the rivers, and the saline groundwater areas cover the central and lower regions of a *doab* (area between two rivers). In saline groundwater areas, which cover a quarter of the Pakistan and Indian Punjabs, and in some three-quarters of Sind, Kutch, and western Rajasthan, fresh groundwater lenses are thin but, according to one estimate, probably store several hundred billion cubic meters of freshwater (Qureshi and Masih 2002). Already, farmers are going after this water, which they have tried to tap through multistrainer shallow tube wells with small bores. However, this method leads to deteriorating quality of pumped water, and large numbers of wells have already been abandoned. Much research is in progress on effective use of marginal water in agriculture; the central issue, however, is institutional: wells pump poor-quality water because too many skimming wells pump from the same lens at the same time.

The use of marginal water in agriculture causes secondary salinization. Every time groundwater is used for crop production, plants extract the freshwater and leave the salts in the soil. If salts are not leached, either by applications of freshwater or through rainfall, they build up in the soil and affect plant growth. Even with leaching, salts enter the top layer of shallow groundwater. Mobilization and subsequent recycling of salts keep degrading soil and groundwater quality. Numerous experiments using water of different quality and reclaiming salt-affected soils have been made, mostly at the field level, but have met with limited success. Mixing marginal groundwater with canal water staves off but does not resolve the problem of soil salinization. Farmers' tendency to apply more frequent irrigation with saline water, far from helping, worsens the situation by increasing salt loading in the root zone. Only a complete change in the farming system, combined with better management of surface water, can improve the situation and make agricultural production more sustainable. Such sweeping change requires not just technology transfer but also the removal of institutional constraints.

Rajasthan is another Indian state where agriculture and dairying have exploited a patently unsustainable tube well irrigation boom. Most of Rajasthan is arid. The Indira Gandhi Canal, one of the early examples of large-scale interbasin water transfer in India after Independence, has created command areas in western desert districts such as Bikaner and Ganganagar. However, well irrigation has contributed even more to expanding irrigated areas. Between 1971 and 1994, the surface-irrigated area increased by 0.7 million ha, from a base of one million ha; but areas irrigated by WEMs soared by 200 percent, from around 1.1 million ha in 1971 to nearly three million ha in 1994 (Shah 1998). According to the latest minor irrigation census (Government of India 2005a), by 2000–01, flow-irrigated area in Rajasthan had grown to 1.31 million ha; but tube well–irrigated area increased to 3.6 million ha.

The Rajasthan example points to an interesting debate in India about the "complementarity" versus "substitutional" impact of public investments in canal irrigation. Researchers like Dhawan (1996b) have argued that public investments in canal irrigation stimulate private investments in WEMs by farmers. Others, notably Mishra and Ramesh Chand (cited in Dhawan 1996b) have argued the opposite, that public investments substitute for private irrigation investments, crowding them out. Complementarity implies widespread conjunctive use of surface and groundwater and more sustainable irrigation regimes in canal commands. Substitution, in contrast, suggests a hydrologic imbalance and little overlap between surface and groundwater irrigation. Complementarity would mean strong positive correlation between canal- and groundwater-irrigated areas; substitution would mean negative correlation between the two. If the complementarity thesis was valid, most Indian districts would have fallen along the line of hydrologic balance (Figure 5.2). This would suggest high net sown area under irrigation from groundwater in districts with large canal-irrigated areas, and vice versa. In actuality, such hydrologic balance is hardly to be found except in a very few

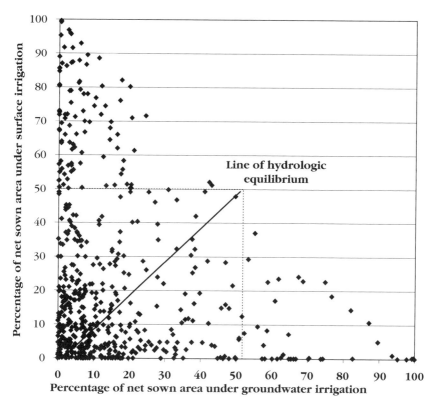

Figure 5.2   Distribution of Indian districts according to percent of net sown area under surface and groundwater irrigation.

Indian districts. Most that have large areas under groundwater irrigation have little surface irrigation, and vice versa.

Unmanaged intensification of groundwater irrigation creates imbalances not only in the groundwater system but also in the social system. In the hard-rock aquifers of peninsular India, Saurashtra peninsula in Gujarat, and hilly parts of Baluchistan and Northwest Frontier Province in Pakistan, the proliferation of wells creates a problem of interference, which leads to strategic gaming behavior among farmers (Chapter 6). The competing parties intensify their efforts to increase and conserve yields of wells with deeper bores within the open well, lateral bores to access untapped fissures, and air compressors to lift water first from the bore to the dug well, from which it is pumped again by a centrifugal pump. Responses to the externalities of well interference also include investments that stretch limited water yields to enhance production by building overhead water tanks and installing microirrigation.

The socioecological impacts of groundwater irrigation excesses in South Asia have been a frequent subject in scientific literature as well as the popular press. Indeed, the prominence of such effects often cloud the socioeconomic welfare that pump irrigation has generated in this poverty-stricken region. To preserve these livelihoods gains, it is important to understand the wider impact of small pumps in South Asia's irrigation economy.

River Basins Reconfigured

Pump irrigation in South Asia has added great complexity to the planning and design of large surface irrigation projects. Such projects take a long time, commonly 15 to 30 years and often more, between conception and completion. Until the mid-1960s, planners could be reasonably confident that the hydraulic mosaic of the river basin or subbasin would remain largely unchanged while the plans were being implemented. Cropping patterns might undergo some change, and so might the cultivated area. More farmers might take to irrigating from wells with bullock bailers, or some small-scale local diversion schemes might come up. However, the layout of hydraulic infrastructure and patterns of water use in the basin would not change so drastically as to falsify planning assumptions, and the project could proceed with planners' reasonable confidence in its success.

The change in this state of affairs explains a significant part of the underperformance of many surface irrigation projects. Figure 5.3 presents an artist's caricature of how expansion in pump irrigation has reconfigured river basins and subbasins, reducing the value of a surface irrigation system even as it is being built. Figure 5.3a shows a river basin in predevelopment state, with some irrigated agriculture along the banks of the river and tributaries upstream. Away from the river, irrigation declined because wells were costly and laborious to operate. Figure 5.3b shows the conception of a surface irrigation project with a reservoir planned at a hydraulically opportune site, complete with a network of canals to transform a hitherto dry area into a compact, prosperous command area, somewhat overdesigned to make the investment pass the cost-benefit rule (Daines and Pawar 1987). When

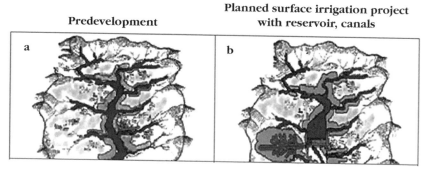

Predevelopment	Planned surface irrigation project with reservoir, canals
Atomistic pump irrigation upstream	Diminished reservoir and reduced canal command

a : Predevelopment river basin with riverine irrigation along the stem and tributaries.
b : A canal irrigation project is planned for intensive irrigation of a compact command area.
c : Numerous pockets of groundwater irrigation develop throughout the catchment reducing inflows into the dam.
d : Pockets of groundwater irrigation expand with numrous water harvesting structures in the uptream; these further reduce inflow into the reservoir and the proposed command area but spread supplemental irrigation all over the river basin.

Figure 5.3   Hypothetical river basin

completed, the actual command area of the project would closely resemble the plan.

Figure 5.3c shows what happens in the basin while the irrigation system is being built. Pockets of WEM irrigation emerge upstream of the reservoir as well as in the proposed command area. Initially, the density of WEMs is high on the banks of the river and tributaries but declines farther away and in upstream catchment areas. Lifting directly from the river and tributaries also accounts for growth in intensive irrigation along the banks. Most of this pump irrigation uses water that would have ended up in the reservoir being built. Because the planners did not allow for this pump irrigation, they assumed a higher water inflow for the reservoir than was actually available.

As a result, the area actually "commanded" by the project turns out to be smaller than planned.

In the midst of most command areas lie "noncommand" areas, high ground that cannot be served by gravity flow. However, using pumps to lift water from canals, noncommand farmers upstream appropriate a sizable portion of the water meant for downstream. Numerous small and medium surface irrigation systems throughout India have fallen prey to such unauthorized lifting of water by noncommand farmers. In these systems, pump irrigation development upstream can make dams useless in most seasons; the reservoirs fill only in years of exceptionally good rainfall in the catchment areas.[5] Even the planning of mega projects is not safe from uncontrolled pump irrigation expansion. The Sardar Sarovar Dam on River Narmada— and the entire hydraulic infrastructure below it—is designed based on the annual allocation of 11 km^3 of water to Gujarat by the Narmada tribunal in 1978. Recent studies have shown that pump irrigation development upstream of the dam has increased annual consumptive use of groundwater by about 5 km^3 during this period (Kumar et al. 2005; Ranade 2005). Singh et al. (2005, 11) report that "there are hundreds of thousands of individual farmers who are lifting water directly from the river or the canals upstream." Since the tribunal award is silent on sharing of groundwater among states, the hydraulic infrastructure below the Sardar Sarovar Dam will have to make do with far less water than it was designed to receive.

Much the same result follows when farmers upstream pump from groundwater instead of from rivers and canals; growth in well irrigation in upper Krishna basin, mostly Maharashtra, reduced the runoff coefficient by a third—from 0.22 to 0.15 between 1971–1974 and 1996–2000—and contributed around half of the 46 percent decline in the inflows into the downstream Sri-Sailam reservoir, from 56 to 30.4 km^3, during that period (Biggs et al. 2007). Unlike the Narmada tribunal, the Bachawat tribunal on the sharing of Krishna waters among Maharashtra, Karnataka, and Andhra Pradesh stipulated that "the use of underground water shall not be reckoned as the use of the water of river Krishna" (Government of India and KWDT 1973, 1976). In 1969, when the tribunal gave its award, the provision seemed inconsequential enough; 30 years later, however, runaway expansion in groundwater irrigation had defeated the spirit of the award.[6]

The development of tube well irrigation within the command areas has also weakened the accountability mechanisms of irrigation bureaucracies because users can choose the "exit" option over the more chancy "voice" option to press for better performance (Chapter 3). In the Indus Basin Irrigation System in Pakistan, systematic deterioration of canal irrigation infrastructure as well as weakening of accountability mechanisms is a cause as well as a result of the rise of tube well irrigation.[7]

Figure 5.3d shows the extreme cannibalization of surface systems by pump irrigation. As farmers in catchment areas expand irrigated agriculture with groundwater, resource depletion in upstream areas creates pressure to increase rainwater harvesting and groundwater recharge. This happens in myriad ways. In many parts of semiarid India, farmers use farm bunds (dikes) to capture and store rainwater to increase soil moisture. Modifying dug wells for localized rainwater recharge is becoming increasingly common in many hard-rock aquifer areas. In Saurashtra and Kutch regions of Gujarat and many areas in Madhya Pradesh and Rajasthan, village communities seeking ways to enhance local groundwater security build a series of small check structures on streams and rivulets. Water harvesting and groundwater recharge on a large scale make pump irrigation sustainable in catchment areas, and farming becomes more drought resilient. But it reduces surface water flows all along the basin. Siltation has been the prime enemy of reservoirs; now, upstream water harvesting and groundwater recharge efforts threaten large reservoirs. Just one million WEMs[8] irrigating two million to 2.5 million ha and supported by decentralized recharge structures upstream of the Sardar Sarovar Dam can use up all 11 km[3] of Gujarat's share of Narmada water. And considering that India has added on average 800,000 new WEMs every year over the 1990–2000 period, there is little doubt that pump irrigation is reducing inflows into reservoirs.

The pace at which such cannibalism is proceeding has increased in recent years. The government of Gujarat initiated the ambitious and innovative Rs. 65 billion Sujalam-Sufalam project to build a 337-km-long elevated earthen canal from Kadana reservoir in the Mahi basin to recharge the parched alluvial aquifers of North Gujarat by filling up 21 dry riverbeds (Chapter 6). Now, with the project half completed, it appears that water may flow into the canal only once in seven to 10 years, and only when the Kadana reservoir is filled to the level of 419 feet can water flow into the canal by gravity; however, since the dam was built in 1977, this has happened only six times. Moreover, groundwater development and decentralized recharge structures are taking water upstream of the Kadana reservoir. NGOs like the Sadguru Foundation have even been setting up live laboratories demonstrating the power of water harvesting for reducing tribal poverty and reviving lost rivers, lowering the chances that Kadana water will ever flow into the canal.

Although pump irrigation makes the planning of large dam and canal projects hazardous, it is not clear whether the basin as a whole is worse off as a result. One view is that upstream diversion by water harvesters leaves downstream users worse off, upholding a kind of prior appropriation rule that became popular in many parts of the New World, especially the western United States and Australia during the nineteenth century. An alternative view begins with the notion of upstream-downstream equity in water allocation in basins where catchment areas are densely populated. Instead of using a river system to create a compact island of agricultural prosperity in the command area, the reconfigured river basin may have the same area, or even more, under supplemental WEM irrigation in the basin as a whole. That these areas are more dispersed and better distributed spatially than in a compact command area may be a socially more desirable outcome. After all, the design intent in many surface irrigation systems in India since colonial times has been to spread available water over as large an area as possible to provide protective irrigation. The reconfigured river basin delivers much the same result without large public investments. Moreover, if a surfeit of water harvesting and groundwater recharge activity in the catchment areas can transform a mostly "giving" river system into a mostly "receiving" one, with recharged aquifers releasing water slowly into the river year-round rather than floodwaters filling the riverbed for only a few months after the monsoon, the reconfigured river basin may be better than the present one, with better environmental flows into estuaries.

A corollary is the sanctity of water-sharing agreements between riparian states. These agreements and tribunal awards commonly concentrate on the sharing of river flows, which are easily measurable. However, if they do not incorporate the potential expansion in groundwater irrigation upstream, downstream states risk getting significantly lower flows simply because it is very difficult for upstream states to control expansion in pump irrigation. By supporting the development of pump irrigation, bad-acting upstream states can kill the intent of the flow-sharing agreement while being faithful to it in a literal sense.[9]

In many parts of the world, catchment areas of river basins are sparsely populated forests with a relatively small human footprint. This was the case in much of South Asia, too, where the central Indian highlands, which are the catchment areas for many large central and peninsular river basins, were thickly forested tribal homelands. This is no longer the case. Large forest areas have been converted into farmland; tribes that once lived by hunting and gathering are increasingly agricultural. Nowhere else in the world are catchment areas of river basins likely to suffer such high population pressures as in South Asia. True, pump irrigation expansion in the central Indian highlands has been slower than in the rest of India, but that is changing, and we should expect the progression outlined in Figure 5.3 to keep playing out.

All in all, the reality of public irrigation projects in South Asia today is that planners propose and pump irrigators dispose. There are two possible solutions: first, the planners of large irrigation projects can recognize, predict, and adapt to the future impact of unregulated expansion in pump irrigation; or second, they can find a way to regulate the pace of pump irrigation expansion upstream—more easily said than done because of the informal nature of the pump irrigation economy.

Informal Water Economy

A major consequence of the pump irrigation boom in South Asia has been the creation of a vast informal water economy that is nearly impossible to govern using direct policy instruments, such as pricing, rights reform, and direct regulation. From the standpoint of effective governance, a water economy is ideal if all or most agricultural, domestic and, industrial users are supplied by a small network of public utilities or private water service providers. This is the case in most industrialized countries. Water laws, water policies, and water administration—the three pillars of water governance in a country—can quickly modify the behavior of water users by influencing water service providers. The toolkit of instruments for managing water demand—volumetric pricing, intersectoral allocation of water at river basin level, specification and enforcement of tradable water rights—constitutes a resource management regime widely understood as integrated water resources management (IWRM). Such highly "formalized" water economies can deploy IWRM tools because water service providers supply most users and are subject to regulation under water law, policy, and administration.

In an "informal" water economy, in contrast, most of the water appropriation occurs directly by millions of self-providing water users who divert water directly from nature; as a result, most water appropriation and use are outside the ambit of the law. The state's writ does not run in informal water economies, where water users rely on self-provision of their water needs (through private wells, streams, ponds) or on informal water markets (Shah 2007a; Shah and van Koppen 2006).[10]

Just how informal the water economy in South Asia can be is revealed by recent nationwide surveys in India. Based on interviews with 78,990 rural households in 5,110 villages throughout India (NSSO 1999b), a 1998 survey showed that only 10 percent of the water infrastructure assets used by survey households were owned and managed by either a public or a community organization; the rest were owned and managed by private households. If receiving domestic water from a tap is an indicator of connection to a formal water supply system, the same survey also showed that more than 80 percent of rural households were not connected to *any* public or community water supply system. They self-supplied their domestic water needs directly from a natural source, mostly aquifers.[11] A 2002 survey (NSSO 2003) showed that of the 4,646 Indian villages covered, only 8.8 percent had a public or community water supply system. In other villages, people depended on wells or open waterbodies for their domestic water supply.

The irrigation economy of South Asia is equally informal. A 1998 survey of 48,419 cultivators around India showed that 65 percent used irrigation for their five major field crops. For half, the source of irrigation was informal, fragmented pump irrigation markets (NSSO 1999a).[12] In the 2002 survey of 4,646 Indian villages (NSSO 2003), 76 percent of the villages reported that some land was irrigated, but only 17 percent had access to a *public* irrigation system; the rest used wells, tube wells, tanks, and streams. These surveys suggest that rural India's water economy—both domestic and irrigation use—is predominantly informal, based on self-supply and local, informal water institutions. It has little connection with public systems and formal organizations through which the three pillars of law, policies, and administration typically operate in industrialized countries.[13] By far the bulk of South Asia's rural water use, based on millions of small, family-owned irrigation and domestic wells, has no direct connection to public systems, nor is it subject to regulatory or economic influence from them.

Things were not always this way, at least for irrigation. Use of natural resources, particularly irrigation water, was once subject to heavy oversight, regulation, and intervention by the ruling classes or local communities in South Asia. A major agenda of colonial engagement in canal irrigation projects was bringing the appropriation and use of land and water under state control. James Thomason, a canny irrigation engineer[14] in colonial India, argued that developing water resources was critical to enhancing state income, but "it was also critical to new forms of state power. Increasing state control over water—and thus over the land—defined new frameworks for exercise of control over the local 'communities' comprising the Indus basin society" (quoted in Gilmartin 2003b, *5057*). When farmers received irrigation water from a canal system centrally operated by an authoritarian bureaucracy for producing agricultural output from which the state claimed a significant portion as land revenue and water charges, agents of the state had various levers to influence the appropriation and use of water by millions of users. In this sense, colonial irrigation economy was more formal than South Asian irrigation is today.

Because of their extractive revenue interests in agriculture, colonial and precolonial states engaged in governing groundwater economies through direct means. Throughout history, recognizing the higher productivity of well irrigation and its revenue potential, ruling classes supported private efforts to increase well irrigation but also taxed it at higher-than-normal rates. In *Arthashastra*, Kautilya asserted groundwater to be state property during the Mauryan rule and suggested calibrated assessment of land revenue to shape peasant incentives in irrigation. Those who practiced irrigation using manual labor had to pay one-fifth of the produce; those who carried water on their shoulders paid one-fourth; water lifts, one-third; and raising water from rivers, tanks, lakes, and wells, one-third or one-fourth. Remission of taxes was granted to those who built their own tanks or lakes or repaired neglected tanks and wells (Raychoudhury 1998). During the medieval era, state support for well irrigation often took the form of remission of land taxes when the wells failed.

During Shahjahan's reign (1666–1707), a royal order prescribed that a person who offered to repair fallen wells should be exempt from land revenue but should pay only a flat tax rate per well (Habib 1999). "In Dakhin [South], when Murshid Quli Khan established the system of crop sharing in the closing years of Shahjahan's reign, he took half the produce from ordinary lands, but one third from those irrigated by wells and still lower proportions (down to one fourth) from high-grade crops" (Habib 1999, *234*). Many rulers encouraged digging of wells by offering land tax remissions but imposed a well tax, too.

Colonial rule is sometimes blamed for today's *laissez-faire* groundwater economy in South Asia. The Easement Act of 1882, which declared all surface water the property of the state but treated groundwater as an easement attached to landownership,[15] is said to be the root cause of groundwater anarchy (Planning Commission 2007). However, the act did not prevent the colonial administration from treating groundwater as a valuable taxable resource for the purposes of revenue administration, and through that, for governing the economy. Hardiman (1998) explores how this was done in Gujarat, and I summarize Hardiman's account in some detail for the insight it offers on the tight hold the state once had over the groundwater economy.

During the early nineteenth century, the British government imposed an irrigation tax on well owners but exempted farmers who dug wells for two to seven years, depending on the depth of the well; in 1846 the period was extended to a maximum of 30 years. To maximize farmer diligence, colonial land revenue assessment taxed the productive potential of land classified into four categories; gardens irrigated with wells (called *bagayat*) were rated the highest, and rain-fed land the lowest. Once assessed, a field was subject to the relevant tax whether it was actually irrigated or not. In addition, every well was subject to a separate tax related to its capacity measured by the number of *kos* (bullock-bailer) that it could support.[16]

The tax on wells led to a 40-year-long heated debate in Bombay newspapers and its eventual abolition and the reaffirmation of landholders' absolute ownership of groundwater. Fields with wells on them, however, were still subject to the highest *bagayat* rate of land tax. By now, groundwater markets had already emerged in central Gujarat, and water buyers could use purchased irrigation water without having to pay the *bagayat* tax, since they had no wells on their fields. The administration noted that this discouraged well construction. To "correct" farmer incentives, in 1890 the revenue officials decided to spread the *bagayat* tax assessed for a village on all land *potentially* irrigable by private wells in the village, not just on lands belonging to the well owners alone. Thus, all land in groundwater-irrigated villages was subject to an extra "subsoil rate"—a kind of aquifer potential tax—on top of the regular land tax rate. The rate was computed on a sliding scale, from a 37.5 percent surcharge for tracts where good-quality groundwater was available at 10 feet or less, to no subsoil tax for tracts where the groundwater level was 40 feet or more. During the survey, water levels were carefully recorded and tracts delineated for different levels of the subsoil rate.

Abolition of the irrigation tax on wells and the imposition of the subsoil tax gave a powerful impetus to well construction as well as to groundwater markets in central Gujarat during the last decade of the nineteenth century. At the same time, as water tables fell during a series of poor rainfall years, the government encouraged boring of tube wells at the bottom of open wells. By 1910, this had taken the form of an official campaign. Boring itself was a costly affair; moreover, with falling water tables, oil engines as big as

26 hp had become necessary. *Taccavi* loans were offered; but many farmers had to borrow from *sahukars* at commercial rates. Such capital investments made it even more imperative for well owners to sell water to recoup their investments. The new technology also offered them the capacity to do so. A single mechanized pump replaced 15 to 18 *kos* and an equal number of pairs of bullocks. In the mid-1920s, it was common for well owners in Kheda district to lay buried cement pipeline networks to convey well water to more than one village. Although northern India waited until the late 1930s for Sir William Stamp to demonstrate the amazing possibilities of mechanized tube wells, the technology was a standard fixture in many villages of central Gujarat during the 1910s.

The end of colonial rule marked a watershed in the revenue relationship between the state and farming communities. Land revenue fell to a token and revenue administration declined, weakening the state's capacity to have its writ run in the agricultural and natural resources economy. Canal commands maintained a semblance of formal relationship between the state and irrigation communities; however, with the ascent of vote-bank politics and the decline of commercial discipline in canal management, even these links slipped. The rise of the informal pump irrigation economy has further weakened the state's grip on water diversions. For one, as we saw in Chapter 3, pump irrigation has been cannibalizing state-run surface irrigation and community-run tank irrigation systems, both of which are losing share in relative and absolute terms to WEMs. Moreover, because WEMs provide a convenient "exit," the disciplining power of the managers of public irrigation systems—and their power to extract the rents from water distribution that Robert Wade (1975, *1982*) had made much of—eroded even within their command areas. Finally, postcolonial regimes failed to establish even skeletal regulatory structures for managing pump irrigation growth. Such structures are best instituted at stage 1 or 2 of development (Figure 5.1), when the number of pumpers is small and pump irrigators have little scope to mobilize for vote-bank politics. But stages 1 and 2 are long since gone in much of South Asia. Indeed, by the time the pump irrigation boom began, South Asia had lost age-old traditions of groundwater governance.

Hardiman's analysis, summarized above, suggests a highly formalized groundwater irrigation economy in which the state administration had an intensive and live engagement of mutuality with groundwater users. It suggests the presence of an administrative apparatus, a structure of rules, and a mechanism for changing the incentives of resource users depending on the priority of the time. None of these conditions obtain today. Instead, the vast number of pump irrigators has made effective governance of pump irrigation economies through direct instruments—rules and administrative orders, direct incentives and disincentives, and laws—extremely difficult, if not impossible. The only link between the state and the millions of pump irrigators is electricity supply, over which the state has control. By maneuvering the pricing and supply of electricity, the state can influence the overall patterns of groundwater withdrawal, but it cannot micromanage local groundwater economies as the colonial state once did. This nexus between electricity supply and irrigation has emerged as the pivot of vote-bank politics in the region and triggered a battle of wits between pump irrigators on one hand and politicians, technocrats, and international agencies on the other.

Bankrupt Electricity Industry

The eighteenth-century German playwright Johann Wolfgang von Goethe once said that the solution of every problem is another problem. The story of South Asia's 40-year-old engagement with the energy-irrigation nexus is testimony to this dictum. During the 1950s and 1960s, when per capita electricity use was considered synonymous with economic progress, the World Bank supported large investments in South Asia's rural electrification infrastructure to energize agriculture. Government-owned power utilities in India and Pakistan pursued farmers unwilling to install electric tube wells. In Indian states like Punjab and Uttar Pradesh, chief ministers gave steep targets to district-level officials to "sell" electricity connections to farmers, and loans and concessions were made available. These policies were vindicated when the Green Revolution was found to follow the tube well revolution with a lag of just three to five years (Dhawan 1982; Shah 2001). Somewhere along the way, the tipping point was reached, and on its own, pump irrigation took off. By the 1970s, the energy-irrigation nexus had become a prominent feature of the region's agrarian boom, and even in canal commands, such as Indian and Pakistan Punjabs, where tube wells were still frowned on by farmers (Shah 1993), their numbers grew rapidly.

By the mid-1970s, however, the enthusiasm of electricity utilities toward agricultural customers had begun to dampen. For India's state electricity boards and Pakistan's Water and Power Development Authority, the transaction costs of serving a large, scattered group of remote consumers were high, and electricity utilities were finding it costly and difficult to manage their metering and billing. The cost of meters and their maintenance was the least of the worry; it was the costs of training meter readers and controlling tampering, pilferage, underbilling, and meter reader corruption that proved problematic.[17] To prevent meter readers from unionizing, some electricity boards, such as that in Uttar Pradesh, farmed out meter reading and billing to village youth on a commission basis, but many of these readers then subcontracted the job. The less honest among them began looting the pump owners under the threat of overbilling.[18] An invidious political economy of metering-and-billing had emerged that threatened to create a major political crisis that both farmers and electricity boards wanted to end (Shah 2001).

A 1985 study by India's Rural Electrification Corporation showed that metering cost alone was 15 to 20 percent of the cost of power supplied to agriculture in Maharashtra (cited in Shah 1993). The introduction of a flat tariff—that is, charging a fixed rate based on the horsepower rating of the WEM—in state after state during the 1970s and 1980s was essentially a response to the high and rising transaction cost of metered power supply.[19] Flat tariffs eliminated the hassle and cost of metering but still afforded scope for illicit practices, such as underreporting the horsepower rating; but controlling this was easier than controlling pilferage. From the electric utilities' viewpoint, the flat tariff could be a solution provided they could (a) raise the tariff levels from time to time such that it broadly covered the average cost of supplying power used by the farmers; (b) ration power supply to ensure that the prevailing flat rates covered the cost of power supplied; or (c) use a combination of both to ensure that power supply to pump irrigation remained financially viable.

In India, however, flat tariffs tended to become "sticky." As power supply to agriculture became a major feature of the region's mass politics, chief ministers found it a powerful weapon to wield in vote-bank politics. Unable to raise the flat tariff for years and pressured to supply abundant farm power, power utilities saw their balance sheets turn red. Around 2001, the World Bank estimated electricity subsidies for pump irrigation in India at US$5 billion (Rs. 240 billion),[20] equivalent to a quarter of India's fiscal deficit.[21] In Madhya Pradesh, Gujarat, Rajasthan, Andhra Pradesh, Haryana, and Tamilnadu, electricity subsidies accounted for half or more of the state government's gross fiscal deficit (Briscoe and Malik 2006). In the early years of the new millennium, the deficits were growing at a rate of 26 percent per year

(Gulati and Narayanan 2003; Lim 2001), and at this rate, it will not be long before power industry finances crash.

Those estimates have been widely contested, and state electricity boards have been accused of hiding their growing transmission and distribution losses in domestic and industrial sectors as agricultural consumption, which is unmetered and thus unverifiable.[22] However, the fact remains that agricultural power supply under the existing regime became the prime cause of the bankruptcy of India's electricity industry. Staff of the World Bank and Asian Development Bank also observe that when a third of electricity use is not measured, it is impossible to manage the electricity industry on a sound commercial basis.

But pushing the genie back into the bottle has proved one of the toughest challenges of mass politics in South Asia. The entire pump irrigation economy in western and southern India depends on subsidized electricity and has steadfastly resisted attempts to end the flat tariff. The battle between pump irrigators and electric utilities has been fought with strikingly different results in three different zones of South Asia (Figure 5.4). In zone 1 (Pakistan Punjab and Sind, Nepal terai, Orissa and Bangladesh), governments have stuck to metering at commercial rates and forced WEM owners to use diesel instead—compelling a "dieselization" of the pump irrigation economy. In zone 2 (eastern India), governments have achieved the same result by whittling down the effective supply of electricity to agriculture. In zone 3 (western and peninsular India), pump irrigators have virtually held governments ransom to prevent them from metering use and charging at commercial rates.

In Pakistan, the Water and Power Development Authority managed to raise the flat tariff three times between 1993 and 1999, hiking it threefold from Rs 176 to 520 per hp per month in Punjab and Sind, and Rs. 146 to 438 in Baluchistan and Northwest Frontier Province (Shah et al. 2000b). By the close of the 1990s, in a bold move, the government of President Musharraf began to enforce an earlier government decision to do away with flat tariffs and began reinstalling meters on tube wells. But with that came all the problems that had prompted many Indian states to abandon metering in the first place.[23] Moreover, farmers responded by switching to diesel WEMs in large numbers. According to Pakistan's agricultural machinery census report of 2004, of the 922,000 WEMs in the country, 833,000 were diesel and only 89,000, less than 10 percent, were electric, down from 40 percent in 1988–89. In India, the groundwater-rich but otherwise poor state of Orissa in eastern India was the sole state to return to metered power supply, which it could do

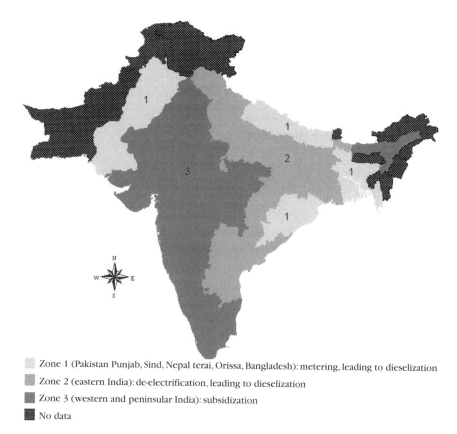

Zone 1 (Pakistan Punjab, Sind, Nepal terai, Orissa, Bangladesh): metering, leading to dieselization

Zone 2 (eastern India): de-electrification, leading to dieselization

Zone 3 (western and peninsular India): subsidization

No data

Figure 5.4   Geography of approaches to electricity supply for pump irrigation

because it had only 4,000 electric WEMs. But the cure proved worse than the disease: farmers deserted electric pumps, and the number quickly fell to 1,100 (Panda 2002). Bangladesh, which began adopting tube wells later than India and Pakistan, never embraced the flat tariff and charged farmers near-commercial rates. As a result, in 2003, Bangladesh had 865,000 diesel WEMs but only 90,000 electric, mostly deep tube wells. Nepal, too, charges metered rates with very little subsidy for tube wells in the Terai area. However, Nepal Terai has hardly any electric WEMs, and the large community-based electric tube wells that were established by international agencies, notably USAID, were patronized as long as the agency absorbed the energy costs; as soon as commercial rates were charged, farmers switched to small diesel pumps. Thus Nepal Terai's nascent pump irrigation economy is almost wholly dependent on diesel pumps. In all these regions, governments and electric utilities forced pump irrigators out of the electricity-irrigation nexus, leaving behind a high-cost, diesel-based pump irrigation economy.

In eastern Indian states, too, pump irrigators have abandoned the electricity-irrigation nexus. Pump irrigation here began with diesel pumps but as rural electrification progressed, electric WEMs proliferated until the early 1980s. State electricity boards' finances began getting squeezed when, because of vote-bank politics, they were allowed neither to raise flat tariffs nor to switch to metering, and they began to neglect rural electricity infrastructure, first by default but then by design (Shah 2001). After 1985, much of eastern India's countryside was progressively deelectrified, as the pump irrigation economy came to depend increasingly on diesel. In West Bengal, Mukherji (2007) found agricultural power supply better than elsewhere in eastern India, but the supply of electricity connections was tightly controlled. Moreover, West Bengal charged among the highest flat tariff in India and, at the time of writing, was planning to move to metering. All these developments mean that West Bengal's pump irrigation economy, already heavily diesel dependent, will likely dieselize further.

In both zone 1 and zone 2, political leaders and electric utilities could cut electricity subsidies by forcing the pump irrigation economy to switch from cheaper, cleaner electricity to costlier and dirtier diesel. A majority of the farmers in these regions already had the option to use diesel pumps, which are best for pumping from shallow depths. In zone 3—arid western and semiarid peninsular India—initial electricity subsidies had created a pump irrigation economy addicted to cheap electricity. As pumping depths increased to 20 meters or more, farmers could no longer rely on centrifugal diesel pumps and were forced to go electric. Metering tube wells and charging pump irrigators the true cost of supplying electricity would make irrigated agriculture totally unviable, and squeezing power supply to cut electricity boards' losses would mean closing down the pump irrigation economy because switching to diesel pumps is no longer feasible in many areas. Preventing a return to metering, not raising flat tariffs, and maximizing daily hours of power supply to pumps became rallying points around which farmers have mobilized in these parts.

It is not that attempts have not been made to break the electricity-irrigation nexus by some astute chief ministers of states in western and peninsular India. But every chief minister who has tried has failed. In Andhra Pradesh, the chief minister had to retract a public announcement of the government's decision to reintroduce metering within a week after he made it, but even the retraction could not help his party from being routed in the *Panchayat* elections that followed. As we saw earlier, his successor wrested power by promising free electricity to farmers and has now promised to extend free electricity up to 2017. In Haryana, farmers held a district magistrate hostage for several days to protest proposed power tariff reforms. In Kerala, the chief minister had to withdraw all his proposals for tariff reforms. In Madhya Pradesh, Chief Minister Digvijay Singh refused to give in and was promptly felled in the following election.[24] In Gujarat, the Electricity Tariff Regulatory Commission had mandated the state government to introduce metering as required by the Asian Development Bank to release a US$350 million loan; however, as soon as Narendra Modi was elected to lead the BJP government, he made it clear he had no intention of metering agricultural pumps. In Pakistan, most farmers who could switch to diesel pumps did so after meters were introduced. But even in the lower Indus basin, there are areas where groundwater lies at considerable depths and can be pumped only with electric WEMs. Some 100,000 such electric WEM owners have been clamoring for "relief," and the government of Pakistan had to declare a 33 percent subsidy on the power tariff.[25] Now, demands to raise this subsidy to 50 percent will likely be met.[26] In Baluchistan, which has more than 15,000 heavy-duty tube well pumps, the Farmers Action Committee has ensured a flat tariff of Rs. 4,000 per month, regardless of not only the actual power consumed but even the size of the pump (Ahmed and Ahmad 2007).

The duels between politicians and pump irrigators in the three energy-irrigation zones of South Asia have created a curious mosaic. In groundwater-rich eastern India, Nepal Terai, and Bangladesh, one of the densest pockets of rural poverty in the world, affordable pump irrigation could have powerful livelihood effects, ease postmonsoon waterlogging, and even moderate annual floods. Here, however, diesel-pump irrigation has been the least affordable, with diesel prices rising eightfold between 1991 and 2007 while rice prices stagnated, pushing smallholders out of the pump irrigation economy (Shah 2007b). A big opportunity for using pump irrigation to alleviate poverty is lost to progressive rural deelectrification of this region.

In Pakistan Punjab and Sind, private pump owners are creating a positive externality in the form of conjunctive use of ground and surface water, achieving the same ends for which the government and donors had spent hundreds of millions of dollars on the failed SCARP tube well programs. If ever there was a case for energy subsidies to encourage pump irrigation, these regions had one, yet governments here have forced the pump irrigators to adopt the costlier and dirtier diesel option.

Western and peninsular India and Baluchistan, which face serious problems of groundwater depletion, in contrast, have witnessed the ascent of electric WEMs based on tariff subsidies. Organizations of pump irrigators have given governments little room to move away from sticky flat tariffs.

Conclusion: Political Stalemate

The pump irrigation boom of South Asia has consequences. Although well irrigation has greatly benefited millions of smallholders, the negative externalities are becoming a real threat to the region's hydrology and to the future sustainability of an agrarian system dependent on a largely ungoverned resource. This threat is much talked about in the popular media as well as in the scientific literature, and Chapter 6 considers these externalities—and farmers' struggle to cope with them. This chapter has highlighted three other side effects of pump irrigation—the reconfiguring of river basins, the informalizing of South Asia's irrigation economy, and the generation of an energy-irrigation nexus and the mass politics surrounding it.

South Asia's energy-irrigation nexus—a mixed bag of problems and opportunities—is anathema to planners and politicians alike. Without exception, commentators on South Asia's groundwater boom have argued that perverse electricity subsidies are a central reason for the widespread depletion of aquifers in western and peninsular India (World Bank 2005a, 2005b). This cause-effect equation was likely true until the mid-1980s. Today, however, electricity subsidies in much of South Asia are a *result* of groundwater depletion as much as the cause. Wherever they could, political leaders and electric utilities have cut electricity subsidies. In Pakistan Punjab and Sind and in Bangladesh, commercial consumption-based rates have priced electricity out of the groundwater economy. In eastern Indian states and parts of northern India, electricity subsidies were curtailed by deelectrifying the whole countryside. In all these regions, groundwater recharge—natural in the Ganga basin and through canal irrigation return flows in Indus basin—has been abundant and its pumping improves agrarian welfare and reduces waterlogging.

Electricity subsidies have been minimized here, but opportunities to enhance the livelihoods of the poor have been lost in the bargain.

Political leaders, electric utilities, and international agencies repeatedly tried the same solution in western and peninsular India during the past decade. Each time, however, pump irrigators quickly mobilized in protest against "reform." Because they must pump groundwater from depths that centrifugal diesel pumps cannot reach, farmers depended on cheap energy for their survival. At US$0.05 (Rs. 2) per kWh of metered electricity charge, pump irrigation would become uneconomic for majority of farmers in North Gujarat, western Rajasthan, Andhra Pradesh, Karnataka, and Tamil Nadu.

In those regions, some of the worst excesses of groundwater depletion are easily stopped; instead they are not only state sanctioned but also state subsidized. The solution to the problem of groundwater depletion in South Asia is surprisingly simple: shut off the oxygen—in the form of electricity supply under a flat tariff—that sustains pump irrigation in western and southern India. If only pump irrigators would let the politicians do so. The irony of the situation is that for centuries, irrigation was associated with violence by ruling classes over peasants, as we saw in Chapter 1. It is a singular outcome of the rise of groundwater irrigation that the tables are turned and it is the irrigators who are now threatening the ruling classes.

Animated political gaming around the energy-irrigation nexus is not unique to South Asia. In 2002, 96,161 tube well owners in Mexico received an annual electricity subsidy of US$159 million at an average of US$1,653 per tube well, four times the per unit subsidy in India. Pina et al. (2006) argue that even decoupling the subsidy from energy use—by making a lump-sum annual payment based on average power consumption—would be opposed: "the political dynamics of the agricultural leaders may generate the opposition even by those who apparently win" because the farmer-leaders who dictate the subsidized rate take the credit for lower electricity charges, where as "the direct transfer . . . 'decoupled' from their decision . . . does not allow them to score points among their constituency."

In South Asia, that political dynamic is magnified a thousand times over, but in essence, it is no different. The electricity-irrigation nexus represents a classic example of public choice in a representative democracy, and the "median voter hypothesis"[27] has been a good predictor of the outcomes so far. Median voter hypothesis—which rests on the premise that preferences of voters on each issue are normally distributed—has been widely used to study the interaction between economic and political behavior in representative democracies (Cukierman and Spiegel 1985). The median voter is not an individual but a position on an issue. The same voter may be at the median on one issue and way off center on another. An electoral candidate perceived by voters to be slightly to the right of the center is likely to get support from all voters on his right and a few on the left, and vice versa. For a politician trying to win an election, then, the trick is to move to the center.

Pump irrigators in western and southern India are in the middle. On their right are commercial and domestic electricity users who are paying for some of the electricity subsidies, and on their left are the rural poor who derive little benefit from electricity subsidies but also share none of the costs. If electricity subsidies to agriculture were put to a vote, those on the right would likely vote against, but those on the left would be indifferent or sympathize with pump irrigators. A weak form of median voter hypothesis asserts that the median voter always votes for a winning policy. But a strong form says her preferred policy tends to win. An implication is that many other voters would be far from fully satisfied with the choice exercised by the median voter. Yet maintaining a flat or even no electricity tariff and guaranteed hours of power supply to farmers has been a preelection promise on which many chief ministers—notably of Punjab, Andhra Pradesh, Gujarat, Tamil Nadu, and Madhya Pradesh—have won elections. After victory, many try to wriggle out of the commitment, but at least so far, pump irrigators have managed to regroup and frustrate such moves.

In the informal water economy of South Asia, cooperation and competition among the users of shared aquifers catalyze intense social and political dynamics that we little understand. Until we develop an understanding of this dynamic, it seems improbable that we can even begin to figure out how to govern this anarchic pump irrigation economy. Although the science of how groundwater behaves is well developed, the social science of how its users behave is still in the making, with just a small number of researchers working on the human dimension of aquifer development. It is to learning from these that we turn in Chapter 6.

CHAPTER 6

AQUIFERS AND INSTITUTIONS

Though this be madness, yet there is method in't.

— *Hamlet (II, ii, 206)*

How do users relate to aquifer development? How do they respond, as individuals and as a group sharing an aquifer, to groundwater depletion or quality deterioration? When do they choose to cooperate and when to compete? Do they actually choose, or are they impelled to behave in a certain way by the natural processes they confront? Are there situations in which they find it easier to cooperate for the greater good? These and many other such questions are crucial for us to explore but require a marriage of hydrogeology and the social sciences—economics, political science, and sociology.

Hydrogeologists have developed a formidable repertoire of models that analyze the complex behavior of aquifers in response to human intervention to develop and use them. However, in a region like South Asia, where millions of smallholders directly interfere with the aquifer processes without let or hindrance, we have little understanding of how users respond to its development and, in due course, its depletion or deterioration. In this chapter,

I explore the effect of aquifer conditions on human behavior, especially the institutional response of groundwater users. By institutional response, I mean the central behavioral tendencies of groundwater irrigators and the social dynamic that results from different aquifer conditions. In keeping with Veblen (1934), the original institutionalist, I treat institutions as "settled habits of thought common to the generality of men" (cited in Paarlberg 1993, 823–27).

The average groundwater user in South Asia has little or no *formal* knowledge of hydrogeology. But farmers certainly have ideas and even theories about how it all works underneath the earth's crust (Rosin 1993; Shah 2000). A lot of these popular theories will not withstand scientific scrutiny, yet farmers' decisions and actions are guided more by their own theories than by formal science. These theories, I suggest, are based on what economist John Muth (1961) called rational expectations, which help people formulate their view of the future state of things. Rational expectations are to be distinguished from adaptive expectations, in which the future is little more than a mechanical reproduction of the past. The *rational expectations model* suggests that people take into account all the information available to them—including the expectations of others they regard highly—to arrive at an expectation that differs from the actual only by a random error (Muth 1961; Sargent 2002[1]). When the behavior of most or all agents is shaped by such rational expectations, self-fulfilling prophecies abound. If a majority of customers expect a bank to fail and begin a run on it, a small bank may actually fail. If most traders expect stock prices to rise and start buying in that expectation, the market will actually skyrocket even when fundamentals suggest no reason for a rally. Likewise, farmers' expectations about how their groundwater source will respond to development or conservation shape their individual or collective behavior toward the aquifer and toward the "aquifer community."

An aquifer community can be viewed as aquifer users in a locality who are aware of their interdependence in their use of a common aquifer or a portion thereof. Researchers from the British Geological Society (2004) put it elegantly when they define it as a group of groundwater users who are "mutually vulnerable and mutually dependent because of the centrality of resource use in supporting livelihoods." The level of awareness of this interdependence is a measure of the strength or weakness of the aquifer community. To understand the institutional dynamic in an aquifer, we must examine representative farmers' rational expectations about the effect of other farmers' withdrawals on their own water availability (s), of the whole community's withdrawals on their water availability (S), of their water conservation efforts on their own water availability (h), and the community's conservation efforts on their water availability (H). Five situations, outlined in Table 6-1, represent the types of institutional dynamic that aquifer conditions generate in response to development in South Asia.

Situation 1: *Atomistic individualism (s=0; S=0; h=0; H=0)*. Each farmer is an insignificant user in an abundantly recharged aquifer; his usage has little impact on himself or other users. Likewise, aquifer development has little discernible impact on the individual user. Interdependence among users goes unnoticed, the aquifer community is nonexistent, and rational expectations fail to generate institutional dynamic of the kind we observe in the remaining four situations.

Situation 2: *Collusive opportunism (s=0; S<0; h=0; H=0)*. Aquifer development sharply raises the cost of groundwater extraction without greatly reducing water supply or quality. Wealthy farmers establish de facto control over the resource and collude against the resource poor but spearhead political mobilization to defend their access to and control over the resource. Irrigators display limited interdependence and are a weak aquifer community.

Situation 3: *Rivalrous gaming (s<0; S<<0; h=0; H>0)*. This kind of gaming occurs when aquifer development sharply raises the cost of water production and also limits the groundwater supply that users compete for. This condition promotes intense and destructive rivalry among competing users. Irrigators display a strong sense of interdependence but are a dysfunctional aquifer community, and sporadic evidence of the beneficial effects of community conservation fails to generate organized collective action.

Situation 4: *Cooperative gaming (s<0; S<<0; h>0; H>>0)*. Under certain catalytic conditions, rivalrous gaming metamorphoses into a cooperative game that reduces the cost and risk of water production and augments water availability to the entire community. The positive expectations that result foster a strong sense of benign interdependence and a highly functional aquifer community. Such aquifer communities are ripe for local groundwater self-governance.

Situation 5: *Exit (s<<0; S<<0; h=0; H=0)*. Groundwater development results in rapid quality deterioration without affecting supply. Costs and risks of groundwater use become prohibitive, and users begin giving up irrigated

Table 6-1   Institutional responses to aquifer development: Five South Asian situations

Institutional response situation	Aquifer characteristic	Impact of aquifer development on typical user	Pump irrigation markets	Example	Ease of political mobilization of farmers	Scope for local aquifer governance
1. Atomistic individualism	High storage; high recharge resources	Insignificant	Efficient, deep and broad; WEM ownership major source of neither power nor profit	Most of Indo-Gangetic basin; alluvial canal commands	Low	Nil
2. Collusive opportunism	High storage; no or limited recharge resources	Sharply rising marginal cost of groundwater	Highly monopolistic, fairly deep and broad; resource-poor elbowed out of pump irrigation economy	North Gujarat; western Rajasthan Baluchistan	High for energy subsidies and surface water imports	Low or nil
3. Rivalrous gaming	Hard-rock aquifer with low aquifer storage; some recharge resources	Rising marginal cost and declining share in limited water	Highly monopolistic; thin and shallow; poor have limited access, on adverse terms	inland peninsular India	High for energy subsidies and recharge resources	Scope for functional aquifer community
4. Cooperative gaming	Alluvial with confining layer, or humid hard-rock environment with low storage	Sharply rising marginal cost and declining share in limited water	Monopolistic; moderate in depth and breadth; access to groundwater more equitable	Eastern Rajasthan; inland Saurashtra	High for energy subsidies and recharge resources	High; functional aquifer community
5. Exit	Fragile aquifers prone to rapid quality deterioration	Sharp deterioration of water quality	Absent or insignificant	Coastal aquifers in Saurashtra; fresh-water lenses in Sind	Low	Nil

farming or farming altogether. Pervasive negative expectations inspire fatal-ism, hopelessness, and despair, which overwhelm the strong sense of inter-dependence. The aquifer community splinters and eventually withers away.

Atomistic Individualism in the Indo-Gangetic Basin

In the vast, continuous, deep alluvial aquifer of the Indo-Gangetic basin and in alluvial command areas of canal irrigation systems, a typical farmer is insignificant in relation to the aquifer. The farmer's extraction has an infin-itesimal effect on the aquifer and its pump irrigation economy. Because groundwater here can be tapped at shallow depths, the cost of entry to the aquifer is small, and so are the externalities of pump irrigation. Broad and deep pump irrigation markets here have the power to extend the benefits of irrigation to a large number of marginal farmers (Kishore and Mishra 2005; Mukherji 2007; Pant 2005; Shah 2001). However, these overheated pump irrigation markets will likely cool and shrink as marginal farmers buy their own pumps and boreholes, a tendency evident throughout the Indo-Gangetic basin (Shah and Ballabh 1997; Mukherji 2005; Steenbergen and Oliemans 1997). Even if this does not happen, not owning a water extrac-tion mechanism (WEM) no longer bars a small farmer's access to ground-water irrigation[2] (Fujita and Hossain 1995; Jacoby et al. 2001; Kishore and Mishra 2005; Shah 1993; Shah and Ballabh 1997). In the lower Indus basin, where alluvial aquifers are continuously recharged by canal irrigation return flows, the conditions are less ideal because of salinity, and there is room for the creation of some monopoly power.[3] This could produce a sub-optimal socioecological outcome because (1) in much of the Indus basin, private groundwater development creates a large positive externality by pro-viding vertical drainage as a joint product of irrigation (Steenbergen and Oliemans 1997); and (2) in Pakistan's unequal agrarian structure, multi-tudes of small and marginal farmers can benefit from vibrant pump irriga-tion markets. Happily, as Jacoby et al. (2001, 2) conclude from a study in the Pakistan Punjab, monopoly power is not a serious issue: "Despite the sub-stantial misallocation of groundwater, a welfare analysis shows that monop-oly pricing has limited effects on equity and efficiency." In Bangladesh, where water transactions are sometimes interlocked with credit or labor, prices may appear to contain monopoly premia. However, as Fujita and Hossain (1995, 456) concluded based on their study of a Bangladeshi vil-lage, when interest on working capital is included in the water price, "the groundwater market cannot be characterized as monopolistic, but rather as competitive and efficient." As we saw in Chapter 4, pump irrigation markets ushered in the *boro* rice revolution in Bangladesh and West Bengal, helping them break out of decades of agrarian stagnation.

Figures 6.1–6.4 and 6.6 represent different kinds of aquifer conditions and their responses to development. In 6.1, the abundantly recharged alluvial aquifers of the Ganga-Brahmaputra basin—with high storage coefficients, infiltration rates, and recharge—promote atomistic individualism among groundwater irrigators. The x-axis indicates the degree of aquifer development, measured as annual groundwater withdrawal as a proportion of long-term annual recharge. The upper half of the y-axis indicates incremental recharge in response to development; the lower half indicates a decline in water quality as well as groundwater level in response to with-

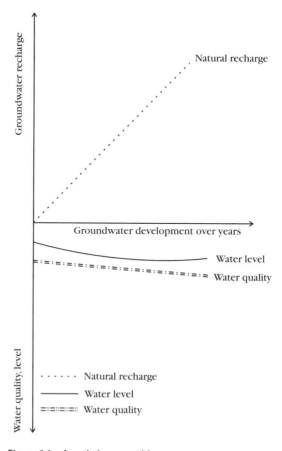

Figure 6.1   Atomistic competition

drawals. In the Ganga-Meghana-Brahmaputra basin, recharge fully compensates withdrawals such that the water level is relatively stable in response to withdrawal, although water quality may slowly decline at high levels of development. An individual user in such an aquifer is little affected by the withdrawals of other users, individually or collectively.

Atomistic competition among numerous small pump owners is the most efficient form of irrigation institution for these aquifers. Governments and donors have tried to reap scalar economies with heavy-duty, deep tube wells (Palmer-Jones 1995; Gautam 2006), public tube wells, SCARP tube wells (Steenbergen and Oliemans 1997), and community tube wells (Pant 1984; Ballabh 1987). These have all been crowded out by the vibrant dynamic of private pump irrigation markets dominated by shallow tube wells. Until now, pump irrigation expansion has produced large socioecological dividends: in the Ganga-Brahmaputra-Meghana basin, it has eased flooding in the eastern parts (Shah 2001); in the Indus basin, widespread waterlogging, a subject of much concern during the 1950s and 1960s, has all but disappeared (Steenbergen and Oliemans 1997; Briscoe and Malik 2006). Further expansion will necessitate managing localized groundwater depletion in summer in the east and secondary salinization in the west. Efficient conjunctive use of surface and groundwater is at the heart of sustaining irrigation agriculture here.

The Indo-Gangetic plains are home to more poor people than all of Africa, and spread of pump irrigation benefits could be a potent weapon against rural poverty here. Yet ironically, the progressive dieselization of pump irrigation, forced upon farmers by deteriorating electricity supply (Chapter 5), has meant a lost opportunity. The victims are marginal farmers who depend on purchased pump irrigation. As diesel prices have increased during recent years, smallholder water buyers are getting priced out of the pump irrigation economy. No one would argue that sellers should not recover fuel costs from buyers. But throughout the Indo-Gangetic basin, each time diesel prices are raised, water buyers are forced to pay a higher monopoly rent *besides* the increased fuel price (Shah 2007b). Water markets here are competitive but not "perfectly competitive" in the Marshallian sense,[4] and every time diesel prices rise, as they frequently have, water prices rise substantially more than necessary to offset the fuel price rise.[5] In 1986, diesel in eastern India cost Rs. 3.5 per liter and shallow tube well irrigation pumped by 5-hp diesel WEMs sold at Rs. 10–15 per hour. In 2007, diesel was selling at Rs. 35 per liter, and pump irrigation, Rs. 90–100 per hour, even though pump prices had actually dropped and five times more wells competed with one another than in the mid-1980s.

Two aspects are pertinent. First, water buyers are under greater pressure to economize on water use than pump owners, and this differential pressure increases with every increase in diesel price. Second, each increase in diesel prices means a transfer of wealth from water buyers to pump owners. Shah and Ballabh (1997) estimated that every hour of pump irrigation sold by diesel WEM owners in eastern India contained a "monopoly rent" of Rs. 10 in 1996; today, this monopoly rent is more like Rs. 42–45, and the poor of the Ganga basin are coughing up something like Rs. 21 billion to 22.5 billion (US$550 million) to diesel WEM owners as monopoly surplus per year.[6] Productivity and equity effects of high water prices in the Indo-Gangetic basin are evident in a host of microlevel studies. With rapid increases in diesel prices, *boro* rice cultivation with pump irrigation purchased from diesel WEM owners has all but come to an end. Recent studies (Mukherji 2007; Shah 2007b) show that buyers can raise *boro* rice only if they buy pump irrigation from a WEM owner who pays a flat electricity rate. Similarly, a survey in eastern Uttar Pradesh, Kishore and Mishra (2005) showed that a marginal farmer using purchased diesel pump irrigation for rice spent 5.5 times what it cost the owner of an electric WEM, and more than twice what it cost a buyer dealing with an electric WEM owner.

WEM owners and their water customers in the Ganga basin can correct this perverse redistribution of irrigation surplus by mobilizing for the electricity supply and pricing policies that farmers have forced governments to adopt in western and southern India (Shah et al. 2004c). The Indo-Gangetic plains are ideally placed to benefit from these (Shah 2001; Kishore and Mishra 2005).[7] However, this is the region least likely to mobilize into a powerful political vote bank around this issue; instead, it will suffer increasingly strident groundwater regulation. Mukherji (2007, 393–94) has recently explored this "strange paradox in India [of] vigorous groundwater regulation where none is needed [as in West Bengal] and virtual free for all access to it where the resource condition is precarious [as in Gujarat]." Her explanation is that Gujarat's politicians and administrators have strong rural roots and therefore sympathy for farmers, whereas those in West Bengal have lost these roots.

An equally plausible explanation may be that the atomistic individualism fostered by the hydrogeology of the Indo-Gangetic basin is a barrier to the emergence of collusion on critical scale necessary for larger-scale political mobilization. In Gujarat, irrigation agriculture would come to a grinding halt in nearly 40 percent of the state were the government to abandon the flat electricity tariff; and it is the collusion among farmers in these parts that is spearheading statewide mobilization and organized protest against electricity pricing reforms. Nowhere in the Indo-Gangetic basin do conditions like those in North Gujarat obtain, which perhaps explains why this region has not witnessed sufficiently strong farmer mobilization for better electricity infrastructure in the countryside, an otherwise eminently justifiable demand. This is likely also why the government of Pakistan was able to reintroduce electricity meters on tube wells without any organized opposition: farmers in the Punjab and Sind have increasingly switched to diesel WEMs (Shah et al. 2004c). Baluchistan, where electric WEMs need 40-hp submersible pumps or more to extract deep groundwater, a relatively small community of 15,000 tube well owners have managed to ensure a flat tariff of Pak Rs. 4,000 per month per tube well (Ahmed and Ahmad 2007).

In summary, then, atomistic individualism in abundantly recharged alluvial aquifers leads to the following conditions:

- users are unaware of their interdependence; as a result, there is no aquifer community, and in most areas, irrigation demand is likely to get saturated before the "safe yield" of the aquifer is exhausted;
- well interference or drawdown externalities are minimal or nonexistent; the desperation caused by aquifer stress, common in varying measures in the other four situations, is not apparent;
- users do not undertake collective action either to secure groundwater or to manage it for sustainability; and
- except under extreme provocation, users are highly unlikely to mobilize into a politically powerful interest group to lobby for their pump irrigation economy.

Collusive Opportunism in Arid Alluvial Aquifers

In arid alluvial aquifers with limited recharge resources, users share the rational expectation that as long as they can chase a falling water level, prolific water supply can be had, but at rapidly rising pumping costs and steadily deteriorating water quality. Like the Indo-Gangetic plains, many parts of western Rajasthan, Kutch, and North Gujarat and much of Baluchistan too have excellent sandy alluvial aquifers with sediment deposits hundreds of meters thick but insufficient rainfall or surface water to recharge the aquifers.

Many of these arid alluvial ecologies sustained small amounts of annual draft for long periods until the 1960s but were no match for modern pump and tube well technologies. In much of Baluchistan, *karezes (qanats)* flowed year-round until the 1960s; since then, the area irrigated by tube wells has grown from 50,000 ha to 250,000 ha in Baluchistan. Today, in Quetta valley, *karezes* are not seen flowing even after the rainy season (Kahlown 2003). In North Gujarat and western Rajasthan, where water was raised by bullock bailers from open wells until 1960s, today tube wells go as deep as 1,000 or 1,500 feet and are mounted with submersible turbine pumps of 75 to 120 hp. A typical tube well involves an investment of Rs. 1.5 million to 2.2 million and is perennially at risk of drying up or collapsing.[8] In North Gujarat, farmers have small landholdings that make the cost and risk of a tube well investment uneconomic. Figure 6.2 illustrates such aquifer conditions. In response to increasing groundwater withdrawals shown by movement along the x-axis, the recharge rate, initially sluggish, declines as groundwater levels drop. Water quality, too, deteriorates, but less rapidly than the water level declines. This is what has happened in the arid alluvial aquifers over the past three decades.

That condition—deep groundwater and small holdings—in North Gujarat's groundwater economy has forced farmers toward opportunistic cooperation to pool capital and spread risks. This unique pattern of organization of groundwater economy—and its many ramifications—have been explored by many researchers (e.g., Dubash 2002; Joshi and Acharya 2005; Kumar et al 2004a, b; Prakash 2005; Shah and Bhattacharya 1993; Shaheen and Shiyani 2005). Most tube wells are organized as "companies" in which farmers own shares, contribute capital, get water, bear profit or loss as well as risk failure of the tube well, all in proportion to the land they have in the command.[9] A tube well company may have five members or a hundred; shareholding by individual members can vary by a factor of 10 or more; each farmer may have shares in different tubewell companies to serve different parcels of his holding. Members get priority in water supply, but surplus water can be sold to nonmembers, sometimes at a premium. Scarcity of electricity as well as groundwater makes water precious despite relatively low marginal energy costs of pumping under the system of flat tariff[10]; as a result, most tube well companies invest in elaborate buried pipelines to distribute water to each farmer's plot. Tube well companies have some assurance that they can get water as long as they keep deepening the well a few meters every year or two (Shah and Bhattacharya 1993; Joshi and Acharya 2005).

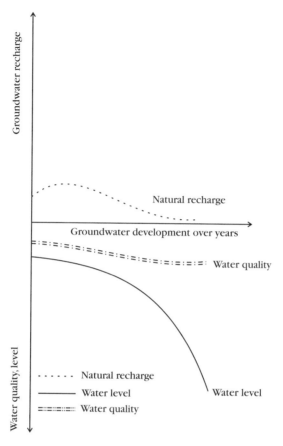

Figure 6.2   Collusive opportunism

Unlike in the Ganga basin, entry to the aquifer here is neither easy nor inexpensive, and therefore, water markets are far from contestable. This implies that tube well companies enjoy a high degree of monopoly power; once a shareholder of a tube well company, a farmer can expect equitable access. But those who are not shareholders end up as "groundwater refugees." Existing shareholders may openly accept the principle of coequal right to all of the aquifer and yet in effect end up excluding nonshareholders from the groundwater economy.[11] When they do have the option to buy water, nonshareholders generally receive poor residual irrigation. The ability to organize and manage a tube well company thus becomes the "groundwater withdrawal permit" for farmers of the *Patidar* community, known for their cooperative entrepreneurship and acumen.[12] Literature offers several nuanced variations of the institutional dynamic that surrounds the pump irrigation economy of North Gujarat (e.g., Dubash 2002; Prakash 2005), but the common theme is domination by the resource-rich in an opportunistic race to the bottom of the aquifer, progressively marginalizing the poor and unorganized in local groundwater economies (Joshi and Acharya 2005).

In Banaskantha district of Gujarat, in western Rajasthan, and in Baluchistan, hydrogeologic conditions are similar, but landholdings get progressively larger and more unequal (Shah and Ballabh 1995). As a result, in a typical village, a small number of large landowners invest in individual deep tube wells, sometimes owned by brothers or other kin and become water sellers. Unlike in canal-recharged central Gujarat or Ganga basin, where water markets are efficient (see Kishore and Mishra 2005; Mukherji 2007; Pant 2004), in Banaskantha and western Rajasthan, they range from imperfect to highly monopolistic, with WEM owners extracting a substantial proportion of the "irrigation surplus" they help buyers create in the form of water charges or crop shares. The consequence of intensive aquifer development in many arid alluvial areas is a rapid decline in water levels resulting in well failures on a massive scale with new, deeper tube wells chasing falling water levels (Sharma and Sharma 2004; Kumar 2007). Only large landholders are able to survive in this game of "creative destruction,"[13] with new, deeper tube wells drying up old ones.[14] Pump irrigation service markets ensure some irrigation to buyers, but prices tend to be high, with substantial monopoly premia; in arid villages, water is often sold for a 33 to 40 percent share in crop output. Under a flat electricity tariff, the incremental energy cost of pumping is zero; however, the relevant costs these WEM owners consider in selling water are the long-run marginal costs, which include the cost of well failure and deepening. Buyers, though seemingly exploited, are often better off than dry-land farmers as in the sample studied by Sharma and Sharma (2004).[15] Researchers also argue that buyers with crop-share contracts may retort to such perceived exploitation by economizing on other inputs, thereby undermining the returns to water sellers.[16,17] In Sangpara village in Mehsana district of North Gujarat, Prakash (2005) found erstwhile buyers reduced to the state of sharecroppers on well owners' land, with the latter taking a two-thirds crop share for land and water. Even so, Prakash noted that the implicit wage rate the buyers earned was double the wage rate paid to a casual farm worker, which was the next best alternative. Moreover, crop sharing guaranteed employment during the entire season.

Since the eventual exhaustion of groundwater is evident to everyone, we would expect farmers to use precautionary logic and choose farming strategies—cropping patterns, water application technologies—consistent with a finite resource subject to rapid depletion. Yet we find hardly any evidence of such choices.[18] In North Gujarat, 78 percent of water use is for water-intensive crops (Kumar 2005). Here, as well as in western Rajasthan and in Baluchistan, there is hardly any spread of drip irrigation or shifting toward water-saving high-value crops (Shaheen and Shiyani 2005). Water buyers and the growing numbers of diesel pump users in Rajasthan should feel the pinch of the high cost of irrigation, but the evidence for this is mixed. In North Gujarat, Kumar (2005) found that water buyers and shareholders in tube well companies achieved significantly higher applied-water productivity[19] than individual owners of WEMs, but he noted that the reason was not so much water-saving crops as more efficient water use. Many studies, however, show little effort by buyers to adopt water-saving strategies. Arguably, buyers may prefer apparently unfair sharecropping because the contract provides them their own weapon against volumetric water pricing; once a crop-share-for-water contract is entered into, the buyer does not have to worry about the marginal cost of irrigation; moreover, the seller has an incentive to provide good irrigation service because he gets paid a crop share. Such a contract acts as water buyers' version of a flat tariff.

How do we explain this propensity toward growing water-intensive, low-value cereal crops and away from water-saving technologies among farmers in arid, alluvial aquifers? One possible explanation is farmers' rational expectations about aquifer behavior. Since nature does not effectively ration water for farmers who can chase falling water tables, users in arid alluvial aquifers are not confronted with here-and-now physical groundwater scarcity,[20] and subsidized, flat electricity tariffs keep them from confronting the *economic* groundwater scarcity (Kumar et al. 2004a).[21] Arguably, the current abundance of a resource that everyone expects to dry up generates a myopic opportunism among farmers, manifest in a perverse tendency to deplete groundwater now to pay for their eventual escape from farming as a livelihood.[22,23] Members of the farming community who display such myopic opportunism are generally those who are most prepared and able to exit from farming; the least prepared are left to bear the brunt.

In North Gujarat, agrarian expansion over the past 150 years has been spearheaded by *Patidars*, who moved there from densely populated central Gujarat in search of farmland. With their access to capital and superior entrepreneurial skills, they soon became the dominant farming class,[24] relegating the native population of Thakors, Prajapatis, and tribals to a secondary role. Patidars were early adopters of tube well technology and reaped the bulk of the benefits, in the process also triggering the race to the bottom of the aquifers. They were, however, quick to realize that with depleted aquifers, agriculture would offer no future in the region. As a result, Patidars began a planned, generational transition out of agriculture, making timely investments in educating their children for nonfarming livelihoods. Many went to Surat and learned diamond cutting; some took trade and government jobs. Others sold their land and purchased farmland in areas with better water prospects (Barry and Issoufaly 2002). The easiest opportunity during the 1970s was to teach in the rapidly expanding school system in Gujarat—a choice taken by Patidars of North Gujarat, in particular Mehsana district, during the 1980s. Today, the children of Mehsana farmers dominate the teacher community in primary and secondary schools throughout Gujarat.

In Sangpura, his study village in Mehsana district, Prakash (2005) found that the popular roadmap out of farming for most Patidars post-1990 has been illegal migration to the United States. There is a hierarchical pattern in this exit plan as well; now that Patidars have mostly moved out, Prajapatis, the next rung, have begun moving to the United States, with help from an elaborate kinship-based, well-lubricated superstructure of illegal migration. Left behind on Sangpura's none-too-promising farms are Thakors, poorer Prajapatis, Harijans, tribal families of various hues, and other original inhabitants who could not plan for this generational transition.

Other consequences are the steady ascent of sedentary pastoralism as the primary economic activity and the growing feminization of household income generation in many arid alluvial areas. While the elite still use groundwater for crop production, those who have been elbowed out of the pump irrigation economy have turned to dairying, which has emerged as the mainstay of the household economy in all arid alluvial areas. In Banaskantha district on the border of the rann (desert) of Kutch, milk purchases by the district cooperative increased more than 10-fold between 1975 and 2000, from 20 million to 210 million kg per year. The growing primacy of dairying has altered the intrafamily decision-making equation, with women now at the center of rural household economies. Dairy farmers, too, need water, for growing green and dry fodder and for watering their herds. In North Gujarat, women pay up to 50 percent of their dairy income to buy tube well water (Lieberand 2004). Dry fodder and cattle feed can be purchased, but availability of green fodder, which needs irrigation, is becoming a constraint for poor households engaged in dairying. So institutions are emerging to meet this need: some village dairy cooperatives are running their own green fodder community farms to supply landless dairy farmers.

In this battle between sustaining livelihoods of the present generation and protecting groundwater for next, the effect of extraction by one farmer on his or her neighbors is neither direct nor easily separable, given the wide spacing of deep WEMs in sandy, alluvial aquifers. As a result, competition among well owners seldom manifests itself in conflict or rivalry, despite their awareness of their interdependence.[25] Instead, WEM owners collude to lobby for importing surface water on a large scale to recharge groundwater[26] or deploy exclusionary mechanisms to monopolize the resource.[27] Because importing water for recharge involves large public investments with long gestation periods,[28] farmers mobilize swiftly and in large numbers against threats of metering of electricity or reduction in power supply. Baluchistan's 15,000 electric tube well owners formed the Farmers' Action Committee to protect the prevailing flat power tariff regime and oppose even a shift to a flat tariff based on horsepower (Ahmed and Ahmad 2007). Joshi and Acharya (2005), who were commissioned by the Gujarat Electricity Regulatory Authority to poll North Gujarat peasants on electricity reforms, concluded, "our perception is that installation of meters is likely to lead to violent opposition."[29] Losing on either of these fronts—importation of surface water or metering of electricity—would end irrigated agriculture. Many realize that this is inevitable, but they will not press the exit button just yet, not while they can still chase falling water levels.[30]

With its strong tribal culture, Baluchistan has a powerful traditional system of governance, and one would expect tribal leadership to catalyze more robust institutions for sustainable groundwater management. Steenbergen (1995) explored, with guarded optimism, the prospects of coordinated groundwater development in Baluchistan, which in many ways is similar to North Gujarat in its hydrogeology and has traveled a similar path. He conceptualized a groundwater development trajectory along three points: a pseudoloss point, when groundwater exploitation begins to cannibalize earlier irrigation structures and regimes (such as *karezes*), prompting pressure groups to install resource management regimes; further development leads to a sustainability point beyond which depletion begins. Steenbergen hypothesized that coordination mechanisms would be most likely to evolve between these two points. Beyond the sustainability point, WEM owners will indulge in self-defeating opportunism of competitive depletion. Then comes the "return point," when the groundwater economy crashes and eventually finds a much lower equilibrium. Baluchistan experienced more extensive attempts to create coordinating mechanisms, including rulemaking by locally credible tribal councils as well as government-instituted permit systems, and even a groundwater rights administration ordinance. Steenbergen's conclusion was that "in general the incipient groundwater management regimes in Baluchistan have not been successful so far and that groundwater 'mining' has reached the level of an ecological crisis" (55).

In sum, then, arid alluvial aquifers have these characteristics:

- weak recognition of interdependence and absence of a strong sense of aquifer community;
- monopolization of groundwater resource by the local elite with the capital and capacity to organize;
- an expanding class of groundwater refugees;
- little or no evidence that farmers are adopting a water-conserving ethic or farming regimens or seeking to maximize cash per drop applied;
- the emergence of myopic opportunism that drives WEM owners to hasten the depletion of an apparently copious resource that must eventually be exhausted; and
- strong and swift political mobilization against metering of electricity and in support of low flat tariffs, extended hours of daily power supply, and importation of surface water.

Rivalrous Gaming in Hard-rock Aquifers

The Latin word *rivalis*—someone who uses the same stream as another[31]— aptly describes the institutional dynamic of groundwater irrigation in hard-rock aquifers. Hydrogeologists consider intensive groundwater use from these aquifers ill-advised because hard-rock aquifers offer very limited storage in pores and crevices through which water cannot move easily. Yet much groundwater irrigation has developed in hard-rock areas of peninsular India. Indeed, the world's only hard-rock areas with large-scale, intensive groundwater development are in South Asia. The challenge for a groundwater user in a hard-rock area is locating a substantial water-bearing formation, which often requires several borings.[32] It is common for farmers to spend heavily on drilling a dozen or more bores before they find water,[33] and quack water diviners do a brisk business in India's hard-rock areas. In the absence of information on water-bearing formations, farmers begin with the rational expectation that the probability of finding water is higher near an already successful well. As a result, new wells tend to cluster around an old well (Shah 1993) or on the rim of a recharge source, such as a tank (Nagaraj and Chandrakanth 1997; Reddy 2005).[34] Wells in hard-rock areas are typically large, open "collector wells" in which water trickling from surrounding fissures accumulates. These are often fortified with horizontal or vertical bores to access untapped water-bearing fractures. Even so, such wells can often be pumped only for an hour or less per day. Farmers sometimes use compressors to pump continuously and store the water in chambers specially built for the purpose, to be pumped out again for later use. Janakarajan (2002) found most wells in Tamilnadu's Noyal basin fitted with compressors. This method is extremely energy inefficient because to provide a small volume of water, the farmer runs the pump at slow speed much longer than needed, first to fill the storage chamber and then to pump it out into the fields. Such practices would not thrive except under a flat electricity tariff.

Successful wells are prized and can make farming profitable. Over generations, land fragmentation here results in well fragmentation, too, leaving large numbers of wells under joint ownership of descendants. Janakarajan (2002) found 43 percent of wells in the Noyal basin of Tamilnadu jointly owned. Sharing these wells, proven for their productivity, creates a unique dynamic. A stable equilibrium is offered by installing a single, jointly owned pump and having time-shares, along the lines of Punjab wells in the nineteenth century (Chapter 1). This often breaks down because of irregular power supply and the arrangements for cost sharing. If all shareholders install separate pumps, the limited water gets used up through competitive pumping. The conflict escalates when one shareholder installs a larger pump than the rest, typically when the land is sold to a farmer outside the kinship group. More often, a resourceful shareholder buys up the shares of poorer shareholders and monopolizes the well. In resolving such conflicts, *Panchayats* (village councils) sometimes divide the well itself, delineating different parts to different shareholders with each having a right to deepen his part of the well or making vertical or lateral bores in it (Janakarajan 2002).

Figure 6.3 depicts the consequences of groundwater development in hard-rock aquifers that suffer from poor storage and low infiltration rates. As well irrigation expands, wells dry up during summer but may come to life again during and after a good monsoon as floodwaters partially replenish

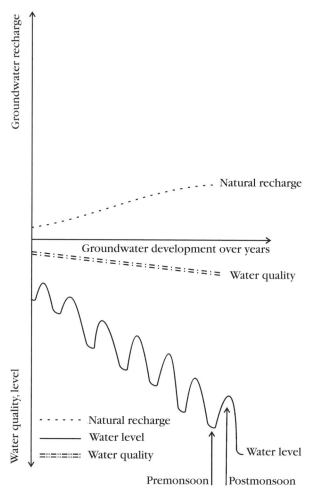

Figure 6.3   Rivalrous gaming

water-bearing pores and crevices. Competitive deepening of wells, however, keeps lowering the premonsoon groundwater levels even as levels temporarily rebound during a good monsoon. The principal visible outcomes of aquifer development here are the growing difference between pre- and postmonsoon water levels and a decline in water quality, especially in the months before the monsoon.

Competitive behavior among users, largely absent in arid and humid alluvial aquifers, is endemic in densely cultivated hard-rock areas. The feature that characterizes WEM owners in the Indo-Gangetic basin—that neither are they affected by the behavior of other WEM owners nor can she influence them—breaks down completely in intensively used hard-rock aquifers, where the share of one WEM owner is generally at the expense of neighboring users. This interdependence creates fertile ground for conflict around aquifer use.[35] The competitive deepening of wells by neighboring WEM owners, described by Janakarajan (1994), Vaidyanathan (1996), Chandrakanth et al. (2004), and Reddy (2005), is akin to the oligopolistic strategies of firms that share a fixed market. A simple model of duopoly published 170 years ago by Augustine Cournot, a French economist, and a similar one by F. Y. Edgeworth can be readily adapted to show how competitive deepening results in a Nash equilibrium in which each player tries to do his or her best given what the competition is doing. Both rivals together spend more on well deepening but get lower yields. Had they cooperated, they could have had higher yields at lower costs.[36]

Researchers in Tamilnadu, Andhra Pradesh, and Karnataka have described how competitive deepening hastens the depletion of aquifers and ruins the farmers engaged in such rivalry. Just to illustrate, in a survey of two areas in Charmarjanagar block of Karnataka, Chandrakanth et al. (1998a) found that 35 to 47 percent of the debt accumulated by farmers surveyed had been incurred for deepening of wells.[37] The higher the congestion of wells, the more intense the competition and the faster the disaster.[38] Under the intense competitive dynamic, well owners sometimes tend toward water-intensive crops to maximize their share the "fastest and mostest" (Wantrup 1968, cited in Chandrakanth et al. 1998a). Selling of water is driven by two opposing sentiments: on the one hand, successful WEM owners want to save all the water for their own needs rather than sell it; on the other, they apprehend that neighbors might deplete the shared water-bearing fissure anyway, which prompts them to sell furiously. Water sales increasingly take place against crop shares, which are generally exploitative for the buyers. Nagaraj et al. (2005) found sharecropping contracts twice as costly for buyers as cash-per-hour contracts.[39] Beyond a stage, resource-poor smallholders give up and fall back on dry-land farming. As Vaidyanathan (1996, 186) notes, "Competitive deepening therefore makes the distribution of access to groundwater irrigation increasingly skewed in favour of large, resource rich farmers leaving small farmers at an increasing disadvantage in sharing the benefits of well irrigation." Reddy (2005) narrates a similar story in three villages he studied in hard-rock Telangana in Andhra Pradesh. When industrial consumers enter, mayhem ensues.

Janakarajan (1994, *55*) illustrates the Hindu notion of *Matsya-nyaya* (big fish eating small fish) in operation: "In many cases, [industry] owners have bought plots of land specifically with a motivation of installing deep bore wells—beating every other well owner in the vicinity by pitching the marginal cost of well digging or deepening disproportionately high—with a view to transporting water."

All things considered, it is surprising that, despite the unstable institutional dynamic of intensive aquifer use in hard-rock areas, well irrigation is not only continuing but even expanding in many places. And despite evidence of widespread misery, some of the worst-exploited districts in southern India still have booming pump irrigation economies. One reason may be that when the competitive deepening game is played over time, providing players time to make a variety of adjustment moves, the worst effects of Nash equilibria are countered or minimized. Vaidyanathan (1996, *189*) gives the example of Coimbatore district of Tamilnadu, where "the government and the farmers have witnessed a progressive increase in wells, lowering of the groundwater level and increasing depth of wells for nearly four decades. However, official statistics do not show any reduction in the total area served by wells. This would suggest that access to well water is more widely dispersed among farmers and though water available per well has declined they have adapted by changing their crop patterns and irrigation practices to conserve water."[40] Vaidyanathan (1996, *185*) also suggests that repetitive play of Nash equilibrium, in which everyone loses from competitive deepening, should provide strong incentives for cooperative arrangements to evolve but recognized that such "arrangements have not developed on a widespread or significant scale."

Besides competing for water-bearing fissures, farmers in these regions are choosing farming systems that maximize returns to water applied. Thus in Coimbatore and Madurai, farmers have taken to irrigating vanilla; in Kolar (Karnataka), scarce groundwater is used to irrigate mulberry for raising silkworms (e.g., Deepak et al. 2005; Nagaraj and Chandrakanth 1997; Shah and Keller 2002) in Shimoga (southern Karnataka), cultivation of betel vine *(Piper betle)* is driving competitive deepening (Chandrakanth et al. 1998a); in Telangana in Andhra Pradesh, Reddy (2005) finds farmers switching from *kharif* and *rabi* rice to sesame, cotton, chili peppers, and groundnuts; and in hard-rock Saurashtra, farmers have begun using wells to irrigate small orchards and *Bt* (pest-resistant) cotton in favor of food grain crops.[41] It is also not surprising that the hard-rock states of Tamilnadu, Andhra Pradesh, Karnataka, and Maharashtra lead India in the spread of microirrigation technologies and account for 90 percent of the country's drip-irrigated areas (Narayanamoorthy 1996). In contrast, the arid alluvial aquifer areas of northwestern India and most of Pakistan have proved resistant not only to microirrigation but even to piped water conveyance. In a water-scarce state like Gujarat, microirrigation is hardly popular, but it has taken off in hard-rock Saurashtra. One reason is that energy subsidies shield farmers in hard-rock aquifers from confronting *economic* water scarcity, but they have no escape from everyday *physical* groundwater scarcity, which creates pressure to maximize cash per drop applied rather than yield per hectare.[42] It is nature's rationing of daily groundwater supply that keeps hard-rock India's pump irrigation economy going.

As for poor farmers, operating as water buyers, it is difficult to say where they are hit hardest. In hard-rock areas, pump irrigation markets shrink, forcing smallholders to compete for water despite their lack of means (Nagraj and Chandrakanth 1997). In arid alluvial aquifers, the illusion of groundwater sufficiency at increasing depth keeps water markets busy, and some small farmers are able to stay in irrigated farming even if on adverse terms (Shah and Ballabh 1995; Kumar 2007).

In sum, then, we can characterize rivalrous gaming in hard-rock areas as follows:

- strong awareness of interdependence among users giving rise to numerous "aquifer communities";
- a near zero-sum game of competitive deepening among well owners with competition increasing in proportion to the congestion around the water-bearing formation;
- a growing class of groundwater refugees excluded from pump irrigation or subjected to exploitive terms;
- a subdued sense of fatalism mixed with opportunism that drives WEM owners to hasten the depletion of a limited, shared resource;
- a propensity to maximize cash per drop applied rather than yield per hectare, inspired by everyday encounters with physical water scarcity; and
- strong and swift political mobilization against metering of electricity and in support of a low flat tariff, extended hours of daily power supply, and development of surface water sources, such as tanks, canals, and watersheds.

Cooperative Gaming in Hard-rock and Confined Aquifers

In the late 1980s, Daniel Bromley, an American natural resource economist, and I spent two weeks working with the Aga Khan Rural Support
Program in Amrapur and Husseinabad, two coastal villages of Junagadh
district in Saurashtra. Our goal was to understand how best to catalyze collective action among farmers to stave off a groundwater disaster—the result
of expansion in groundwater extraction through 1970s and 1980s. Amrapur,
about 10 km inland, had a bowl-shaped limestone aquifer with a confining
layer; Husseinabad was closer to the sea and had a sandy alluvial aquifer with
a very high groundwater yield during the 1960s. Amrapur's problem was the
high rate of well failures, declining yields of wells, and growing well interference. In Husseinabad, wells in a third of the village seaward had already
turned saline; away from the sea, wells were saline in summer and farmers drew pipelines from wells further inland, keeping ahead of salinity
ingress.

We found that farmers in Amrapur, distressed but hopeful, had been
experimenting with methods to improve the productivity of their wells.
Making lateral bores inside dug wells was already common, some farmers
making more than one well in the same field. These were private options.
But recognizing their limits, they had begun cooperatively building check
dams and other structures to improve the groundwater regime in the entire
village. In Husseinabad, in contrast, distress was mixed with fatalism, hopelessness, and despair. William Barber, an American hydrogeologist, had vis-
ited and declared that salinity could be pushed out from Husseinabad but
only if there was complete cessation of groundwater abstraction for
30 years. The only alternative the people in Husseinabad had was bringing
fresh water from outside, which many affluent farmers did by buying small
plots of land farther inland with the sole purpose of making wells in them.
They saw no point in building recharge structures, whose efficacy was
unknown to them, or in instituting demand restrictions, because they did
not understand that the water they saved today would be available tomor-
row (Shah 1992).

Fifteen years later, Husseinabad's depopulation is nearly total, as with
scores of "ghost" villages along the Saurashtra coast from Madhavpur to Una.
Even the large landowners had left the village because their wells had turned
saline, joining the unemployed in towns like Junagadh and Keshod. Some
farmers still go back during monsoon, when wells have fresh water, and

take a *kharif* crop (Shah and Desai 2002). Amrapur, in contrast, is now more vibrant and better off, with more orchards. Barber had told its people there was a hole in the bottom of their aquifer, so there was no point in building recharge structures. But the people of Amrapur went ahead all the same and built a profusion of check and recharge structures; they cooperated in doing this because they could see for themselves the private benefits of coopera- tive action, something that farmers in Husseinabad did not. What seemed to happen in Amrapur is depicted in Figure 6.4. As groundwater with- drawals expanded, the annual difference between pre- and postmonsoon water levels amplified even as both levels began to decline. With intensifica- tion of recharge activity, however, the interyear decline in postmonsoon water levels lessened; as a result, although wells continued to remain dry in

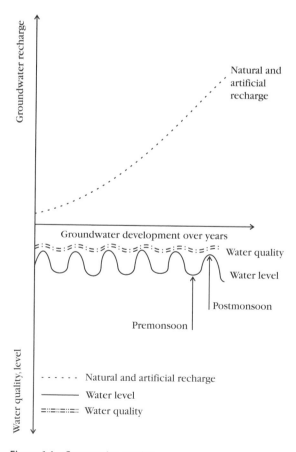

Figure 6.4   Cooperative gaming

late summer, after a good monsoon they remained live until late weeks of monsoon season, and many had water even during winter and early summer months. This was reflected in fluoride concentrations, too, which were high during late summer but declined during monsoon and post-monsoon periods.

Groundwater recharge in decentralized, cooperative fashion evolved as a mass movement throughout hard-rock Saurashtra. The stimulus came, strangely, from spiritual leaders who, after a bad drought in 1987, instructed their followers: "Quench the thirst of Mother Earth, and she will quench yours." People responded haltingly, first by modifying their dug wells to receive floodwaters that they had previously let into their neighbors' fields, and then by building small check structures through community effort. Capturing even a small proportion of rainfall (which would otherwise run off to the sea in flash floods because of the area's inverted saucer topography) is enough to fill Saurashtra's wells to the brim. Hydrogeologists consider these overflowing wells a sign of the poor capacity of Saurashtra's limited aquifers (Sakthivadivel and Nagar 2003), but to water-harvesting farmers, the number of times their wells overflow during a monsoon provides some basis for a rational expectation about how much water they can retrieve later in the season for an emergency irrigation or two. As of 2007, some half a million dug wells in Saurashtra had been modified for recharge and more than 100,000 check structures had been built; these probably recharge 1 to 2 km^3 of water, a small fraction of what the controversial Sardar Sarovar Dam on River Narmada will hold at full capacity. Hydrologists consider this too much effort and expense—without much science[43]—to produce such a small amount of additional water. But this small amount of water has spelled the difference between ruin and prosperity for Saurashtra, whose farmers can now count on one *kharif* crop, whereas in the past, if the monsoon departed earlier than expected, wells would not have sufficient water to save the crop (Shah 2000; Shah and Desai 2002; Talati 2004). In a year of good rainfall, wells in many parts of Saurashtra now have water for *rabi* and even a small summer irrigated crop.

Prolific hands-on experimentation with groundwater recharge technologies and contraptions—and vigorous propagation of the results through pamphlets and manuals in the vernacular—by individual farmers, NGOs, schoolchildren, scientists, religious leaders, retired industrialists, diamond merchants, teachers, local aid workers, former princes and underworked bureaucrats has created a veritable subaltern hydrology of groundwater recharge in Saurashtra and Kutch. These efforts revive and build upon a forgotten tradition of local water management that existed in much of arid and semiarid South Asia, a tradition that *The Dying Wisdom* (Agarwal and Narain 1977) documented and ethnographer Thomas Rosin (1993) explored in great detail in Aravalli hills in Rajasthan.[44] Even though this people's movement, which began and ran on its own steam for nearly a decade, was coopted by government and vote-bank politics, one can confidently assert that the people of Saurashtra pieced together a working response to their groundwater depletion challenge in cooperative action for rainwater harvesting and recharge.

Gujarat Government's Sardar Patel Participatory Water Conservation Program deprived Saurashtra's decentralized recharge movement of its spontaneity and popular initiative, but still it attracted 40 percent contributions of labor and material for water-harvesting structures from people while the government contributed the balance. By 2000, more than 10,700 check dams had been constructed in Gujarat under the scheme, against requests for 25,300 check dams by village communities. In 2000, the Indian Institute of Management at Ahmedabad studied a stratified sample of 102 of these check dams in 96 villages of Saurashtra and compared them with a control of 11 villages without check dams (Shingi and Asopa 2002). The study estimated that these check dams could recharge some 300 million m^3 of water during a normal year, for an estimated net gain in increased agricultural output of 30 percent. An average check dam benefited seven wells and 200 *bigha*[45] of farmland, and the extent of benefit was determined by the distance between the well and the check dam. The study projected that 10,700 check dams in Saurashtra helped drought-proof 320,000 ha of farmland in Saurashtra, and that even if just crop-related benefits were counted, the payback period for a check-dam investment was between two and three years. A third of the check-dam beneficiaries reported increases in land values of the order of Rs. 19,244 per *bigha*, on average. Detailed hydrological studies concluded that the water recharge was modest, thanks to poor aquifers (Sakthivadivel and Nagar 2003); however, field studies that asked farmers whether check dams had eased their water woes returned unequivocally favorable reports (Shah and Desai 2002; Shah 2000). Based on a more recent study, Gandhi and Namboodiri (2007, *17*) found that the recharge movement "appears to have had a huge impact on water availability and agricultural incomes in this area" and positively influenced "irrigated area, participation, empowerment, village development and environment." The

Gujarat government's groundwater department staff regularly talk to news-papers about the beneficial impact of check dams using observation well data of the kind shown in Figure 6.5. This helps keep popular faith alive in the efficacy of local resource management.

There are few places in the world where water has become "everybody's business" quite like it has in Saurashtra and Kutch. Here, community water management has replaced farmers' widespread despondence and fatalism with hope and optimism; this may promote investment in land care, enhance farm productivity, and improve on-farm water management.[46] It has also created a climate for the emergence of local water governance insti-tutions and for widespread uptake of water-saving irrigation technologies and farming systems (Shah and Desai 2002).

In Saurashtra, groundwater intensification led to mass construction of water-harvesting structures. In South India, which already has a profusion of tanks, the pull for groundwater recharge has encouraged communities to reinvent them. In Rayalaseema, Andhra Pradesh, a local NGO persuaded a tank community to permanently seal its sluice gate and convert the tank into a recharge structure. This threatened to make a common-property tank a

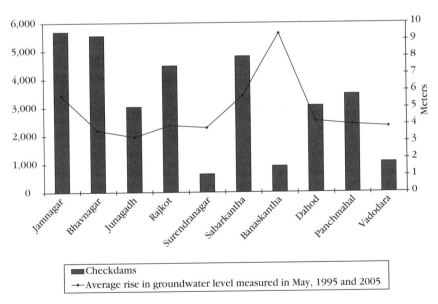

Source: Gujarat Minister of Water Resources, quoted in *Gujarat Samachar*, Ahmedabad edition, 14 6 April 2006

Figure 6.5   Checkdams and premonsoon water levels in Gujarat

resource only for well owners. Negotiations ensued between those who owned wells and those who did not, and eventually the well owners agreed to sell pump irrigation to nonowners at a third of the prevailing price for the first crop and two-thirds for the second crop. Another 22 villages turned 33 irrigation tanks into recharge tanks, but the move failed for the lack of agreement between well owners and nonowners. Once the two groups agreed on the distribution of gains from the new use of the tank, vigorous and methodical desilting of tank beds and inflow channels ensued, with fuller participation from well owners as well as nonowners. In many villages, such as Adepalli, tank conversion unleashed unprecedented prosperity, thanks to higher cropping intensity, increased dairy production, and intensive diversification to vegetable and flower cultivation. The distributive impact of this movement suggests the power of the "recharge pull" that groundwater intensification has generated (Rao 2003). The government of Andhra Pradesh has already called for all irrigation tanks to be transformed into percolation tanks. According to Sakthivadivel (2007, 197), "this trend has essentially become a movement by itself and even some state governments as Karnataka are encouraging this proactively through enactment of laws."

The cooperative gaming situation, then, is characterized by the following:

- hard-rock aquifers with low storage capacity or alluvial aquifers with an impervious confining layer accompanied by the availability of some recharge resources—conditions analogous to those where we find rivalrous gaming;
- a strong recognition of interdependence and a full-developed sense of aquifer community;
- visible benefits of groundwater conservation by individual harvesters on their own wells, and rapid magnification of these positive effects as neighbors join conservation;
- a collective sense of confidence and exuberance about individual and collective water futures;
- ease of collective action on increasing groundwater recharge leading to endogenous efforts at demand management; and
- a growing societal perception of the aquifer as a collectively managed but limitedly private bank account drawn down in times of need and replenished at the first opportunity.

Exit

Henry Vaux asserted that in the U.S. West, groundwater overexploitation was self-terminating because the costs of pumping from great depths make it uneconomic to continue groundwater irrigation. Economics have forced farmers in large areas of Arizona, Texas, Colorado, and elsewhere in the United States to exit from groundwater irrigation, as we reviewed in Chapter 2. In South Asia, this situation would have resulted in many parts of western and peninsular India but for energy subsidies. In North Gujarat, even with electricity subsidies, irrigating a hectare of wheat costs about US$300; without subsidy, Kumar et al. (2005) estimated the cost would be twice as high, making farming and dairying unviable.

With electricity subsidies, farmers using arid alluvial aquifers manage to survive. However, in some coastal aquifers, exit from pump irrigation may be swift and immiserating because saline intrusion renders irrigated agriculture highly unproductive. Mobilizing for electricity subsidies is of no avail here, since pumping deeper produces only more saline water. Equally hapless is the predicament of farmers whose groundwater is polluted by industrial effluents, as analyzed by Janakarajan in Tamilnadu. In such situations, when pump irrigators have little or no hope of subsisting on pump irrigation, institutional responses become indeterminate. Even where there might be some hope of preserving farming livelihoods through mobilization and collective action, instances of such mobilization are few. In coastal Saurashtra, Gujarat, where salinity intrusion desiccated a 300-km strip of coastal farms known during the 1960s as *Lili Nagher* (Green Creeper),[47] one finds no evidence of endogenous collective action toward sustainable pump irrigation. Instead, throughout this region, there is large-scale desertion of farmland, with people moving to nearby towns and rebuilding their lives outside farming. My conjecture is that when people see little or no hope in the medium to long run of preserving pump irrigation-based livelihoods by mobilizing for specific demands—such as electricity subsidies—the foresighted among them exit, starting a trickle that gradually builds into an river.

The predicament of Saurashtra's Green Creeper is played out on a far bigger scale in western Rajasthan, Haryana, Sind and the Punjabs, even though the underlying hydrogeology is different. A considerable area in these states lies above saline aquifers. All the groundwater development we are witnessing in these parts has been aimed at 20- to 150-meter-thick lenses of

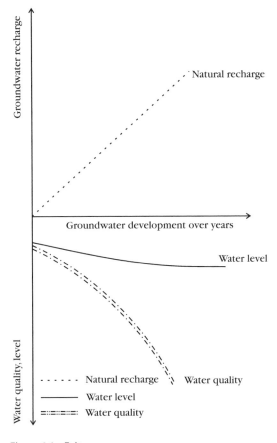

Figure 6.6   Exit

freshwater that lie above these saline aquifers. Farmers here use skimming wells with horizontal bores, as farmers do in hard-rock areas of southern India. The latter use them to source water-bearing fractures; the former use them to increase the flow of fresh water from the lenses. The rivalry for capturing fresh water is much the same in both the situations; however, the hard-rock equilibria are arguably likely to be more stable than for the saline aquifers because of the latter's extreme fragility in the face of congestion and ultimate unsustainability.[48]

In the case of saline arid alluvial aquifers, the rational expectations of users would very likely lead them to conclude that fresh water would be exhausted sooner rather than later and prompt sufficient numbers of them to hasten to capture their share in it, thereby creating a disastrous self-fulfilling prophecy. The rational expectations model also suggests that interventions to correct the situation may prove self-defeating. If the government plans a large-scale recharge project, rational expectations may lead users to expand their ground-water withdrawals to the extent of recharge; similarly, by propagating drip irrigation, policymakers would lead farmers to irrigate larger areas to use up the water saved.

The features of the exit groundwater socioecology can be summarized as follows:

- good aquifers with prolific water yields that rapidly turn saline upon development;
- awareness among pumpers of their interdependence;
- despair among users about individual or collective efforts to conserve or revive the aquifer;
- the general failure of local effort to bring fresh water from afar; and
- aquifer communities incapable of cooperating locally or mobilizing politically.

Experiments in Moral Water Economy

The pace of groundwater abstraction has created in South Asia an irrigation economy where irrigators are driven essentially by short-term self-interest and desperation, with little regard for third-party effects, future generations, nature, or even their own future prospects. Moving from traditional community management of water and land during precolonial times (as described in Rosin 1993) to today's atomistic pump irrigation economy has led, among other things, to the erosion of reciprocity and connectedness and shared values—something in the nature of Putnam's (1993) "social capital."

Against this backdrop is a groundswell of spontaneous social experiments: groundwater depletion and the consequent misery have triggered attempts to create a new social order and a kind of "moral economy" (Scott 1976). The extended moral economy argument supposes that certain kinds of cooperation and solidarity within village communities can and do occur, and they are sustained endogenously or with stimulus from outside. These ideas are echoed in experiments by social entrepreneurs like Anna Hazare in Ralegaon Siddi and Popat Powar in Hivre Bazaar in Ahmednagar district in Maharashra, Hardevsingh Jadeja in Rajsamadhiala village near Rajkot, Rajendra Singh and the *Tarun Bharat Sangh* in Alwar district of eastern Rajasthan, and Salunke's *Gram Gaurav Pratishthan* near Pune, not to mention the work done by religious Hindu organizations like the *Swaminarayana Sampradaya* and *Swadhyaya Pariwar* in Saurashtra, Gujarat. All these experiments were triggered by groundwater scarcity, but all went far beyond just harvesting rainwater to invoke visions of moral economy. Each in its own way, the experiments attempted to create a social ethic in which actors were exposed to new—or long-forgotten—social and environmental values. In particular, five aspects are common to all these experiments.

New water ethic based on intuitive hydrology. All the experiments attempted to propagate simple, intuitive notions of how water scarcity can be countered by popular action. Pandurang Athavale of *Swadhyaya Parivar* enjoined his many followers, "Quench the thirst of Mother Earth, and she will quench yours" (Shah 2000). Rajendra Singh called on village people to change rainwater's habit of breaking into a sprint at the first opportunity and teach it to trot or even take a leisurely walk. Anna Hazare was fond of saying "water on the surface is no good; it best stays below the ground" (Sharma 2006). Popat Powar allowed open wells but banned bore wells in Hivre Bazaar (Deulagaonkar 2004). Saurashtra's recharge movement created a popular hydrogeology with treatises written in the vernacular on how to site subsurface check dams (Shah 2000).

Community self-help. Most experiments placed great emphasis on community self-reliance over government programs. Community labor was invariably mobilized to build water-harvesting and recharge structures, and although some experiments used external finances or material support, *Swadhyaya Parivar* insisted on total self-help from within the community—the only acceptable help from outside being voluntary labor (Shah 2000).

Equitable sharing. Each experiment emphasized the common property nature of groundwater and introduced new norms for equitable sharing of the resource. Salunke's experiment was notable in this respect because it emphasized water allocation per person rather than per acre of land owned (Chambers et al. 1989). But rather than employing positive discrimination or some other kind of affirmative action, most experiments promoted equitable access by creating redundancies in their natural resource systems, best exemplified in Raj Samadhiala in Saurashtra (Tilala and Shiyani 2005) and Hivre Bazaar (Sangameshwaran 2006).

Community-sanctioned norms of demand management. Typically, cultivation of water-loving crops—notably, sugarcane and banana—that were inconsistent with local water endowments was banned. Hivre Bazaar also sealed all existing bore wells at a certain depth and banned new ones. Many experiments banned pumping of water directly from recharge structures. *Tarun Bharat Sangh* created the Aravari River Parliament as a small-scale basin governance structure.

Nonwater values. Finally, after "fixing" water, many leaders found themselves working on a far bigger moral economy agenda; a natural extension for many was reforestation and other larger aspects of the local environment. Some, like Hazare in Ralegaon Siddi, Popat Pawar in Hivre Bazaar, and Hardev Singh of Raj Samadhiala, built village communities, styled around personal values of virtuous living. Hazare and Pawar each adopted *Panchasutri* (five rules of noble living; Sangameshwaran 2006); banned tobacco, alcohol, and gambling; and mandated all able-bodied to work for a living. Jadeja did much the same in Raj Samadhiala. Popat Pawar promoted the values of community life in Hivre Bazaar. Others promoted somewhat less stringent nonwater values; Saurashtra Jaldhara Trust, an NGO, campaigned against dowries and wedding festivities and suggested the money saved be used to build check dams instead.[49] The entrepreneurs, and their chroniclers and critics, all stressed the moral dimensions that helped the community rise above the pursuit of narrow, shortsighted self-interest and create a new village order based on caring and sharing, on solidarity and cooperation, on love of nature and concern for future generations. Above all, in a climate of despondence and fatalism inspired by dried-up wells and desiccated surface water bodies, these experiments generated hope that with cooperative husbanding of resources, a superior and secure rural economy could be created.

Whether such communities will survive their creators, only time will tell. However, numerous studies have produced evidence to suggest that together, the supply- and demand-side interventions they have introduced had a profound impact on the water situation in their areas, on the agrarian economy, and somewhat less clearly on the equitable sharing of water. Indeed, most popular accounts emphasized how these experiments began by trying to ease water scarcity but ended up resurrecting dying agrarian communities and transforming them into vibrant economies. In a decade, Hivre Bazaar was rejuvenated (Vijapurkar 2000).[50] Raj Samadhiala near Rajkot and Ralegaon Siddhi near Ahmednagar have become prosperous focal points for water-harvesting tourism. It was nobody's prediction that Saurashtra would become a Punjab, but it is widely said that the mass-based recharge movement has "drought-proofed" Saurashtra's main *kharif* crop, assuring a minimum agricultural production of Rs. 30 billion to 40 billion even during dry years.

It is interesting that all these moral water economy experiments have occurred in hard-rock areas or places with an impermeable confining layer a few meters below the vadoz zone of the aquifers.[51] Although the Saurashtra experience inspired local communities elsewhere in hard-rock Gujarat, North Gujarat, whose groundwater crisis is deeper than Saurashtra's, failed completely to forge its own mass-based recharge movement, much as government, NGOs, and local leaders tried to trigger it. Gandhi and Namboodiri (2007), who extolled the impacts of village-level water-harvesting institutions in Saurashtra, in the same study looked at many tube well companies in arid alluvial North Gujarat and found them unconcerned about groundwater depletion and disinterested in water harvesting. Similarly, *Tarun Bharat Sangh's* success in reviving Arwari River as well as the agrarian life around it failed to spread to Jodhpur, Bikaner, and Jaiselmer. Many parts of Punjab, Haryana, and western Rajasthan are experiencing rapid decline in groundwater (Sidhu and Bhullar 2005); however, nowhere in these parts do we hear about anyone trying a moral irrigation economy experiment.

The reason, in large part, is hydrogeology and its influence on rational expectations. In unconfined alluvial aquifers, no farmer expects recharge efforts at the individual or village level to increase the yield of his or her own well, which drives the decision to cooperate or defect, especially when recharge resources in terms of rainfall are limited. Here, it would be very difficult to catalyze mass mobilization for recharge. These regions are, however, ripe for mass mobilization for surface water import projects (such as Gujarat's Sujalam Sufalam scheme, described in Chapter 5) and for electricity subsidies under a flat tariff. The provincial government and the World Bank invested in 160 delayed-action dams for enhancing groundwater recharge in Baluchistan. But groundwater irrigators have little interest in recharge because they do not see it translate into improved water availability for themselves.

In alluvial aquifers with a shallow confining layer, as in the Alwar district of Rajasthan, individual farmers water harvesting may not improve the yield of their wells, but coordinated effort at the level of the village community can have *some* effect, which may multiply when the wider aquifer community joins such effort. Here, farmers on their own are unlikely to take to ground-water recharge, but with high-quality catalytic intervention that produces results convincing enough to generate positive expectations, large-scale mobilization for water harvesting and recharge is a feasible proposition in such areas, as Tarun Bharat Sangh has demonstrated in Rajasthan.

Water harvesting and decentralized groundwater recharge on a mass basis have best payoffs in hard-rock areas with low storage capacity and reasonable rainfall, especially of the monsoon kind. Here, even individual farmers' recharge can increase, albeit minutely, the on-demand yield of their wells; this gain multiplies as the village and aquifer community join the effort. It is here that we find fertile ground for mass-based water conservation and recharge effort, and therefore, it is here that groundwater irrigation in an atomistic mode is most likely to be sustainable in the long run. Over time, we can expect a movement toward both a steady state with greater community effort to increase recharge and endogenous norms for demand management.

Conclusion: Predictable Human Dynamics

Understanding the "settled habits of thought common to the generality of men" about aquifers is a crucial aspect of the challenge of making South Asia's atomistic pump irrigation economy sustainable. This chapter has sought to explain how the rational expectations that irrigators form about an aquifer's behavior under intensive development shape their own interactions, producing widely differing productivity, equity, and sustainability results under different hydrogeological settings.

The analysis places in bold relief the chasm between formal hydrology and popular hydrology, between how we scientists would like things to be and what people actually want:

- Scientists would advocate urgent restrictions on groundwater abstractions in arid alluvial areas. Farmers would militate against such restrictions, and collusive opportunism drives them to draw down the aquifers in a hurry.
- Scientists tend to consider water table aquifers with coarse sandy material the best available, but in South Asia, it may well be poor hard-rock aquifers where groundwater use may eventually be sustainable. In the former, there is little indication of farmers worrying about sustainability; in the later, there is sporadic and growing evidence of farmers struggling to increase the recharge and the efficiency of its application because of their daily struggle with physical water scarcity.

- In good alluvial aquifers in arid regions, regulating groundwater demand as well as importing surface water for recharge necessitate intensive external intervention; in poor hard-rock aquifers, supporting village communities in water harvesting and recharge efforts can go a long way.
- To scientists, the measure of a good recharge project is the maximum volume of surplus water available that can be put into roomy aquifers. To farmers, a good recharge structure is one that can deliver crop saving irrigation on demand.
- Scientists consider the proliferation of small recharge structures the root cause of upstream-downstream externalities. To water-harvesting village communities in Saurashtra and elsewhere in hard-rock South Asia, everyone lives downstream.
- Scientists look for appropriate recharge zones to site recharge structures. Farmers build recharge structures close to their wells because experience tells them that water availability in their wells is determined by proximity to recharge structures.
- Scientists aim at planning basin-level water storage, but as a Saurashtra farmer told me in an interview, "a farmer considers one cubic meter of water in his well equal to ten in the village tank, a hundred in a canal and a thousand in a distant government reservoir." Like the notions of "effective rainfall" and "effective irrigation efficiency" (Keller and Keller 1995), there is something like "effective recharge efficiency"—the ratio of usable recharge available on demand to a community to the volume of water put into the aquifers—that appears to convey farmers' idea of efficient recharge strategy in hard-rock South Asia. Farmers' participation will be high where such "effective recharge efficiency" is seen to be high.

To create a platform for scientists and farmers to work together, it is critical that these two worldviews merge. Failing that, chances are that scientists will try to meet the "unfelt" needs of irrigators. And farmers will seek to meet their immediate felt needs. The core groundwater governance challenge, then, differs from one groundwater socioecology to another, and we can categorize five situations.

Situation 1. In amply recharged humid alluvial aquifers, as in the Ganga-Meghna-Brahmaputra basin, where s=0, S=0, h=0, H=0, the challenge is planning expansion of groundwater irrigation for maximum social welfare and poverty reduction while addressing local negative externalities of intensive use.

Situation 2. In arid alluvial aquifers, the primary need is improved conjunctive management of ground, surface, and rain water. In much of South Asia's arid west and northwest, where s=0, S<0, h=0, H=0, demand regulation needs to be combined with importation of water to promote conjunctive use through recharging of the aquifers as well as for surface irrigation in lieu of pumping groundwater; demand restriction alone is certain to be frustrated by farmers.

Situation 3. In all hard-rock areas with reasonable rainfall, where s<0, S<0, h=0, H >0, there is potential to transform rivalrous gaming into cooperative gaming. The challenge is mobilizing users for water harvesting and decentralized recharge as well as instituting local demand management institutions; these have much scope because a good deal hinges on transforming h=0 into h>0. Here too, attempts to restrict groundwater abstractions per se are likely to meet stiff resistance.

Situation 4. In hard-rock regions where water harvesting is already a popular practice, and where s=0, s<0, h>0 and H>0, the priority is to institutionalize the positive experiences and build upon them. There is also need for their lateral spread; continued focus on demand management is the key to future sustainability.

Situation 5. In arid alluvial aquifers with acute salinity problems, where s<0, S<0, h=0, H=0, large-scale public intervention on the supply as well as the demand side may help stem the exodus. Where copious fresh surface water is available, the solution to groundwater problems lies in improved management of surface water.

A great deal of global understanding of sustainable groundwater management is based on Situation 2 (intensive groundwater irrigation in arid alluvial aquifers) and Situation 5 (exploitation of coastal aquifers for urban and industrial water needs, as in South Africa). Elsewhere in the world, humid alluvial areas and places with abundant surface water rarely have large pockets of intensive groundwater irrigation, as we saw in Chapter 2 (Situation 1) and as we find in the Ganga-Brahmaputra-Meghana basin. Likewise, in no other hard-rock areas elsewhere in the world do we find as much land under groundwater irrigation, running into several million hectares, as we find in central and peninsular India (Situations 3 and 4). In learning from global experience in groundwater governance, which we take up in Chapter 7, it is important to bear in mind these unique features of South Asia's groundwater irrigation economy.

CHAPTER 7

CAN THE ANARCHY BE TAMED?

Laws do not persuade just because they threaten.

— *Seneca,* A.D. *65*

Social scientists have long debated what, if anything, anarchy describes. However, there is no semantic ambiguity in the epithet "functioning anarchy," which John K. Galbraith, economist and one-time U.S. ambassador, gave to India. It conveys more than tomes written about how India—indeed, South Asia as a whole—works. As one writer summed up, it meant that whatever happens here does "not depend upon the government but on the energy and ingenuity of its people" (Thakurta 2005).

Nothing describes the pump irrigation revolution in South Asia better than the label Galbraith gave to India. This vast functioning anarchy, today the mainstay of South Asia's smallholders, is essentially a product of the energy and ingenuity of its people. Public policy worked when it ran along with the energy and ingenuity of farmers but came unstuck when it tried to regulate this economy. Indeed, many policies widely considered perverse— such as electricity subsidies—have persisted because of mass politics rather than expert advice or rational decision making, as we reviewed in Chapter 5.

Despite the social dividend that pump irrigation has bestowed on South Asia's poor, there are frequent calls to replace the present irrigation anarchy with orderly governance. The calls have become increasingly urgent with mounting evidence of groundwater overexploitation and depletion, drawdown externalities, deterioration in water quality deterioration, and all the other unseemly outcomes of unregulated development discussed in Chapters 5 and 6. A bigger concern is sustaining the social dividend already created: as more smallholders seek a share, the groundwater juggernaut may just cave in, as is increasingly evident in many parts of the region. The parable of the Prisoners' Dilemma (PD) leading to the tragedy of the commons is nowhere more fitting on so vast a scale as in the groundwater economy of South Asia. Considering the overwhelming—and still rising—influence of groundwater irrigation, clearly the agricultural future of the region rests on how well it governs its atomistic groundwater irrigation economy.

As in the first two chapters, in these two concluding chapters I seek to situate the South Asian discussion within the global context. Many countries experienced unregulated private development of groundwater for irrigation decades before South Asia and faced many of the consequences visible in South Asia today. They responded to the threats posed by groundwater overdevelopment, and the lessons that emerged from their experiments have contributed much to the global pool of ideas about approaches to groundwater governance. This chapter offers an overview of international experience and its profound impact on national thinking (see, e.g., Romani et al. 2007) as well as the new global discourse around integrated water resources management (IWRM). My premise is that, although international experience offers valuable guidance, the approach most likely to work in South Asia will be the one adapted to the unique dynamic and drivers of the groundwater revolution in South Asia and the North China Plain.

Groundwater governance is about creating institutional structures, processes, mechanisms, and policy tools for harmonizing the interests of resource users and the wider interests of society and future generations. It is not only about control and regulation. Where groundwater is undeveloped, governance is about developing the resource in an orderly, equitable, and planned manner to enhance material well-being and alleviate agrarian poverty. Where groundwater is overexploited, governance is about regulating its extraction to minimize third-party externalities and social "illfare." In the language used by Lipton (1985), it is about moving society from

Prisoner's Dilemma (PD) outcomes to Coase outcomes. When numerous users partake of a natural resource like groundwater (or ocean fisheries or grazing land) under open access, the tragedy of the commons unfolds, manifest in myriad externalities, positive or negative,[1] in the form of unintended third-party impacts of private economic activity that remains uncompensated. This is the proverbial PD outcome, which leaves a society materially worse off than it can be with good governance.

The state can use coercion to stamp out economic activities that generate negative externalities and undertake public production of those that produce positive externalities. However, a similar effect can be achieved through economic incentives. Arthur Pigou, writing on the problem in 1930s, suggested a tax to neutralize negative externalities or a subsidy to maximize positive externalities. This Pigovian tax is at the root of the popular "user pays" and "polluter pays" principles. Nobel laureate economist Ronald Coase, however, showed that in a regime with clearly specified credible property rights, creators of externalities and affected third parties would arrive, through negotiation and bargaining, at a mutually satisfactory and socially optimal arrangement.[2] Such results, which Lipton called Coase outcomes, would not be possible, however, and externalities would remain "uninternalized," in an open-access, laissez-faire regime. Transforming PD into Coase outcomes requires clearly specified property rights, credible enforcement mechanisms, and an efficient court system to resolve disputes—in sum, a regime that can enforce rules and norms, manipulate economic incentives, and deploy the authority of the state.

Instruments of Water Governance

Water governance discourse worldwide is a product of the growing threat of water scarcity, which has made the transition from resource development to resource management mode critical. In this transition, groundwater—an invisible, fungible resource—has proved particularly difficult, and although the western United States, Spain, Mexico, and other countries offer lessons about attempts to craft groundwater governance regimes, nowhere are the outcomes fully satisfactory (Shah et al. 2007). However, as the groundwater question becomes more pressing, South Asian policymakers must understand what has been tried elsewhere and ask what has (or has not) worked and why (or why not). To this end, the following sections briefly review the experience with five major groundwater governance instruments, each of which seeks to directly influence the actions and behavior of users.

1. *Direct regulation through administrative action.* Claims of eminent domain and use of governmental administrative apparatus to regulate groundwater extraction characterize the groundwater governance regime in many countries, notably the Sultanate of Oman, Iran, Saudi Arabia, Israel, and the western United States. In South Asia, too, groundwater departments in most Indian states as well as Bangladesh have norms for siting irrigation wells and minimum spacing to be maintained to minimize well interference externalities. India has had a draft groundwater law for more than 30 years, and several state governments have passed groundwater laws providing regulatory powers (Planning Commission 2007). Regulatory effectiveness, however, has remained limited, primarily because popular support, political will, and enforcement capacity commensurate with the enforcement challenge are lacking.

Countries like Oman have nevertheless used government instruments with greater vigor and seriousness. The hallmark of Oman's groundwater governance regime is the strong and very visible hand of the state. Without much concern for property rights, entitlements, or incentives, the Oman government, with the personal initiative of the sultan, instituted demand-side measures, such as obligatory well registration, permits, metering, prohibition of wells within 3.5 km of the mother wells of some 4,000 *aflaj* *(kareze, or qanat)* systems supplying 30 percent of Oman's irrigation (World Bank and SDC (2000, 20)), filling up of illegally constructed wells, confiscation of the equipment of contractors involved in illegal drilling, and wellfield protection zoning (Abdel-Rahman and Islam Abdel-Magid 1993; Al-Ajmi and Abdel-Rahman 2001; Jack van der Gun in Shah et al. 2007). Saudi Arabia, Jordan, and Iran have taken a similar path with varying levels of commitment and success.

The experience with implementing direct regulation has been generally poor, as was concluded by a conference on Middle Eastern and North African countries in 2000 (World Bank and Swiss Agency 2000). Elsewhere, even talk about regulation has generated a groundswell of opportunistic response from farmers. In Mexico, political leaders have issued, from time to time since 1949, "regularization" deadlines after which new tube wells would be banned in stressed aquifers. Every time, however, the threat has set off a well-boring spree; the last time a deadline was issued, in 1997, tube well numbers doubled in the central Mexican province of Guanahuato (Scott et al. 2003). A leading Mexican practitioner of groundwater governance concluded that regulation would not work "unless social and economic realities are taken into account" (Sandoval 2004).

2. *Economic instruments.* Economic instruments are attractive because they can influence the behavior of numerous economic agents without having to coerce them or invoke eminent domain. Using a price or a Pigovian tax is the basic economic instrument to signal scarcity value. The problem in pricing groundwater is often the high transaction costs of metering, monitoring, and charge collection; as a result, pricing is effectively used when it can be levied on bulk users or service providers who can transmit the price signals to users. In the U.S. West, a pump tax, generally higher for industries than for agricultural users, was widely used to control groundwater overdraft (Turral 1998). In China, water pricing—for cost recovery as well as demand management in cities—has worked because municipalities collect them from a handful of water service providers; however, collecting water withdrawal fees, under the 1995 Water Law, from millions of scattered agricultural tube well owners has proved far more challenging (Shah et al. 2004a). In a new Law of the Nation's Waters, Mexico, like China, has imposed water resource fees— besides service charges—on all users including irrigators. However, Mexico too has found implementation difficult (Shah et al. 2004b).

The best-known case of water pricing for agricultural use is Israel, where all irrigation diversion and delivery points are metered and closely monitored (Feitelson 2006). Jordan has introduced a groundwater withdrawal charge of US$0.40 per cubic meter on industrial users, but its extension to agriculture invited much resistance. Jordan had to use force in installing meters on deep tube wells and create a quasi "water police" to enforce pumping quotas (World Bank and SDC 2000, 22).

Pricing has met with greater success when used to create incentives for moving water to higher-value uses. Saudi Arabia and Yemen have tried paying farmers to sell groundwater to towns rather than using it for irrigation (Abderrahman 2003; Briscoe 1999). In India, Metro-water, the water service provider for Chennai, also did this successfully. In the industrialized world, compensating farmers to reduce negative third-party externalities is common. Some German cities have been paying periurban farmers to reduce chemical use and thus nonpoint source pollution of groundwater (Shah et al. 2001a), and in the western United States, it is common for cities to buy up groundwater rights from farmers or for the federal government to pay groundwater irrigators in overdrafted areas to switch to dry-land farming. Direct scarcity pricing of groundwater use in irrigation in developing countries is rare, however, not because the principle is in doubt but its actual practice has proved difficult.

3. *Tradable property rights.* The conceptual foundation of the tradable property rights discussion rests on the premise that under open access, a groundwater resource would always be open to depletion and degradation.[3] To move from PD to Coase outcomes, one road is creating enforceable private property rights, preferably tradable. Tradable water rights modify the outlook of the users as well as third parties about externalities, leading to more efficient allocation—though not necessarily conservation—of the resource. The historical foundation of tradable rights, however, rests in the history of European settlements in the New World, where secure property rights were essential to encourage settlers to make private investments in land and water development (Chapter 1). The idea of the groundwater governance regimes in the United States and Australia then rests on the concept that users *can* evolve mechanisms for self-governance of the resource, with the state providing an overarching regulatory and facilitative framework. The actual experience with such collective self-governance is a matter of much debate even within these countries; however, their experience has given birth to a growth industry for promoting tradable water rights as a one-stop solution to groundwater malgovernance. The virtues of tradable property rights are widely advertised and commended (Rosegrant and Gazmuri 1994). The outcome of an innovative project of introducing tradable water rights in Chile has been vigorously lauded (Rosegrant and Gazmuri 1994) as well as roundly criticized (Bauer 2004; Boelens and Bustamante 2005; Global Water Partnership 2006).

At the conceptual plane, there is little to gainsay the hypothesis that tradable property rights result in superior allocation of scarce water. The real problem of using this approach effectively, however, is again the transaction costs, which rise in geometric progression with the increase in the number of users. Although the property rights protagonists have not paid much heed to transaction costs, these were central in the scheme of Ronald Coase, who warned that the assignment of property rights would be of little avail under three circumstances: if the information available to contracting parties was less than perfect, if transactions costs were high, and if the number of contracting parties was too large to permit easy negotiations among them. As Armen Alchian,[4] another prominent property rights theorist, similarly argued,

The cost of establishing private property rights—so that I could pay you a mutually agreeable price to pollute your air—may be too expensive. Air, underground water, and electromagnetic radiations, for example, are expensive to monitor and control . . . When private property rights are unavailable or too costly to establish and enforce, substitute means of control are sought. Government authority, expressed by government agents, is one very common such means.

Even where transactions costs are manageable, results are not uniformly satisfactory. Fertile ground for studying the impacts of a variety of tradable water rights regimes is the U.S. West. In Kansas and Colorado, groundwater management is centrally about proactive demand management,[5] and third-party externalities generate massive amounts of litigation. In Texas, which has embraced the "rule of capture," the situation can be nearly as anarchic as in South Asia. Even where the resource is threatened, demand management by reducing irrigated areas or groundwater withdrawals through rights administration is more an exception than a rule. When groundwater pumping is restricted to meet a threat to the aquifers, it is often because a new water supply is offered in lieu of pumping of groundwater or because soaring pumping costs make groundwater irrigation economically unviable.

According to Henry Vaux only 19 of 431 groundwater basins in California are "actively managed," with some restrictions on pumping. In all the rest, groundwater management is passive, basically involving federal government grants to build infrastructure to import surface water and supply it to groundwater users in lieu of pumping. Here, nobody is expected to reduce groundwater use. Vaux also suggests that active management basins are generally overlain by highly urbanized areas where governments or municipalities can easily buy water rights to serve high-paying urban consumers.[6] U.S. groundwater management districts are held out as a model of collective action to achieve Coase outcomes in which members make and enforce norms for withdrawals; however, such is seldom the case. In a study of local resource management in eight groundwater basins in California, Blomquist found that collective action was mostly about implementing supply-side interventions, much like those the Indian farmer communities have evolved in hard-rock areas of Saurashtra and eastern Rajasthan (Chapter 6).[7]

All in all, it is by no means clear that the rich institutional and regulatory activity of the western and central United States has created a wholesome groundwater governance regime. The Ogallala aquifer continues to be depleted; Kansas experiences "widespread falls in groundwater level of significant magnitude [that are] non-recoverable in large areas"; in Arizona, overexploitation and falling water levels are addressed by legislation that mandates balancing extraction with recharge, but it is "not clear that targets will be met;" in California, courts have determined "equitable distribution" over large areas, but "it may not lead to sustainable use" (Kalf and Woolley 2005, 299). In Texas, James Nachbaur found that irrigation interests always defeated laws designed to regulate them (Shah 2006b). Allan (2007, 75) suggests, "Even in economies that had the political and economic space to pursue knowledge-based groundwater management policies, both renewable and non-renewable aquifers have been seriously depleted. Overuse of the aquifers of the High Plains of Texas is a sorry tale." The U.S. experience inspires little faith in demand management; its lesson is that the practical way to protect a stressed aquifer is to ease pressure on it by developing alternative supply sources.

Groundwater institutions in the United States and Australia also tend to be highly sensitive to transaction costs. This is why they are careful to "exempt" numerous relatively small—*de minimis*—users so that the groundwater governance regime has to contend only with a small number of large users. Kansas thus exempts *de minimis* users, defined as those who divert no more than 15 acre feet of groundwater. In Nebraska, only wells that pump 50 gallons or more per minute need a permit, a meter, and an allocation (Nagaraj et al. 2000). In Australia, too, those irrigating up to 2 ha are exempted as *de minimis* users (Macdonald and Young 2000). An extreme case of minimizing transaction costs is Texas, which has deliberately embraced groundwater anarchy by adopting the principle "let the locals figure it out for themselves." If India and China were to undertake institutional management of the Colorado and Kansas kind, the resources they would need, in terms of money and manpower, would be considerable. And if they were to exempt *de minimis* users by Kansas, Nebraska, and Australian standards, more than 95 percent of users would fall through the groundwater governance sieve.

4. Community aquifer management. In evolving their groundwater governance regimes, Mexico and Spain have adapted the U.S. experience of tradable water rights and groundwater management districts. The underlying premise—somewhat along the Coasean logic—is that if groundwater users are organized around aquifers for self-governance, they will internalize third-party externalities through bargaining and negotiation, collectively monitor the behavior of the groundwater as well as its users, and ensure the long-term sustainability of both. A more practical consideration was to use groundwater associations as agents in monitoring and enforcement of government policies and laws. The idea of groundwater organizations has a wide appeal; it was advocated to India by a British Geological Survey (2004) study. And in South India, the FAO-supported Andhra Pradesh Farmer Managed Groundwater Systems Project has organized groundwater users in 650 habitations in 66 hydrological units (Knegt and Vincent 2001). Spain and Mexico have, however, embraced groundwater organizations as the central element of their official national water governance strategy.

Until 1985, Spain, like Texas, followed the rule of capture. However, the intensification of groundwater stress under unregulated agricultural use prompted stern measures. The 1985 Water Act nationalized groundwater and gave river basin management agencies *(confederacions hidrograficas)* an active role in managing groundwater. These were vested with the power to grant permits for groundwater use, declare an aquifer overexploited, and formulate a management plan for its recovery. The typical plan involved reduction in the volume of withdrawals by rights holders and rejection of new applications for wells. To encourage participation, all users of the aquifer were organized into groundwater user associations.

An assessment of the results of groundwater reforms in Spain by Spanish researchers suggests a rather gloomy picture. For one, even after 20 years, recording of groundwater rights remains incomplete; worse, less than a quarter of all groundwater structures have been registered. Intensive groundwater governance does not come cheap: recording the rights and monitoring them require far more human and other resources than the implementing agency can afford. Thus, Spain, with some half a million irrigation wells,[8] is still grappling with the most basic issue of identifying and recording groundwater users. Given Spain's long tradition of successful surface water users' associations (some in Valencia are centuries old), similar associations were assumed to work for aquifers as well. But even though thousands of small groundwater user associations have been "registered" on paper, only a handful have made some movement toward collective management of aquifers, and even fewer have met with some success.[9] Villaroya and Aldwell (1998, 111) concluded that in Spain, groundwater overexploitation "is dealt with in the water act and implemented by the regulations that enforce that act. Experience has shown that without the cooperation of the water users themselves, good results are not obtained." Lopez Gunn and Llamas (1999, 5) were more severe:

> With the passing of the 1985 Water Law, [groundwater] was declared as of "public ownership." This represented a fundamental change in relation to water rights. Yet this drastic change . . . has led to many situations of "hydrologic disobedience" in relation to water rights and abstraction in almost every stressed aquifer. Indeed the question remains as to what came first, hydrologic disobedience or stressed aquifers.

Mexico followed in Spain's footsteps and had a similar experience (Scott et al. 2003). By the Law of the Nation's Waters of 1992, the National Water Commission *(Comision Nacional del Agua)* declared water a national property and required existing users to legitimize their rights by procuring "concessions" (in effect, volumetric rights). A regulatory structure was authorized to enforce and monitor the concessions granted and collect a volumetric water fee from all except small users. Aquifer management councils, known as COTAS, were promoted by the commission as structures for collective, participatory self-governance of aquifers (Sandoval 2004).

Results of Mexico's groundwater reforms fell far short of expectations. The challenge, as in Spain, has been registering the water rights of some 96,000 tube well irrigators who account for 80 percent of Mexico's groundwater withdrawals. Irrigators had to be enticed to apply for concessions through the "carrot" of an electricity subsidy worth US$1,600 per year, high enough to make registration profitable. Even so, eight years later, only 55,000 of Mexico's 96,000 tube well owners were concessioned, and more than 80 percent of Mexican tube wells pumped more groundwater than their quotas (Pina et al. 2006). Monitoring actual withdrawals has been far trickier. COTAS, which were expected to do this, steered clear of the task.

"COTAS were intended to be consensus-building spaces where integrated water management models are to be implemented" (Sandoval 2004, *10*), institutions where the users would self-monitor their extraction and help reduce groundwater overexploitation. The problem is that even though they are farmers' organizations in name, COTAS survive because the National Water Commission has been paying all their bills, and as it runs out of funds—and patience—there is little likelihood that farmers will contribute to sustain organizations whose ultimate goal, they perceive, is to limit their immediate economic opportunities.

Concessions have created a new dynamic of opportunism. Recently, the National Water Commission announced its intention to withdraw unused portions of groundwater quotas, creating a perverse "use it or lose it" situation. Luis Marin, a Mexican researcher, reported,

In Mexico, the government has tried to give the stakeholders the responsibility for managing aquifers by establishing COTAS. However, COTAS depend financially on subsidies from . . . governments . . . Under the new law, stakeholders who don't use all of the volume that they have a permit for, stand to lose the unused volume the following year. As a result, stake holders extract their full volumes, even if much of this water is wasted, only not to have their concessions reduced. (2005, pers. comm.)

5. *Crowding out tube wells through supply augmentation.* One of the most common, successful, and time-tested approaches to easing pressure on stressed aquifers is to develop alternative water sources. As I write this in June 2007, Gujarat, in western India, inaugurated a 335-km recharge canal built at a cost of US$1.5 billion to take the floodwaters of Mahi and Narmada rivers to ease the stress on the parched aquifers of North Gujarat, one of the world's worst groundwater cases. Most arid states of western and central United States, where irrigation depends on depletion mostly of the High Plains aquifer, the importation of surface water to substitute for groundwater draft is widely used to wean farmers off groundwater use. Indeed, in the U.S. West, water augmentation by local agencies but with federal funding preceded demand management by decades and remains the central feature of groundwater governance. The Central Arizona Project is one example. In Southern California, the city of Pasadena began spreading water to increase groundwater recharge as early as in 1914, and efforts continue to date. Government funding of local agencies and management districts to build groundwater recharge and flood storage projects increased annual water yield by 300,000 acre feet in California during recent years (Department of Water Resources 2003). Many of the projects constructed by California's local districts are comparable to the decentralized recharge movement in Saurashtra (Chapter 6; Blomquist 1992). The Orange County water district's aggressive program to enhance recharge to the groundwater basin included construction of levees in river channels, artificial recharge basins within the forebay, and use of imported water from the state water project and the Colorado River (Blomquist 1992). Costlier projects include recycling of reverse osmosis–treated wastewater to create a seawater intrusion barrier. Imported surface water to substitute for groundwater pumping near coastal areas and for recharge, too, is widely used by many districts.

Spain's much-proposed water transfer project from Ebro River, China's south-to-north water transfer project, and India's proposed project to link Himalayan with peninsular rivers are all inspired in part by water scarcity, manifested in groundwater depletion and stress. Smaller interbasin water transfer projects are implemented even by provincial governments using their own funds, as with Jiangsu Province in China and Gujarat in India. Worldwide, pressures on urban aquifers have been eased primarily by importation of surface water from distant sources and less by proactive demand management. Chinese cities, especially in rapidly growing Shaanxi and Jiangsu provinces in the eastern parts, have used supply augmentation to crowd out groundwater wells and to sugarcoat an Oman-like groundwater governance regime, at least in their urban and industrial sectors (Shah et al. 2004a).

IWRM and Groundwater Governance

Water governance means different things to different people. According to a widely used definition by the Global Water Partnership (2002, 2), it refers to "the range of political, social, economic and administrative systems that are in place to develop and manage water resources, and the delivery of water services, at different levels of society." The operational counterpart of this somewhat philosophical notion, integrated water resources management (IWRM), is understood as "a process which promotes coordinated development and management of water, land and related resources, in order to maximize the resultant economic and social welfare in an equitable manner without compromising the sustainability of vital ecosystems" (Global Water Partnership 2000).

Since it means different things to different people, IWRM has become a catchall phrase. Mollinga (2006, 21) described it as a "concept looking for a constituency." But the concept is also impossible to evaluate, much less critique. IWRM protagonists dismiss criticism by insisting that the version being critiqued is not the *original* idea of IWRM.

As Cicero once said, ideas are judged by results, not by intentions. In the hands of operational managers, especially of international lending and donor agencies, the IWRM philosophy morphed into a package designed to produce results. To national policymakers in many poor countries, the package—derived from the Global Water Partnership's IWRM toolkit[10]— held out special appeal, especially as part of a large loan. The IWRM package turned out to be a mix of policy instruments, like those reviewed above, and is centrally about readying developing countries' water economies for integrated and direct management of water demand by strengthening the role of water policy, law, and administration, the three pillars of water governance. And since this is the version that got applied, the "IWRM package" began to overshadow the original philosophy.

IWRM has generally included the following: (1) enunciation of a national water policy that declares water as national property (as in Mexico and Spain) and presents a cohesive, well-understood normative framework to guide all players in the sector; (2) a water law that provides the legal framework for implementing the water policy (Mexico's Law of the Nation's Water of 1992; South Africa's Water Law of 1995); (3) acceptance of the principle of water as an economic good by pricing water resource as well as services, especially outside lifeline uses, to reflect its scarcity value so that it is efficiently used and allocated to high-value uses (Israel, Mexico, China, South Africa); (4) recognition of the river basin as the unit of water and land resources planning and management and creation of river basin organizations in place of territorial or functional departments, and treating ground and surface water as a part of the same system; (5) creation of water rights, preferably tradable, by instituting a system of water withdrawal permits (Australia, United States, Spain, Mexico); and (6) participatory water resource management, with involvement of women, so that water becomes "everybody's business."[11]

If IWRM were viewed as a long-term dialectical process, the IWRM package, suitably adapted to local context, would be its end result. However, during the past decade, a dozen or so countries in Asia and Africa have witnessed efforts to impose the package itself, as if doing that would somehow help these societies leapfrog their water economies from anarchy to order, from nongovernance to good governance.

The results of introducing the end as an entry-point intervention generally have been disappointing, however (Shah and van Koppen 2006). A good example is Sri Lanka. During the past decade, its government has made two bold but abortive attempts to push through a regulation IWRM package that would establish state ownership of all water, institution of water use rights through withdrawal permits, pricing of water in all uses, transferable permits to encourage trade in water rights, and replacement of existing water organizations by river basin organizations. Sri Lanka's media and civil society, however, bitterly opposed the very logic underlying the proposed reforms (Samad 2005), and the government, which had given little thought to how the provisions would have been implemented anyway, withdrew.

Many Southeast Asian countries—notably Thailand, Indonesia, and Vietnam—faced no such opposition from media and civil society and swiftly adopted the IWRM package (Molle 2005), with little effect. Researchers called for "reforming reforms" (Merrey et al. 2007). Molle (2005, 13) found little connection between the reality of the water economies of these countries and the reforms borne out of "a global water discourse largely driven by international organizations." His review of the IWRM experience in Mekong led him to emphasize "a gap between formal and state-centered initiatives, and reality on the ground, which proceeds at a different pace. Lessons learned elsewhere are certainly important but cannot be adopted indiscriminately and must not be allowed to crowd out the emergence of endogenous and condition-specific solutions." The IWRM package left Asian water economies untouched, like raindrops rolling off the lotus leaf. But when similar reforms were rammed home in African countries hard pressed for international aid, they only worsened the situation, uprooting traditional customary rights and institutions without creating alternative arrangements (Shah and van Koppen 2006).

With the exception of Sri Lanka, South Asia has so far managed to steer clear of the IWRM package. But its groundwater crisis keeps prompting calls for stern measures from the IWRM package. In helping India's water economy in "bracing up for a turbulent future," a 2006 World Bank report urged policymakers to undertake wide-ranging reforms through "systemic sets of legislation, capacity building, organizational change, and the use of entitlements, pricing and regulatory instruments" (Briscoe and Malik 2006, 71). In November 2006, Ahluwalia, the deputy chairman of India's Planning Commission, told a large conference of hydrogeologists[12] to "consider levying a cess [special tax] on groundwater extraction" and called for "changes in the legal framework" to "prevent over-use of groundwater." He convened an expert group[13] to "review the issue of groundwater ownership in the country" and recommend a "proper and rational policy for water management." The proceedings of the conference he addressed had 20-odd papers on groundwater governance, each advocating IWRM-style tools of direct groundwater demand management without addressing the logistics of actually implementing the proposals (Romani et al. 2007).

Appeals for strong groundwater laws, backed by requisite authority, have a long history. Indeed, in 1996 the Supreme Court of India, acting on a public interest litigation, designated the Central Groundwater Board as India's central groundwater authority, charged with halting the abuse of groundwater resources in the country. Yet even the court did not address the logistics, and its orders remained largely unimplemented 10 years later.

Can a groundwater cess or a system of groundwater entitlements or a powerful groundwater law restore order in South Asia's irrigation economy? In theory, yes. The problem is how to make any or all of these actually work on the ground, given the atomistic nature of the subcontinent's irrigation economy. In Mexico, Spain, and even the United States, according to their own researchers, practice has defeated the precept, even though their groundwater economies are much smaller and simpler than South Asia's. Consider the organization of groundwater economies of the six countries listed in Table 7-1, with India on one extreme and the United States on the other. Indian farmers withdraw around 230 billion m³ of groundwater annually, more than twice as much as the U.S. users do, but India has 100 times more independent diverters of groundwater. In addition, more than half of all Indians—compared with less than two percent of Americans—will proactively oppose or frustrate any groundwater governance regime that hits their livelihoods.

The Australian Groundwater School at Adelaide says, "Groundwater will be the enduring gauge of this generation's intelligence in water and land management." Many observers have considered Australia, especially the Murray-Darling basin, the showcase of the IWRM package in operation, overlooking the fact that the institutional arrangement Australia has today is the result of a dialectical process initiated in the early years of the twentieth century by the likes of Prime Minister Alfred Deakin, as we saw in Chapter 1. In learning

Table 7-1   Organization of groundwater irrigation economies of selected countries, c. 2000

Country	Annual groundwater use (km³)	Agricultural groundwater structures (million)	Average extraction/ structure (m³/year)	Population dependent on groundwater irrigation (percentage)	Average annual farm income per farmworker (US$)
India	210	17.5	12,000	55–60	~350
Pakistan	55	0.9	60,000	60–65	~400
China	105	4.5	23,000	22–25	~458
Iran	29	0.5	58,000	12–18	~2,200
Mexico	29	0.07	414,285	5–6	3,758
United States	100	0.2	500,000	<1–2	67,800

Sources: www.agnet.org/library/stats/2003/24.html; Pina et al. 2006.

from the Australian experience, South Asian water policy students must also pay attention to other differences. Just 5.5 percent of Australia's irrigated area depends on groundwater compared with more than 60 percent in India and 90 percent in Bangladesh. The 285 to 300 km^3 of groundwater that South Asia withdraws every year to water crops is 50 times what Australia uses. But most importantly, South Asia has 20 million groundwater diverters—5,000 times more people to whom groundwater governance must speak.

The organization of a country's groundwater economy is central to understanding how it might be governed. China is discovering the implementation challenge of the IWRM package in a vast and atomistic groundwater economy. Just issuing water withdrawal permits to some 7.5 million tube well owners is a logistical nightmare, let alone monitoring their withdrawals. Not surprisingly, Wang et al. (2007, 53), who recently surveyed 448 villages and 126 townships from 60 counties in Inner Mongolia, Hebei, Henan, Liaoning, Shaanxi, and Shanxi, found that:

> inside China's villages few regulations have had any effect . . . despite the nearly universal regulation that requires the use of a permit for drilling a well, less than 10% of the well owners surveyed obtained one before drilling. Only 5% of villages surveyed believed their drilling decisions needed to consider spacing decisions . . . Even more telling was that water extraction was not charged in any village; there were no physical limits put on well owners. In fact, it is safe to say that in most villages in China, groundwater resources are almost completely unregulated.

If India or Pakistan, "softer," less regulated states than China, were to assign water entitlements or water withdrawal permits, as is widely suggested, for groundwater alone, it would have to issue permits to more than 20 million tube well owners, a number growing at 800,000 a year, and monitor their activities. If marginal farmers who buy groundwater were included, some 40 million more permits would be needed. Imposing a groundwater cess would be simple enough, but collecting it would require an army of water cess collectors, even if farmers were willing to pay. Maharashtra made a law with a specific, limited, and noble purpose of keeping irrigation wells from drying up nearby drinking water wells; more than a decade after the law came into force, researchers could not find a single case of the use of the law to protect a drinking water well (Phansalkar and Kher 2006). In its 2007 report, the Expert Group on Groundwater Ownership surveyed the experience of six Indian states that had experimented with groundwater regulation through law and concluded, with characteristic understatement, "From the experience of the six states it can be surmised that the enforceability of the Act has been a problem" (Planning Commission 2007, 48).

Conclusion: Limits to Leapfrogging

Water economies of countries differ in a variety of ways; but one dimension of critical importance is their degree of formalization, itself a function of the degree of "intermediation" in water service provision. Most water users in a highly formal water economy are secondary users, connected with the water governance regime through a battery of organized service-providing primary users amenable to regulation; those in a predominantly informal water economy are mostly primary users, drawing water directly from nature to meet their personal water requirements. "Governing an informal water economy" is a contradiction in terms, for by definition, an informal system is outside the legal, regulatory, and administrative ambit of the state. In a formal water economy, the state "steers" the water economy by means of water law, policy, and administration—the three pillars of water governance that institutional economists call the *institutional environment*. They distinguish this from *institutional arrangements*, which "are the structure that humans impose on their dealings with each other" (North 1990). In highly formalized water economies, the institutional environment dominates while institutional arrangements are marginal; in informal water economies, the opposite obtains.

In South Asia, institutional arrangements include entities like pump irrigation service markets and tube well cooperatives (Chapter 4), water user associations under participatory irrigation management and private lift irrigation provisioning from canals in Gujarat (Chapter 3), Tarun Bharat Sangh's water-harvesting movement in Alwar and the groundwater recharge movement in Saurashtra (Chapter 6), urban tanker water markets and peri-urban wastewater irrigation economies proliferating throughout South Asia (Londhe et al. 2004), informal institutions for tank fishery management (Shah 2003a), and the reverse-osmosis cottage industry in fluoride-affected North Gujarat that markets fluoride-free drinking water to households (Indu 2002). If we took a close look at the water economy of Cambodia or Ethiopia, we might find different institutional arrangements, but the poorer a country, the more such arrangements dominate water affairs. In contrast, in a European country, the institutional environment handles most service provision.

What determines whether a country has a highly formal water economy or not? Figure 7.1 presents empirically verifiable hypotheses—iron laws of water sector transformation—about how the organization of a country's water economy metamorphoses in response to economic growth. Poor countries' water economies everywhere are dominated by self-provision of water services (with most users being primary water diverters), low presence of public or formal water service providers, low intermediation between water users and water producers, customary rights regimes, and self-help and mutual-help community organizations. At the other extreme, affluent countries' water economies are dominated by a fully developed water industry,

	Stage I: completely informal	Stage II largely informal	Stage III formalizing	Stage IV: highly formal water industry
Percentage of water users in the formal sector	<5 percent	5–35 percent	35–75 percent	75–95 percent
Examples	sub-Saharan Africa	India, Pakistan, Bangladesh	Mexico, Thailand, Turkey, Eastern China	USA, Canada, western Europe, Australia
Dominant mode of water service provision	Self-supply; and informal mutual help institutions	Partial public provisioning but self-supply dominates;	Private-public provisioning with attempts to improve service and resource management.	Rise of the modern water industry; high level of intermediation; self-supply disappears
Human, technical and financial resources used by water sector ■ - ■				
Percentage of total water use self-supplied ▬ ▬ ▬				
Rural population as percentage of total ▬▬▬				
Cost of domestic water as percentage of per caput income ••••				
Cost of water service provision ▬▬▬▬				
Concerns of the governments	Infrastructure creation in a welfare mode	Infrastructure and water services, especially in urban areas.	Infrastructure and services in towns and villages, cost recovery, resource protection	Integrated mgt. of water infrastructure, service and resource. High level of service and resource protection
Institutional arrangements	Self-help and mutual help and feudal institutions dominate	Informal markets; mutual help and community mgt. institutions	Organized service providers; self-supply declines as do informal community institutions.	Self-supply and informal institutions disappears as all users get linked to a modern water industry.

Figure 7.1   Transformation of informal water economies during overall economic growth

formal water service providers, a high degree of intermediation between water users and water producers, and a water economy that is highly monetized. Between these two extremes lies a continuum that I have artificially collapsed into two intermediate stages of "largely informal" and "formalizing" water economies (Figure 7.1).

It is difficult to find a country in, say, sub-Saharan Africa with a modern water industry of the kind we find in a European country, and vice versa. South Africa is the exception that tests the rule that overall economic prosperity drives the formalization of a water economy. White South Africa—inhabiting its towns and operating large commercial farms in the countryside—is served by what approximates a modern water sector. However, the former homelands, where 90 percent of South Africans live, are served by a water economy even more informal than India's. Much the same can be said about Brazil and even Chile. Within South Asia itself, the dependence of water users on public systems and formal water providers rises as one moves from a poor province or district to a rich one, from villages to cities, and from poor villages to well-off villages (Shah 2006b).

The trouble with the IWRM package, and indeed the global water governance debate as a whole, is its intent to transform, all at once, a predominantly informal water economy into a predominantly formal one—something that would normally be the result of a long process of economic growth and the transformation that comes in its wake. In the IWRM discourse, formalizing informal water economies *is* improving water governance. But evidence across the world suggests that there is no shortcut for a poor society to morph its informal water economy into a formal one; the process by which this happens is organically tied to wider processes of economic growth. When countries try to force the pace of formalization, as they will no doubt do, interventions come unstuck. Interventions are more likely to work if they aim to improve the working of a water economy while it is informal.

Groundwater governance worldwide is a work in progress. Countries like the United States, Spain, Australia, and Mexico struggled with orderly governance of their agricultural groundwater economies for decades before South Asia and the North China Plain had to worry about these problems. And their experience is valuable capital from which the latter societies can draw important lessons. The pioneer countries' experience does not offer solutions, given developing countries' early stage of economic growth, vast number of small, dispersed water abstractors, and highly informal, atomistic irrigation economies. The solutions would work in portions of water economies, such as urban areas and industrial sectors, that are already formal or easy to formalize. Here, water pricing and regulation must certainly be the way to go. But in a diffuse, atomistic irrigation economy, more inventive approaches are called for. The lesson that developing countries need to draw from the pioneer countries is the value of actively engaging with the expanding but unregulated atomistic irrigation economy.

Three distinctive aspects set South Asia's groundwater revolution apart from the pioneer countries. First is the transaction costs, with millions of dispersed users directly withdrawing water from nature. Using pricing, tradable water rights, or even policing and administrative regulation here is infinitely more difficult in logistical terms than in most other countries.

Second is the agrarian poverty aspect. Over the past three decades, the farmer-based groundwater revolution has provided more relief—if not a lasting solution—to millions of the region's agrarian poor than most public policies and programs. Until population pressure on agriculture eases, public policy will involve tightrope walking to balance conflicting objectives. The government will simultaneously persist with the power subsidies responsible for groundwater depletion and implement watershed development intended to recharge aquifers. This apparent incoherence is symptomatic of the dilemma of groundwater governance in South Asia. Efforts to cope with or alleviate depletion through supply-side strategies will tend to be preferred over aggressive demand-side strategies that threaten livelihoods.

Finally, the large numbers of dispersed users over a vast countryside present not only a constraint but also a great opportunity for land and water care that sparsely populated countries do not have. The institutional environment here can often achieve more by joining forces with farming communities and institutional arrangements than by taking a command-and-control position. Rogers and Hall (2003, 10) ask, "can the state steer the society?" In most developing countries "which typically have a strong society and a weak state," the challenge of steering lies in the state's making common cause with the multitudes. The mass-based groundwater recharge movement in Saurashtra (Chapter 6) is but one example of what the state can do in partnership with people. The trouble with regulatory zeal is that it puts the institutional environment and the people in rivalrous relationships when they should be comrades-in-arms.

Bearing the experiences of the pioneer countries in mind, South Asian countries need to look within to find ways of turning PD outcomes in Coase outcomes. In so doing, they can derive useful guidance from the original IWRM philosophy—which emphasized participation and dialectics, enjoined societies to move from a resource development to resource management, highlighted the insight that a natural resource cannot long remain both scarce and free, and encouraged a process for evolving water governance structures tailored to the local context. By so doing, South Asia may not tame its irrigation anarchy, but it can achieve a better compromise between its conflicting priorities—providing succor to its agrarian poor, and protecting its natural resources and environment.

CHAPTER 8

THRIVING IN ANARCHY

Anarchy is order.

— *Pierre-Joseph Proudhon*

In an oft-quoted piece, Ashis Nandi, one of India's best-known socio-logists, once said about India what is true of South Asian society as a whole:

> In India the choice could never be between chaos and stability, but between manageable and unmanageable chaos, between humane and inhumane anarchy, and between tolerable and intolerable disorder. (cited in Guha 2007, 575)

Nandi's characterization also sets limits on the degree of order that can be imposed on irrigation anarchy. The IWRM package—indeed, the water governance discourse—assumes it can tame the anarchy in South Asia's water economy even as the anarchy spreads. IWRM discourse is also inward looking, seeking to redress water sector anomalies by acting within the water sector itself. It seeks shortcuts to formalizing an informal water economy—something that only decades of economic progress can accomplish. But groundwater stress in South Asia is merely a symptom of population overload on farmlands: that is the real problem, and it can hardly be resolved by acting only within the water economy, no matter how improved its governance.

Some strategic indirect approaches may, however, help impose some order in an informal irrigation economy without formalizing it. In these lie important possibilities for South Asia. *Strategic* here implies acting outside a "problem-shed"[1] to produce an impact within it, often using a not-so-obvious cause-effect relation.[2] *Indirect* means not targeting each individual's actions directly.[3] Taming the irrigation anarchy may be impractical, but managing it, or even thriving in it, may be practical. Transforming chaos into stability may prove impossible, but transforming inhumane anarchy into humane anarchy through adaptive approaches may be well within the realm of possibility (see Moench 2007).

My argument in this concluding chapter is threefold. First, in South Asia, IRWM water governance—with a groundwater cess (user charge) that is collected, entitlements that are credible, laws and regulations that are vigorously enforced—should be viewed, at best, as a long-term project, with a timeframe of 30 to 50 years. Second, in the interim, South Asia should explore a range of indirect strategies to influence, shape, and steer its atomistic irrigation economy in a problem-solving mode. Third, the first step in this direction is for policymakers to step out of the colonial irrigation mindset, recognize and understand the new irrigation reality of the region, and forge a groundwater governance regime rooted in this reality.

Ironically, devising *indirect* approaches requires taking a far more integral view of the operating system of a country's water economy than does the IWRM thinking, which is preoccupied with *direct* instruments within the water economy. It requires discovering ways of solving problems without directly touching their cause. It involves exploring the true nature of the water economy and its driving forces, and understanding the backward and forward linkages that connect the water economy with the larger socioeconomic and political fabric. Such explorations may yield ideas for indirect strategies to move from intolerable to tolerable disorder.

Political theorist Theodore Lowi (1972) asserted that the most important thing about governments is that they coerce, and the different ways in which governments coerce generate different kinds of politics, depending on the likelihood of coercion and how coercion is likely to work. Coercion can be positive (sanction) or negative (reward); it can be remote or immediate. More importantly, coercion can work through individual conduct (e.g., withdrawal permit) or through the environment of conduct (e.g., electricity pricing and supply policies).

In analyzing how different policies work, Lowi (1972, 299) writes,

> ... some policies do not come into operation until there is a question about someone's behavior ... In strong contrast, some policies do not need to wait for a particular behavior, but rather do not touch behavior directly at all. Instead they work through the environment of conduct. For example, a minor change in the Federal Reserve discount rate can have a major impact on my propensity to invest, yet no official need know of my existence.

Indirect strategies operate through the environment of conduct. These may be potent, even if imprecise; their main advantage, however, is their ease—their low transaction costs,[4] which are best viewed in a broad sense as the costs of running an economic system (Arrow 1969, cited in Brennan 2002, 21). Politicians, operating from a higher vantage point, think of such strategies more readily than water researchers and managers. And it is following their often contradictory stances that one gleans ideas about indirect strategies. Chief Minister Amarinder Singh's answer to groundwater stress in the Indian Punjab was to wean farmers away from the rice-wheat system to high-value orchard crops amenable to microirrigation. Similarly, Chief Minister Raj Sekhar Reddy of Andhra Pradesh came to power on the promise of free farm electricity but soon imposed a seven-hours-a-day power ration and launched a campaign to propagate a system of rice intensification intended to reduce rice irrigation needs as well as electricity subsidies.

Bigger changes in the local or global theater may open new windows of opportunity for groundwater governance. In the not-so-distant future, global farm trade can offer a powerful tool for national water management through virtual water trade. Of the many benefits of shifting the geography of South Asia's rice-wheat system from northwestern parts of the Indo-Gangetic basin to eastern parts by redesigning the support prices and the government procurement system, an important one would be easing groundwater stress in the former regions, something that regulating pumping by farmers may not achieve. Expansion of rural employment in Bangladesh's garment manufacturing industry helped ease water stress in agriculture; so did the rise of the remittance economy and the shift from paddy to plantation crops in Kerala. The Chinese leaders' 30-year plan to move the country's 400 million farming population to off-farm livelihoods may be part of a larger development strategy, but it will work wonders in easing groundwater stress in the North China Plain. These examples require changes in a larger system that may, as a spillover, correct anomalies in a particular subsystem, such as the water economy.

Also available are indirect levers of influencing a system by acting on a subsystem. In controlling new tube wells in South Asia, it may be easier to regulate and police the activities of drillers than those of farmers, who are far more numerous and dispersed. Electricity managers may have greater leverage in the groundwater economy than even groundwater managers. Subsidizing the raw materials that go into the manufacture of water-saving microirrigation systems may reduce their prices to farmers more than direct subsidies targeted to adopters. Small catalytic action and support may unleash vast energies and resources of farming communities in groundwater stressed hard-rock regions to improve groundwater balance. Looking outside the water sector to devise levers to manipulate the agricultural water economy can help policymakers devise unconventional interventions that fit the unique context of the region. Such interventions may not have precision, in the sense of influencing the behavior of a particular user in a particular area in a desired direction; however, they can be potent in bringing about large-scale changes in desired direction at the sectoral level.

Over the past few years, the International Water Management Institute (IWMI)[5] has explored opportunities for strategic indirect approaches that have proved politically feasible and have technoeconomic merit. Based on this work, I have come to believe that for designing practical approaches to groundwater governance, this is the way to go. In the next three sections, I offer three brief cases that illustrate how happenings outside South Asia's groundwater economy have influenced its inner workings. The first describes how the state of Gujarat has begun to use electricity policies to reshape its groundwater economy. The second outlines a strategic intervention designed to mobilize farmers' energies and resources in a mass-based groundwater recharge program. The third illustrates a "butterfly effect;" it shows how the emergence of a particular pattern of pump industry organization in China after 1970 fueled a pump irrigation revolution in Bangladesh, Vietnam, and Cambodia, while a policy designed to support smallholder irrigation sustained the monopoly of an inefficient domestic pump industry that condemned India's smallholders to heavy, expensive, and fuel-wasting pumps for 30 years.

Gujarat's *Jyotirgram* Scheme

In large swaths of India, groundwater aquifers are under threat from an energy-irrigation gridlock that has become a political conundrum (Shah et al. 2004c). In Chapter 5, I argued that arresting groundwater depletion in much of western and peninsular India is, in principle, surprisingly easy: eliminate farm power subsidies, and the groundwater use would shrink in quick time. The human cost in terms of agrarian livelihoods, however, would be massive, since irrigated agriculture would come to a grinding halt in most areas where well irrigation at commercially priced electricity would become unviable (Somanathan and Ravindranath 2006). Electricity subsidies began as the cause of widespread groundwater depletion in South Asia, but now, they are its result, too. The large-scale political mobilization of farmers and the powerful vote-bank politics aimed single-mindedly at preserving farm-power subsidy are an indication of how central the energy-irrigation nexus has become in South Asian agriculture and its mass politics.

Direly needed in South Asia is a politically feasible conjoint solution that must achieve three objectives at once: first, ease the deadweight subsidy burden on the electricity industry and nonfarm electricity users; second, protect agrarian livelihoods and social stability; and third, ease groundwater stress by controlling overdraft. The solution long favored is to revert to metering farm power and charge farmers at the commercial rate. The problem has been the political feasibility of doing this. Farmers foresaw, correctly, that metering of tube wells was the proverbial camel to be kept out of the tent. Several chief ministers of Indian states announced metering but met opposition on unprecedented scale; one, in Madhya Pradesh, even found his party voted out. In Andhra Pradesh, a chief minister got elected on the promise of free farm power and then entrenched his position by extending his promise to 2017. For more than a decade now, the energy-groundwater nexus has stood at an impasse.

In Gujarat, the government has moved to break this impasse by acting on a second-best strategy. In recent years, throughout South Asia, electric tube well owners who pay a flat tariff use 25 to 40 percent more energy and groundwater per hectare than diesel tube well owners because of the illusion of free power[6] (Shah et al. 2004c; see also Shah et al. 2006); some of this excess water and power use involves waste, and in curtailing this waste lies a big opportunity to dent the three problems at once. IWMI researchers argued for a flat farm power tariff but with intelligent rationing of supply based on the notion that farmers' demand for power is derived from their demand for irrigation: their irrigation needs peak on the 30 to 40 days of the year when crops face moisture stress, and if farmers receive full power supply on these days, they can make do with a small maintenance ration of three or four hours daily during the remainder of the year. This would be like mimicking a high-performing canal irrigation system, and in regions where electric pumps are the only means to draw groundwater, electricity rationing also implies groundwater rationing. To make such rationing possible, the researchers suggested separating feeders supplying power to tube wells from other rural feeders. Farmers, researchers asserted, would oppose rationing but could be won over by a more predictable and reliable power supply, improved quality (in terms of voltage, frequency, and minimum interruptions), and power supply schedules better matched to periods of moisture stress.

That scheme was to be implemented in the complex political economy of farm power supply. In Gujarat, as elsewhere in India, since the 1980s, the energy-irrigation nexus has degenerated into a prolonged war of wits between the government and increasingly organized farmer lobbies. A major fallout was serious deterioration in the quality of rural life and stagnation in the non-farm rural economy. Over the years, to control farm power subsidies, the government began reducing the hours of three-phase rural power supply, used by tube well owners, while maintaining 24-hour single- or two-phase power, sufficient for most rural domestic users. Farm power quality also deteriorated as electricity board officials began treating agriculture as a loss leader and farmers as residual customers; power came to farms with low voltage and frequent trips, generally at night without any prior announcement of schedule. Farmers reconciled themselves to poor-quality power as the price of subsidy. However, all nonfarm cottage enterprises, schools, health clinics, and shops were hit by the rationing of three-phase power, even though they paid metered charge. Worst of all, farmers began rampant use of phase-splitting capacitors (locally called *tota*) to run their motors on two- or even single-phase power supply. This practice helped them beat the power rationing but reducing the voltage for all the rural power users downstream. Ironically, the poorest of Gujarat farmers—the landless sharecroppers and marginal farmers—benefited from the scourge of the capacitors because tube well owners sold them irrigation aplenty at a low price with the help of "stolen power."

In 2003, the government of Gujarat pioneered a bold plan—the *Jyotirgram* ("Lighted Village") scheme—which incorporated the core ideas of the second-best strategy of intelligent rationing suggested by IWMI researchers (Figure 8.1). During 2003–2006, it invested around US$260 million to separate farm feeders from nonfarm feeder lines that served domestic and nonfarm commercial users in rural areas. By 2006, Gujarat covered almost all its 18,000 villages under the *Jyotirgram* scheme. Under the new regime, the villages get 24-hour three-phase power supply for domestic uses, schools, hospitals, and village industries, and farmers get eight hours of full-voltage three-phase power, but on an announced schedule. Because feeders supplying farms are shut off, the capacitors no longer work, and the rationing of farm power supply to eight hours a day is nearly complete.

A recent appraisal of the impact of the *Jyotirgram* scheme (Shah and Verma 2008), carried out with the help of local researchers in 11 districts of Gujarat, showed that it has produced profound impacts—intended and otherwise. The biggest success was insulating homes and the nonfarm rural economy from the invidious energy-irrigation nexus. The largest class of beneficiaries proved to be rural women and schoolchildren, who suddenly experienced a quantum jump in quality of life and productivity from uninterrupted 24-hour three-phase power supply. Other beneficiaries are nonfarm enterprises and village institutions, such as dairy cooperatives, schools, health centers, cottage industries, shops, and workshops, all of which experienced increased output and employment and reduced costs with 24/7 three-phase power supply. Our interactions with some 300 respondents in 11 districts of Gujarat suggested different groups of winners and losers from *Jyotirgram*, as set out in Table 8-1.

Tube well owners gave a mixed response: power rationing had reduced irrigated areas, but better-quality power according to a fixed, announced schedule helped them stretch the power ration. The power economy of the state began looking up, too. During the past five years, Gujarat's electricity board has improved its financial performance more than those of most other Indian states, thanks to a clutch of reforms of which *Jyotirgram* scheme is a major component. Aggregate use of power in groundwater irrigation fell 37 percent, from 15.7 billion units per year in 2001 to 9.9 billion units in 2006, which also meant reduced groundwater draft. The effect was a halving of aggregate farm power subsidy, from US$788 million in 2001–2002 to US$388 million in 2006–2007.

Above all else, *Jyotirgram* pioneered real-time comanagement of electricity and groundwater of the kind found nowhere else in the world. It created an on-off groundwater economy that is amenable to vigorous regulation at

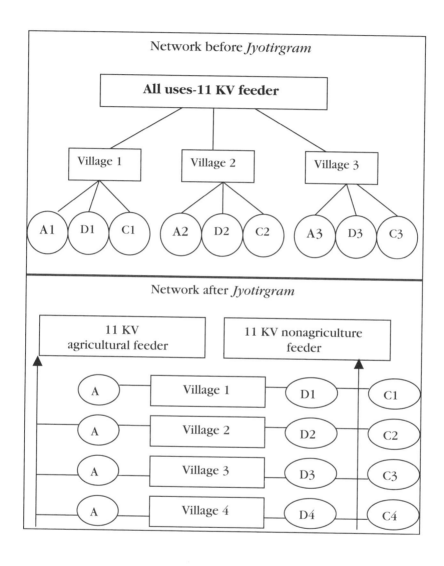

A= WEM owners
D= Domestic power consumers
C= Commercial power consumers

Figure 8.1   Rewiring of rural electricity infrastructure under *Jyotirgram* ("lighted village")
scheme, Gujarat

Table 8-1   Impacts of *Jyotirgram* scheme on Gujarat's rural society

Stakeholder group	Impact
Rural housewives, domestic users	+++++
Students, teachers, patients, doctors	+++++
Nonfarm trades, shops, cottage industries, rice mills, dairy co-ops, banks, cooperatives	+++++
Pump repair, motor rewinding, tube well deepening	-----
Tube well owners: quality and reliability of power supply	+++
Tube well owners: hours of power supply	---
Water buyers, landless laborers, tenants	-----
Groundwater-irrigated area	---

different levels. Arguably, there is nothing that the IWRM instruments—water laws, tradable groundwater rights, groundwater cess—can do that *Jyotirgram* cannot do better and quicker. Skeptics argued that groundwater management through electricity pricing and rationing would be too gross an approach, incapable of being fine-tuned to local situations (Moench 1995). Experience shows that *Jyotirgram* is capable of sophisticated groundwater management, and in sheer regulatory power and simplicity, it makes other approaches—such as Mexico's COTAS and groundwater districts—look like Rube Goldberg[7] contraptions. In hard-rock areas, farmers were frustrated with eight hours of power supply in one spell; here, wells need time to recoup after pumping for a few hours and cannot be pumped for eight hours continuously. Gujarat's electricity companies have responded by dividing their power ration into two or three daily installments, with a time interval for wells to recoup. Post-*Jyotirgram* in Gujarat, electricity supply can be used to reduce groundwater draft in resource-stressed areas and stimulate it in water-abundant or waterlogged areas, to encourage conjunctive use of ground and surface water; and to reward "electricity feeder communities" that invest in groundwater recharge and penalize villages that overdraw without regard for future needs. In this sense, *Jyotirgram* has transformed what was a highly degenerate electricity-groundwater nexus into a rational one.

Especially in groundwater-stressed areas, even while complaining about power rationing, farmers recognized that unbridled competitive pumping of groundwater must eventually lead to disaster, and that on their own, farmers would not forge collective self-regulation. *Jyotirgram* put a cap on collective groundwater withdrawal in a manner most farmers considered fair and just. Many therefore welcomed *Jyotirgram* for limiting competitive pumping and addressing the common-property externality inherent in groundwater irrigation.

As it is managed now, *Jyotirgram* has a big downside: its brunt is borne largely by marginal farmers and the landless, who must buy tube well irrigation. Since power rationing is effective, groundwater markets have shrunk, with water prices soaring by 35 to 40 percent and driving many agrarian poor out of irrigation, and thus farming. Many tube well owners have discontinued water selling altogether. There is no way of completely eliminating the burden on the agrarian poor except by increasing hours of power supply— and increasing the subsidy—that tube well owners everywhere want.

In this context, the only recommendation of the original second-best proposal of IWMI researchers that *Jyotirgram* has not acted on opens a window of opportunity: it can significantly reduce the misery of the agrarian poor by replacing the present rationing scheme of eight hours of daily power supply by a demand-adjusted scheme. An assessment by Shah and Verma (2008) asked more than 200 tube well owners from different parts of Gujarat how they would like their power ration allocated across the year; the results are summarized in Figure 8.2, which suggests that a demand-adjusted supply schedule would be more consistent with irrigation requirements than the

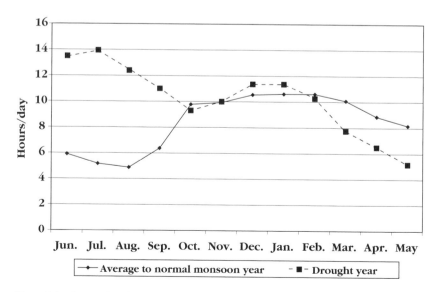

Figure 8.2   Farmers' preferred monthly power allocations under *Jyotirgram* scheme, Gujarat

present policy of providing eight hours daily. This would stimulate water markets and benefit the sharecroppers and marginal farmers without compromising the other gains of the scheme.

Many other regions in South Asia are waking up to the potential offered by intelligent comanagement of electricity and groundwater. Andhra Pradesh offers free power but rations it for seven hours a day. Punjab has begun whittling down farm power supply in summer to compel farmers to delay paddy transplantation by a month to reduce groundwater stress. In contrast, Baluchistan, which levies a flat rate of Rs. 4,000 per year per tube well regardless of pump size or utilization and without effective power rationing, offers an example of how farm power policies can ruin aquifers and bankrupt the electricity industry. Indeed, under some conditions, intelligently rationed power supply under a flat tariff may be a better solution than a metered tariff with unlimited power supply, as the current received wisdom suggests.

Recharge Program for Peninsular India

Besides alluvial western and northwestern South Asia, the hard-rock peninsular region, some 65 percent of India's territory, is the region's other major groundwater "hotspot." Farmers in this mostly semiarid region have become highly dependent on groundwater and are now coming to grief. A former chairman of India's Central Groundwater Board once said that the region's miseries were well deserved: the aquifers just did not have the groundwater the farmers had been developing all these years. However, as we saw in Chapters 2 and 6, smallholders throughout South Asia have held on to their wells as drowning men would clutch straws to survive. Rapid expansion of groundwater irrigation in peninsular India has meant that of the 1,065 blocks[8] (of India's total 6,572 blocks) that the Central Groundwater Board has identified as critical or overexploited groundwater areas, more than 80 percent are in the seven problem states of Andhra Pradesh, Gujarat, Karnataka, Madhya Pradesh, Maharashtra, Rajasthan, and Tamilnadu. Together, these account for some 100 billion m^3 of groundwater withdrawals per year, mostly for irrigating (a conservatively estimated) 15 million ha. This is an important groundwater problem shed of South Asia (Table 8-2).

South Asian thinking on groundwater recharge is often swayed by the grandiose western U.S. experiments with water banking or the Australian

Table 8-2   Geographic distribution of boreholes and dugwells in India

	Irrigation wells (million)	Dugwells (%)	Bore/ tube wells (%)
Indo-Gangetic Basin states: Assam, Bihar, Haryana, Punjab, Uttar Pradesh, Uttaranchal, West Bengal	6.07	5.1	94.9
Hard-rock areas of western and peninusular India[a]: Andhra Pradesh, Chhatisgarh, Gujarat, Jharkhan, Karnataka, Kerala, Madhya Pradesh, Maharashtra, Orissa, Rajasthan, Tamilnadu	12.55	62.9	37.1

[a]Chhattisgarh, Jharkhand and Orissa have mostly hard-rock aquifers but little groundwater use in agriculture.
Source: Third Minor Irrigation Census of India, 2000–01

"ASR" projects of aquifer storage and recharge, using water-spreading or injection techniques. These often involve resourceful commercial or public organizations that transform vast, unpeopled swaths of sandy alluvial areas into recharge basins to create substantial groundwater storage available for withdrawal and transport elsewhere in times of need. In South Asia, this model requires considerable adaptation to local conditions, primarily because it is difficult to find large unpeopled territories suitable for large-scale recharge. Equally constraining is the lack of commercial possibilities that make such investments worthwhile, at least for the present. Because of the organization of its water economy and the nature of aquifers, the model that makes the best sense in South Asia involves in situ recharge technologies deploying the energies and enterprise of its people.

Compared with the alluvial aquifers of Ganga basin, hard-rock aquifers offer smaller storage and lower recharge rates. Scientists therefore tend to be lukewarm about large-scale recharge projects in hard-rock areas. However, as we saw in Chapter 6, the limitations of hard-rock aquifers can actually turn into advantages for a mass-based, decentralized recharge program in at least three respects. First, even a small recharge volume shows up in overbrimming wells, creating a "recharge illusion" that sustains a mass movement.[9] Second, during a dry spell, at least some part of the recharged water can be retrieved by owners of recharge-enabled wells. Finally, hard-rock areas in India are speckled with millions of large, open dug wells with a diameter of five to 12 meters and a depth of up to 60 meters or even more, used as storage chambers or collector wells; water trickles into the empty well from nearby fractures and fissures all night for the owner to withdraw the following morning. As we saw in Chapter 6, with groundwater depletion, farmers have begun, besides deepening their wells, making horizontal and vertical bores—often 200 feet or longer—within their dug wells to enhance their "connectivity" with water-bearing formations. Dug wells used for water extraction can also be excellent vehicles for distributed groundwater recharge.

Hard-rock India is also the major site of the energy-irrigation nexus, with electricity subsidies playing a critical role in smallholder survival strategies but also in impeding the emergence of a healthy power economy. With falling water levels, diesel pumps have rapidly given way to submersible electric pumps. Now more than 80 percent of the irrigation wells here are fitted with electric pumps, and 62 percent of India's electrified wells are concentrated in the seven problem states (Shah 2006b). These also account for the bulk of the estimated US$5 billion annual power subsidy to agriculture, which is directly linked to groundwater depletion. These seven states therefore have to be the focus of the country's groundwater recharge strategy.

In a unique scenario, the seven hard-rock Indian states have, among them, 8.2 million dug wells, many going out of use because of groundwater depletion but still worth some US$20 billion in terms of replacement value (see Table 8-2). Among these seven states, there are 100 districts that account for more than 60 percent of India's critical and overexploited blocks. These have seven million of India's 10 million dug wells, and at rate of 1,000 m³ each time they are filled with monsoon water, they can dispatch seven billion m³ of monsoon floodwater to water-bearing hard-rock formations. Here is where falling water tables have the most serious impact, drying up wells and forcing farmers to revert to rain-fed farming. Outside the Punjab, most recent farmer suicides are reported from these districts, and groundwater stress is commonly an important source of agrarian distress in these regions. It is in these 100 districts that the Government of India has launched a US$450 million pilot scheme for a recharge movement involving dug wells, based on the IWMI research summarized below (Shah 2006b).

IWMI researchers have argued that much of the distress of these 100 districts can be alleviated—at a relatively minor cost—by catalyzing a well-designed people's program that adopts the dug well as the recharge vehicle and its farmer owner as its driver, as in Saurashtra. Watershed development programs and tank desilting, often suggested, are only a limited answer to groundwater depletion in hard-rock India. Tanks, small water-harvesting structures with poor surface-area-to-depth ratio, often act as evaporation pans, losing more water to evaporation than is available for recharging the aquifers. This is especially the case because they are not regularly desilted. In the old times, when groundwater withdrawal was a small fraction of what it is today and population density was much smaller, irrigation tanks made sense, but today, they need to be reinvented. On their own, farmer communities in many of these districts are converting their centuries-old irrigation tanks into percolation tanks to increase recharge to their wells, and governments have begun supporting their efforts. Even at the river basin level, storing monsoon flood waters in groundwater makes better sense than surface storage because "it is effective in minimizing water loss due to evaporation . . . [it involves] no loss of . . . land by inundation . . . [and] where channels are used for groundwater recharge, 'multiple use' benefits have also been achieved" (Sakthivadivel 2007, *200*). As Keller et al. (2000) have shown, groundwater offers the best form of storage on all criteria barring one: the slow rate of natural recharge. Aggressive mass-based dug well recharge can help overcome this limitation.

Moreover, watershed programs have an incentive compatibility problem: they demand collective community action to create groundwater recharge that gets captured largely by well owners. This is why watershed programs will always need external catalysis and support. Dug well recharge programs have an opposite incentive structure: private well owners invest in dug well recharge for a share in creating common pool recharge that all groundwater users benefit from. Once dug well owners begin to value their share, it can become a self-sustaining movement.

What prevents the momentum of a dug well-based groundwater recharge program from building up might be called an unlearning barrier. The Indian farmer has been accustomed, from time immemorial, to viewing the muddy floodwaters of monsoon rains as a nuisance, to be diverted in a hurry to the field downstream and never allowed near his dug well, lest it get silted up. This thinking was appropriate when wells were few and aquifers full, but not any longer. Dug well owners in hard-rock areas need to learn to view monsoon floodwaters as a resource, to be desilted and diverted into the dug well. They also need to accept well desilting every three or four years as a standard operating procedure of well irrigation, as has happened in Saurashtra. If Saurashtra's experience over the past 15 years is any guide, a dug well-based groundwater recharge program can revive the agrarian economies of the seven hard-rock aquifer states. True, hard-rock aquifers so recharged cannot ensure year-round groundwater availability, but if done on a large enough scale, *kharif* crop insurance from frequent dry spells is a certain and substantial benefit.

Shah (2006b) has suggested a five-point program to kickstart a dug well recharge movement in hard-rock India: (1) a massive education, information, and communication campaign with the help of NGOs and local community organizations, to reeducate farmers about the value of monsoon floodwaters and the benefits of dug well recharge; (2) technical and other support to help farmers construct desiltation chambers and redirect field drains to bring runoff to the wells rather than carry it away; (3) incentives to help farmers deepen their dug wells and make lateral bores within wells to enhance their connectivity with water-bearing formations, both to improve well yield and to increase the recharge capacity of dug wells; (4) undertaking dug well recharge in a campaign mode because when most or all dug wells in a locality are recharged, the impact is much greater than when scattered dug wells are recharged; and (5) integrating dug well recharge as a core element of ongoing watershed and tank rehabilitation programs.

With effective education, dug well recharge is likely to be well received for many reasons. For one, modifying a well for recharge costs little (US$40–$100), and the structures are also easy and inexpensive to maintain. Then, farmers in hard-rock regions will easily see the recharge-ready dug well as a partial bank account and visualize its potential private benefit. If all the seven million wells in 100 groundwater-stressed hard-rock districts of India are fitted with recharge shafts, in a normal monsoon with three or four big rainfall events, they can augment natural groundwater recharge by 20 to 30 km^3 and substantially ease the groundwater stress in these districts. Dug well recharge will also help reduce fluoride concentration in groundwater, as evident from the experience from Saurashtra. This may be a major benefit in terms of public health, especially for the poor and women, who are particularly at risk of dental and skeletal fluorosis because of the calcium deficit in their diets. Finally, at the national level, the economics of dug well recharge are highly favorable. US$1 billion invested in modifying 10 million dug wells for recharge could provide *kharif* crop insurance for some 25 million ha in the seven states. This is US$40 per ha, compared with the US$4,000 required to create an additional ha of canal command. The savings in electricity subsidies from reducing the pumping head itself would pay for the dug well recharge program many times over.

Groundwater recharge programs in South Asia cannot work in a central-ized mode; they have to run on the same popular energy that created South Asia's atomistic irrigation anarchy in the first place. Central to making a suc-cess of groundwater recharge in South Asia, then, is finding common ground between formal hydrology and "popular hydrology" (Chapter 6). Scientists want recharge structures sited near recharge zones; villagers want them close to their wells. Scientists recommend injection tube wells to counter the silta-tion that impedes recharge; farmers just direct floodwaters into their wells after filtering. Scientists worry about upstream-downstream externalities; farmers believe that everyone lives downstream. Scientists write off hard-rock aquifers for having too little storage to justify the prolific growth in recharge structures; farmers say a recharge structure is worthwhile if the well provides even 1,000 m^3 of irrigation per ha in a drought. Hydrologists keep writing the obituary of the recharge movement, but the movement has spread from eastern Rajasthan to Gujarat, thence to Madhya Pradesh and Andhra Pradesh. Protagonists think that with better planning and larger coverage, a decentralized recharge movement can be a major response to India's groundwater depletion because water tables in pockets of inten-sive use could rebound close to predevelopment levels at the end of a good monsoon season.

Daxi to the Aid of the Agrarian Poor in Bangladesh

The quarter-century from 1975 to 2000 was the golden age of smallholder irrigation in the Ganga-Meghna-Brahmaputra basin, encompassing Bangla-desh, Nepal Terai, and eastern India. The basin floats over one of the most abundant aquifer systems in the world; it is also home to one of the largest concentrations of agrarian poverty that is rapidly turning even more adverse. Stimulating groundwater use to improve livelihoods has been one of the regional governments' top rural development priorities. And this was achieved to some extent with rapid expansion in shallow tube wells powered with diesel engines. As we saw in Chapter 5, the politics of the energy-irrigation nexus led to "dieselization" of the groundwater irrigation economy of the entire Indo-Gangetic basin (Table 8-3), and we saw in Chapter 4 that during the 1980s and 1990s, "diesel shallows" powered a *boro* rice revolution that transformed Bangladesh from a rice deficit country to a rice exporter; these also helped West Bengal overcome its century-old agrarian stagnation and achieve front-ranking agrarian growth rates.

Table 8-3   Geographic distribution of electric and diesel irrigation pumps in South Asia

	Number of irrigation pumps (million)	Diesel (%)	Electric (%)
Pakistan	0.93	89.6	10.4
Bangladesh	1.18	96.7	3.3
Eastern India: Assam, West Bengal, Bihar, Orissa, Jharkhand, Orissa, Uttar Pradesh, Uttaranchal, West Bengal	5.09	84.0	16.0
Western and Southern India: Andhra Pradesh, Gujarat, Haryana, Karnataka, Kerala, Madhya Pradesh, Maharashtra, Punjab, Rajasthan, Tamilnadu	11.69	19.4	80.6

Sources: 1. Pakistan figures are from Pakistan Agricultural Machinery Census 2004.
2. Bangladesh figures are from Mandal 2006.
3. Figures for Indian states are from the third Minor Irrigation Census 2000–01.

Since 2000, however, the region's pump irrigation economy has begun shrinking in response to a growing energy squeeze. This squeeze is a combined outcome of the utilities' progressive reduction in the quantity and quality of power supplied to agriculture as a desperate means to contain farm subsidies, the growing difficulty and capital cost of acquiring new electricity connections, and an eightfold increase in the nominal price of diesel during 1990–2007, when the nominal rice price rose by less than 50 percent. In 1990, in eastern India and Bangladesh, a liter of diesel cost a kilogram of rice; in 2007, a liter of diesel took six kg of rice. And since the groundwater economy of the Indo-Gangetic basin has come to depend on diesel, as evident in Table 8-3, it has been hit hard by soaring oil prices.

Of even greater significance for the poor is the response of groundwater markets to the rise in diesel prices because the poorest strata of the region's peasants depend on purchased irrigation. Because groundwater markets are natural oligopolies (Shah 1993), pump owners use diesel price increases to raise their pump rental rates in tandem with every major rise in diesel price, even though pumps themselves became cheaper during 1990–2007. In Mirzapur, Uttar Pradesh, between 1990 and 2007, diesel prices rose from US$0.11 to $0.85 per liter, but the rate buyers incur per hour of pump irrigation with a five-hp pump increased from US$0.59 to $2.30 an hour, far more than needed to cover the increase in fuel cost. Another characteristic of this relationship has been the downward stickiness of pump irrigation prices:

every time there is a big increase in diesel price, pump irrigation price tends to jump, but the reverse is never the case.

A reconnaissance of the impoverishing impact of the energy squeeze on the agrarian poor in more than 20 villages scattered over eastern India, Pakistan, Nepal Terai and Bangladesh found that economizing on diesel—by irrigating less and taking the yield cut—was a common response (Shah 2007b; Ul Hassan et al. 2007). But many smallholders changed crops, took up vegetable cultivation, and entered into crop-sharing contracts with water sellers in which they became laborers on their own fields. Owners of electric tube wells, wherever we could find some, experienced hardening of their monopoly power vis-à-vis their customers. A very common response of the poor, however, was to give up pump irrigation and revert to rain-fed farming, or quit farming altogether and migrate.

The most preferred way out of the energy squeeze for eastern India's farmers would be rapid expansion of electricity connections for shallow tube wells. It is a travesty that parts of South Asia—mostly the Indo-Gangetic basin, where groundwater irrigation could do most good—are practically deelectrified. As Table 8-3 shows, diesel pumps are increasingly the mainstay of groundwater irrigation in the basin, whereas electric pumps dominate in western and peninsular India. In Chapter 5, we explored the underlying political economy and the potential gains of promoting electric pumps in the basin. However, this is unlikely to happen soon, if at all. Temporary relief has come from unlikely quarters: China. The diesel pump market in the basin was long dominated by the Indian pump industry, with the most popular brand being Kirloskar, whose five-hp diesel engine was the industry standard for decades. Thanks to an oligopolistic market structure and protection offered by government subsidies on tube well irrigation bolstered by import restrictions, the Indian pump industry faced little incentive or pressure to invest in innovation and product improvement. The typical Indian diesel pump cost US$350 or more, weighed up to 325 kg, needed a bullock cart to move around, and burned one liter of diesel an hour.

The story was entirely different in China, where the pump industry was differently organized. Until the 1970s, China's pump industry specialized in heavy-duty irrigation pumps for collectives. Then there emerged demand for small pumps, as Chinese agriculture was decollectivized and numerous very small farms appeared under the Household Responsibility System. At the same time, industrial reforms allowed the emergence of small, profit-oriented rural manufacturers. As trade liberalization in South and Southeast

Asia reduced tariffs and opened up markets, there was further impetus for an export-oriented pump industry. The combined result was the rise in China of a fiercely competitive pump industry organized in distributed production clusters, exemplified in the city of Daxi, "the home of China's small water pumps," as it is described in Huang et al. (2007). Daxi has thousands of cottage-scale, owner-operated manufactories of pumps and components. Most units are tiny, unregistered family firms with but a few workers. Having emerged as a city of pump manufacture, Daxi has attracted a rich pool of skills and cheap labor. Close proximity of production units has resulted in both intense competition and cooperation. Since manufacturers achieve a high level of specialization, costs are pared to the minimum. This has meant that even compared with pumps manufactured elsewhere in China, the costs of Daxi pumps are a good 30 percent lower. A Daxi pump is small, weighs only 45 kg, and costs just US$90. It runs on diesel or kerosene and is fuel efficient compared with Indian engines, running for two hours per liter of fuel.

Bangladesh and Vietnam were among the early beneficiaries of the Daxi-type pumps. When Bangladesh liberalized trade and imports in irrigation equipment in late 1970s, its farmers had a choice between heavy, fuel-inefficient Indian pumps and efficient, light, but expensive Japanese Honda pumps. But then came the Chinese pumps, which were lighter, cheaper, more fuel efficient, and less expensive to maintain than either Indian or Japanese pumps. By the 1990s, more than 90 percent of the diesel pumps purchased in Bangladesh were Chinese.

Chinese pumps only recently arrived in eastern India, through an osmotic process rather than a planned move. Some second-hand Chinese pumps smuggled across the Bangladesh border attracted farmers' attention, and soon enough, there followed a deluge of smuggled second-hand Chinese pumps. Official imports began in 1998. Now, of every 100 new diesel pump assemblies purchased in West Bengal, more than 90 have Chinese engines. Kolkatta has emerged as the epicenter of Chinese pump diffusion. Most Chinese brands sell at 35 to 40 percent of the price of erstwhile market leader Kirloskar and Honda 4-hp pumps. Interviews with pump dealers in Kolkatta confirmed that farmers preferred the Chinese pumps for their low price, much higher fuel efficiency, and ability to run on kerosene, which is cheaper than diesel.

The benefits provided by Chinese pumps to Ganga basin's agrarian poor will likely not last beyond the next one or two major diesel price increases. Nevertheless, the account illustrates the importance of indirect strategic linkages. India's policymakers were thinking all along that their pump subsidies were helping small and marginal farmers. In reality, they entrenched the monopoly of an inefficient pump industry and deprived the Indian farmer of Daxi pumps long after the Bangladeshi farmers had begun realizing their benefits.

Building on Local Institutional Arrangements

Exploring the maze of backward and forward linkages that drive the operating system of atomistic irrigation economy is necessary to devise a practical groundwater governance regime capable of solving problems without touching their causes. Separating the feeders that convey power to tube wells from nonfarm consumers, reeducating farmers about the power of dug wells as recharge structures, and liberalizing trade in irrigation equipment—each represents an indirect intervention capable of producing sectorwide change. Such strategies are seldom the outcomes of discussions about water governance or IWRM, however, because of the preoccupation with direct instruments. In Lowi's words, the indirect approaches work by intervening in the environment of conduct rather than by trying to modify individual conduct. Their strength is low transaction cost.

Contrast that with three arenas in which South Asia's water policy needs rethinking. The first is the arena of *tokenism,* where policy action entails low transaction costs but is cosmetic. Tokenism creates a façade of action but in fact detracts from it. India's water policy statements of 1987 and 2002 are classic examples of nonpolicies setting "targets without teeth": little or nothing has been implemented.[10] Water policies issued by various Indian states, likewise, are not designed to materially change anything. Similar is the fate of a clutch of new water laws made in response not so much to a local buy-in as to international debates or donor conditions. In informal water economies like South Asia's, the high transaction costs of enforcing strong water laws and regulations render these ineffectual. To reduce transaction costs and still meet donors' demands, clauses that are likely to have effect (and therefore be violated) are often progressively removed, or enforcers shy away from enforcement.

The second is the arena of *institutional innovation.* Here, action is dominated by ideas that survive not because they have worked but because they have become "development narratives" (Roe 1991). The challenge in dealing with these, as Roe points out, is either improving an obsolete narrative or proposing a counternarrative. A fertile arena for such engagement is policy-makers' and social researchers' attachment to the "communitarian ideal"—the notion that people readily cooperate to take over the responsibility of participatory, democratic management of virtually anything, whether groundwater, watersheds, forests, irrigation systems, or river basins. Its having worked—or even been tried—in a few situations in exceptional conditions becomes the basis for designs of major programs of institutional reform, commonly bankrolled by international donors and lenders. Participatory irrigation management (of canal systems, tanks, lift irrigation systems) is one such development narrative. Management of aquifers by groundwater user organizations, such as Mexico's COTAS (Chapter 7), is another. What is wrong about these defunct development narratives is that they discourage innovative ideas. What is worse, they overshadow spontaneous, *swayambhoo* (self-creating) local institutional formation and preclude the learning of lessons these offer about what might work and why.

That leads to the third arena, *learning and action:* opportunities to hone indirect strategic approaches by learning from institutional arrangements created by a strong society confronted with a weak state. When perceived payoffs are high and transaction costs low, people devise efficient institutional arrangements that serve purposes important to them. However, rather than studying, nurturing, engaging with, influencing, and replicating these institutions, the dominant discourse, preoccupied with its development narratives, has kept these spontaneous institutions at arm's length, when it has not weakened them.

Table 8-4 describes a sample of four such local institutional arrangements in India that the water policy discourse has bypassed. The rapid rise of reverse osmosis plants as a cottage industry in rural Gujarat is a powerful response to the rising fluoride levels in drinking water, a negative externality created by tube well irrigation. Goverment agencies should nurture this industry as a working alternative to hundreds of failed community-managed water treatment plants, but in Gujarat, the fledgling rural industry got nearly closed down because the Bureau of Indian Standards required each small plant to invest in a laboratory costing more than the plant itself instead of allowing clusters of units to share one (Indu 2002).

Tube well companies in North Gujarat offer a contrasting example. Throughout India, efforts to turn over unprofitable government tube wells to idealized farmer cooperatives have proved resounding failures. After a similar experience, Gujarat learned from the experience of its informal tube well

Table 8-4 Characteristics of some spontaneous water institutions in Gujarat

	Reverse osmosis plants in North Gujarat's cottage industry	Tube well companies of North Gujarat and Gujarat's public tube well transfer program	Irrigation institutions unfolding in Narmada command and Upper Krishna Basin	Decentralized groundwater recharge movement of Saurashtra
Scale of the institution	Around 300 plants in Gujarat	8–10 thousand companies in North Gujarat	Several thousand new pumps installed annually	300,000 recharge wells; 100,000 check dams
Economic contribution	Operate water treatment capacity to provide fluoride-free water	Create irrigation potential where individual farmers cannot	Private investment in water distribution infrastructure; expansion of Narmada irrigation	Improved greatly security of *kharif* crop, possible *rabi* crop; stabilized the regional farm economy
Raison d'être	To profit from serving emerging demand for fluoride-free water by investing in reverse-osmosis plant	To pool capital and share risks of tube well failure in over-exploited aquifer	To profit by distributing Narmada water by lifting water from canals and transporting it by rubber pipe	To improve water availability in wells for emergency irrigation
Mode of emergence	Spontaneous	Spontaneous	Spontaneous	Spontaneous with community support
Strategy of reducing transaction and transformation cost[a]	Cultivating annual customers	Vesting management roles in members with largest share in command area	Saving land and effort needed for subminors and field channels, reducing seepage, overcoming topography	Reducing transaction costs of cooperative action (with help of NGOs and Hindu religious sects)
Incentive structure	Payoff concentration	Payoff concentration	Payoff concentration	Self-interest blended with missionary zeal
Response of the establishment	Negative	Negative	Negative to neutral	Initially skeptical, then piggybacked
Preferred alternative in institutional environment	Community reverse-osmosis plants	Idealized water user associations	Idealized water user associations	Narmada project, scientific recharge

aTransformation cost includes cost of labor and materials in making subminor and field channels plus cost of acquiring land. Transaction cost involves persuading farmers to give up their land for channels and permit right-of-way to carry water to downstream farmers.

companies to design robust, self-sustaining member organizations to take over government tube wells. With a few simple modifications to its scheme, Gujarat government then turned over 3,500 public tube wells to farmers in a five-year period (Shah and Bhattacharya 1993). Mukherji and Kishore (2003) showed that within a year, the performance of these tube wells, in terms of area irrigated, hours of operation, quality of service, operation and mainte-nance, and financial results, had improved. Two years after the turnover, it had improved dramatically.

Examples abound of cases in which "social energy" and the state work at cross-purposes rather than as comrades-in-arms. In Gujarat's much-planned Sardar Sarovar Project on River Narmada, farmers have been lukewarm about sparing land, money, and labor to dig distribution systems but are enthusiastic about achieving the same purpose by investing in thousands of low-lift diesel pumps and rubber pipes to distribute canal water on their own as well as their customers' fields. However, this model does not conform to the "command" and "duty" notions of the irrigation department, which insists on a conventional distribution system, thereby forfeiting a potential opportunity for people's participation (Talati and Shah 2004). As a result, the project is stuck in gridlock. In contrast, neighboring Maharashtra has made an opportunity of a similar situation. In the North Krishna basin, the government has used a similar groundswell of numerous private irrigation service providers to replace public investment and management and has has-tened irrigation development through a public-private partnership. In the command of one small reservoir, Padhiari (2005) found 1,200 such private irrigation service providers. These entrepreneurs did better than irrigation departments on all counts: they collected 25 percent of the output value as irrigation charge against the three to five percent that irrigation departments were unable to collect. They irrigated more area than was designed. And they did a better job of providing irrigation on demand. What, one might ask, is this if not participatory irrigation management?

Finally, the mass-based groundwater recharge movement of Saurashtra (Chapter 6) is another *swayambhoo* institutional arrangement exemplify-ing a people-driven move from PD to Coase outcomes. Unlike the cases above, in which people are driven by opportunism, the recharge move-ment is driven by more complex motives as well, including long-term, col-lective self-interest (Shah 2000). Religious leaders ennobled the work in their public discourses by imbuing it with a larger social purpose. The gathering movement generated enormous local goodwill and released philanthropic energies on unprecedented scale, with diamond merchants—originally from Saurashtra but now settled in Surat and Belgium—offering cash, cement companies offering cement at discounted prices, and communities offering millions of days of voluntary labor. Saurashtra's recharge movement was truly multicentric, unruly, spontaneous, and wholly internally funded, with no support from government, international donors, or the scientific community (Shah 2000; Shah and Desai 2002). The government of Gujarat coopted the movement in 1998, and it became a government program more than a people's movement. However, even in its new incarnation, groundwater recharge activity has engaged the local people and mitigated the groundwater depletion problem. I argue that for this reason alone, it is possible to replicate a mass-based recharge movement throughout hard-rock India with intelligent catalytic action.

The examples of institutional arrangements spontaneously evolved by the society described in Table 8-4 operate on a large scale, are adaptive (Moench and Dixit 2004), and are capable of further scaling up and out. They exemplify high-payoff, low-transaction-cost institutions and represent examples of "things working out in the best *feasible* manner" (Dixit 2004, 4). If we judge institutions by their contributions to productivity and welfare, all these are successful. A notable aspect is that each institution has arisen spontaneously and flourished as an instrument of the society, serving a purpose important to people—though not necessarily of the institutional environment with its irrigation departments, lenders, and scientists. Each has its own methods to reduce transaction costs and manage incentive structure. Finally, each is widely viewed in the institutional environment—by government officials, NGOs, researchers, international experts, and even local opinion leaders—as a *subaltern*, or inferior, arrangement to some "ideal" depicted in a development narrative.

Imposing Discipline on a Screwy Site

Designing a school, Donald Schon (1983, *306, 311*) said, should be thought of as "imposing discipline on a screwy site," and he characterized the problem of malnutrition as "gaps in a process of nutrient flow." The challenge of governing informal water economies likewise needs to be thought of in these terms: creating mechanisms and processes to influence millions of atomistic water-scavenging irrigation economies. Understanding how best to proceed can also fruitfully follow the Schon steps: first, bounding the phenomena to which we should pay attention, then building a repertoire of possible interventions, and finally, generating action theories about working through the *environment of conduct.*

One way to summarize the last two chapters is to describe (and critique) the labels that current global and local discourses of groundwater governance use for bounding the phenomena: entitlements, tradable water rights, water pricing, IWRM, multistakeholder platforms, laws and regulations, permits, and prices. My critique is not that they, and the underlying ideas, are invalid. It is that they do not provide a frame that can center the anarchy that South Asia's atomistic irrigation economy represents. Over a sufficiently long period, it is likely that the site itself will change to fit the frame.

This book is an attempt at such a frame analysis, offering an alternative reading of evidence on how South Asian irrigation is actually working and where it is headed. In distilling a repertoire of ideas and action theories from this frame analysis, a primary consideration is who is driving the action on the ground. The land-starved smallholder is the actor-in-chief in the current irrigation drama; the institutional environment has been largely a bystander and will remain on the sidelines unless it engages in arenas where South Asian farming communities are putting their resources and energy. No matter where the global discourse on IWRM, property rights, groundwater withdrawal permits, and pricing is headed, the machinations of irrigation mass politics in South Asia will play out in five theaters of irrigation governance, outlined in Figure 8.3. My hypothesis is that proactively engaging in these is the best way for water policymakers to bring a modicum of order and method to the region's water-scavenging irrigation economy.

Managing the energy-irrigation nexus is the region's principal tool for groundwater demand management. The current challenge is twofold. First, diesel-based groundwater economies of the Indo-Gangetic basin are in the throes of an energy squeeze; some of IWMI's recent studies (Shah 2007b; Ul Hassan et al. 2007) show that, with further rise in diesel prices, the social consequences of a large-scale exodus of marginal and small farmers from farming will make the social costs of electricity subsidies to agriculture look like small change. Electrification of the groundwater economy of these regions combined with a sensible scheme of farm power rationing may be the most feasible way of stemming distress outmigration of the agrarian poor.

Second, in the electricity-dependent groundwater economy of western and peninsular India and in Baluchistan, the challenge is to transform the

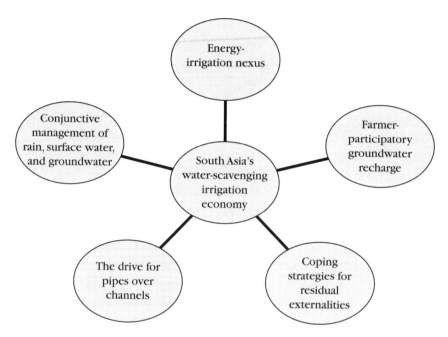

Figure 8.3   Irrigation governance in South Asia

current degenerate electricity-groundwater nexus into a rational one. Gujarat's ongoing experience, as discussed in this chapter, illustrates an approach based on intelligent rationing of power supply. But other states in the region also are moving in the direction of demand management by rationing power. Punjab has effectively used stringent power rationing in summer to encourage farmers to delay rice transplantation by a month and in the process significantly reduced groundwater depletion.[11] Andhra Pradesh gives farmers free power but has now imposed a seven-hour ration. Baluchistan has been charging a heavily subsidized flat tariff without any rationing; however, a case is being made there, too, for intelligent rationing of the kind tried under Gujarat's *Jyotirgram* scheme (Ahmad 2005). My surmise is that power rationing can be a simple and effective instrument for groundwater demand management.

In hard-rock South Asia, together with intelligent management of the energy-irrigation nexus, mass-based decentralized groundwater recharge offers a major short-run supply-side opportunity. Public agencies are likely to attract maximum farmer participation in any programs that augment "scavengable" water around farming areas. Large numbers of dug wells per 1,000 ha in hard-rock areas are viewed as threats but offer great opportunities for decentralized recharge. Experience suggests that once recharge-enabled private dug wells show up as partial bank accounts, farmer communities move on to larger common-property recharge structures, such as check dams. Experience also shows that engaging in groundwater recharge is often the first step for communities to evolve norms for local, community-based demand management, thus moving from PD toward Coase outcomes.

In alluvial aquifer areas, conjunctive management of rain, surface water, and groundwater is the big hitherto—underexploited opportunity for supply-side management. For reasons discussed in Chapter 6, mass movements for groundwater recharge are unlikely to materialize in alluvial aquifers of northwestern India, Pakistan Punjab, and Sind. Massive investments being planned for rehabilitating, modernizing, and extending gravity-flow irrigation from large and small reservoirs need a major rethink. Regardless of the noisy debates about their environmental and displacement impacts, most surface irrigation projects are just poor economic propositions; they cost more than US$4,000 per ha to bring under irrigation, but there are few places in South Asia where incremental annual net return per ha from gravity-flow irrigation amounts to even five percent of the capital cost, when the maintenance itself needs three to 3.5 percent annually. The current orthodoxy is that South Asia needs more reservoir storage because it has only 262 m³ per capita, compared with 6,103 m³ in Russia, 3,145 m³ in Brazil, 1,964 m³ in the United States, 1,111 m³ in China, and 753 m³ in South Africa (Malik in Briscoe and Malik 2007). This is an inappropriate cross-country comparison, for it fails to answer why India, with among the world's smallest per capita storage, has one of the world's largest irrigation areas.

Over the past 40 years, the South Asian landmass has been turned into a huge underground reservoir, more productive, efficient, and valuable to farmers than surface reservoirs. For millennia, it could capture and store little rainwater because in its predevelopment phase it had little unused storage. The pump irrigation revolution has created 285 to 300 km³ of new, more efficient storage in the subcontinent. Like surface reservoirs, this is good in some places and not so good in others. To the farmers, this reservoir is more valuable than surface reservoirs because they have direct access to it and can scavenge water on demand. Therefore, they are far more likely to collaborate in managing this reservoir if it responds to their recharge pull. Indeed, they would engage in participatory management of a canal if it served their recharge pull. This is best illustrated by the emergence of strong canal water user associations of grape growers in the Vaghad system in Nasik district of Maharashtra. Vineyards under drip irrigation in this region need to be watered some 80 to 100 times a year, but canals are useless: they release water for a maximum of just seven times. Yet grape growers have formed some of the finest water user associations in the region for proactive canal management here mostly because they value canals as the prime source of recharging the groundwater that sustains their high-value orchards (Bassi 2006, pers. comm.).

In mainstream irrigation thinking, groundwater recharge is viewed as a byproduct of flow irrigation, but in South Asia today, this equation needs to be stood on its head. Increasingly, the region's 450-odd km^3 of surface storage makes economic sense only for sustaining water-scavenging irrigation in extended command areas. A cubic meter of recharged well water, scavengeable on demand, is valued many times more than a cubic meter of water in surface storage. Farmers' newfound interest in local waterbodies throughout semiarid South Asia reflects the value of groundwater recharge. This is evident in South Indian tank communities that are converting irrigation tanks into percolation tanks, and in Saurashtra and Kutch, where a new norm intended to maximize groundwater recharge forbids irrigation from check dams.

In areas of South Asia with massive evaporation losses from reservoirs and canals but high rates of infiltration and percolation, the big hope for surface irrigation systems—small and large—may be to reinvent them to enhance and stabilize scavengeable water supply close to points of use, permitting frequent and flexible just-in-time irrigation of diverse crops. Already, many canal irrigation systems create value not through flow irrigation but by supporting well irrigation. In the Mahi Right Bank system in Gujarat, with a command area of about 250,000 ha, it is the more than 30,000 private tube wells—each complete with heavy-duty motors and buried pipe networks to service 30 to 50 ha—that really irrigate crops; the canals merely recharge the aquifers.[12] An elaborate study by India's Central Groundwater Board (1995) lauded the Mahi irrigation system as a "model conjunctive use project" in which 65 percent of water was delivered by canals and 35 percent was contributed by groundwater wells. However, what conjunctive use was occurring was more by default than by design: the then-chairman of the board wrote in the preface (ii), "The credit . . . [goes to] the enterprising farming community of the area who have taken the initiative and who realize fully the advantages of adopting the conjunctive use techniques for reaping optimal benefits." In a study of conjunctive use in the Mahi system around the same time, I had argued that while farmers were doing their bit, the management of the system itself was antithetical to optimal systemwide conjunctive use (Shah 1993, *176–201*).

One aspect of the pentagram (Figure 8.3) is the recognition of changing roles and protocols for designing and managing surface waterbodies for maximum impact on groundwater recharge. Surface systems in water-stressed regions of western India are already being remodeled to mimic the on-demand nature of groundwater irrigation. In Rajasthan's Indira Gandhi Canal, the government is subsidizing farmers to make farm ponds, to be filled by canal once a month and then used to supply water on demand. Gujarat is following suit through a new program of supporting farmers in command areas to build on-farm storage from which they can irrigate on demand. Integrating large canal irrigation projects into the atomistic pump irrigation economy may support the case for rethinking their modernization in ways previously unimagined. Replacing lined canals with buried perforated pipes that connect with irrigation wells or farm and village ponds, creating recharge paths along the way, may be a more efficient way of using surface storage than flow irrigation.

There is a new groundswell of enthusiasm for pipes rather than open channels to transport water. South Asia's irrigation boom, based on the triad of mechanical pumps, boreholes, and rubber pipes, is quintessentially the smallholders' response to the age-old hydraulic constraints imposed by gravity and open channel flow (Chapter 2). But the use of pipes for water transport is also valued for at least two other benefits: first, saving scarce farmland otherwise used for watercourses and field channels, and second, microirrigation. In the Sardar Sarovar Project, the major reason water user associations refused to build water distribution systems was land scarcity. In an agrarian economy with already high population pressure on farmland, flexible pipes for water distribution make more sense than surface channels, and buried pipes are even better. Pipes also support microirrigation technologies. This is what explains a boom in the use of plastics in many parts of South Asian agriculture. And if China's experience is any guide, this boom will continue to generate water as well as energy savings.

Promoting piped water conveyance aggressively can be a win-win strategy in South Asia's pump irrigation economy. Recent discussion has cast doubts on whether microirrigation offers real water savings at the basin level or not. Regardless, the appeal of microirrigation to farmers derives not from water savings but from reduced cultivation costs, higher yields, and better product quality.[13] To the extent that microirrigation improves smallholders' livelihoods from available land and water, it deserves aggressive promotion, with energy savings thrown in as a bonus. The primary reason microirrigation technology is not spreading as fast as it could is, paradoxically, the government subsidy intended to promote it. Drip irrigation companies can manipulate the subsidy scheme to make money without having to promote the technology to farmers, as they would have done in a subsidy-free market. Microirrigation markets can grow in South Asia if subsidies are abolished all together, and it can boom if subsidies are redesigned so that instead of shrinking the market for these technologies, as they now do, they begin growing it.

South Asian policymakers need to reinvent public irrigation systems. Retrofitting large reservoirs and canals as piped systems delivering water for pressurized irrigation, somewhat like Qaddafi's Great Manmade River project in Libya, has never received serious consideration because of the high capital cost of piped water transport. But in South Asia today, this idea deserves to be explored for its countless advantages. Four to seven percent of the land in the command area of a canal irrigation system is used up by the canal network itself. In a land-scarce region like South Asia, land acquisition itself is the major cause of cost and time overruns, not to mention widespread farmer unrest and opposition from civil society groups. Then, pump irrigators in many South Asian canal commands expend more energy on their wells and tube wells than the hydropower that reservoirs generate. Using the weight of the water in the reservoir, closed systems of buried pipes below the reservoir[14] could run turbines as well as provide pressurized irrigation service. On a microscale, this is already practiced by water sellers in Gujarat, who use overhead tanks and buried pipelines to deliver pressurized irrigation to their customers.

Small irrigation systems in the U.S. South, Canada, and Spain are converting water transport from surface canals to rubber-gasketed jointed reinforced concrete pipes.[15] A similar retrofit could transform many of South Asia's reservoir irrigation systems to pressurized systems providing on-demand, just-in-time irrigation, as frequently as needed, and mimic atomistic pump irrigation. Water would be delivered under pressure to retailers or water user associations, which would then distribute it to farmers through their own buried pipe networks. Such a system would also permit volumetric water pricing and use of drip and sprinkler irrigation, encourage private investment in water distribution, generate massive rural employment in water distribution, create spaces for viable public-private partnerships, reduce energy use in groundwater irrigation, ease pressure on groundwater, reduce evaporation from open canals, save scarce land, and serve larger areas from the same storage. It could also reduce the redundancy of separate water delivery systems—surface canals for irrigation and pipes for domestic water supply—common in South Asia. The value of the productive land released, improved water availability, energy savings, and carbon credits earned may pay for much of the retrofitting costs.

Why, one might ask, has such a system not been tried more extensively elsewhere in the world? The answer comes in two parts: first, it is indeed being tried in many developed countries simply for the water savings and pressurized irrigation that piped systems offer; second, nowhere do we find a boom in groundwater irrigation within canal commands as we find in South Asia. From society's viewpoint, there is little justification for investing in expensive surface canal systems if farmers are going to use them predominantly for groundwater recharge.

Finally, many negative externalities associated with the pump irrigation boom are impossible to internalize fully anytime soon and are best coped with. A good example is arsenic in the eastern Ganga basin and fluoride in western and peninsular India. These contaminants of drinking water are geogenic, and their links with irrigation development seem neither clear nor straightforward. Even if the link is strong, restoring aquifers to their predevelopment stage by banishing groundwater irrigation would be an unrealistic response. A more practical approach is to enhance social capacity to cope with and adapt to these contaminants. Doing this is as much a socioeconomic issue as a scientific and technological one. Notably, the society is quicker and more savvy in responding to these threats than the state, as the small-scale reverse—osmosis industry in North Gujarat would suggest. NGOs in Saurashtra, too, have noted that one spillover benefit of the decentralized recharge movement is a reduction in fluoride concentration in groundwater. Although there is no systematic supporting evidence, it stands to reason that fluoride concentrations might be greater when water is pumped from greater depths in hard-rock aquifers than from closer to the surface.

Summary Propositions

In choosing directions for strategic change, leaders and policymakers often undertake an "environment scan" to get a bird's-eye view of the situation and how it is changing. This book is an attempt at an environment scan of South Asia's irrigation economy, looking at the major changes under way and the position of the public systems. I begin concluding the book by briefly summarizing in a dozen propositions the highlights of this environment scan.

Proposition 1. For centuries until 40 years ago, the irrigation initiative in South Asia rested first with farming communities and later with an autocratic state. The rise, since 1970, of an atomistic mode of irrigation, teeming with millions of tiny pump irrigation economies untrammeled by the state and its regulatory apparatus, is the distinctive feature that sets irrigation in South Asia (and North China) apart from its own past and from the rest of the irrigating world (Chapter 1).

Proposition 2. The geography of global groundwater use in agriculture can be usefully divided into four socioecologies with distinct characteristics: (1) small-holder intensive farming systems, which emerged in South Asia and North China after 1970; (2) arid agrarian systems of western Asia and North Africa; (3) industrial agriculture systems of the U.S. West, Spain, Mexico, and Australia; and (4) groundwater-supported extensive pastoralism in Africa and Latin America. The drivers and the dynamics of groundwater use in each of these socioecologies are materially different; as a result, each will chart a different trajectory. This makes reflective cross-learning a profitable enterprise—and copybook transplantation of lessons counterproductive (Chapter 2).

Proposition 3. Intensive groundwater irrigation around the world is a reflection of water scarcity; however, in South Asia, it is more a response to land scarcity. As population pressure on farmland has grown, smallholders locked into South Asia's unviable agriculture have been drawn to pumps, wells, and flexible pipes—water extraction mechanisms (WEMs)—for their land-augmenting and labor-absorbing power. WEMs enable multiple cropping and increased food and income per m^2 of farmland, they permit intensive use of underemployed family labor and scavenged water, and they afford farmers a level of control—the ability to mobilize and apply small quantities of water with high frequency on demand, year-round—that flow irrigation cannot (Chapter 2).

Proposition 4. Strong direct links between groundwater irrigation and agrarian poverty are the hallmark of the water-scavenging irrigation economy that has come to dominate South Asian agriculture. In its early stages, pump irrigation created value by enhancing land-use intensity, but now it is creating livelihoods by supporting value-added intensive diversification of agriculture even outside the command areas of large canal systems (Chapter 4).

Proposition 5. The booming groundwater economy is eroding the canal and tank irrigation capital South Asia inherited and exposing its internal contradictions. Globally, surface irrigation thrives when the irrigation system (including its management regime) serves a small number of large customers (fewness, as in Australia); ensures homogeneous cropping, planting, and irrigation schedules on the entire command (homogeneity, as in rice irrigation systems); commands the power to enforce operational discipline on users (authority, as in the Gezira scheme in Sudan); and holds irrigators captive to an "irrigation culture" and creates an "irrigation community" (captivity, as in traditional hill irrigation systems in Nepal). Many other irrigating regions of the world meet one or more of these preconditions; so did India in both the colonial and the precolonial eras. Postindependence South Asia increasingly meets none. As a result, despite sustained investments, surface irrigation is losing out to pump irrigation, in both relative and absolute terms (Chapter 3).

Proposition 6. Flow irrigation as a technology is in decline in South Asia, and irrigation management transfer to farmers' organizations and participatory irrigation management of canal and tank systems are proving feeble responses. Therefore, it is unlikely that institutional reforms of the participatory management genre will arrest or reverse the atrophy in flow irrigation. Future relevance of tanks and canal systems lies in reinventing them from a technology to deliver gravity-flow irrigation to one that can increase the supply of scavengeable ground and surface water close to farming communities (Chapter 3).

Proposition 7. But for the groundwater revolution, which has acted as something of a safety valve, South Asia would have arguably experienced far greater social and political instability in the countryside than it has so far. Whereas public irrigation systems could reach out to less than a 10th of the region's smallholders, small pumps and tube wells have democratized irrigation in South Asia just as personal computers have democratized computing worldwide. Thanks to its myriad and widespread benefits, the pump irrigation revolution, aided by irrigation service markets, has alleviated more poverty than most government programs (Chapter 4).

Proposition 8. Against those livelihood benefits, the pump irrigation revolution has produced four profound impacts on a subcontinental scale. First is *environmental:* in ever-growing areas, unmanaged ground-water development is putting aquifers at risk of depletion and/or quality deterioration, with collateral damage in the form of dried-up wetlands and reduced lean-season flows downstream. Second is *institutional:* pump irrigation has left the subcontinental water economy more informal than it was in the 1950s, implying that a larger proportion of water diversion, use, and users in agriculture are outside the regulatory ambit of the state than was the case 50 years ago. Third is *hydronomic:* it is leaving river basins reconfigured such that public investments in surface water infrastructure begin depreciating in value even as projects are being planned and constructed. The last impact is *fiscal:* electricity subsidies began as the central cause of the pump irrigation boom during the 1970s but have now ended up as their result throughout western and peninsular India (Chapter 5).

Proposition 9. The behavior of aquifers is better understood than the behavior of aquifer communities in South Asia. However, observing the way users respond to groundwater development and overdevelopment does suggest unmistakable patterns. With intensive development, different aquifer conditions produce different institutional dynamics. In heavily recharged alluvial aquifers with no quality concerns, users fail to form an aquifer community and are unable to organize *(atomistic individualism).* In poorly recharged alluvial aquifers, where users can maintain well yields by progressively deepening their wells, the resource-rich collude to monopolize access to groundwater, exclude the poor, and mobilize into powerful pressure groups to secure favorable policies through mass-based political action *(collusive opportunism).* In seemingly robust aquifers susceptible to rapid water quality deterioration during development, as in coastal aquifer systems, fatalism sets in early and users fail to organize for collective self-restraint, instead destroying the aquifer and moving on to other livelihoods *(exit).* In hard-rock (and some confined) aquifers, which confront their users with physical water scarcity on a daily basis, interdependence among users can lead to destructive *rivalrous gaming* within close-knit aquifer communities, but it is also here that there are maximum prospects for *cooperative gaming,* as the experience in India over the past decade shows. With effective catalysis, users of such aquifers cooperate and mobilize to secure accelerated natural and induced recharge, evolve *some* demand management regime, and take their pump irrigation closer to sustainability (Chapter 6).

Proposition 10. The technology of groundwater governance arising from the experience of industrialized countries includes five instruments: economic incentives, allocation of property rights, direct legal and administrative regulation, participatory aquifer management, and supply augmentation. The review of experience around the world suggests that groundwater governance is still a work in process; nowhere do we find a regime that has succeeded, in unequivocal terms, in taming the anarchy endemic to groundwater irrigation. This applies even where groundwater users number just a few tens of thousands. Trying these instruments in South Asia with more than 20 million tiny, scattered groundwater diverters presents a logistical challenge on a colossal scale (Chapter 7).

Proposition 11. Constructs like integrated water resources management, which is held out as a new "philosophy of water governance," in reality do nothing more than recycle the instruments tried by the industrialized world. The problem with IWRM-as-applied is twofold. First, it seeks to transform, abruptly, predominantly informal irrigation economies into highly formalized ones, even though global experience suggests that this is a long process in which the overall economic growth of a country plays a central role. Second, by promoting a formulaic approach, it discourages homegrown approaches to groundwater governance with a better contextual fit (Chapter 7). In governing its irrigation economy, South Asian policymakers should instead consider a repertoire of indirect interventions that operate through the environment of conduct rather than through individual conduct. The operational water governance pentagram in South Asia—which can make a difference to the region's irrigation anarchy on a here-and-now basis—suggests five arenas of action: the energy-irrigation nexus; conjunctive use of rain, surface water, and groundwater; mass-based groundwater recharge; supporting water transport and distribution by pipes instead of channels; and helping communities, in the short run, cope with negative externalities rather than trying to eliminate those externalities altogether.

Proposition 12. The biggest barrier to effective groundwater governance in South Asia—and mainstreaming the work on the groundwater governance pentagram—is institutional lock-in: the region's irrigation thinking and planning are stuck. Since colonial times, irrigation policy has been dominated by "command" and "duty" thinking in a civil engineering mode, and groundwater, soil, and water conservation were secondary considerations. Today, South Asia's irrigation economy is vastly different in its structure and organization from what the British left behind, yet mainstream irrigation policy is still steeped in the colonial mode. South Asian smallholders have now figured out to mobilize, store, scavenge, and apply water largely outside the purview of the mainstream irrigation thinking and practice. The region's irrigation planners and managers need to come to terms with the new reality.

Conclusion: Outgrowing Path Dependence

In his *Seeing Like the State*, James C. Scott (1998) analyzes how the mainstream or official conception of forests in many colonized countries like India during the nineteenth century was shaped by the German foresters' obsession with the idea of revenue yield as the central objective of managing forests. This obsession encouraged single-minded conversion of natural forests into monoculture timber plantations. Scott argued that, long after colonialists withdrew, forest management for revenue yield remained the defining logic of local forest bureaucracies, themselves the product of the idea.

Strikingly similar has been the evolutionary trajectory of official irrigation thinking in South Asia. Like revenue yield of forests, command and duty in flow irrigation system dominated irrigation planning during the colonial era. The atomistic irrigation economy is making these notions irrelevant, and a new model is needed. The state and the water establishment have become mute spectators in the unfolding irrigation drama, whereas they should be its proactive *Sutradhar*, who in traditional Indian theater provided the link among the performer, the performance, and the audience.

If the state is to emerge as the *Sutradhar* in a changing environment, its irrigation thinking and planning must change and its institutions must adapt. But irrigation thinking and policymaking in South Asia have remained path dependent. The fractured policymaking institutions, obsolete mandates of strategic organizations, and outmoded competencies of water planners have only helped deepen the region's irrigation anarchy. Managing the vast underground reservoir that South Asia's farmers have created must be the priority for thriving in the anarchy that the state has neither the power nor the wherewithal to tame. This is especially so in view of the increased hydrological variability and uncertainty that the region is destined to face in the wake of climate change. We saw in earlier chapters that for decades, groundwater, and not surface storage, has been the principal recourse of South Asia's smallholders during drought; this is evident in the fact that well-drilling activity peaks during drought years. Managing South Asia's vast underground reservoir has to be a core element of the region's survival strategy of bracing up to the challenge of global warming.

Outgrowing path dependence implies rewriting the mission statement of water resources managers in South Asia. Instead of building surface reservoirs and creating command areas, the mission should now be helping maximize supplies of water that farmers can scavenge close to their farms. Outgrowing path dependence means going beyond traditional notions of conjunctive management of surface and groundwater, by adapting surface water management to the atomistic irrigation economy. It means transforming rivalrous gaming among aquifer communities into cooperative gaming in hard-rock aquifers, reining in collusive opportunism in alluvial aquifers, and minimizing exit in saline aquifers. Carving out a meaningful and significant role for the state in this new drama demands creativity.

Instead, South Asia's planners are doing more of the same. Government planners in India are already writing new canal irrigation projects in their 11th five-year plan, and in Pakistan, billions of dollars are earmarked for restoring the Indus Basin Irrigation System. These planners refuse to see that flow irrigation in South Asia will increasingly have social uses only if it effectively responds to the recharge pull. Jettisoning path dependence implies giving up on meeting people's unfelt needs, as constructive imperialism did. It implies redesigning water governance to meet, in a sustainable manner, the felt needs of smallholders, increasingly expressed by their recharge pull. Jettisoning path dependence demands new forms of partnership between state and society for governing atomistic irrigation.

The question currently posed is, *"Can society coordinate and manage itself?"* This is the essence of *distributed governance*. It looks at coordination and the various forms of formal and informal types of State/society interactions and the role of civil society and policy networks. This is more society centered and less statist, with governance systems providing the power balance, recognizing of course that political power is derived essentially from economic resources and instruments (Rogers and Hall 2003).

Above all, outgrowing path dependence means inventing mechanisms for distributed governance of groundwater socioecologies, and in so doing, building on *swayambhoo* (spontaneous) institutions that people themselves have created to meet their felt needs. Outgrowing path dependence demands a change in our view—*weltanschauung*, as the Germans would say—of how South Asia's irrigation is actually functioning, and how best can we build on it.

ENDNOTES

Introduction

1. FAO Aquastat (2004) figures updated by the author for revised national estimates for selected countries, including India.

Chapter 1

1. "Those who control the hydraulic network are uniquely prepared to wield supreme power" (Wittfogel 1957, 47).

2. Hardiman (2002, 113) likewise brushes aside the Wittfogel thesis: "Wittfogel's proposition was strongly materialistic . . . In fact, polities are shaped in much more complex ways—being a congeries of histories of conflict and their resolution."

3. Wittfogel's ideas are likely more true of China, whose emperors and warlords did more than their counterparts elsewhere to manipulate rivers for irrigation as well as warcraft. China also had much more canal irrigation than South Asia. Wittfogel cites F. H. King, an American agronomist, who estimated the combined length of man-made watercourses in China, Korea, and Japan c. 1900 at 200,000 miles.

"Forty canals across the United States from east to west and sixty from north to south would not equal in number of miles those in these three countries today. Indeed, it is probable that this estimate is not too large for China alone" (Wittfogel 1957, 34).

4. "[T]he Oriental Despot reigns with foremost authority in the realms of fiction" (Steadman 1969 cited in Christensen 1998, 16).

5. This view is being increasingly questioned. See, for example, Raychaudhury (1998).

6. The state's claim over the produce of land ranged from a low of one-quarter to two-thirds or sometimes even more under rulers like Alau-din-Khilji, Marathas, and the Hindu kings of Vijayanagara (Randhawa 1982).

7. Numerous such accounts exist in the literature. As a typical example, Hatekar (1996, 452) suggests that in response to attempts by British revenue collectors to rigorously collect land revenue in the Deccan during the late 1820s, "A large number of cultivators simply abandoned their homes and fled to neighboring provinces. Large tracts of land were thrown out of cultivation; and in some districts no more than a third of the cultivable area remained in operation."

8. For western Punjab before the construction of the British system of Indus canals during 1892–1916, Agnihotri (1996, 42–43) writes, "Cultivation . . . was by and large confined to a strip varying from 3 to 15 miles in width along the river bank. The cultivation zone was divided into the *Hithar* and *Nakka*, of which the former constituted the alluvial tract bordering the rivers. This contained the finest villages where almost every acre was brought under cultivation during the *rabi* without any irrigation being required to bring the crops to maturity." Further, "Apart from the natural drainage that Shahpur benefited from, it had a network of inundation canals . . . Multan, like Shahpur, depended heavily on river action and inundation canals."

9. Some observers argue that India had devices like the Persian wheel long before West Asians began invading northern India (see, e.g., CBIP 1953; Basham 2001). Bagchi (1995) cites a 14th-century stone inscription in a Jodhpur temple to suggest that the Persian wheel was in use in North India before the coming of Islamic influence. However, it is widely agreed that the technology came from West Asia (Mate 1998).

10. Hardiman (1998) suggests that wells were the prime mode of irrigation in Gujarat in the 19th century and earlier. Islam (1997), Dutt (1989), the first Indian Irrigation Commission (IIC 1903), and CBIP (1953) all emphasize the tradition of well irrigation in today's Indian and Pakistan Punjab, Haryana, parts of Rajasthan, Sind, and Gujarat. Stone (1984) and other historians who wrote about western parts of Ganga basin also consider well irrigation prevalent in western districts of the United Province. About colonial Punjab, Islam (1997, 36) suggests, "At the time of the annexation of the province and for many years thereafter wells constituted the most important source of artificial water supply in the province." Habib (1999, 28) believes that "In the Upper Gangetic plains as also in parts of Dakhin, wells must have provided the chief source of irrigation."

11. According to Islam (1997), the number of wells in undivided Punjab increased from 137,000 in 1848–49 to 347,000 in 1943–44; and the capital value of wells

in 1943–44 was Rs. 278,000,000 compared with Rs. 345,000,000 in the major irrigation works.

12. FAO uses "water-managed agriculture" to refer to areas where water other than direct rainfall is used for agricultural production. Irrigated areas, in contrast are those which are "equipped to supply water to crops" (FAO 2005a).

13. Writing about Krishna basin of the mid-1850s, R. Biard Smith, a lieutenant colonel from Bengal Engineers who toured Madras in 1853, called the profusion of tanks "so truly stupendous as not to be looked at without wonder." Ten years later, Major Richard Sankey wrote about Mysore that "it would take some ingenuity to discover a site within this great area suitable for a new tank." Colonel J. P. Grant, Superintendent of Mysore Revenue Survey, asserted that tanks are the life of the people (Wallach 1985).

14. In Gorakhpur, Buchanan estimated that 10 men could water 3,000 to 5,000 square feet per day using swing baskets.

15. Bengal then included today's West Bengal, Bihar, coastal Orissa, Assam, and most of Bangladesh.

16. Willcocks (1984, 14) also saw in Tanjor's medieval irrigation systems the imprint of the overflow irrigation in Bengal: "Let anyone follow the long-continued, well-spaced alignments of these seven canals, of the main canals in Central Bengal, and in the Tanjore delta, and he will not be surprised to learn that history tells us that the Chola kings of Bengal conquered Southern India, became masters of Tanjore and introduced their system of irrigation there."

17. Whitcombe (2005) notes that the company investments on Grand Anicut and related works brought a return on investment of 69.5 percent over 14 years. The investments in Jumna canals were less profitable.

18. That Pol Pot's irrigation adventure was inspired by Angkor is evident in the following description: "There is no comparison between the present day rice fields of Cambodia and those of the time of Angkor. In those days, permanent irrigation allowed three or four harvests a year. The rice fields were regularly demarcated, in perfect squares, framed by small raised dykes. The region chosen by the king for the establishment of a city soon became an opulent rice loft, thanks to this system of exploitation . . . The existence of dykes presupposes earthworks, solid embankments which also served as routes . . . In every place where the king erects a linga and constructs a monument, he irrigates and nourishes . . . As soon as he was invested with royal power he made this promise: in five days from now, I will begin to dig . . ." (Thierry 1997: 64–65). As soon as he came to power, Pol Pot mobilized his people to begin digging.

19. The key elements of the program were a nationwide chessboard of leveled 1-ha plots in productive areas and in the reclaimed forest; irrigation and drainage developed in a rectangular pattern of ditches and canals; canals in a 1-by-1 km grid following the coordinate lines shown on the 1:50,000 topographical maps (or aligned with the national roads) and with a base width of 3 to 5 m; within each 1-by-1 km grid, ditches each 200 m surrounding a unit of 4 ha; the creation of reservoirs, equipped with pumping stations, by constructing long dykes along depressions or by damming natural depressions and alleys, with dykes often projecting along a canal at the coordinate lines of the 1-by-1 km grid; and the

construction of river closures with control structures to divert water into reservoirs or the canal-ditch system (Himel 2007).

20. This was also the strategy the British used in sparsely populated Punjab, where preexisting nomadic communities were dispossessed and became the "oppressed underclass in the colonies" (Hardiman 2002, *118*).

21. Expressing a similar sentiment, David Hardiman (1999) wrote, "Despite the sophistication of many of the pre-existing systems, the colonial rulers held them to be rudimentary, 'primitive,' and unchanging, trapping the people in a culture of backwardness. The new rulers believed that they had a superior knowledge which was scientific, and that they could transcend these supposed limitations through technology. Nature could be mastered, transformed and thus exploited in the context of global markets. 'Natives' were expected to conform to this new, more 'rational' scheme of resource use" (http://www.iwha.net/events/events-1999/hardimanpolitics.htm).

22. A good example of this unequal mutuality is provided by Niranjan Pant (1998, *3133*) in showing how the *zamindars* maintained the *ahar-pyne* systems that irrigated nearly a million hectares in south Bihar during the first two decades of the 20th century: "Tenants were required to pay gilandazi (improvement of irrigation works) charges." Pant suggests that the return on the *zamindars'* investments on maintenance of *ahar-pyne* systems were as high as 40 to 50 percent.

23. Land revenue constituted 60 percent of East India Company's total income in the 1840s (Banerjee and Iyer 2002); though its share declined somewhat, it hovered around 50 percent through the 19th century.

24. Three main types emerged: permanent settlement (*zamindari,* or landlord) areas, in which a landlord was given charge of revenue collection and the state had no direct dealings with peasants; *raiyatwari* areas, where each cultivator was assessed for revenue directly by state revenue administration; and *mahalwari* areas, where the village bodies jointly collected the land revenue. These different systems created a different dynamic of land and water management, whose impacts survived long after these institutions were abolished (see, e.g., Banerjee and Iyer 2002). While they were in force, their impact was of course decisive.

25. In effect, as Deakin had done in Victoria, Australia, the colonial state in India too had imposed a kind of compulsory water right. As Hardiman (2002, *114*) remarks, in the canal commands the canal water "tax had to be paid regardless of whether or not use was made of the canal in a particular year or whether or not there was a reliable supply from the canal." This, according to him, encouraged and even forced farmers to grow valuable commercial crops.

26. In a study of irrigation economics in Bihar, R. Bhatia (1991) showed that total irrigation dues were so small that it made eminent sense to reallocate the 5,000-strong force deployed in their collection to other gainful activities and abolish irrigation fees altogether.

27. That irrigation was a cash cow for the colonial government is evident in the fact that in 1927–28, of the total revenue receipts of the government of Punjab from all sources, Rs. 157.98 million, the net irrigation receipts (after meeting the expenses of irrigation administration) were Rs. 46.74 million, 10 times the income tax receipts and twice the income from land revenue (Paustian 1968).

28. See http://www.indianpumps.org/history.asp.

29. Khan (1994, *81*), however, asserted that "in 1990–91, the minor irrigation lifting devices provided irrigation water to about 88 percent of irrigated area" in Bangladesh.

30. "The character of [irrigation] works was largely conditioned by the physiographical features of the area in which they were located. In the arid and semi-arid plains of North India, perennial rivers like the Indus and the Ganga made it relatively easy to divert flood flows through inundation channels. In the peninsula, where the rainfall is scanty, the practice of trapping storm water in large tanks for domestic and agricultural purposes was widespread. In areas where a high groundwater table permitted lift irrigation, wells were common" (Government of India 1972, *61*).

31. Some Chinese scholars call this "fragmentary" irrigation (see Zhou 1997).

Chapter 2

1. For example, "Groundwater development . . . has grown dramatically in the last fifty years, especially in arid and semi-arid regions" (Llamas and Custodio 2003, *xi*). "The much drier climate of arid and semi-arid regions as compared with the climates in the industrialized countries is an important reason why groundwater in (semi-) arid areas is used for irrigation in the first place" (Schrevel 1997, 4).

2. See www.fao.org/docrep/W7314E/w7314e0t.htm.

3. Inner Mongolia, Hebei, Henan, Liaoning, Shaanxi, and Shanxi.

4. Burke (2003, *59*), for example, notes, "Much of this success [in groundwater irrigation] has occurred as an indirect result of hydraulic engineers continuing to promote the expansion of irrigated agriculture through surface command areas."

5. See, for example, Gilbert Etienne (2003) for one such view.

6. Henry Vaux, of the University of California at Berkeley, asserts, "Persistent groundwater overdraft is self-terminating" (2005, pers. comm.).

7. This too is likely an underestimate. Wijesinghe (1994, *12*), a onetime chairman of Sri Lanka's Water Resources Board, had suggested back in 1993 that "Although no precise data [are available] . . . it is reasonable to believe that over 115,000 engine pump sets are in use in the country."

8. See www.ficci.com/ficci/media-room/speeches-presentations/2003/sep/sep5-asean-kirloskar.htm.

9. Around 1980, India and China each produced about 0.8 million diesel pumps a year. The Indian industry still manufactures diesel engines that weigh 325 kg and cost US$350. The Chinese captured 90 percent share in global diesel pump market by marketing 45-kg portable pumps at US$90 apiece (*Gujarat Samachar* 2006).

10. See Bhamoriya (2004) for a study of the wastewater economy of Vadodara City in Gujarat, and Buechler and Devi (2004) for a study of the wastewater irrigation economy of Hyderabad City.

11. See, for example, the data compiled by the International Commission on Irrigation and Drainage (www.icid.org) on agricultural population and farmland in 101 countries.

12. With rising global food prices since 2007, this scenario is changing. Small holders in South Asia have begun increasing food grain production.
13. Virtual water is the water embedded in agricultural products. Importing a ton of rice is equivalent to importing the volume of water needed to grow it at home. Water-scarce regions can conserve their water resources through imports of water-intensive farm produce.
14. Hydrogeologists consider groundwater use intensive when "the natural functioning of aquifers is substantially modified by groundwater abstraction" (see the introduction in Llamas and Custodio 2003, 3).

Chapter 3

1. Cost was an issue, too. The Agriculture Commission's cost estimates were Rs. 7–20 per ha for canal irrigation and Rs. 54 per ha from a well. "In view of such a large difference in cost, it was not surprising that wells were superseded by canals as the source of water supply in areas supplied by canals" (Randhawa 1983, *vol. 3, 291*).
2. Dhawan (1996a, *537*) called this the "substitutional effect" of public irrigation works; it caused among farmers well-placed in new command areas a "disinclination even to maintain their own sources of irrigation of pre-canal vintage, not to mention that they drastically cut back on new investments in such means of irrigation."
3. In the Indian Punjab, growth in tube well irrigation during the 1960s and 1970s helped a great deal in arresting and reversing the waterlogging tendencies that the Bhakra and Pong dams had created. Soon, however, concerns about waterlogging were replaced by groundwater depletion issues (Dhawan 1995). The same phenomenon is seen in the Pakistan Punjab as well (World Bank 2005b).
4. *Kareze*, or *qanat*, is a 3,000-year-old system, popular in Asia and North Africa, of delivering groundwater by gravity flow via gently sloping underground tunnels that convey water to the surface. A mother well is dug to the depth of the water table at the top of an alluvial fan and an underground tunnel several miles long is constructed. Vertical shafts are dug along the length of the tunnel to provide ventilation and room for desilting. *Karezes* are found from Baluchistan to Iran, Oman, and Yemen. Similar structures are also found, and are still in use, in Kerala, India, where they are called *surangams*.
5. Between 1962–63 and 1985–86, 1.7 million ha of tank-irrigated area was lost, implying a capital loss of Rs. 51 billion (Athavale 2003). Since 1985–86, tank irrigated areas have declined by 2.6 million ha more.
6. "Since the number of wells located in tank commands is significant, the tank is losing its place as an important source of irrigation." Moreover, they argue, "Since high yielding varieties require more assured, controlled and timely application of water and since the available tank water is inadequate to raise three short duration [high-yielding] crops, wells have a major advantage over surface sources."
7. See *Divya Bhaskar*, Ahmedabad edition, 4 September 2007, 3.
8. Thakkar (1999) cites World Bank studies that show a major decline in areas served by canal systems in Andhra Pradesh, Tamilnadu, and Gujarat during the early 1990s.

9. Dhawan (1993, *2371*) suspected 15 years ago that a major reappraisal of the area actually irrigated by public canals "might lead to drastic reduction in our plan achievements in this sphere." He went on: "For example, when the government of Kerala state did such bold reappraisal in respect of its irrigation works in mid-1970s, the state's estimate of net irrigated area nosedived from 4.7 to 2.3 lakh [0.47 million to 0.23 million] hectares. A like reduction, but of a much smaller magnitude, occurred when the estimates of our created irrigation potential from major and medium irrigation works were critically reviewed by a working group of the planning commission."

10. Indeed, the rise of well irrigation and its significance sometimes went unnoticed even in detailed field research. Mollinga (2003) is a good example. Based on more than two years of fieldwork in the command of Tungbhadra Left Bank Canal during early 1990s, this book provides a rich account of the social and political dynamic around canal irrigation but glosses over—even in footnotes—the rise of groundwater wells, which served more than 60 percent of Raichur district's irrigated area, according to the 1993–94 minor irrigation census (Government of India 2001).

11. South Asian surface irrigation systems were mostly designed for protective irrigation over large areas. Operating these required a highly refined orchestration between system design and management; moreover, it was assumed "that farmers will stick to subsistence production of food crops, when supplementary irrigation is made available to them" (Jurriens et al. 1996, *26*). Thus, the cropping patterns and intensities that surface irrigation was designed to support have become increasingly unrealistic during recent decades, making it impossible to operate the systems as originally envisaged.

12. See also Mollinga (1992) for an analysis of how irrigation systems designed for supplying protective irrigation over large areas are in effect transformed into rice irrigation systems in the context of Tungabhadra Left Bank Canal.

13. The Haryana study defined flow irrigation deprivation as 50 percent or less of the canal irrigation received by the best-off farmer in a watercourse.

14. "Anarchy in an irrigation system results where group norms and values are not observed" (Pradhan 1989, *18*). In a study of a Philippine irrigation system, Oorthuizen (2003, *207*) notes, "Long before 'turn over' was introduced . . . farmers and their political representatives were actively 'messing up' the management of the main system. They disregarded the National Irrigation Agency rules and regulations, guarded or destroyed main gates, diverted water to non-programmed areas, and even managed to redesign the layout of the system."

15. The best-known examples of successful PIM on large irrigation systems in India are Ozar on Waghad project in Nashik, Maharashtra; Dharoi in North Gujarat; and Pingot and a few more medium schemes in Bharuch district. The high level of investment made of motivation, skill, time, effort and money is unlikely to be replicated on a large scale, however. In catalyzing Ozar cooperatives, Bapu Upadhye, Bharat Kawale, two local leaders and researchers of SOPPEKOM, a research group, invested years of effort (Paranjapye et al. 2003). In Gujarat, between Aga Khan Rural Support Program and Development Support Centre, Anil Shah and Apoorva Oza invested at least 30 professional field staff for more than 10 to 15 years to organize 20,000 to 30,000 flow irrigators into functional

water user associations. No government agency in South Asia has the quality and scale of human and other resources needed to implement PIM on 35 million to 40 million ha.

16. In the Philippines' National Irrigation Administration, Oozrthuizen (2003, *303*) found that the transfer led to more inequity rather than less and a decline in irrigated area; the program "became a tool to solve the [administration's] financial problems."

17. Local farmer cooperatives have traditionally managed midsized paddy irrigation systems in Java. Fed by rain, these systems involve weirs that divert streams into tunnels and channels leading to paddy fields. Farmers are organized into *subaks* for the maintenance of the system and for orderly water distribution.

18. Transaction costs include search and information costs; bargaining, negotiation, and contracting costs; and policing and enforcement costs (Dahlman 1979).

19. Cubbie Station is a 14,000-ha cotton farm with a captive private irrigation system, complete with its own reservoir of 500 million m^3 (Pearce 2006).

20. Boyce (1988, *A-11*) notes, "A small scale river diversion project will be easier to organize if 50 households are involved than if 500 are involved."

21. A public good has the features of nonrivalry and nonexcludability in consumption. Nonrivalry means that its enjoyment by one member of a society does not in anyway reduce its availability to others; nonexcludability means that once available, nobody can be kept from consuming it.

22. Turral (1998, *65*) reviews the experience of IMT in the Colombia basin and notes "a relatively homogeneous and small group of farmers who are well educated and commercially oriented" as a factor in its success.

23. Turral (1995, *3*) raised the same concern when he said, "There is a significant problem in evaluation [of the potential and performance of IMT] at the moment, in that most experience comes from countries such as the US, Australia and Chile where functional systems are handed over to relatively small numbers of well-capitalized farmers, operating within a well-established legal framework."

24. Even in middle-income countries, unequal landholdings and high-value export crops have helped IMT. For evidence on the Andean region of Colombia, see Ramirez and Vargas (1999); for Turkey, see Svendsen and Nott (1997).

25. In 1943–44, nearly 500,000 acres in British Punjab were irrigated by private canals captive to one or a few farmers. In Shahpur district, where the government encouraged construction of private canals, all were owned by just two families, Noon and Tiwana (Islam 1997).

26. Land grants to bureaucrats, doctors, and lawyers were a minimum of 50 acres; horse-breeding yeoman grants were 55 to 110 acres; landed gentry grants were 150 to 350 acres; and capitalist grants were 160 to 540 acres. Even peasant grants, the smallest, were seldom smaller than 55 acres (Islam 1997).

27. Many researchers have noted the impact of heterogeneity in raising anarchy levels. See the brief survey by Schlager (2007).

28. "Hydraulic rulers were sufficiently strong to do on a national scale what the feudal lords could accomplish only within the boundaries of their domains." Further, the "hydraulic state prevented the non-governmental forces of society

from crystallizing into independent bodies strong enough to counterbalance or even control the political machine" (Wittfogel 1957, 47).

29. Wade (1984) recounts how challenging even simple changes in water allocation rules proved in their actual enforcement in a southern Indian irrigation system because of a "well-institutionalized system of corruption."

30. Wade (1986, 248) echoed this sense when he said, "I do not think a sense of obligatory group membership or a belief in cooperation as a desirable way to live are important factors."

31. See www.headwater.nve.no/abstractShowSession.php?id=32.

32. However, with intensification and intensive diversification, that is changing rapidly (Facon 2002; Renault and Facon 2004). A World Bank study of rice irrigation systems in Thailand in the mid-1980s noted that "the emerging trend towards crop diversification . . . raises many questions . . . diversified field crops do not accommodate over-irrigation and continuous irrigation which are common practices in irrigating rice in Thailand" (Plusquellec and Wikham 1985, 7).

33. In a study of cooperation around surface irrigation in 48 villages of Tamilnadu, Bardhan (1999) found more rampant violation of rules of water distribution and allocation made and enforced by the Public Works Department than when these were formulated by village elders.

34. A detailed discussion of the Narmada evidence follows in Chapter 5.

35. In a series of papers, von Oppen and Subba Rao analyzed the distribution of the number and area irrigated by tanks in 165 districts of India and found several determinants of variations in tank density. The presence of a hard-rock substratum, levels of average annual humidity and postmonsoon and total rainfall, and the low moisture-holding capacity of soils explained half of the variation in tank-irrigated area. Districts in former princely states had distinctly higher dependence on tanks than in the former British territory. In the former princely districts, the other major determinant was population density: "The human pressure on land transforms the environment and affects the performance of irrigation tanks; vegetation in catchment areas decreases because of over-utilization; subsequent erosion and flash run-off cause siltation in tank-beds and breaches of tanks" (1987, 36).

36. As Boyce (1988, A-10) points out, "In the first approach [bottom up], the cultivators are the initiators of irrigation development; in the second [top down] they are treated as instruments."

Chapter 4

1. US$1 = Indian Rs. 44 in 2003.

2. South Asian crop farming, especially under irrigation, is predominantly a male-dominated affair, although women traditionally play important roles in specific operations, especially rice transplanting and weeding. Household dairy farming, in contrast, is a female-dominated livelihood system.

3. www.worldbank.org/wbi/pimelg/pim.htm.

4. The IWMI survey of 2600 WEM owners in South Asia suggested that 58 percent in India, 74 percent in Pakistan, 76 percent in Bangladesh and 39 percent in Nepal received no government support for establishing their WEMs but used their own savings and borrowed from friends and relatives. The minor irrigation census of 1993–94 for India suggests the figure for self-financing WEM owners was lower, 47 percent.

5. The Bhairahawa Lumbini Groundwater Irrigation Project in Nepal Terai analyzed by Gautam (2006) is a good example of the fate of government-run tube wells in the region. At US$5,200 per ha, no farmer group would have the courage or resources to build such a scheme. As long as the project was operated by USAID, water was free and farmers used it in plenty, but when the donors wanted out, farmers were unwilling to take over the white elephant and its utilization dropped by 90 percent.

6. Marketing professionals view market penetration as the percentage share of all possible sales represented by the actual sale of their products.

7. Early writings called these groundwater markets, a usage that has come to be widely questioned because what the WEM owner sells is not groundwater, which belongs to all, but merely the service of pumping it and conveying it to the buyer's field (Saleth 1994; Palmer-Jones 1994). Therefore, some researchers now call the institution pump rental markets, and I have chosen to call it irrigation service markets. Despite all this hairsplitting, farmers in most parts of South Asia call their pump irrigation transactions water purchases and water sales.

8. With a high level of land fragmentation, it is not economic for a farmer to install a WEM in each parcel. What most farmers do is install a WEM in the largest and best parcel and depend on purchased irrigation in other parcels. This implies that most sellers of pump irrigation services are buyers, too.

9. Despite widespread support for this position, many studies, some of which I explore in Chapter 6, show that under a flat electricity tariff, interlocked water transactions are often as beneficial to buyers as to sellers, or even more.

10. Wilson's critique of pump irrigation markets is illustrative of the nature of debates on welfare effects on buyers. Wilson grants their contribution in making WEM irrigation accessible to the poor; however, she found them exploitative because pump-owning large farmers were able to extract monopoly premia from their poorer clients. Shah and Ballabh (1997), who studied water markets in six villages a hundred kilometers away, also found monopoly profits being charged by sellers; however, they concluded that the rise of water markets had opened up new production possibilities for the poor, improving their lot and thereby imparting a new dynamism to the region's peasant economy. In a critique of Shah and Ballabh, however, Wilson (2002) argued that the impact of pump rental markets on poor buyers reflects not dynamism but a desperate attempt to survive, usually through intensive exploitation of family labor.

11. Mukherji's (2007) West Bengal survey suggests an ideal situation where water buyers are not obliged to economize on pump irrigation but WEM owners are. However, in the Meerut survey, pure buyers harvested lower yields of sugarcane and wheat than WEM owners because they economized on irrigation more than on N-P-K fertilization, suggesting that the irrigation price they faced was in the "pinching" range (Singh and Singh 2003).

12. In Navli village in Anand district of central Gujarat, which I studied in the late 1980s, 23 WEM owners had invested in laying 65 kilometers of buried pipeline networks to cover all 1,100 ha of the village's farmland. Buyers were supreme, with outlets from four or five WEMs opening into each field. WEM owners here have little room to exercise any monopoly power in their dealings with their customers, who receive pump irrigation service of extremely high quality (Shah 1989).

13. Fujita and Hossain (1995) record six ways in which pump irrigation exchange transactions were designed in a single village in northern Bangladesh: for *boro* rice, (1) a buyer leases his land to the shallow tube well owner and accepts 40 percent crop share as land rent (2) the tube well owner supplies water for a fixed 33 percent crop share or (3) a fixed amount; (4) a part of the fixed payment is made as a cash advance and the rest is paid as crop share (5) in addition, for *aman* rice, the buyer pays a fixed cash price for a supplementary irrigation at early stages; and (6) the tube well owner pays a 50 percent crop share to the landowner as a tenant-cum-water seller.

14. Droughts are generally considered to be of four types. Meteorological drought is caused by lack of precipitation. Prolonged meteorological drought leads to agricultural drought, which starts when crops suffer growing moisture stress; available water in surrounding waterbodies is marshaled to save the dying crops. When these waterbodies dry up for lack of replenishment, a hydrological drought occurs. And a series of such hydrological droughts may leave a region's economy sapped and diminished, causing misery all around—a phase referred to as socioeconomic drought (IWMI 2005).

15. The Ginny ratio is an index of inequality with values ranging from zero to one. The higher the value, the greater the inequality.

16. For the mid-1980s, Daines and Pawar (1987) placed the economic rate of return on investment in Andhala command in Maharashtra at 15 to 16 percent with well irrigation and 8.5 percent with just flow irrigation. The incremental rate on well development exceeded 120 percent.

17. Recent discussions in water resources management distinguish between human-managed water (i.e., flow and pump irrigation), called blue water, and rainfall and soil moisture used by crops directly from rainfall, called green water.

18. Based on a review of several systems, Daines and Pawar (1987, *100*) concluded that "40–50% might be a reasonable estimate of utilization for India as a whole." And later, "While India claims to have approximately 35 million ha of surface irrigation 'potential' created as of 1980, at current performance levels less than half of that area is actually irrigated in an average rainfall year. Project designers 'manufactured' almost 17 million ha of fictitious potential." The situation now is much worse in view of the shrinking of flow irrigation commands (Chapter 3).

Chapter 5

1. Whether arsenic in irrigation water translocates in the rice plant is a critical issue on which the jury is still out. If it does, shallow tube well irrigation in the Ganga-Brahmaputra-Meghana basin is up against some serious questions. Norra et al.

(2005) found that grains of rice and wheat crops irrigated with high-arsenic water were free of arsenic, but roots and stems did show traces.

2. Thus, Gujarat has the pumping capacity to irrigate 4.364 million ha against a potential of 2.76 million ha; Haryana has 2.4 million ha against a potential 1.46 million ha; Maharashtra has 4.57 million ha against a potential of 3.65 million ha; in Rajasthan 5.84 million ha against 1.78 million ha; and in Tamilnadu, the potential created was 2.96 million ha against an assessment of 2.83 million ha (Government of India 2005a).

3. Blocks that draw less than 70 percent of their assessed potential and suffer no significant pre- and postmonsoon long-term decline in water levels are considered safe, or white. Those that have developed more than 70 but less than 90 percent of their resource potential and register significant long-term decline in water levels before or after the monsoon are considered semicritical, or gray. Those that use more than 90 percent but less than 100 percent of their assessed resource potential and face significant long-term decline in water levels are colored dark. Finally, blocks with more than 100 percent resource development, which invariably show long-term declines, are considered overexploited.

4. The evidence on the net effect on water quality from expansion of tube well irrigation is by no means unequivocal, however (see Steenbergen and Oliemans 1997 for a review).

5. Gidwani (2002) shows how well irrigation in upstream areas has been an old and foolproof device to sabotage surface-water sharing agreements by analyzing the disputes around Khari River in Gujarat.

6. An excellent account by Neelakantan (2003) of the socioeconomic transformation in Chettipalayam, a Tamilnadu hamlet, and its surrounding areas over the past 50 years offers a vivid case study of how the arrival of pump irrigation made short work of the original engineering and institutional design of a public irrigation project, including a long-defended system of riparian rights. The same dynamic is described by Steenbergen (1995) to explore the decline of *karezes (qanats)* in Baluchistan.

7. See Van Halsema (2002) for an analysis of this aspect in the Indus Basin Irrigation System.

8. Each is assumed to pump an average of 15,000 m³ per year, and two-thirds of the pumped water is consumptively used.

9. Even as the chinks in Sujalam Sufalam project's feasibility came to light, for example, Gujarat's minister for Water Resources bitterly complained that "Rajasthan has been conveniently blocking the flow of waters into North Gujarat dams with check dams upstream" (*Times of India* 2006).

10. Formal and informal economies are a matter of elaborate study in institutional economics. Fiege (1990) summarizes a variety of notions of informality deployed by different researchers. According to Weeks (1975), cited in Fiege (1990, *footnote 6*), "The distinction between a formal and informal sector is based on the organizational characteristics of exchange relationships and the position of economic activity vis-à-vis the State. Basically, the *formal sector* includes government activity itself and those enterprises in the private sector which are officially recognized, fostered, nurtured and regulated by the State . . . Operations in the informal sector are characterized by the absence of such benefits." According to

Portes et al. (1987, cited in Fiege 1990, *footnote 6*), "the informal sector can be defined as the sum total of income generating activities outside the modern contractual relationships of production." According to Portes and Saassen-Koo (1987, cited in Fiege 1990, *footnote 6*) informal sector activities are "not intrinsically illegal but . . . production and exchange escape legal regulation." To most researchers, an informal economy is marked by the "absence of official regulation" or "official status."

11. In urban households (sample = 31,323 households), the situation was the opposite; three-fourths were connected to a public water supply system.

12. NSSO (1999a) also reported on irrigation. Some 36 percent of rural households (a category that includes farmers, farm laborers, and households dependent on off-farm livelihoods) used some means of irrigation. Of the irrigators, 37 percent used their own source (well or tube well), 42.5 percent purchased pump irrigation, and 36 percent used a government tube well, canal, or river. Of the 78,990 households interviewed, 48 percent reported no "availability of community and government water resources in villages of their residence;" another 42 percent reported the presence of community or government source but "without local management." Only 10 percent of households reported living in villages with access to community or government water sources "with local management" by community or government or both (NSSO 1999a, 44).

13. This informal organization of South Asia's water economy is in sharp contrast to water economies of industrialized countries, where IWRM-type interventions work smoothly. Consider a recent account by Luís-Manso (2005) of the highly formalized water economy of Switzerland: 98 percent of the Swiss are linked to public water supply networks and 95 percent with wastewater treatment facilities; all water users are served by a network of municipal, corporate, or cooperative water service providers; and stringent laws and regulations govern withdrawals from any waterbody, requiring formal concessions. Because these concessions are held only by *formal* service-providing public agencies, their enforcement entails little transaction costs.

14. What is today Roorkee Engineering College was originally named for him.

15. The 1882 law, however, made a distinction between water flowing in "defined channels" underground and percolating water. One interpretation of the law is that landowners are entitled to whole of the latter but none of the former (Planning Commission 2007).

16. Many Mughal rulers also imposed a tax on wells independent of the land tax on cultivated area irrigated by the well. This implied that the state claimed ownership of groundwater distinct from the overlying land.

17. Wide geographic dispersion of tube well connections was a major reason for the high transaction costs of metering, billing and collection. According to Rao and Govindarajan (2003, 23), "To illustrate, a rural area of the size of Bhubaneshwar, the capital city of Orissa state, will have approximately 4000 consumers. Bhubaneshwar has 96,000. The former will have a collection potential of Rs. 0.7 million a month; for Bhubaneshwar, it is Rs. 22.0 million a month."

18. The tyranny of arbitrary meter reading has been the major reason for the failure of electricity boards' schemes in recent years to encourage farmers to move from a fairly high flat tariff to a highly subsidized metered tariff. The reason farmers

prefer the flat tariff is freedom from having to deal with meter readers and other staff of the electricity boards (Shah and Ballabh 1995; Shah 1993).

19. Many researchers argue that flat tariffs for farmers began as a populist handout (Joshi and Acharya 2005). Vote-bank politics was certainly implicated, but a compelling need to address the problems of metering was the major stimulus that led to the adoption of flat tariffs.

20. US$ = Ind. Rs. 48 in 2001.

21. This estimate makes sense only if the opportunity cost of power supplied to agriculture is about Indian Rs. 5 per kWh. According to the 2001 minor irrigation census, India had 10.27 million electric WEMs at the turn of the millennium. The figure of Rs. 240 billion per year would mean an average electricity subsidy of Rs. 23,369 per WEM per year. Assuming an average WEM operates for 1000 hours a year, this implies an electricity subsidy of Rs. 23.4 per hour, which can buy 4.68 kWh of power at Rs. 5 per kWh, enough to operate an average Indian electric WEM of 6.5 horsepower. Many people argue that power supplied to farmers is mostly off-peak and of poor quality, and its opportunity cost is more like Rs. 1.8–2 per kWh. The real economic subsidy may thus be more like Rs. 100 billion.

22. See Briscoe and Malik (2006). Shah (2001) has analyzed this aspect for Uttar Pradesh State Electricity Board, and based on a World Bank study in Haryana, Kishore et al. (2003) found that actual agricultural power consumption was 27 percent less than reported, and the overall T&D losses were 47 percent; the official figure was 36.8 percent, making the electricity board appear more efficient than it actually was. The power subsidy ostensibly meant for the agricultural sector but actually accruing to other sectors was estimated at Rs. 5.5 billion a year for Haryana alone.

23. In their paper on the energy-irrigation nexus in Pakistan, Qureshi and Akhtar (2004, 7) lamented, "Power theft and meter tempering is a pressing issue . . . The total power theft was estimated at seven billion units worth Pak Rs. 14 billion. Finally, the army was called in to look for illegal connections and rigged meters. By March 2001, the army has lodged 5687 complaints."

24. As soon as the chief minister announced a sixfold hike in the flat tariff, there was a realignment of forces within his own ruling party, and senior cabinet ministers began clamoring for leadership change. Subhash Yadav, the deputy chief minister, lamented in an interview with *India Today*, "A farmer who produces 10 tonnes of wheat earns Rs. 60,000 and he is expected to pay Rs. 55,000 to the electricity board. What will he feed his children with and why should he vote for the Congress?" (*India Today* 2002, 32).

25. See www.dawn.com/2003/05/01/ebr1.htm.

26. See www.southasianmedia.net/cnn.cfm?id=296859&category=Economy&Country =PAKISTAN.

27. This is widely used to study preelection politics. In this hypothesis, the primary role of elections is to choose policies via the choice of candidates who are known to be committed to certain policy positions. The aim of the analyst is to predict the policy that will be implemented, or the candidate who will be elected given the voters' variety of preferences on any policy (Dharmapala and Lehman 2003).

Chapter 6

1. See www.econlib.org/library/Enc/RationalExpectations.html.

2. Sind may be an exception. Here, large landlords have such large landholdings that they neither have the surplus pumping capacity nor feel the need to sell water to their poorer neighbors. Steenbergen and Oliemans (1997, 9) report that only two percent of tube well owners in Moro and Sakrand sold water, generating a regime of groundwater appropriation that is exclusive and skewed even though groundwater is abundantly recharged in many canal irrigated areas where it is not saline.

3. However, in the late 1970s, 22 percent of the Indus basin had water table at 6 feet, and 30 percent more, at 10 feet, conditions analogous to those in Ganga basin (Steenbergen and Oliemans 1997). Water tables throughout the Indus Basin Irrigation System have dropped since as the number of WEMs in Pakistan soared sixfold from around 150,000 during the mid-1970s to 930,000 in 2004, besides 15,000 heavy-duty SCARP tube wells.

4. This is Perry and Hassan's (2000) implicit assumption in a Pakistan study. They argue that energy cost increases have little effect on water use by buyers by showing that even when fully passed on to the water buyers, increases in energy prices have a minimal effect on demand for water. These authors overlook the fact that when diesel prices rise by 10 percent, water prices rise by substantially more than 10 percent. In a perfectly competitive market, prices would rise just enough to cover the increased cost of fuel.

5. The relationship between energy cost and pump irrigation prices is approximated by

$$w = e/(e-1) \ c$$

where w is the price of pump irrigation (Rs./hour), c is the incremental cost (Rs./hour) of pumping facing the seller (of which, in the case of diesel pumps, a large part is the cost of diesel used per hour), and e is the price elasticity of demand for pump irrigation facing a seller (see Shah 1993 for the derivation). $e/(e-1)$, the index of monopoly power, provides the multiple by which water price will exceed the *incremental* pumping cost. If water sellers behaved as if under perfect competition, e becomes infinity, monopoly multiple approaches zero, and water price charged equals marginal cost. In such a situation, every time the diesel price increases, sellers would raise their pump irrigation price only enough to cover the increased fuel cost. In reality, the value of e in Indo-Gangetic plains is more like 1.5–1.6, and the multiple, 2.7–3. Recent evidence suggests that with growing tube well density, monopoly power is declining.

6. This assumes that 10 million ha of buyers' gross cropped area is irrigated at an average rate of 50 hours per ha through pump irrigation sold by owners of diesel WEMs in eastern India, Nepal Terai, and Bangladesh.

7. Comparing the working of water markets in villages dominated by electric and diesel pump sets in eastern Uttar Pradesh, Kishore and Mishra (2005, 1) concluded that "water buyers, most of whom are marginal and sub-marginal farmers, are hit the hardest by high energy cost for groundwater pumping." And that

shifting pump irrigation from diesel to electricity "will have a huge redistributive impact in Uttar Pradesh since 57 percent of all food crop cultivators in this state are water buyers." This holds true for all of Ganga basin.

8. Farmers in parts of North Gujarat assert that the most common reason for failure of tube wells is breakage of the coupling that bears the weight of all the pipes that have been inserted in course of successive deepening.

9. "Finding single owners of tubewells is becoming increasingly difficult especially in Mehsana . . ." (Joshi and Acharya 2005, 15).

10. The long-run marginal cost is high, however, because farmers expect to have to deepen their tube wells by several feet every year or two. In Mehsana, Joshi and Acharya (2005) say that water tables are receding by up to 20 feet every year. Kumar (2007) notes that water level declines in several *talukas* range from two to six meters per year. Farmers expect this rate of decline and anticipate by making new tube wells deeper and installing pumps bigger than necessary.

11. I have never come across any attempt by an existing tube well company to thwart the formation of another one in its neighborhood. Even so, it is likely the recognition of the inherent inequity of the situation caps blatant profiteering by water sellers. Dubash (2002) hints at some kind of social contract in operation in the two villages he studied in North Gujarat. In a recent study in a sugarcane-growing village in western Uttar Pradesh, Banerji et al. (2006) show that WEM owners sell water even when the pump irrigation price is lower than the marginal value product of water on their own fields, suggesting the operation of some kind of a "social contract" or a "moral economy" in pump irrigation markets.

12. And holding on to this "permit" is not always easy, even when groups of non-*Patidar* poor organize to own a tube well. In his seminal study in two North Gujarat villages, Dubash (2002) found that a group of *Harijans* had organized to own a tube well but had to hand over its control to upper-caste *Patidar* or *Chaudhary* farmers because they could not sustain the business.

13. This phrase was introduced by economic philosopher Joseph Schumpeter (1942) to describe how new technologies enjoy a monopoly and use it to drive out older ones in the process of economic growth.

14. In their sample of 280 farming households, Sharma and Sharma (2004) found that 80 percent of tube wells were owned by medium and large farmers, who also owned more than 80 percent of the WEM-irrigated area belonging the sample households.

15. Among the equity benefits of the flat tariff, one is the subsidy WEM owners in arid alluvial areas provide to small farmers in growing risky cash crops with occasional high payoffs. Shah and Ballabh (1995) argued that in Banaskantha, larger farmers who owned WEMs provided small farmers irrigation to grow highly profitable cumin crops against a one-third crop share. In three of every four or five years, the WEM owner got next to nothing because the buyers' crop failed. He could never afford this under metered tariff.

16. In a study in Madhya Pradesh, Kei and Takeshi (1999), however, found "no significant inefficiency on the farms managed by output sharing water buyers" because the output risk sharing and interest cost on deferred payment for water charges at informal interest rates made up for the higher water price implicit in the output share. In Pakistan Punjab, Jacoby et al. (2001) similarly concluded

that "in a monopolized input market, such as groundwater, inter-linked tenancy contracts actually enhance efficiency." They also show that WEM owners treat tenants at par with themselves but discriminate against buyers who pay cash.

17. Despite palpable exploitation, buyers sometimes seem to benefit as much from well irrigation in arid alluvial aquifers as WEM owners. In a study of Banaskantha, Kumar et al. (2004) found buyers deriving more of their agricultural income from well irrigation than even WEM owners.

18. Shaheen and Shiyani (2005) do find some changes in cropping patterns in Mehsana and Banaskantha districts of North Gujarat over the four decades ending in 2000, but the marked trend is for fodder millet to expand during *kharif* as well as *rabi* to support rapidly growing dairy production.

19. This is distinguished from basin water productivity—that is, output per m^3 of consumptive water use.

20. In North Gujarat, farmers' expectations are strongly influenced by the reports about copious aquifers deep down under the region from India's Oil and Natural Gas Commission, which has drilled deep throughout the region in search of oil and gas.

21. Although low private costs may be the case for WEM owners, pump irrigation buyers bear a much higher irrigation cost, and yet there is no significant move among them, either, toward water-saving crops.

22. In an optimal control theory model that Shaheen and Shiyani (2005) used to understand the myopia of pump irrigators in Banaskantha and Mehsana district, they found that if WEM owners followed a collective optima, average well life could increase to 15 years and present a value of benefits 20 percent higher compared with the present well life of three years resulting from myopic opportunism.

23. Pina et al. (2006, *12*) in Mexico found, "The more overexploited the aquifer is the more water is extracted. This can be explained by the fact that . . . since they do not perceive any damage in the short term, they do not vary their extraction levels. [Also] . . . overexploited aquifers are seen as a type of public good; . . . farmers perceive the water as a very scarce resource, giving them the incentives for extracting as much water as they can before it is exhausted."

24. Absentee water lords are an important group of water service providers in North Gujarat. Shah and Ballabh (1995) interviewed an entrepreneur who had no land of his own but owned seven tube wells and irrigated 200 acres of cumin for one-third crop share contracts. They estimated that some 60 WEM-owning families in that village supported 2,000 acres of cumin irrigation for one-third crop shares, gaining complete virtual control over the village irrigation economy. Interestingly, the buyers interviewed by Shah and Ballabh were not unhappy with this state of affairs. Elsewhere in Banaskantha, Shah and Ballabh recorded cases of schoolteachers, government employees, and bank clerks who invested in diesel pumps and rubber pipes and rented them to farmers against a one-third crop share. There were complex problems of moral hazard in the contracts because these investors had no way of monitoring diesel consumption, which they had to pay for. So specialist agents emerged who would mobilize 60 to 70 acres of potential cumin cultivators and then invite the water lord to invest in a diesel pump and pipes. The agent and his principal would share equally the cost of diesel and the one-third crop share, thus creating a win-win deal for the investor, the agent, and the small farmers (Shah and Ballabh 1995).

25. In Mehsana and Banaskantha districts of North Gujarat, Shaheen and Shiyani (2005) were told by an overwhelming majority of a sample of 180 WEM owners that a new tube well drilled in the neighborhood of an existing one substantially reduced the latter's yield, sometimes even causing it to fail. However, even when specifically asked, very few farmers said they tried to negotiate with the new entrant for an amicable settlement; only three suggested "there is need for a law to space wells and regulate pumping;" and only one farmer said that his neighbor had asked him to reduce his pumping. "More than 50 percent of the farmers were insensitive towards the neighbor's behavior and opted for taking no alternative strategy/action."

26. The major plank on which successive governments in Gujarat have been able to mobilize massive popular support around the Sardar Sarovar Project on River Narmada is sustaining pump irrigated agriculture in arid Saurashtra, North Gujarat, and Kutch, besides drinking water security for the bulk of the state.

27. I have come across no such example in South Asia, but Riaz (2002, 99), writing about cooperation among groundwater irrigators in Yemen, refers to the Al-Sinah community, which bought up the land near its water source, drilled wells and capped them so that well-spacing restrictions could be used to prevent new well development within 500 to 1,000 meters of existing wells.

28. But Joshi and Acharya (2005) do mention that farmers they met in Sabarkantha are resentful that Meshvo water from a dam in their district is dispatched to Kheda and "threatened that if their problem is not solved they would destroy the canal which is connected to Kheda district."

29. Just how serious farmers are in mobilizing against electricity reforms is evident in some random quotes from the study by Joshi and Acharya (2005, passim), who interviewed 400 farmers in North Gujarat about electricity-irrigation issues: "Electricity is an extremely sensitive issue here and farmers become aggressive as soon as one starts discussing [it]. Every week we could see some rally, *dharana*, etc. in front of the Gujarat Electricity Board (GEB) offices. GEB officials fear to enter many villages . . . they [farmers] perceive GEB as their enemy number one . . . [Farmers] feel it is their right to get free electricity . . . Most farmers are not only against the idea of fixing meters but even threaten to damage them . . . [They] either want to continue with this system or want free electricity . . . Farmers have developed some sort of an allergy for meters. They apprehend that GEB officials might tamper with the meter and the blame might fall on [them]. [So], attempts to fix meters are likely to be met with stiff resistance . . . 'What we require is water; give us water and we don't want electricity . . .' Some also demanded that electricity rates should be fixed as per the level of water tables . . . [The leader of the Bharatiya Kisan Sangh (Indian Farmers Federation) said that] any attempt to fix meters or to increase the flat rates will be opposed by all 25 district presidents of BKS . . ."

30. See Karami and Hayati (2005) for an analogous dynamic among groundwater irrigators in two villages in Iran.

31. Chambers 21st Century Dictionary (1999).

32. In a 1998 survey of borewell owners in a hard-rock dry zone of central Karnataka, Nagaraj et al. (2000) found that the cost of exploration—that is, finding water—was a quarter of the capital cost of making a new borewell.

33. In peninsular India and Saurashtra, drilling such bores has become a specialized and hazardous vocation. Journalist Sree Padre narrates the amazing story of Mohammad—nicknamed *adda-bore* (horizontal bore)—in Vittal, a Dakshin Kannada town in Karnataka. See www.indiatogether.com/2006/apr/env-addabore.htm.

34. In a survey of betel vine growers in southern Karnataka, Chandrakanth et al. (1998b) found that 40 percent of their sample farmers had made wells up to 5 km away from their fields to find groundwater.

35. Janakarajan (1994) suggests that overt and covert conflict over a declining resource gets reflected in (1) fragmentation of wells into different shares along with land and the emerging conflicts between different sharers of the same well; (2) competitive deepening of wells and the emerging conflict between well owners who share a common aquifer; (3) trading in groundwater and the emerging conflicts between water seller and water purchaser; and (4) unregulated pumping contributing to the drying up of the surface waterbodies.

36. Each player in the Cournot-Edgeworth model assumes that his rival will not react to his moves. Two well owners sharing the same water-bearing fissure assume that each can increase the yield of his well because he naively expects the other will not follow suit. To begin with, A deepens his well, but his gain is promptly shared by B, who deepens his well, following which A deepens his well again. Each time this happens, combined yields of both the wells increases, but each gets half the yield increase he expected from his investment.

37. Many researchers argue that besides high costs of pesticides and failures of the cotton crop, a major factor that explains the increase in suicide rates among farmers, especially in peninsular India, is heavy debt accumulated by small farmers in coping with well-interference externalities (Reddy 2005).

38. In the well-congested area in their study, well yields declined, on average at 12 percent per year; as a result, 79 percent of dug-cum-boreholes and 38 percent of tube wells were abandoned. In a low-congestion area, in contrast, the average well yield fell only one percent per year; as a result, only 17 percent of dug-cum-boreholes had failed. The average capital investment incurred to cope with well interference was twice as high in the high-congestion area compared with the low-congestion area (Chandrakanth et al. 1998a, 14).

39. But the advantage of the crop-share contract is that payment is deferred until the crop is harvested, and the water seller shares the risk of crop failure. These authors also note the presence of water sales-for-labor contracts. In a similar study in the same area, Nagaraj et al. (2005) found buyers with crop-sharing agreements better off. In all their studies, Chandrakanth and colleagues found that buyers were generally more efficient water users than WEM owners.

40. See also Chandrakanth et al. (1998b) for a similar trend in Shimoga district in southern Karnataka.

41. Deepak et al. (2005) surveyed 120 farmers in Sidlaghatta block of dry Karnataka, where they found that household income from dairying and sericulture, which have derived demand for irrigation for growing fodder and mulberry on small plots, was 1.5 to five times the income derived from field crops, which use much more water because they are grown on larger areas.

42. Among Shimoga's betel vine farmers, Chandrakanth et al. (1998a, *18*) found the "coping mechanisms involved are the use of drip irrigation, conveying water through PVC pipes laid two feet below the ground over long distances of 2–5 km from the borewell located outside the farm, surface water tank, covering the on-farm water tank with polythene sheet to reduce percolation losses and drilling additional wells to meet the acute groundwater scarcity."

43. The ultimate value of decentralized recharge is still a matter of much debate. Some scientists argue that (*1*) water stored in numerous small structures is subject to higher evaporation than one large reservoir with a small exposed surface; and (*2*) in closed river basins, check dams in catchment areas reduce inflows to large government reservoirs downstream. In response to (*1*), others report many years' experimental results by scientists working in arid and semiarid areas showing that collection efficiency has an inverse relationship to the size of the catchment area, and harvesting water from small catchments yields more because water that travels long distances to a large reservoir suffers evaporative losses en route. In response to (*2*), it is suggested that most large dams in South Asia store only a small fraction of the total monsoon discharge because the runoff hydrograph peaks during a short period during the monsoon. Many dams get filled up with just three days of peak flow; in such a situation, water harvesting upstream is unlikely to affect inflows in downstream reservoirs except during drought years (Athavale 2003, *67–68*).

44. Rosin (1993) explored how, over centuries, many arid alluvial regions with an impervious layer have supported population densities unusually high for their climate through intensive groundwater use matched by intensive local management of the resource. In the village of Gangwa in the Aravalli hills, the transition from a rainfed-crop and pastoral economy to a two-crop settled agriculture was supported by an increasingly complex adaptive pattern involving progressive expansion of water-harvesting facilities and a "proliferation of craft, service and ritual specialties from a diverse set of castes" (*59*).

45. Bigha = 0.4 acre = 0.16 hectare.

46. In documenting his visit to village Vikadia, Talati (2004) analyses the experience of the village community using 400- to 600-foot-deep boreholes to recharge water accumulated in newly constructed check dams during the good monsoon of 2003. The community was dismayed when they found they were recharging a saline aquifer. Therefore, it was decided by unanimous vote to seal all boreholes at a depth of 200 feet. Next monsoon, all wells yielded fresh water during *kharif* as well as *rabi*. The value of recharged water established, the community has now turned its attention to bringing all farmland under drip irrigation.

47. Here, some government-built tidal regulators and check dams to recharge coastal aquifers succeeded in staving off salinity and restoring irrigated farming (Shah and Desai 2002).

48. In some arid alluvial areas of Banaskantha district, Shah and Ballabh (1995) had found temporary shallow wells dug by farmers at low cost along the rims of village tanks and used them for irrigation. These would turn saline in a short period, but because they were easy and cheap to dig, farmers would abandon them and make new ones in the expectation that over the next few years, tank recharge would stave off salinity from the abandoned wells. Broad understanding of this

pattern and relatively low congestion had created what was thought in 1991 to be a sustainable pattern.

49. Achieving large-scale water management reform was higher on the Saurashtra Jaldhara Trust's agenda than working on a deep moral economy program. A small NGO founded by a diamond merchant, this trust has taken upon itself the task of rejuvenating dry Gujarat "by making check-dams, ponds and reservoirs in each of 5600 villages and surrounding areas of the villages of Saurashtra and Kutch region. The gist of the activities is to raise ground-water table . . ." To this end, the trust began by giving away free cement to 200 village communities who were ready to build check dams through *sharma-dan* (voluntary labor). Later, it purchased 20 loader-backhoe machines and began giving away 500 hours of machine time per village to all those who were willing to find diesel to run them. In its 2002–2012 business plan to rejuvenate 4,000 villages of Saurashtra and Kutch, the trust has calculated that 100 earthmovers working for 10 years at full utilization could create enough rainwater harvesting and groundwater recharge capacity to increase agricultural production by Rs. 1,850 million per year with a one-time investment of Rs. 980 million, besides making the region drought proof, reducing electricity use for irrigation, making villages tanker-free for their domestic water needs, and greening the entire landscape (*Saurashtra Jaldhara* Trust 2002, pers. comm.).

50. In another study of Hivre Bazaar, Deulagaonkar (2004) asserts, based on a government survey, that a decade ago 90 percent of Hivre Bazaar's households lived in abject poverty; today, none does. The survey showed that the area under summer irrigation jumped more than tenfold and the area under horticulture, sevenfold; milk production increased 25-fold and average household income, 16-fold. Hivre Bazaar has all the characteristics of a dream village. It now has, besides its water success story, active self-help groups, biogas plants, dairy development, and community farming, and the village and its leader, Popat Pawar, have been honored with numerous awards.

51. "Particularly where the impact of recharge or pumping is immediate and dramatic, self-regulation has developed" (Steenbergen and Shah 2003, *242*).

Chapter 7

1. Private tube wells' lowering of water levels in waterlogged areas, making others' farms productive, is an example of a positive externality. New, deep tube wells' drying up of preexisting shallow wells is an example of a negative externality.

2. For example, if a new, deep tube well were to dry up neighboring shallow wells, the tube well owner would compensate shallow well owners enough for them to allow him to dry up their shallow wells, or they will compensate him enough to give up the deep tube well project.

3. The historical antecedent of the idea of water rights through permits is, however, entirely different in the former colonies and far less innocent. As van Koppen (2007, 46) has shown, in former European colonies, "in middle-and low-income countries in Latin America and sub-Saharan Africa, permit systems were introduced

by the colonial powers with the primary goal of dispossessing indigenous water users of their prior claims to water." This colonial idea has acquired new legitimacy in recent years.

4. See www.econlib.org/library/Enc/PropertyRights.html.

5. For example, Colorado decommissioned about 1,000 irrigation wells by decree (Olinger and Plunkett 2005), and Idaho purchased water rights from irrigators and closed 2,000 irrigation wells (Pence 2005). In Colorado, many irrigators had to quit farming or switch to dry-land crops, supplemented by nonfarm income. In Idaho, in contrast, groundwater pumping from increased depths became so expensive that the irrigators were more or less ready to have their operations bought out.

6. From a presentation made by Henry Vaux at the summer school on "Groundwater Intensive Use in South Asia: Food Security, Livelihoods Security and the Challenge of Sustainability," El Escorial, Complutense University of Madrid, 19 June 2005.

7. To quote Blomquist (1992, *303*), "water users in most of these basins originally undertook collective action not in order to enhance efficiency of water use or to implement an 'optimal' management regime but to keep the water supplies . . . Water users in all the seven basins have augmented local water supplies by instituting natural and artificial replenishment programs, and by acquiring access to imported water for direct use."

8. According to Ramon Llamas, this figure could be as high as two million, suggesting that even building an inventory of groundwater irrigators is not easy.

9. An oft-cited success case is Upper Guadiana, a 16,200-km² basin with severely overexploited aquifers. However, what has eased overextraction here is not collective action but the European Union's Income Compensation Programme, with subsidies of up to €420 per ha for giving up irrigation (Hernandez-Mora et al. 2003; Lopez-Gunn 2003). At one-third of that subsidy per ha, many South Asian farmers would willingly give up farming.

10. See www.gwptoolbox.org.

11. Van Koppen et al. (2007, *2*) offers an alternative but similar formulation of the IWRM package: "the role of the state has shifted more towards that of regulator, promoting decentralization and users' participation. In order to fulfil their regulatory role, states have promoted measures such as the strengthening of formal administrative water rights systems, cost-recovery and water pricing ('the user pays' principle), the creation of new basin institutions, and better consideration of the environment (the 'polluter pays' principle). Together, this set of regulatory measures is usually referred to as 'Integrated Water Resources Management' (IWRM)."

12. Inaugural address to the 12th National Symposium on Hydrology with focal theme "Groundwater Governance: Ownership of Groundwater and Its Pricing," organized by the Central Ground Water Board and National Institute of Hydrology, Roorkee, India, 14–15 November 2006 at New Delhi.

13. The author was a member of this group.

Chapter 8

1. Merrey et al. (2007, *209*) argue for replacing watersheds (and other hydrologic units) as unit of analysis and management to "problem-sheds" a term they use to describe "the boundaries of a particular problem as defined by a network of issues."

2. According to Collins' Concise Dictionary (1995 edition), a strategic weapon is "directed against the enemy's homeland rather than used on a battlefield."

3. Also, see Kemper (2007).

4. Transaction costs are often viewed in narrow terms as the costs of accomplishing a transaction. In understanding economy-wide reforms, however, transaction costs are better viewed as the economic equivalent of friction in physical systems (Williamson 1985). More strikingly, Cheung (1974) defines transaction costs as costs impossible to imagine in a Robinson Crusoe economy.

5. Disclosure: the author is employed by IWMI.

6. Under a flat tariff, once a tube well owner pays his fixed monthly charge, the marginal cost of irrigation approaches zero; as a result, farmers keep their pumps running as long as electricity is available because of their illusion that it is free, when actually the cost to society—of the water as well as the power they use—is significant.

7. The famous American cartoonist best known for his complex machines that performed simple tasks in an indirect and convoluted manner.

8. A block is a subdistrict territorial unit with 100 to 150 villages.

9. Farmers are led to believe that more water is being recharged and stored than is actually the case. In Saurashtra, scientists found volumes recharged were small, but farmers were elated because wells were brimming over.

10. The 1987 Water Policy is "such a simple non-binding policy statement" (Saleth 2004, *29*), and it is "occasionally vague" (Mohile, in Briscoe and Malik 2007, *11*).

11. See, www.downtoearth.org.in/cover_nl.asp?mode=3, downloaded 31 July 2007.

12. B. D. Dhawan showed for Mula command and then for Punjab that the indirect benefits of canal irrigation from groundwater recharge are far in excess of the direct benefits of flow irrigation.

13. See, for example, Narayanmoorthy (1996).

14. Using Pascal's principle that pressure throughout a closed system remains constant.

15. See, www.cocef.org/aproyectos/ExComHidalgo2003_05ing.htm. This 20,000-acre irrigation system in Hidalgo County, Texas, has proven viable, with water and energy savings, reduced health risks, and improved vector control. Spain has similarly retrofitted its 1,000-year-old Mula system (see www.fao.org/docrep/004/ac799e/ac799e03.htm), and so has Alberta in Canada (see www1.agric.gov.ab.ca/$department/deptdocs.nsf/all/irr7197/$FILE/irrigationinalta-part2.pdf).

GLOSSARY OF HINDI
AND OTHER TERMS

ahar-pyne: a floodwater-harvesting system
aman: see kharif
bagayat: a garden irrigated with well water
begar: institution of forced labor
bigha: a unit of farmland
boro: rice harvested before summer
brinjal: eggplant
charasa: a leather bucket
chud-pon: a water administrator
dhenkuli: a bamboo basket device for lifting water
doab: the area between two rivers
hilandazi: an irrigation improvement tax; also *gilandazi*
gingili: sesame
kareze: a tunnel that carries groundwater from a well to a series of surface
    outlets

kharif: an autumn harvest of a crop planted at the start of the rainy season
kos: a bullock-bailer
kuchcha: earthen
lambardar: a major local landowner who collected government revenues, including irrigation charges
mesqa: a ditch
moga: an outlet
neerkatti: a water manager
osra bandi: water supplied based on orders placed by farmers
Panchayat: village council
Pani Panchayat: water assembly
Panchayati Raj: local government by elected village councils
Panchasutri: five rules of noble living
prahara: one-eighth of a day
pucca: made with cement and concrete
qanat: see *kareze*
rabi: a spring harvest of a crop grown during the winter
sailab: flood
sakiya: Persian wheel; also *rahat*
Sinchai Samiti: irrigation committee
swayambhoo: self-creating
taccavi: a low-interest agricultural loan
thooti: a village guard
tota: capacitors
wara bandi: a system of rotational water supply
zamindar: a landlord

REFERENCES

Abdel-Rahman, H. A., and Abdel-Magid, I. M. 1993. Water Conservation in Oman. *Water International* 18(2): 95–102.

Abderrahman, W. A. 2003. Should Intensive Use of Non-Renewable Groundwater Always Be Rejected? In *Intensive Use of Groundwater: Challenges and Opportunities*, edited by M. R. Llamas and E. Custodio. Rotterdam, Netherlands: A. A. Balkema Publishers, 191–206.

Adnan, S. 1999. Agrarian Structure and Agricultural Growth Trends in Bangladesh: The Political Economy of Technological Change and Policy Interventions. In *Sonar Bangla? Agricultural Growth and Agrarian Change in West Bengal and Bangladesh*, edited by B. Rogaly, B. Harris-White, and S. Bose. New Delhi: Sage Publications, 177–228.

Agarwal, A., and Narain, S. 1997. *Dying Wisdom: Rise, Fall and Potential of India's Traditional Water Harvesting Systems*. New Delhi: Centre for Science and Environment.

Agnihotri, I. 1996. Ecology, Land Use and Colonization: The Canal Colonies of Punjab. *The Indian Economic and Social History Review* 33(1): 37–58.

Ahluwalia, M. S. 1978. Rural Poverty and Agricultural Performance in India. *Journal of Development Studies* 14(2): 298–323.

Ahmad, S. 2005. Irrigation and Energy Nexus: Managing Energy and Water Use for Reducing Subsidy on Electric Tubewells in Balochistan. *Water for Balochistan Policy Briefings* 1(1), TA-4560. http://brmp.gob.pk, accessed 2 July 2007.

Ahmed, I., and Ahmad, S. 2007. Performance of Diesel and Electric Tubewell Farms and Issue of Subsidy: Lessons from Farmers' Survey. *Water for Balochistan Policy Briefing*, 3(1), TA-4560. http://brmp.gob.pk, accessed 2 July 2007.

Al-Ajmi, H. A., and Abdel Rahman, H. A. 2001. Water Management Intricacies in the Sultanate of Oman: The Augmentation-Conservation Conundrum. *Water International* 26(1): 68–79.

Allan, J. A. 2003. Virtual Water: The Water, Food, and Trade Nexus—Useful Concept or Misleading Metaphor? *Water International* 28 (1): 106–12.

———. 2007. Rural Economic Transitions: Groundwater Use in the Middle East and Its Environmental Consequences. In *The Agricultural Groundwater Revolution: Opportunities and Threats to Development*, edited by M. Giordano and K. G. Villhoth. Wallingford, U.K.: CAB International, 63–78.

Ashley, J. S., and Smith, Z. A. 2001. Western Groundwater Wars. *FORUM for Applied Research and Public Policy* Spring 2001: 33–39. http://forum.ra.utk.edu/Archives/Spring2001/ashley.pdf, accessed 30 January 2008.

Athavale, R. N. 2003. *Water Harvesting and Sustainable Supply in India.* Ahmedabad, India: Centre for Environment Education.

Aung, M. U. 1994. Improved Operation and Maintenance of Lift Irrigation Systems and Management of Groundwater Resources in Myanmar. In *Water Lifting Devices and Groundwater Management for Irrigation*. Report of the Expert Consultation of the Asian Network on Water Lifting Devices for Irrigation, Bangkok, 27 September–1 October 1993. Bangkok: FAO, Regional Office for Asia and the Pacific (RAPA), 185–91.

Bagchi, K. S. 1995. *Irrigation in India: History and Potentials of Social Management.* Delhi: Upalabdhi Trust for Development Initiatives.

Ballabh, V. 1987. Decline of a Novel Experiment: A Case Study of Group Irrigation Tubewells in Deoria District. Anand, India: Institute of Rural Management Anand (typescript).

Ballabh, V., Choudhary, K., Pandey, S., and Mishra, S. 2003. Groundwater Development and Agriculture Production: A Comparative Study of Eastern Uttar Pradesh, Bihar and West Bengal. Paper presented at Annual Partners' Meet of the IWMI-Tata Water Policy Research Program, Anand, India, February 2002.

Banerjee, A., and Iyer, L. 2002. History, Institutions and Economic Performance: The Legacy of Colonial Land Tenure Systems in India. Working Paper 02-27. Boston: MIT.

Banerji, A., Meenakshi, J. V., and Khanna, G. 2006. Groundwater Irrigation in North India: Institutions and Markets. Working Paper 19-06. Kathmandu: SANDEE.

Bangladesh Bureau of Statistics. 2000. *Statistical Yearbook of Bangladesh.* Dhaka, Bangladesh.

Bardhan, K. 1973. Factors Affecting Wage Rates for Agricultural Labour. *Economic and Political Weekly* 8(26): A56–A64.

Bardhan, P. K. 1999. Water Community: An Empirical Analysis of Co-operation on Irrigation in South Asia. Berkeley: University of California.

Barry, E., and Issoufaly, H. 2002. Agrarian Diagnosis of Kumbhasan in North Gujarat, India. Anand, India: IWMI-Tata Water Policy Research Program, and Paris-Grignon, France: National Institute of Agricultural Sciences.

Basham, A. L. 2001. *The Wonder That Was India*. New Delhi: Rupa & Co.

Bassi, N. 2006. Personal communication, 5 December.

Bauer, C. 2004. *Siren Song: Chilean Water Law as a Model for International Reform*. Washington, D.C.: Resources for the Future Press.

Bernal, V. 1997. Colonial Moral Economy and the Discipline of Development: The Gezira Scheme and 'Modern' Sudan. *Cultural Anthropology* 12(4): 447–79.

Bhalla, G. S. 1995. Agricultural Growth and Industrial Development in Punjab. In *Agriculture on the Road to Industrialization*, edited by J. W. Mellor. Baltimore and London: Johns Hopkins University Press, 67–112.

Bhamoriya, V. 2004. Wastewater Irrigation in Vadodara, Gujarat, India: Economic Catalyst for Marginalized Communities. In *Wastewater Use in Irrigated Agriculture: Confronting the Livelihood and Environmental Realities*, edited by C. A. Scott, N. I. Faruqui, and L. Raschid-Sally. Wallingford, U.K.; Colombo; and Ottawa: CAB International, IWMI, and IDRC, 127–34.

Bhatia, B. 1992. Lush Fields and Parched Throats: Political Economy of Groundwater in Gujarat. *Economic and Political Weekly* 27(51–52): A142–A170.

Bhatia, R. 1991. Irrigation Financing and Cost Recovery Policy in India: Case Studies from Bihar and Haryana. In *Future Directions for Indian Irrigation: Research and Policy Issues*, edited by R. Meinzen and M. Svendsen. Washington, D.C.: International Food Policy Research Institute, 168–213.

Biggs, D. 2001. The Problem with Thinking like a Network in the Regional Development of the Mekong Delta. In *Conflict and Cooperation Related to International Water Resources: Historical Perspectives*, edited by S. Castelein and A. Otte. Selected papers of the International Water History Association's Conference on the Role of Water in History and Development, Bergen, Norway, 10–12 August. Paris: UNESCO, 105–120.

Biggs, T. W., Gaur, A., Scott, C. A., Thenkabail, P., Rao, P. G., Krishna Gumma, M., Acharya, S. K., and Turral, H. 2007. Closing of the Krishna Basin: Irrigation, Streamflow Depletion and Macroscale Hydrology. Research Report 111 Colombo: International Water Management Institute.

Blomquist, W. A. 1992. *Dividing the Waters: Governing Groundwater in Southern California*. San Francisco: ICS Press.

Boelens, R., and Bustamante, R. 2005. Formal Law and Local Water Control in the Andean Region: A Field of Fierce Contestation. In *African Water Laws: Plural*

Legislative Frameworks For Rural Water Management in Africa, edited by B. V. Koppen, J. A. Butterworth, and I. Juma. Proceedings of a workshop held in Johannesburg, 26–28 January. Pretoria: International Water Management Institute.

Bose, S. 1999. Agricultural Growth and Agrarian Structure in Bengal: A Historical Overview. In *Sonar Bangla? Agricultural Growth and Agrarian Change in West Bengal and Bangladesh,* edited by B. Rogaly, B. Harris-White, and S. Bose. New Delhi: Sage Publications, 41–59.

Boserup, E. 1999. *My Professional Life and Publications 1929–1999.* University of Copenhagen: Museum Tusculanum Press.

Boyce, J. K. 1988. Technological and Institutional Alternatives in Asian Rice Irrigation. *Economic and Political Weekly* 23: 13: A6–A22.

Brennan, D. 2002. *Water Policy Reform: Lessons from Asia and Australia,* Canberra: Australian Centre for International Agricultural Research.

Briscoe, J. 1999. Water Resources Management in Yemen: Results of a Consultation. Office memorandum from John Briscoe, World Bank, to Doris Köhn, Jean-Claude Villiard, Inder Sud, Salah Darghouth, Jamal Saghir and Mena Water Staff, Water Resources Sector Board members, World Bank, Washington, D.C., 1 November.

Briscoe, J., and Malik, R. P. S. 2006. *India's Water Economy: Bracing for a Turbulent Future.* New Delhi: Oxford University Press.

———. 2007. *Handbook of Water Resources in India.* New Delhi: World Bank and Oxford University Press.

British Geological Survey. 2004 *Community Management of Groundwater Resources: An Appropriate Response to Groundwater Overdraft in India?* London.

Brown, L. 2003. *Plan B: Rescuing a Planet under Stress and a Civilization in Trouble.* New York: Worldwatch Institute and W. W. Norton.

Buechler, S., and Devi, G. M. 2004. Innovations among Groundwater Users in Wastewater Irrigated Areas near Hyderabad, India. Paper presented at Annual Partners' Meet of the IWMI-Tata Water Policy Research Program, Anand, India, February.

Burke, J. J. 2003. Groundwater for Irrigation: Productivity Gains and the Need to Manage Hydro-Environmental Risk. In *Intensive Use of Groundwater: Challenges and Opportunities,* edited by M. R. Llamas and E. Custodio. Rotterdam, Netherlands: A. A. Balkema Publishers, 59–92.

Burke, J. J., and Moench, M. 2000. *Groundwater and Society: Resources, Tensions and Opportunities.* New York: United Nations Publications, Sales E.99.II.A.1.

Burt, C., and Styles, S. 1999. Modern Water Control and Management Practices in Irrigation: Impact on Performance. In *Modernization of Irrigation System Operations,* edited by D. Renault. Proceedings of the Fifth International IT IS Network Meeting, Aurangabad, India, 28–30 October 1998. Bangkok: Food and Agriculture Organization, RAP Publication 99/43, 93–114.

Central Board of Irrigation and Power (India). 1953. *Irrigation in India through Ages,* second edition. New Delhi: Government of India.

———. 1992. *History of Irrigation in Indus Basin.* Publication 230. New Delhi: Government of India.

Central Ground Water Board (India). 1995. *Studies on Conjunctive Use of Surface Water and Ground Water Resources in Mahi-Kadana Irrigation Project, Gujarat.* Faridabad, India: Central Ground Water Board.

Chambers, R. 1988. *Managing Canal Irrigation: Practical Analysis from South Asia.* Cambridge: Cambridge University Press.

Chambers, R., Saxena, N. C., and Shah, T. 1989. *To the Hands of the Poor: Water and Trees.* Delhi, India: Oxford University Press and IBH, London: Intermediate Technology Publications.

Chandrakanth, M. G., Shivakumaraswamy, B., and Ananda, K. K. 1998a. *Economic Implications of Unsustainable Use of Groundwater in Hard Rock Areas of Karnataka.* Report submitted to Ford Foundation, New Delhi, Department of Agri Economics, UAS, Bangalore, March 1998.

Chandrakanth, M. G., Sathisha, K. M., and Ananda, K. K. 1998b. *Resource Economics Study of Valuation of Well Interference Externalities Central Dry Zone of Karnataka.* Report submitted to Ford Foundation, New Delhi, Department of Agri Economics UAS, Bangalore, March 1998.

Chandrakanth, M. G., Bisrat A., and Bhat, M. G. 2004. Combating Negative Externalities of Drought: A Study of Groundwater Recharge Through Watershed. *Economic and Political Weekly* 39(11): 1164–70.

Changming, L., Jingjie, Y., and Kendy, E. 2001. Groundwater Exploitation and Its Impact on the Environment in the North China Plain. *Water International* 26(2): 265–72.

Cheung, S. N. S. 1974. Structure of a Contract and the Theory of Nonexclusive Resources. In *The Economics of Property Rights,* edited by E. G. Furubotn and S. Pejovich. Cambridge, Mass.: Ballinger Publishing.

Choudhury, N. 2006. Irrigation Service Delivery in Canal Systems: A Study of Eight Canal Commands in India. Discussion Paper for ITP 2006, Anand, India: IWMI-Tata Water Policy Program.

Choudhury, N., and Kher, V. 2006. Public Private Partnership in Surface Irrigation: A Case in Kolhapur. Discussion Paper for ITP 2006, Anand, India: IWMI-Tata Water Policy Program.

Christensen, P. 1998. Middle Eastern Irrigation: Legacies and Lessons. In *Transformations of Middle Eastern Natural Environments: Legacies and Lessons,* edited by J. Albert, M. Nernhardsson and R. Kenna. New Haven, Conn.: Yale School of Forestry and Environmental Studies, Bulletin 103, 15–30.

Copestake, J. G. 1986. Finance for Wells in a Hardrock Area of Southern Tamil Nadu. ODAI/NABARD Research Project, Credit for Small Farmer and Rural

Landless, Mumbai: National Bank for Agricultural and Rural Development (NABARD).

Coward, E. W. 1983. Property in Action: Alternatives for Irrigation Investment. Paper presented at Workshop on Water Management and Policy at Khon Kaen University, Khon Kaen, Thailand, September.

―――. 1985. Traditional Irrigation Systems and Government Assistance: Current Research Findings from Southeast Asia. Paper presented at Symposium on Traditional Irrigation Schemes and Potential for Their Improvement, organized by German Association for Water Resources and Land Development, Darmstadt, Germany, April.

Cukierman, A., and Spiegel, Y. 1985. When Is the Median Voter Paradigm a Reasonable Guide for Policy Choices in a Representative Democracy? *Economics and Politics* 15(3): 247–84.

Dahlman, C. J. 1979. The Problem of Externality. *Journal of Law and Economics* 22(1979): 141–61.

Daines, S. R., and Pawar, J. R. 1987. Economic Returns to Irrigation in India, SDR Research Groups Inc. & Development Group Inc. Report prepared for U.S. Agency for International Development Mission to India. New Delhi.

Davis, M. 2001. *Late Victorian Holocausts: El Nino Famines and the Making of the Third World.* London: Verso.

Davis, P. 1968. Australian and American Water Allocation Systems Compared. *Boston College Industrial and Commercial Law Review* 9(1): 647–710.

Dawe, D. 2004. Water Productivity in Rice-Based Systems in Asia: Variability in Space and Time. In *New Directions for a Diverse Planet,* edited by T. Fischer, N. Turner, J. Angus, L. McIntyre, M. Robertson, A. Borrell, and D. Lloyd. Proceedings of Fourth International Crop Science Congress, 26 September–1 October. Gosford, NSW, Australia: The Regional Institute Ltd., www.cropscience.org.au.

DebRoy, A., and Shah, T. 2003. Socio-Ecology of Groundwater Irrigation in India. In *Intensive Use of Groundwater: Challenges and Opportunities,* edited by R. Llamas and E. Custodio. Lise: Netherlands Swets and Zetlinger Publishing Co., 307–35.

Deepak, S. C., Chandrakanth, M. G., and Nagaraj, N. 2005. Groundwater Markets and Water Use Efficiency: The Case of Karnataka. Water Policy Research Highlight 12. Anand, India: IWMI-Tata Water Policy Program.

Delgado, C., Rosegrant, M., Steinfed, H., Ehui, S., and Courbois, C. 2003. Livestock to 2020: The Next Food Revolution. Food, Agriculture and Environment Discussion Paper 28. Washington, D.C.: International Food Policy Research Institute.

Department of Water Resources (California). 2003. *California's Groundwater Update.* Bulletin 118, update 2003. Sacramento: Resources Agency, Department of Water Resources.

Depeweg, H., and Bekheit, K. H. 1997. Evaluation of Proposed Mesqa Improvements. *Irrigation and Drainage Systems* 11: 299–323.

Deulagaonkar, A. 2004. A Monsoon Dream. *Frontline*, 21(14), 3–16 July.

Dharmadhikari, S. 2005. *Unravelling Bhakra: Assessing the Temple of Resurgent India*, Bhopal, India: Manthan Adhyayan Kendra.

Dharmapala, D., and Lehman, E. 2003. A Median Voter Theorem for Post-Election Politics. Working Paper 2003-47. Storrs, Conn.: University of Connecticut.

Dhawan, B. D. 1982. *The Development of Tubewell Irrigation in India*. New Delhi: Agricole Publishing Academy.

———. 1989. *Studies in Irrigation and Water Management*. New Delhi: Commonwealth Publishers.

———. 1993. Reassessment of Irrigation Potential. *Economic and Political Weekly* 28(43): 2371–72.

———. 1995. *Groundwater Depletion, Land Degradation and Irrigated Agriculture in India*. New Delhi: Commonwealth Publishers.

———. 1996a. Trends and Determinants of Capital Investments in Agriculture. *Indian Journal of Agricultural Economics* 541(4): 529–42.

———. 1996b. Relationship between Public and Private Investments in Indian Agriculture with Special Reference to Public Canals. *Indian Journal of Agricultural Economics* 51(1/2): 209–19.

Dhawan, B. D., and Satya Sai, K. J. 1988. Economic Linkages among Irrigation Sources: A Study of the Beneficial Role of Canal Seepage. *Indian Journal of Agricultural Economics* 43(4): 569–79.

Dixit, A. K. 2004. *Lawlessness and Economics: Alternative Modes of Governance*. New Delhi: Oxford University Press.

Down to Earth. 2005. The Lie of the Land. 31 May, 36–38.

D'Souza, R. 2006. Water in British India: The Making of a 'Colonial Hydrology.' *History Compass* 4(4): 621–28.

Dubash, N. 2002. *Tubewell Capitalism: Groundwater Development and Agrarian Change in Gujarat*. Bombay: Oxford University Press.

Dutt, R. 1904 (reprint 1989). *The Economic History of India*, volumes I and II. New Delhi: Government of India, Ministry of Information and Broadcasting.

Dutt, U. 2004. Punjab: Turning into Land of Dark Zones—Need of People's Movement for Water Conservation. *Dams, Rivers & People* 2(2-3-4): 4–5.

Ebrahim, A. 2004. Institutional Preconditions to Collaboration: Indian Forest and Irrigation Policy in Historical Perspective. *Administration and Society* 36(2): 208–42.

Ertsen, M. W. 2003. The Gezira Irrigation Scheme in Sudan: Result or Source of Colonial Irrigation Policies in Africa. Paper presented at Third International Water History Association Conference. Alexandria, Egypt, December.

Etienne, G. 2003. Major Versus Minor Hydraulic Works: Some Critical Issues in Asia. In *Water Resources and Sustainable Development: Challenges of 21st Century*, edited by K. Prasad. Delhi: Shipra Publications, 47–54.

Facon, T. 2002. Asian Irrigation in Transition: Service Orientation, Institutional Aspects, and Design, Operation, Infrastructure Issues. Paper presented at the Conference on Asian Irrigation in Transition-Responding to the Challenges Ahead, 22–23 April, Asian Institute of Technology, Bangkok. http://www.watercontrol. org/tech/files/Asain%20Irrigation%20in%20Transition%20.pdf, accessed 30 January 2008.

Fan, S., Peter, H., and Thorat, S. 1999. *Government Spending, Growth and Poverty: An Analysis of Inter-Linkages in Rural India*. Washington, D.C.: International Food Policy Research Institute.

Food and Agriculture Organization (FAO). 2003. Aquastat.

———. 2004. Aquastat. http://www.fao.org/nr/water/aquastat/dbase/index.stm, accessed 30 January 2008.

———. 2005. Aquastat database.

Faures, J. M., Svendsen, M., Turral, H., et al. (2007). Reinventing Irrigation. In *Water for Food, Water for Life: A Comprehensive Assessment of Water Management in Agriculture*, edited by D. Molden. London: Earthscan, and Colombo: International Water Management Institute, 353–94.

Feitelson, E. 2006. Impediments to the Management of Shared Aquifers: A Political Economy Perspective. *Hydrogeology Journal* 14(3): 319–29.

Fiege, E. L. 1990. Defining and Estimating Underground and Informal Economies: The New Institutional Economics Approach. *World Development* 18(7): 989–1002.

Freeman, D. M., Bhandarkar, V., Shinn, E., Wilkins-Wells, J., and Wilkins-Wells, P. 1989. *Local Organizations for Social Development: Concepts and Cases of Irrigation Organizations*. Boulder, Colo.: Westview Press.

Fujita, K., and Hossain, F. 1995. Role of Groundwater Market in Agricultural Development and Income Distribution: A Case Study in a Northwest Bangladesh Village. *The Developing Economies* 33(4): 442–63.

Gandhi, V., and Namboodiri, N. V. 2007. Groundwater Irrigation: Gains, Costs and Risks. In *Water Policy in India: Context, Issues and Options*, edited by R. M. Saleth. Washington, D.C.: Resources for the Future Press (forthcoming).

Gautam, S. R. 2006. *Incorporating Groundwater Irrigation: Technology Dynamics and Conjunctive Water Management in the Nepal Terai*. Hyderabad, India: Orient Longman.

Gidwani, V. 2002. The Unbearable Modernity of 'Development'? Canal Irrigation and Development Planning in Western India. *Progress in Planning* 58(1): 1–80.

Gilmartin, D. 2003a. Imperial Rivers: Irrigation and British Visions of Empire. Paper presented at Center for South Asia Studies conference on How Empire Mattered: Imperial Structures and Globalization in British Imperialism, University of California–Berkeley, 4–5 April. http://www.ias.berkeley.edu/southasia/Gilmartin. doc, accessed 30 January 2008.

———. 2003b. Water and Waste: Nature, Productivity and Colonialism in the Indus Basin. *Economic and Political Weekly* 38(48): 5057–65.

Giordano, M. 2006. Agricultural Groundwater Use and Rural Livelihoods in Sub-Saharan Africa: A First-Cut Assessment. *Hydrogeology Journal* 14(3): 310–18.

Global Water Partnership. 2000. Integrated Water Resources Management. TAC Background Papers 4(67). Stockholm. www.gwpforum.org/gwp/library/Tacno4.pdf.

———. 2002. *Dialogue on Effective Water Governance*. Stockholm. www.gwpforum.org.

———. 2006. *Water and Sustainable Development: Lessons from Chile*. Policy Brief 2. Stockholm.

Government of India. 1972 *Report of the Irrigation Commission,* Ministry of Irrigation and Power. New Delhi.

———. 2001. Report on Census of Minor Irrigation Schemes (1993–94). New Delhi: Ministry of Water Resources, Minor Irrigation Division.

———. 2005a. Report on Third Census of Minor Irrigation Schemes (2000–01). New Delhi: Ministry of Water Resources, Minor Irrigation Division.

———. 2005b. Net Area Irrigated from Different Sources of Irrigation and Gross Irrigated Area in India during 1950–1951 to 2000–2001. New Delhi: Ministry of Agriculture. http://www.indiastat.com, accessed 30 January 2008.

Government of India and Krishna Water Disputes Tribunal (KWDT). 1973, 1976. The Report and the Further Report of the Krishna Water Disputes Tribunal with the Decision. New Delhi: Central Water Commission.

Government of Indonesia. 2004. *Statistics of Indonesia.* Central Bureau of Statistics.

Government of Pakistan. 2001. Exploitation and Regulation of Fresh Groundwater: Interim Report. Lahore: Ministry of Water and Power.

———. 2003. Pakistan Statistical Year Book 2003. Islamabad: Federal Bureau of Statistics.

———. 2006. *Pakistan Census of Agricultural Machinery.* Islamabad: Census Organization. http://www.statpak.gov.pk/depts/aco/publications/publications.html, accessed 30 January 2008.

Grey, D., and Sadoff, C. 2005. *Water Resources, Growth and Development.* Working Paper for Discussion at U.N. Commission on Sustainable Development, Panel of Finance Ministers. Washington, D.C.: World Bank.

Guha, R. 2007. *India after Gandhi: The History of the World's Largest Democracy.* New Delhi: Pan MacMillan.

Gujarat Samachar. 2006. Rajkot Market Ne Chibi Dragon Thi Saat Udyogkaaro no Prayog. 27 August, 7.

Gulati, A., and Narayanan, S. 2003. The Subsidy Syndrome in Indian Agriculture. New Delhi: Oxford University Press.

Gupta, R., and Tiwari, S. 2002. At the Crossroads: Continuity and Change in the Traditional Irrigation Practices of Ladakh. Paper presented at The Commons in an Age of Globalisation, Ninth Conference of the International Association for the Study of Common Property. Victoria Falls, Zimbabwe, June.

Habib, I. 1999. *The Agrarian System of Mughal India 1556–1707.* New Delhi: Oxford University Press.

Hardiman, D. 1998. Well Irrigation in Gujarat: Systems of Use, Hierarchies of Control. *Economic and Political Weekly* 33(25): 1533–44.

——. 1999. The Politics of Water in Colonial India. Paper presented at Water in History: Global Perspectives An International Historical Conference. University of Wales, Aberystwyth, July. http://www.iwha.net/events/events-1999/hardiman-politics.htm, accessed 30 January 2008.

——. 2002. The Politics of Water in Colonial India, in South Asia. *Journal of South Asian Studies* 25(2): 111–20.

Hatekar, N. 1996. Information and Incentives: Pringle's Ricardian Experiment in the Nineteenth Century Deccan Countryside. *The Indian Economic and Social History Review* 33(4): 438–53.

Hayami, Y., and Ruttan, V. 1971. *Agricultural Development: An International Perspective.* Baltimore, Md.: Johns Hopkins University Press.

Hernandez-Mora, N., Martinez, C. L., and Fornes, J. 2003. Intensive Groundwater Use in Spain. In *Intensive Use of Groundwater: Challenges and Opportunities*, edited by M. R. Llamas and E. Custodio. Rotterdam, Netherlands: A. A. Balkema Publishers, 387–414.

Himel, J. 2007. Khmer Rouge Irrigation Development in Cambodia. *Deathpower in Cambodia.* http://leahbowe.com/deathpower/2007/04/12/khmer-rouge-irrigation-projects/, accessed 3 May 2007.

Hirschman, A. 1965. Exit, Voice and Loyalty: Responses to Decline in Firms, Organizations and States. Boston: Harvard University Press.

Huang, Q., Rozelle, S., and Hu, D. 2007. Pumpset Clusters in China: Explaining the Organization of the Industry that Revolutionized Asian Agriculture. Unpublished draft report. St. Paul: University of Minnesota, Department of Economics.

Hunt, R. C. 1986. Canal Irrigation in Egypt: Common Property Management. In *Proceedings of the Conference on Common Property Resource Management*, 21–25 April 1985. Washington, D.C.: National Academy Press, 199–215.

——. 1988. Size and the Structure of Authority in Canal Irrigation Systems. *Journal of Anthropological Research* 44(4): 335–55.

——. 1989. Appropriate Social Organization? Water User Associations in Bureaucratic Canal Irrigation Systems. *Human Organization* 48(1)(Spring): 79–89.

Hunter, W. W. 1997. *A Statistical Account of Bengal: Midnapur*, volume III. Calcutta: West Bengal District Gazetteers, Government of West Bengal.

India Today. 2002. Running for Cover: Demand for a Tribal Chief Minister and a Proposed Hike in Power Tariffs Pose a Serious Challenge to Digvijay Singh's Leadership. 27(47) (19–25 November): 32.

Indian Irrigation Commission. 1903. Report of the Indian Irrigation Commission 1901–03. Calcutta: Office of the Superintendent of Government Printing.

Indu, R. 2002. Fluoride-Free Drinking Water Supply in North Gujarat: The Rise of Reverse Osmosis Plants as a Cottage Industry: An Exploratory Study. Anand, India: IWMI-Tata Water Policy Program.

Intercooperation in India. 2005. Tradition Meeting Modernity: A Case Study on the Management of Mudiyanur Tank, Kolar District Karnataka. Working Paper 2. Hyderabad, India: Intercooperation Delegation.

International Water Management Institute (IWMI). 2003. Confronting the Realities of Wastewater Use in Agriculture. Water Policy Briefing 9. Colombo.

———. 2005. Drought Assessment and Mitigation in Southwest Asia: A Synthesis Report. Colombo.

Ishikawa, S. 1967. *Economic Development in Asian Perspective.* Tokyo: Kinokuniya.

Islam, M. M. 1997. *Irrigation Agriculture and the Raj, Punjab, 1887–1947.* New Delhi: Manohar Books.

Jacoby, H. G., Murgai, R. and Rehman, S. 2001. Monopoly Power and Distribution in Fragmented Markets: The Case of Groundwater. Policy Research Working Paper 2628, Development Research Group, Rural Development. Washington, D.C.: World Bank.

Jairath, J. 1985. Technical and Institutional Factors in Utilization of Irrigation: A Case Study of Public Canals in Punjab. *Economic and Political Weekly* 20(3): A2–A10.

———. 2001. *Water User Associations in Andhra Pradesh: Initial Feedback.* New Delhi: Concept Publishing Co.

Janakarajan, S. 1994. Trading in Groundwater: A Source of Power and Accumulation. In *Selling Water: Conceptual and Policy Debates over Groundwater Markets in India,* edited by M. Moench. Ahmedabad, India: VIKSAT, 47–58.

———. 2002. Wells and Illfare: An Overview of Groundwater Use and Abuse in Tamil Nadu, South India. Paper presented at Annual Partners' Meet of the IWMI-Tata Water Policy Research Program, Anand, India, February.

Janakarajan, S., and Moench, M. 2006. Are Wells a Potential Threat to Farmers' Well-Being? Case of Deteriorating Groundwater Irrigation in Tamil Nadu. *Economic and Political Weekly* 41(37): 3977–87.

Joseph, C. J. 2001. *Beneficiary Participation in Irrigation Water Management: The Kerala Experience.* Discussion Paper 36. Thiruvananthapuram, India: Centre for Development Studies.

Joshi, V., and Acharya, A. 2005. Addressing Agricultural Power Subsidy: A Case Study of North Gujarat. Working Paper 2. Surat, India: Center for Social Studies. www.esocialsciences.com.

Joshi, P. K., Gulati, A., Birthal, P. S., and Tewari, L. 2004. Agriculture Diversification in South Asia: Patterns, Determinants and Policy Implications. *Economic and Political Weekly* 39(24): 2457–69.

Jurriens, M., Mollinga, P., and Wester, P. 1996. *Scarcity by Design: Protective Irrigation in India and Pakistan.* Wageningen, Netherlands: Liquid Gold 1996 Paper 1.

Kahlown, M. A. 2003. Depleting Aquifers in Baluchistan. *The Dawn,* 6 October.

Kahnert, F., and Levine, G. 1993. Overview. In *Groundwater Irrigation and the Rural Poor: Options for Development in the Gangetic Basin,* edited by F. Kahnert, and G. Levine. Washington, D.C.: World Bank.

Kalf, F. R. P., and Wooley, D. R. 2005. Applicability and Methodology of Determining Sustainable Yield in Groundwater Systems. *Hydrogeology* 13(1): 295–312.

Karami, E., and D. Hayati. 2005. Rural Poverty and Sustainability: The Case of Groundwater Depletion in Iran. *Asian Journal of Water, Environment and Pollution* 2(2): 51–61.

Kei, K., and Takeshi, S. 1999. Price Determination under Bilateral Bargaining with Multiple Modes of Contract: A Study of Groundwater Market in India. http://www.fasid.or.jp/english/surveys/research/program/research/pdf/discussion/2000-002.pdf, accessed 1 November 2006.

Keller, A., and Keller, J. 1995. *Effective Efficiency: A Water Use Concept for Allocating Freshwater Resources.* Water Resources and Irrigation Division Discussion Paper 22. Arlington, Va.: Winrock International.

Keller, A., Sakthivadivel, R., and Seckler, D. 2000. Water Scarcity and the Role of Storage in Development. Research Report 39. Colombo: International Water Management Institute.

Kemper, K. E. 2007. Instruments and Institutions for Groundwater Management. In *The Agricultural Groundwater Revolution: Opportunities and Threats to Development,* edited by M. Giordano and K. G. Villhoth. Wallingford, U.K.: CAB International, 153–72.

Kendy, E., Molden, D. J., Steenhuis, T. S., and Liu, C. 2003. Policies Drain the North China Plain: Agricultural Policy and Groundwater Depletion in Luancheng County, 1949–2000. Research Report 71. Colombo: International Water Management Institute.

Khan, H. R. 1994. Operation and Maintenance of Lift Irrigation Systems in Bangladesh. In *Water Lifting Devices and Groundwater Management for Irrigation.* Report of the Expert Consultation of the Asian Network on Water Lifting Devices for Irrigation, Bangkok, 27 September–1 October 1993. Bangkok: FAO, Regional Office for Asia and the Pacific, 81–91.

Khaneiki, M. L. 2007. Traditional Water Management: An Inspiration for Sustainable Irrigated Agriculture in Central Iran. Paper presented at International History Seminar on Irrigation and Drainage, Tehran, May. http://www.irncid.org/

pim2007/DownloadFileArticle.aspx?FileName=681329675930457635.pdf, accessed 30 January 2008.

Kikuchi, M., Weligamage, P., Barker, R., Samad, M., Kono, H., and Somaratne, H. M. 2003. Agro-Well and Pump Diffusion in the Dry Zone of Sri Lanka: Past Trends, Present Status and Future Prospects. Research Report 66. Colombo: International Water Management Institute.

Kishore, A. 2002. Social Impact of Canal Irrigation: A Review of 30 Years of Research. Paper presented at First Annual Partners' Meet of the IWMI-Tata Water Policy Research Program, Anand, India, February.

Kishore, A., and Mishra, K. N. 2005. Cost of Energy for Irrigation and Agrarian Dynamism in Eastern Uttar Pradesh. Water Policy Research Highlight 21. Anand, India: IWMI-Tata Water Policy Program.

Kishore, A., Sharma, A., and Scott, C. A. 2003. Power Supply to Agriculture: Reassessing the Options. Water Policy Research Highlight 7. Anand, India: IWMI-Tata Water Policy Program.

Klein, G. K. and Ramankutty, N. 2004. Land Use Changes during the Past 300 Years. In *Natural Resources Policy and Management,* edited by W. Verheye. Encyclopedia of Life Support Systems. Oxford: EOLSS Publishers. http://www.eolss.net, accessed 30 January 2008.

Kloezen, W. H. 2002. *Accounting for Water: Institutional Viability and Impacts of Market-Oriented Irrigation Interventions in Central Mexico.* Ph.D. Thesis, Rural Development Sociology Group, Wageningen University, Netherlands.

Knegt, J. F., and Vincent, L. F. 2001. From Open Access to Access by All: Restating Challenges in Groundwater Management in Andhra Pradesh. *Natural Resources Forum* 25(4): 321–31.

Kolavalli, S., and Atheeq, L. K. 1990. *Groundwater Utilization in Two Villages in West Bengal.* Ahmedabad, India: Centre for Management in Agriculture, Indian Institute of Management.

Kolavalli, S., Kalro, A. H., and Asopa, V. N. 1989. *Issues in Development and Management of Groundwater Resources in East Uttar Pradesh.* Ahmedabad, India: Centre for Management in Agriculture, Indian Institute of Management.

Kuhn, T. 1962. *The Structure of Scientific Revolutions.* Chicago: The University of Chicago Press.

Kumar, D. 1974. Changes in Income Distribution and Poverty in India: A Review of the Literature. *World Development* 2(1): 31–41.

Kumar, M. D. 2005. Impact of Water Prices and Volumetric Water Allocation on Water Productivity: Comparative Analysis of Well Owners, Water Buyers and Share-Holders. Water Policy Research Highlight 11. Anand, India: IWMI-Tata Water Policy Program.

———. 2007. *Groundwater Management in India: Physical, Institutional and Policy Alternatives.* New Delhi: Sage Publications.

Kumar, M. D., and Singh, O. P. 2005. Virtual Water in Global Food and Water Policy Making: Is There a Need for Rethinking? *Water Resource Management* 19(6): 759–89.

Kumar, M. D., Iyer, B., and Agarwal, V. 2004a. Can North Gujarat's Agrarian Economy Thrive with Less Groundwater Use? A Simulation Study Using Linear Programming in Banaskantha District. Paper presented at Annual Partners' Meet of the IWMI-Tata Water Policy Research Program, Anand, India.

Kumar, M. D., Singhal, L., and Rath, P. 2004b. Value of Groundwater: Case studies in Banaskantha, Gujarat. *Economic and Political Weekly* 39(31): 3498–503.

Kumar, M. D., Ghosh, S., Singh, O. P., Ranade, R., and Ravindranath, R. 2005. Changes in Groundwater Ecology and Its Implications for Surface Flows: Studies from Narmada River Basin, Madhya Pradesh, India. Water Policy Research Highlight 25. Anand, India: IWMI-Tata Water Policy Program.

Kumar, M. D., Singh, O. P., Sinha, S. K., Jos, C. R., Sreeja, K. G., and Joji, A. O. 2007. Planning for Integrated Water Management in Bharatapuzha River Basin: Report of a Research Study Undertaken in Kerala Part of the Basin. Report submitted to Kerala State Planning Board, Trivandrum.

Le Van Hien. 1994. Water Lifting Devices Development in Vietnam. In *Water Lifting Devices and Groundwater Management for Irrigation.* Report of the Expert Consultation of the Asian Network on Water Lifting Devices for Irrigation, Bangkok, 27 September–1 October 1993. Bangkok: FAO, Regional Office for Asia and the Pacific (RAPA), 249–52.

Lieberand, J. W. 2004. Drip for Cows or Crops: What Gender Issues and New Livelihoods Strategies Mean for Water Saving Technologies. Paper presented at Annual Partners' Meet of the IWMI-Tata Water Policy Research Program, Anand, India, February.

Lim, E. R. 2001. Address to the World Bank Conference on Distribution Reforms, October 12–13, http://www.ficci.com/media-room/speeches-presentations/2001/oct/oct-power-lim.htm, accessed 30 January 2008.

Lipton, M. 1985. The Prisoners' Dilemma and the Coase Theorem: A Case for Democracy in Less Developed Countries? In *Economy and Democracy,* edited by R. C. O. Matthews. London: Macmillan.

Llamas, R., and Custodio, E. 2003. *Intensive Use of Groundwater: Challenges and Opportunities.* Rotterdam, Netherlands: A. A. Balkema Publishers.

Londhe, A., Talati, J., Singh, L. K., Dhaunta, S., Rawlley, B., Ganapathy, K. K., and Mathew, R. 2004. Urban-Hinterland Water Transactions: A Scoping Study of Six Class I Indian Cities. Paper presented at Annual Partners' Meet of the IWMI-Tata Water Policy Research Program, 2004, Anand, India, February.

López-Gunn, E. 2003. The Role of Collective Action in Water Governance: A Comparative Stay of Groundwater Uses Association in La Mancha Aquifer in Spain. *Water International* 28(3): 367–78.

López-Gunn, E., and Llamas, M. R. 1999. New and Old Paradigms in Spain's Water Policy. Paper presented at Forum of the UNESCO International School of Science for Peace Meetings on Water Security in the Third Millennium, Mediterranean Countries as a Case, Villa Olmo, Como, Italy, April. UNESCO Science for Peace Series.

Lowdermilk, M. K., Earley, A. C., and Freeman, D. M. 1978. *Farm Irrigation Constraints and Farmers: Responses: Comprehensive Field Survey in Pakistan.* Water Management Research Project Technical Reports 48A–48F. Fort Collins: Colorado State University.

Lowi, T. J. 1972. Four Systems of Policy, Politics and Choice. *Public Administration Review* 32(4): 298–310.

Ludden, D. 1999. *An Agrarian History of South Asia.* Cambridge: Cambridge University Press.

Luís-Manso, P. 2005. Economic Risks in the Drinking Water Sector. Paper presented at International Conference on Water Economics, Statistics and Finance, IWA, Rethymno, Greece, July.

Macdonald, D. H., and Young, M. 2000. A Case Study of the Murray-Darling Basin. Natural Resource Management Economics 01_001, Policy and Economic Research Unit, CSIRO Land and Water, Adelaide, Australia.

Madhav, R. 2007. *Irrigation Reforms in Andhra Pradesh: Whither the Trajectory of Legal Changes?* Working Paper 2007–04. Geneva: International Water Law Research Center. http://www.ielrc.org/content/w0704.pdf, accessed 30 January 2008.

Mahendra, D. S., and Rao, C. N. 2005. Food Processing and Contract Farming in Andhra Pradesh: A Small Farmer Perspective. *Economic and Political Weekly,* 40(26): 2705–713.

Malthus, T. 1798. *An Essay on the Principles of Population, as It Affects Future Improvement of Society.* London: St. Paul's Church-Yard. http://www.econlib.org/Library/Malthus/malPlong.html, accessed 30 January 2008.

Mandal, M. A. S. 1989. Groundwater Irrigation by Landless Pump Group in Bangladesh. Paper presented at Workshop on Groundwater Management at the Institute of Rural Management, Anand, Gujarat, India, 30 January–1 February.

———. 2000. Dynamics of Irrigation Water Markets in Bangladesh. In *Changing Rural Economy of Bangladesh,* edited by M. A. S. Mandal. Dhaka, Bangladesh: Economic Association, 118–28.

———. 2006. Groundwater Irrigation Issues and Research Experience in Bangladesh. Paper presented at International Workshop on Groundwater Governance in Asia, IIT, Roorkee, India, 12–14 November.

Mandal, M. A. S., and Palmer-Jones, R. W. 1987. Access of the Poor to Groundwater Irrigation in Bangladesh. Paper presented at Roorkee University Workshop on Common Property Resources with Special Reference to Access of the Poor to Groundwater, Rourkee, India, February.

Marin, L. E. 2005. Personal communication, 5 July.

Masiyandima, M., and Giordano, M. 2007. Sub-Saharan Africa: Opportunistic Exploitation. In *The Agricultural Groundwater Revolution: Opportunities and Threats to Development*, edited by M. Giordano and K. G. Villhoth. Wallingford, U.K.: CAB International, 79–99.

Mason, P. 2006. *The Men Who Ruled India*. New Delhi: Rupa & Co.

Mate, M. S. 1998. *A History of Water Management and Hydraulic Technology in India, 1500 B.C.–1800 A.D.* New Delhi: B.R. Publishers.

Mehanna, S., Huntington, R., and Rachad, A. 1984. Irrigation and Society in Rural Egypt. *Cairo Papers in Social Science* 7(4).

Meinzen-Dick, R. 1996. *Groundwater Markets in Pakistan: Participation and Productivity*. IFPRI Research Report 105. Washington, D.C.: International Food Policy Research Institute.

Meinzen-Dick, R. and Sullins, M. 1994. *Water Markets in Pakistan: Participation and Productivity*. EPTD Discussion Paper 4. Washington, D.C.: International Food Policy Research Institute.

Merrey, D. J., Meinzen-Dick, R., Mollinga, P. P., Karar, E., et al. 2007. Policy and Institutional Reform: The Art of the Possible. In *Water for Food, Water for Life: A Comprehensive Assessment of Water Management in Agriculture*, edited by D. Molden. London: Earthscan, and Colombo: International Water Management Institute, 193–231.

Ministry of Agriculture Bangladesh. Handbook of Statistical Year Book 2005. Dhaka, Government of the People's Republic of Bangladesh.

Ministry of Water Resources (India). 1999. *Integrated Water Resource Development: A Plan for Action*. Report of the National Commission for Integrated Water Resources Development, volume I. New Delhi: Government of India.

Moench, M. 1992. Chasing the Water Table: Equity and Sustainability in Groundwater Management. *Economic and Political Weekly* 27(51–52): 171–77.

———. 1995. *Electricity Pricing: A Tool for Groundwater Management in India?* Ahmedabad, India: VIKSAT-Natural Heritage Institute.

———. 2003. Groundwater and Poverty: Exploring the Connections. In *Intensive Use of Groundwater: Challenges and Opportunities*, edited by M. R. Llamas and E. Custodio. Rotterdam, Netherlands: A. A. Balkema Publishers, 441–55.

———. 2007. When the Well Runs Dry but Livelihood Continues: Adaptive Responses to Groundwater Depletion and Strategies for Mitigating the Associated Impacts. In *The Agricultural Groundwater Revolution: Opportunities and Threats to Development*, edited by M. Giordano and K. G. Villhoth, K. G. Wallingford, U.K.: CAB International, 173–92.

Moench, M., and Dixit, A. 2004. Adaptive Capacity and Livelihood Resilience: Adaptive Strategies for Responding Floods and Droughts in South Asia. Kathmandu: Institute of Social and Environmental Transition.

Mohanty, N. 2005. Moving to Scale. Background Paper for India's Water Economy: Bracing for a Turbulent Future. Report 34750-IN. Agriculture and Rural Development Unit, South Asia Region. Washington, D.C.: World Bank.

Molle, F. 2005. *Irrigation and Water Policies in the Mekong Region: Current Discourses and Practices.* Research Report 95. Colombo: International Water Management Institute.

Molle, F., Shah, T., and Barker, R. 2003. The Groundswell of Pumps: Multi-Level Impacts of a Silent Revolution. Paper presented at ICID-Asia Meeting, Taipei, November.

Mollinga, P. 1992. *Protective Irrigation in South India: Deadlock or Development?* DPP Working Paper 24. Development Policy and Practice Research Group. Milton Keynes, U.K.: Open University.

———. 2003. *On the Water Front: Water Distribution, Technology and Agrarian Change in a South Indian Canal Irrigation System.* New Delhi: Orient Longman.

———. 2006. IWRM in South Asia: A Concept Looking for a Constituency. In *Integrated Water Resources Management: Global Theory, Emerging Practice and Local Needs,* edited by P. P. Molling, A. Dixit and K. Athukorala. New Delhi: Sage Publications, 21–37.

Mukherji, A. 2005. The Spread and Extent of Irrigation Rental Market in India, 1976–77 to 1997–98: What Does the National Sample Survey Data Reveal? Water Policy Research Highlight 7. Anand, India: IWMI-Tata Water Policy Program.

———. 2007. *Political economy of groundwater markets in West Bengal, India: Evolution, extent and impacts.* PhD thesis, University of Cambridge, United Kingdom.

Mukherji, A., and Kishore, A. 2003. Tubewell Transfer in Gujarat: A Study of the GWRDC Approach. Research Report 69. Colombo: International Water Management Institute.

Muth, J. A. 1961 Rational Expectations and the Theory of Price Movements. *Econometrica* 29(6): 315–35.

Nagaraj, N., and Chandrakanth, M. G. 1997. Intra and Inter-Generational Equity Effects of Irrigation Well Failures: Farmers in Hard Rock Areas of India. *Economic and Political Weekly* 32(13): 41–44.

Nagaraj, N., Frasier, W. M., and Sampath, R. K. 2000. A Comparative Study of Groundwater Institutions in the Western United States and Peninsular India for Sustainable and Equitable Resource Use. Paper presented at Constituting the Commons: Crafting Sustainable Commons in the New Millennium, Eighth Conference of the International Association for the Study of Common Property, Bloomington, Ind., May–June.

Nagaraj, N., Kumari, S. A. H., and Chandrakanth, M. G. 2005. Institutional and Economic Analysis of Groundwater Markets in Central Dryzone of Karnataka.

Paper presented at Annual Partners' Meet of the IWMI-Tata Water Policy Research Program, Anand, India, February.

Narain, V. 2004. Crafting Institutions for Collective Action in Canal Irrigation: Can We Break the Deadlocks? Paper presented at Silver Jubilee Symposium on Governance Issues in Water, Institute of Rural Management, Anand, India, December.

Narayanamurthy, A. 1996. *Evaluation of Drip Irrigation in Maharashtra.* Pune, India: Gokhale Institute of Politics and Economics.

———. 2006. State of India's Farmers. *Economic and Political Weekly* 41(6): 471–73.

———. 2007. Does Groundwater Irrigation Reduce Rural Poverty? Evidence from Indian States. *Irrigation and Drainage* 56(2–3): 349–62.

Narayanamoorthy, A., and Deshpande, R. S. 2003. Irrigation Development and Agricultural Wages: An Analysis Across States. *Economic and Political Weekly* 38(35): 3716–22.

National Sample Survey Organization (NSSO). 1999a. *Cultivation Practices in India:* NSS 54th Round, January–June 1998, Report 451. New Delhi: Department of Statistics, Government of India.

———. 1999b. *Common Property Resources in India:* NSS 54th Round, January–June 1998, Report 452. New Delhi: Department of Statistics, Government of India.

———. 2003. *Report on Village Facilities.* NSS 58th round, July–December 2002, Report 487(58/3.1/1). New Delhi: Department of Statistics, Government of India.

———. 2005. *Situation Assessment Survey of Farmers: Some Aspects of Farming.* 59th Round, January–December 2003, Report 496(59/33/3). New Delhi: Department of Statistics, Government of India.

Neelakantan, S. 2003. *A Gossipmonger's Revisit to Chettipalayam: Water Conflict and Social Change in Amaravathi Basin.* Working Paper 182. Chennai: Madras Institute of Development Studies.

Neetha, N. 2003. Irrigation Institutions in Canal Command: The Case of Chalakkudy River Diversion Scheme in Kerala, South India. Ph.D. Thesis, Centre for Development Studies, Thiruvanthapuram, India.

Nijman, C. 1993. A Management Perspective on the Performance of the Irrigation Subsector. Ph.D. Thesis, Agricultural University. Wageningen, Netherlands.

Norra, S., Berner, Z. A., Agarwala, P., Wagner, F., Chandrasekharam, D., and Stüben, D. 2005. Impact of Irrigation with as Rich Groundwater on Soil and Crops: A Geochemical Case Study in West Bengal Delta Plain, India. *Applied Geochemistry* 20 (10): 1890–906.

North, D.C. 1990. *Institutions, Institutional Change, and Economic Performance.* New York: Cambridge University Press.

Olinger, D., and Plunkett, C. 2005. Law Makes, Breaks Men. *Denver Post,* 23 November.

Olson, M. J. 1965. *The Logic of Collective Action: Public Goods and the Theory of Groups.* Cambridge, Mass.: Harvard University Press

O'Malley, L. S. S. 1995a. *Bengal District Gazetteers: Bankura.* Calcutta: West Bengal District Gazetteers, Government of West Bengal.

———. 1995b. *Bengal District Gazetteers: Midnapur.* Calcutta: West Bengal District Gazetteers, Government of West Bengal.

———. 1996. *Bengal District Gazetteers: Birbhum.* Calcutta: West Bengal District Gazetteers, Government of West Bengal.

———. 1997. *Bengal District Gazetteers: Murshidabad.* Calcutta: West Bengal District Gazetteers, Government of West Bengal.

———. 1999. *Bengal District Gazetteers: Santhal Paragana.* Calcutta: West Bengal District Gazetteers, Government of West Bengal.

Oorthuizen, J. 2003. *Water, Works and Wages: The Everyday Politics of Irrigation Management Reform in the Philippines.* New Delhi: Orient Longman.

Oweis, T., Hachum, A., and Kijne, J. 1999. Water Harvesting and Supplemental Irrigation for Improved Water Use Efficiency in Dry Areas. SWIM Paper 7. Colombo: International Water Management Institute.

Paarlberg, D. 1993. The Case for Institutional Economics. *American Journal of Agricultural Economics* 75(3): 823–27.

Padhiari, H. K. 2005. Water Management in Upper Krishna Basin: Issues and Challenges. Paper presented at FPRM Research Workshop, Institute of Rural Management, Anand, India, October.

———. 2006. Water Service Markets in Surface Irrigation Systems: Institutions and Socio-Economic Impact. Paper presented at Annual Partners' Meet of the IWMI-Tata Water Policy Research Program, Anand, India, March.

Palanisami, K., and Ranganathan, C. R. 2004. *Value of Water in Tank (Surface) Irrigation Systems.* Coimbatore, India: Water Technology Center, Tamil Nadu Agricultural University.

Palmer-Jones, R. W. 1987. Share Cropping with Water in Bangladesh: Imperfect Institutional Innovation? Agricultural Economics Unit, Oxford University, London.

———. 1994. Groundwater Markets in South Asia: A Discussion of Theory and Evidence. In *Selling Water: Conceptual and Policy Debates over Groundwater Markets in India,* edited M. Moench. Ahmedabad, India: VIKSAT, 11–46.

———. 1995. Deep Tubewells for Irrigation: Efficiency, Equity and Sustainability. School of Development Studies, University of East Anglia, U.K.

———. 1999. Slowdown in Agricultural Growth in Bangladesh: Neither a Good Description Nor a Description Good to Give. In *Sonar Bangla? Agricultural Growth and Agrarian Change in West Bengal and Bangladesh,* edited by B. Rogaly, B. Harris-White, and S. Bose. New Delhi: Sage Publications, 92–136.

Panda, H. 2002. Energy-Irrigation Nexus: Orissa's Power Sector Reforms and Its Groundwater Economy. Paper presented at Annual Partners' Meet of the IWMI-Tata Water Policy Research Program, Anand, India, February.

Pant, N. 1984. Community Tubewell: An Organizational Alternative to Small Farmers' Irrigation. *Economic and Political Weekly* 19(26): A59–A66.

———. 1991. *Development of Groundwater Markets in Eastern Uttar Pradesh. Indo-Dutch Uttar Pradesh Tubewell Project.* Lucknow, India: Centre for Development Studies.

———. 1992. *New Trends in Indian Irrigation: Commercialization of Groundwater.* New Delhi: Ashish Publishing House.

———. 1994. Performance of the World Bank Tubewells in India. In *Groundwater Irrigation and the Rural Poor, Options for Development in the Gangetic Basin,* edited by F. Kahnert and G. Levine. Washington, D.C.: World Bank, 119–30.

———. 1998. Indigenous Irrigation in South Bihar: A Case of Congruence of Boundaries. *Economic and Political Weekly* 33(49): 3132–38.

———. 2004. Trends in Groundwater Irrigation in Eastern and Western UP. *Economic and Political Weekly* 39(31): 3463–68.

———. 2005. Control and Access to Groundwater in UP. *Economic and Political Weekly* 40(26): 2672–80.

Pant, N., and Rai, R. P. 1985. *Community Tubewell and Agricultural Development.* New Delhi: Ashish Publishing House.

Paranjapye, S., Joy, K. J., and Scott, C. 2003. The Ozar Water User Societies: Impact of Society Formation and Co-management of Surface Water and Groundwater. Paper presented at National Seminar on Water, Pune: India, July. http://www.cess.ac.in/cesshome/wp/VUMURHJ1.pdf, accessed 30 January 2008.

Paustian, P. W. 1968. *Canal Irrigation in the Punjab: An Economic Inquiry Relating to Certain Aspects of the Development of Canal Irrigation by the British in the Punjab.* New York: AMS Press.

Pearce, F. 2006. *When Rivers Run Dry: What Happens When Our Water Runs Out.* London: Transworld Publishers.

Pence, J. 2005. Bell Rapids Farmlands to be Dried Up . . . State Makes Historic Move to Buy Back Water Rights. Fairfield, ID, *Times-News,* March 10.

Perry, C., and Ul-Hassan, M. 2000. Control of Groundwater Use: The Limitations of Pricing, and a Practical Alternative. Paper presented at GWP, Groundwater Management Seminar, Islamabad, October.

Phansalkar, S. J., and Kher, V. 2006. A Decade of the Maharashtra Groundwater Legislation: Analysis of the Implementation Process. *Law, Environment and Development Journal* 2(1): 67–83.

Pina, C. M., Sara, A. F., Luis, A. J. M., Jaime, S. S., and Adán, M. C. 2006. Agriculture Demand for Groundwater in Mexico: Impact of Water Right Enforcement and Electricity User-Fee on Groundwater Level and Quality. Paper presented at Stockholm Water Symposium, Stockholm, August.

Planning Commission (India). 2007. *Report of the Expert Group to Review the Issue of Groundwater Ownership in the Country.* New Delhi: Government of India.

Plusquellec, H. 1989. *Two Irrigation Systems in Colombia: Their Performance and Transfer of Management to Users' Associations.* Working Paper 264. Washington, D.C.: World Bank.

———. 1990. *The Gezira Irrigation Scheme in Sudan: Objectives, Design and Performance.* Technical Paper 120. Washington, D.C.: World Bank.

Plusquellec, H., and Wikham, T. 1985. *Irrigation Design and Management: Experience in Thailand and Its General Applicability.* Technical Paper 40. Washington, D.C.: World Bank.

Postel, S. 1999. *Pillar of Sand: Can the Irrigation Miracle Last?* New York: W. W. Norton & Company.

Prabowo, A., Handaka, and Maria, C. R. 2002. *Development of Groundwater for Agricultural Irrigation in East Java Region.* Indonesian Center for Agricultural Engineering Research and Development.

Pradhan, P. 1989. *Patterns of Irrigation Organization in Nepal: A Comparative Study of 21 Farmer Managed Irrigation Systems.* Colombo: International Irrigation Management Institute.

Prakash, A. 2005. *Dark Zone: The Groundwater Irrigation, Politics and Social Power in North Gujarat.* Wageningen University Water Resources Series. Hyderabad, India: Orient Longman.

Prasad, K. 2003. *Water Resources and Sustainable Development,* New Delhi, India: SHIPRA Publications.

Prasad, R. K., and Sarkar, T. K. 1994. Management of Groundwater Resources in India. In *Water Lifting Devices and Groundwater Management for Irrigation.* Report of the Expert Consultation of the Asian Network on Water Lifting Devices for Irrigation, Bangkok, 27 September–1 October 1993. Bangkok: FAO, Regional Office for Asia and the Pacific (RAPA), 144–66.

PSCST. 2005. *State of the Environment, Punjab: 2005.* Chandigarh: Punjab State Council for Science and Technology.

Putnam, R. 1993. *Making Democracy Work: Civic Traditions in Modern Italy.* Princeton, N.J.: Princeton University Press.

Qureshi, A. S., and Akhtar, M. 2004. Energy-Irrigation Nexus: Impact of Energy Pricing on Groundwater Management in Pakistan. Paper presented at Third South Asia Water Forum. Dhaka, Bangladesh, July.

Qureshi, A. S., and Masih, I. 2002. Modeling the Effects of Conjunctive Water Management on Secondary Salinization. In *Sustaining Surface and Groundwater Resources: Proceedings of the International Workshop on Conjunctive Water Management for Sustainable Irrigated Agriculture in South Asia,* edited by A. S. Qureshi, A. Bhatti, W. A. Jehangir. Lahore: International Water Management Institute, 73–81.

Qureshi, A. S., and Mujeeb, A. 2004. The Groundwater Management in Pakistan: Issues and the Way Forward. Paper presented at National Symposium on World Water Day, University of Agriculture, Faisalabad, Pakistan, April.

Qureshi, A. S., Shah, T., and Akhtar, M. 2003. *The Groundwater Economy of Pakistan*. Working Paper 64, Pakistan Country Series 19. Lahore: IWMI.

Qureshi, R. H., and Barrett-Lennard, E. G. 1998. *Saline Agriculture for Irrigated Land in Pakistan: A Handbook*. Monograph 50. Canberra, Australia: ACIAR.

Raj, A. B. S., and Sundaresan, D. 2005. Declining Trend in Tank Irrigated Area: Is There a Way to Arrest? Paper presented at Annual Partners' Meet of the IWMI-Tata Water Policy Research Program, Anand, India, February.

Ramirez, A., and Vargas, R. 1999. Irrigation Transfer Policy in Colombia: Some Lessons from Main Outcomes and Experiences. Paper presented at International Researchers' Conference on the Long Road to Commitment: A Socio-Political Perspective on the Process of Irrigation Reform, Hyderabad, India, December.

Ranade, R. 2005. "Out of Sight, Out of Mind": Absence of Groundwater in Water Allocation of Narmada Basin. *Economic and Political Weekly* 40(21): 2172–75.

Randhawa, M. S. 1982. *A History of Agriculture in India*, volume II. New Delhi: Indian Council of Agricultural Research.

———. 1983. *A History of Agriculture in India*, volume III. New Delhi: Indian Council of Agricultural Research.

Rao, D. N., and Govindarajan, S. 2003. Community Intervention in Rural Power Distribution. Water Policy Research Highlight 12. Anand, India: IWMI-Tata Water Policy Program.

Rao, G. B. 2003. Oases of Rayalaseema: SPWD's Tank Restoration Program in Southern Andhra Pradesh. *Wastelands News* 19(1): 64–72.

Rao, P. P., Birthal, P. S., Joshi, P. K., and Kar, D. 2004. *Agricultural Diversification in India and the Role of Urbanization*. MSSD Discussion Paper 77. Washington, D.C.: International Food Policy Research Institute.

Rao, R. M. M. S., Batchelor, C. H., James, A. J., Nagaraja, R., Seeley, J., and Butterworth, J. A. 2003. *Andhra Pradesh Rural Livelihoods Programme Water Audit Report*. Rajendranagar, Hyderabad, India: APRLP.

Rap, E. R. 2004. *The Success of a Policy Model: Irrigation Management Transfer in Mexico*. Ph.D. Thesis, Rural Development Sociology Group, Wageningen University, Netherlands.

Raychaudhuri, T. 1998. The Agrarian System of Mughal India: A Review Essay. In *The Mughal State 1526–1750*, edited by A. Muzaffar and S. Sanjay. New Delhi: Oxford University Press, 259–83.

Reddy, A. M. 1990. Travails of an Irrigation Canal Company in South India, 1857–1882. *Economic and Political Weekly* 25(12): 619–28.

Reddy, V. R. 2003. Irrigation: Development and Reforms. *Economic and Political Weekly* 38(12–13): 1178–89.

———. 2005. Costs of Resource Depletion Externalities: A Study of Groundwater Overexploitation in Andhra Pradesh, India. *Environment and Development Economics* 10(4): 533–56.

Renault, D. 1998. Modernization of Irrigation Systems: A Continuing Process. In *Modernization of Irrigation System Operations,* edited by D. Renault. Proceedings of the Fifth International IT IS Network Meeting, Aurangabad, India, 28–30 October. Bangkok: FAO, RAP Publication 99(43): 7–12.

Renault, D., and Facon, T. 2004. Beyond Drops for Crops: The Systems Approach for Water Value Assessment in Rice-Based Production Systems. *International Rice Commission Newsletter* 53(2004). http://www.fao.org/rice2004/en/pdf/renault. pdf, accessed 30 January 2008.

Repetto, R. 1986. *Skimming the Water: Rent, Seeking and the Performance of Public Irrigation Systems.* Research Report 4. Washington, D.C.: World Resources Institute.

———. 1994. *The "Second India" Revisited: Population, Poverty, and Environmental Stress over Two Decades.* Washington, D.C.: World Resources Institute.

Riaz, K. 2002. Tackling the Issue of Rural-Urban Water Transfers in the Ta'iz region, Yemen. *Natural Resources Forum* 26(22): 89–100.

Rice, E. B. 1996. *Paddy Irrigation and Water Management in Southeast Asia.* Washington, D.C.: World Bank.

Roe, E. M. 1991. Development Narratives, Or Making the Best of Blueprint Development. *World Development* 19(4): 287–300.

Rogaly, B., Harris-White, B., and Bose, S. 1999. Introduction: Agricultural Growth and Agrarian Change in West Bengal and Bangladesh. In *Sonar Bangla? Agricultural Growth and Agrarian Change in West Bengal and Bangladesh,* edited by B. Rogaly, B. Harris-White and S. Bose. New Delhi: Sage Publications, 11–38.

Rogers, P., and Hall, A. W. 2003. *Effective Water Governance.* Novum, Sweden: Global Water Partnership.

Romani, S., Sharma, K. D., Ghosh, N. C., and Kaushik, Y. B. 2007. *Groundwater Governance: Ownership of Groundwater and Its Pricing.* New Delhi: Capital Publishing Company.

Ronghan, H. 1988. Development of Groundwater for Agriculture in the Lower Yellow River Alluvial Basin. In *Efficiency in Irrigation: The Conjunctive Use of Surface and Groundwater Resources,* edited by G. T. O'Mara. Washington, DC: World Bank, 80–84.

Rosegrant, M. and Gazmuri, R. 1994. *Reforming Water Allocation Policy through Markets in Tradable Water Rights: Lessons from Chile, Mexico and California.* EPTD Discussion Paper 6. Washington, D.C.: International Food Policy Research Institute.

Rosin, T. 1993. The Tradition of Groundwater Irrigation in Northwestern India. *Human Ecology* 21(1): 51–86.

Roy, K. C., and Mainuddin, M. 2003. Socio-Ecology of Groundwater Irrigation in Bangladesh. Paper presented at Workshop on Groundwater Socio-Ecology of Asia: Governing a Colossal Anarchy, IWMI-Tata Water Policy Program, Anand, India, January.

Roy, T. 2000. *The Economic History of India 1857–1947*. New Delhi: Oxford University Press.

———. 2007. Roots of Agrarian Stagnation in Interwar India: Retrieving a Narrative. *Economic and Political Weekly* 41(52): 5389–401.

Sakthivadivel, R. 2007. The Groundwater Recharge Movement in India. In *The Agricultural Groundwater Revolution: Opportunities and Threats to Development*, edited by M. Giordano and K. G. Villhoth. Wallingford, U.K.: CAB International, 195–210.

Sakthivadivel, R., and Nagar, R. K. 2003. Private Initiative for Groundwater Recharge: Case of Dudhada Village in Saurashtra. Water Policy Research Highlight 15. Anand, India: IWMI-Tata Water Policy Program.

Sakthivadivel, R., Gomathinayagam, P., and Shah, T. 2004. Rejuvenating Irrigation Tanks through Local Institutions. *Economic and Political Weekly* 39(31): 3521–26.

Saleth, R. M. 1994. Groundwater Markets in India: A Legal and Institutional Perspective. In *Selling Water: Conceptual and Policy Debates over Groundwater Markets in India*, edited by M. Moench. Ahmedabad, India: VIKSAT, 59–71.

———. 1998. Water Markets in India: Economic and Institutional Aspects. In *Markets for Water: Potential and Performance*, edited by K. W. Easter, M. W. Rosegrant, and A. Dinar, A. Dordrecht. Netherlands: Kluwer Academic Publishers, 187–205.

———. 2004. Strategic Analysis of Water Institutions in India: Application of a New Research Paradigm. Research Report 79. Colombo: International Water Management Institute.

Samad, M. 2005. Water Institutional Reforms in Sri Lanka. *Water Policy* 7(1): 125–40.

Sandoval, R. 2004. A Participatory Approach to Integrated Aquifer Management: The Case of Guanajuato State, Mexico. *Hydrogeology Journal* 12(1): 6–13.

SANDRP. 2006. Accelerated Irrigation Benefit Program: Why It Is a Complete Misnomer: No Acceleration, Little Irrigation, Minuscule Benefits. *Dams, Rivers and People* 4(7–8): 8–9.

Sangameshwaran, P. 2006. Equity in Watershed Development: A Case Study in Western Maharashtra. *Economic and Political Weekly* 41(21): 2157–65.

Sargent, T. J. 2002. Rational Expectations. *The Concise Encyclopedia of Economics*, edited by D. R. Henderson. Indianapolis: Liberty Fund, Inc. http://www.econlib.org/LIBRARY/Enc/RationalExpectations.html, accessed 25 August 2006.

Saul, S. B. 1957. The Economic Significance of "Constructive Imperialism. *Journal of Economic History* 17(2): 173–92.

Saurashtra Jaldhara Trust. 2002. Personal communication, 15 October.

Schlager, E. 2007. Community Management of Groundwater. In *The Agricultural Groundwater Revolution: Opportunities and Threats to Development*, edited by M. Giordano and K. G. Villhoth. Wallingford, U.K.: CAB International, 131–152

Schon, D. 1983. *Reflective Practitioner: How Professionals Think in Action*. New York: Basic Books.

Schrevel, A. 1997. Managing an Open Access Resource: Groundwater. In *Groundwater Management: Sharing Responsibility for an Open Access Resource: Proceedings of the Wageningen Water Workshop 1997*, edited by A. Schrevel. Netherlands: ILRI, 1–18.

Schumpeter, J. A. 1942. *Capitalism, Socialism and Democracy*. New York: Harper & Row.

Scott, C. A., Shah, T., and Buechler, S. J. 2003. Energy Pricing and Supply for Groundwater Demand Management: Lessons from Mexican Agriculture. Water Policy Research Highlight 3. Anand, India: IWMI-TATA Water Policy Program.

Scott, J. C. 1976 *The Moral Economy of the Peasant: Subsistence and Rebellion in South East Asia*. New Haven, Conn.: Yale University Press.

———. 1998. *Seeing Like a State: How Certain Schemes to Improve the Human Condition Have Failed*. Yale ISPS Series and Yale Agrarian Studies. New Haven, Conn., and London: Yale University Press.

Seckler, D., Barker, R., and Amarasinghe, U. 1999. Water Scarcity in the Twenty-First Century. *Water Resources Development* 15(1–2): 29–42.

Seenivasan, R. 2003. *Neerkattis: The Rural Water Managers*. Madurai, India: DHAN Foundation.

Selvarajan, S. 2002. *Sustaining India's Irrigation Infrastructure*. Policy Brief 15. New Delhi: National Center for Agricultural Economics and Policy Research.

Shah, A. 2003. Tail-Enders and Other Deprived in Canal Irrigation Systems: Gujarat. Paper presented at National Workshop on Tail-Enders and Other Deprived in Canal Irrigation Systems, Ahmedabad, India, November.

Shah, M., Banerji, D., Vijayshankar, P. S., and Ambasta, P. 1998. *India's Drylands: Tribal Societies and Development through Environmental Regeneration*. New Delhi: Oxford University Press.

Shah, T. 1989. Groundwater Grids in the Villages of Gujarat: Evolution, Structure, Working and Impacts. *Wamana* 14–29.

———. 1992. *Sustainable Development of Groundwater Resource: Lessons from Junagadh District. Economic and Political Weekly* 27(10–11): 515–20.

———. 1993. *Groundwater Markets and Irrigation Development: Political Economy and Practical Policy*. Bombay: Oxford University Press.

———. 1996. *Catalysing Co-operation: Design of Self-Governing Organizations*. New Delhi: Sage Publications.

———. 1998. *Elixir or Opiate? An Assessment of Minor Irrigation Policies in North Bengal*. Policy School Working Paper 3. Anand, India: Policy School.

———. 2000. Mobilizing Social Energy against Environmental Challenge: Understanding the Groundwater Recharge Movement in Western India. *Natural Resource Forum* 24(3): 197–209.

———. 2001. *Wells and Welfare in Ganga Basin: Public Policy and Private Initiative in Eastern Uttar Pradesh, India.* Research Report 54. Colombo: International Water Management Institute.

———. 2003a. Who Should Manage Chandeli Tanks? Water Policy Research Comment 1. Anand, India: IWMI-TATA Water Policy Program.

———. 2003b. Governing the Groundwater Economy: Comparative Analysis of National Institutions and Policies in South Asia, China and Mexico. *Water Perspectives* 1(1): 2–27.

———. 2004. Water and Welfare: Critical Issues in India's Water Future. *Economic and Political Weekly* 39(12): 1211–13.

———. 2005. Groundwater and Human Development: Challenges and Opportunities in Livelihoods and Environment. *Water, Science & Technology* 51(8): 27–37.

———. 2006a. Institutional Groundwater Management in United States: Lessons for South Asia and North China. *Kansas Journal of Law and Public Policy* 15(3): 567–71.

———. 2006b. Note for the Planning Commission, Government of India Groundwater Regulation: International Experience.

———. 2007a. Issues in Reforming Informal Water Economies of Low-Income Countries: Examples from India and Elsewhere. In *Community-Based Water Law and Water Resource Management Reform in Developing Countries,* edited by B. V. Koppen, M. Giordano, and J. Butterworth. Wallingford, U.K.: CAB International, 65–95.

———. 2007b. Crop per Drop of Diesel? Energy Squeeze on India's Small-Holder Irrigation. *Economic and Political Weekly* 42(39): 4002–4009.

Shah, T., and Ballabh, V. 1995. The Social Science of Water Stress: An Exploratory Study of Water Management Institutions in Banaskantha District, Gujarat. In *Groundwater Management: The Supply Dominated Focus of Traditional NGO and government efforts,* edited by M. Moench. Ahmedabad, India: VIKSAT, 42–61.

———. 1997. Water Markets in North Bihar: Six Village Studies in Muzaffarpur District. *Economic and Political Weekly* 32(52): A183–A190.

Shah, T., and Bhattacharya, S. 1993. *Farmer Organisations for Lift Irrigation: Irrigation Companies and Tubewell Cooperatives of Gujarat.* Network Paper 26. London: Overseas Development Institute.

Shah, T., and Desai, R. 2002. Creative Destruction: Is That How Gujarat Is Adapting to Groundwater Depletion? A Synthesis of ITP studies. Paper presented at Annual Partners' Meet of the IWMI-Tata Water Policy Research Program, Anand, India, February.

Shah, T., and Keller, J. 2002. Micro-Irrigation and the Poor: A Marketing Challenge in Smallholder Irrigation Development. In *Private Irrigation in Sub-Saharan Africa: Regional Seminar on Private Sector Participation and Irrigation Expansion in Sub-Saharan Africa*, edited by H. Sally and C. L. Abernethy. Colombo: International Water Management Institute, 165–84.

Shah, T., and Raju, K. V. 1988. Working of Groundwater Markets in Andhra Pradesh and Gujarat: Results of Two Village Studies. *Economic and Political Weekly* 26(3): 23–28.

———. 2001. Rethinking Rehabilitation: Socio-Ecology of Tanks in Rajasthan, India. *Water Policy* 3(6): 521–36.

Shah, T., and Singh, O. P. 2004. Irrigation Development and Rural Poverty in Gujarat, India. A Disaggregated Analysis. *Water International* 29(2): 167–77.

Shah, T., and van Koppen, B. 2006. Is India Ripe for Integrated Water Resources Management (IWRM)? Fitting Water Policy to National Development Context. *Economic and Political Weekly* 41(31): 3413–21.

Shah, T., and Verma, S. 2008. Real-Time Co-management of Electricity and Groundwater: An Assessment of Gujarat's Pioneering *Jyotirgram* Scheme. *Economic and Political Weekly* 43(7): 59–66.

Shah, T., Alam, M., Dinesh K. M., Nagar, R. K., and Singh, M. 2000a. *Pedaling Out of Poverty: Social Impact of a Manual Irrigation Technology in South Asia*. Research Report 45. Colombo: International Water Management Institute.

Shah, T., Hussain, I., and Saeed ur, R. 2000b. *Irrigation Management in Pakistan and India: Comparing Notes on Institutions and Policies*. IWMI Working Paper 4. Colombo: International Water Management Institute.

Shah, T., Molden, D., Sakthivadivel, R., and Seckler, D. 2001a. Global Groundwater Situation: Opportunities and Challenges. *Economic and Political Weekly* 36(43): 4142–50.

Shah, T., Seenivasan, R., Shanmugam, C. R., and Vasimalai, M. P. 2001b. Sustaining Tamilnadu's Tanks: Fieldnotes on PRADAN's Work in Madurai and Ramnad Districts. In *Institutionalizing Common Property Management*, edited by D. Marothia. Delhi, India: Concept Publishing Company.

Shah, T., Koppen, B. V., Merrey, D., Lange, M. D., and Samad, M. 2002. *Institutional Alternatives in African Smallholder Irrigation: Lessons from International Experience with Irrigation Management Transfer*. Research Report 60. Colombo: International Water Management Institute.

Shah, T., Giordano, M., and Wang, J. 2004a. Irrigation Institutions in a Dynamic Economy: What Is China Doing Differently from India? *Economic and Political Weekly* 39(31): 3452–61.

Shah, T., Scott, C., and Buechler, S. 2004b. Water Sector Reforms in Mexico: Lessons for India's New Water Policy. *Economic and Political Weekly* 39(4): 361–70.

Shah, T., Scott, C., Kishore, A., and Sharma, A. 2004c. *Energy-Irrigation Nexus in South Asia: Improving Groundwater Conservation and Power Sector Viability.* Research Report 70. Colombo: International Water Management Institute.

Shah, T., Singh, O. P., and Aditi Mukherji. 2006. Some Aspects of South Asia's groundwater Irrigation Economy: Analyses from a Survey in India, Pakistan, Nepal Terai and Bangladesh. *Hydrogeology Journal* 14(3): 286–309.

Shah, T., Burke, J., Villholth, K., et al. 2007. Groundwater Use in Agriculture: A Global Assessment of Scale and Significance for Food, Livelihoods and Nature. In *Water for Food, Water for Life: A Comprehensive Assessment of Water Management in Agriculture,* edited by D. Molden. London: Earthscan, and Colombo: International Water Management Institute, 395–23.

Shaheen, F. A., and Shiyani, R. L. 2005. Equity Redistribution: Groundwater Bore-Wells in North Gujarat. *Economic and Political Weekly* 40(4): 307–12.

Shankar, K. 1987. Working of Private Tubewells in Phulpur Tehsil of Allahabad District in UP. Paper presented at Workshop on Common Property Resources: Groundwater, Rourkee, India, February.

Sharma, C. V. J. 1989. *Modern Temples of India: Selected Speeches of Jawaharlal Nehru at Irrigation and Power Projects.* New Delhi: Central Board of Irrigation and Power.

Sharma, B. R., Rao, K. V., Vittal, K. P. R., and Amarasinghe, U. 2007. Potential of Rainfed Agriculture in India: How Critical Is the "Critical Irrigation"? Water and People: Reflections in a Turbulent Pool. Compendium of the Sixth IWMI-Tata Annual Partners Meet, Anand, India, 8–10 March.

Sharma, M. 2006. The Making of Moral Authority: Anna Hazare and Watershed Management Programme in Ralegan Siddhi. *Economic and Political Weekly* 41(20): 1981–88.

Sharma, P., and Sharma, R. C. 2004. Groundwater Markets across Climatic Zones: A Comparative Study of Arid and Semi-Arid Zones of Rajasthan. *Indian Journal of Agricultural Economics* 59(1): 138–50.

Shi, Y. 2000. Groundwater Development in China. Paper presented at Second World Water Forum, The Hague, March.

Shiklomanov, I. A. 1993. World Fresh Water Resources. In *Water in Crisis: A Guide to the World's Fresh Water Resources,* edited by P. H. Gleick. New York, U.S.: Oxford University Press, 13–25.

Shingi, P. M., and V. N. Asopa. 2002. *Independent Evaluation of Checkdams in Gujarat: Strategies and Impacts,* volume 1, Executive Summary. Ahmedabad, India: Indian Institute of Management, Center for Management in Agriculture.

Short, P. 2004. *Pol Pot: The History of a Nightmare.* New York: Henry Holt and Company.

Shukla, P. 2004. Exposure cum Training Visit to Participatory Irrigation Management (PIM) Project Ahmedabad, Gujarat. *Letters* 1(3): 12–14. http://www.srijanindia.org/imgs/Letters%20July%2004.pdf, accessed 30 January 2008.

Sidhu, R. S., and Bhullar, A. S. 2005. Patterns and Determinants of Agricultural Growth in the Two Punjabs. *Economic and Political Weekly* 40(53): 5620–27.

Sikka, A., and Gichuki, F. 2006. *Indo-Gangetic Basin: Enhancing Agricultural Water Productivity through Strategic Research*. Technical Report 2. Colombo: Challenge Program on Water and Food.

Singh, D. R., and Singh, R. P. 2003. Groundwater Markets and the Issues of Equity and Reliability to Water Access: A Case of Western Uttar Pradesh. *Indian Journal of Agricultural Economics* 38(1): 115–27.

Singh, K. K., and Satish, S. 1988. Public Tubewells in Uttar Pradesh: Performance and Management. Paper presented at Workshop on the Development and Management of Groundwater Resources in Eastern Uttar Pradesh, Gaziabad, India, April.

Singh, O. P., Kumar, M. D., and Ghosh, S. 2005. Changing Water Use Hydrology of Narmada River Basin: Implications for Basin Water Allocation. Water Policy Research Highlight 19. Anand, India: IWMI-Tata Water Policy Program.

Singh, S. 2006. Credit, Indebtedness and Farmer Suicides in Punjab: Some Missing Links. *Economic and Political Weekly* 41(3): 3330–31.

Somanathan, E., and Ravindranath, R. 2006. Measuring the Marginal Value of Water and Elasticity of Demand for Water in Agriculture. *Economic and Political Weekly* 41(26): 2712–15.

Sonou, M. 1994. *An Overview of Low-Lift Irrigation in West Africa: Trends and Prospects*. RAPA Publication. Regional Office for Asia and the Pacific (RAPA). Bangkok: FAO.

State Statistical Bureau (People's Republic of China). 2000. China Statistical Year Book 2000. Beijing: National Bureau of Statistics of China, China Statistical Publishing House.

———. 2002. China Statistical Year Book 2002. Beijing: National Bureau of Statistics of China, China Statistical Publishing House.

Steenbergen, F. van. 1995. The Frontier Problem in Incipient Groundwater Management Regimes in Balochistan (Pakistan). *Human Ecology* 23(1): 53–74.

Steenbergen, F. van, and Oliemans, W. 1997. Groundwater Resource Management in Pakistan. In *Groundwater Management: Sharing Responsibility for Open Access Resource: Proceedings of the First Wageningen Water Workshop, October 1997*, edited by A. Schrevel. Special Report. Wageningen: International Land Reclamation Institute, 93–109.

———. 2002. A Review of Policies in Groundwater Management in Pakistan 1950–2000. *Water Policy* 4(4): 323–44.

Steenbergen, F. van, and Shah, T. 2003. Rules Rather Than Rights: Self-Regulation in Intensively Used Groundwater Systems. In *Intensive Use of Groundwater: Challenges and Opportunities*, edited by M. R. Llamas and E. Custodio. Rotterdam: A. A. Balkema Publishers, 241–56.

Stone, I. 1984. *Canal Irrigation in British India: Perspectives on Technological Change in a Peasant Society.* Cambridge: Cambridge University Press.

Svendsen, M., and Nott, G. 1997. Irrigation Management Transfer in Turkey: Process and Outcomes. Paper presented at International Workshop on Participatory Irrigation Management: Benefits and Second Generation Problems, Cali, Colombia, February.

Talati, J. 2004. Water Revolution through Rainwater Harvesting in Gujarat. Working Paper. Anand, India: IWMI-Tata Water Policy Program.

Talati, J., and Shah, T. 2004. Institutional Vacuum in Sardar Sarovar Project: Framing "Rules-of-the-Game." *Economic and Political Weekly* 39(31): 3504–509.

Tata, M. 2007. Switch on the Charm. *Outlook Magazine,* 30 July. http://outlookindia.com/full.asp?fodname=20070730&fname=Andhra+Pradesh+%28F%29&SID=1, accessed 29 July 2007.

Thakkar, H. 1999. Assessment of Irrigation in India. Contributing Paper for World Commission on Dams (WCD) Thematic Review IV.2 Irrigation Options. http://www.dams.org/docs/kbase/contrib/opt161.pdf, accessed 1 November 2006.

Thakurta, P. G. 2005. Ending Poverty Still a Goal. *The Tribune,* Chandigarh, 24 September.

The Age. 1891. Deakin on Irrigation. 7 February 1891. http://150.theage.com.au/view_bestofarticle.asp?straction=update&inttype=1&intid=437, accessed 1 November 2006.

Thierry, S. 1997. *The Khmers.* Pondicherry, India: Kailash Editions.

Thorner, D. 1956. Feudalism in India. In *Feudalism in History,* edited by R. Coulborn. Princeton, N.J.: Princeton University Press, 133–50.

Tilala, H., and Shiyani, R. L. 2005. Small Water Harvesting: A Sustainable Way for Equity and Income Generation. Water Policy Research Highlight 17. Anand, India: IWMI-Tata Water Policy Program.

Times of India. 2006. Ahmedabad edition, 31 May.

Tiwari, R. 2007. From Persian Wheels to Submersible Pumps: Social Organisation of Shared Ground Water Irrigation in Punjab. Paper presented at Annual Partners' Meet of the IWMI-Tata Water Policy Research Program, Anand, India, March.

Trist, E. 1991. *The Evolution of Socio-Technical Systems,* Occasional Paper No 2. Toronto: Ministry of Labour.

Tsur, Y. 1990. The Stabilization Role of Groundwater When Surface-Water Supplies Are Uncertain: The Implications for Groundwater Development. *Water Resources Research* 26(5): 811–18.

Tucker, S. P. 2005. Innovations in Financing of Irrigation Projects. Paper presented at Workshop on Financing Irrigation Infrastructure, New Delhi, May.

Turral, H. 1995. Recent Trends in Irrigation Management: Changing Directions for the Public Sector. *ODI Natural Resource Perspectives* 5. London: Overseas Development Institute.

———. 1998. *Hydro Logic? Reform in Water Resources Management in Developed Countries with Major Agricultural Water Use.* London: Overseas Development Institute.

Ul Hassan, M. 2006. Personal communication with the author, 26 April.

Ul Hassan, M., Shah, T., Rehman, S., Khattak, M. Z., Tanwir, F., Saboor, A., Lashari, B., and Ashraf, S. 2007. Impacts of Diesel Price Increases on Small-Holder Irrigation in Pakistan. Draft Paper. Lahore: International Water Management Institute.

Umrani, N. K. 1999. Development of Dryland Technologies across Five Foundation Locations: Historical Perspective. In *Fifty Years of Dryland Agricultural Research in India,* edited by H. P. Singh, Y. S. Ramakrishna, K. L. Sharma, and B. Venkateswarlu. Hyderabad, India: Central Research Institute for Dryland Agriculture.

Uphoff, N. 1986. *Improving International Irrigation Management with Farmer Participation: Getting the Process Right.* Studies in Water Policy and Management 11. Boulder, Colo.: Westview Press.

Vaidyanathan, A. 1996. Depletion of Groundwater: Some Issues. *Indian Journal of Agricultural Economics* 51(1–2): 184–92.

Vakulabharanam, V. 2004. Agricultural Growth and Irrigation in Telangana: A Review of Evidence. *Economic and Political Weekly* 39(13): 1421–26.

Van Halsema, G. E. 2002. *Trial and Retrial: The Evolution of Irrigation Modernization in NWFP, Pakistan.* Ph.D. Thesis, Wageningen University, Netherlands.

Van Koppen, B. 2007. Dispossession at the Interface of Community-Based Water Law and Permit Systems. In *Community-Based Water Law,* edited by B. V. Koppen, M. Giordano, and J. Butterworth. Wallingford, U.K.: CAB International (forthcoming).

Van Koppen, B., Giordano, M., Butterworth, J., and Mapedza, E. 2007. Community-Based Water Law and Water Resources Management Reform in Developing Countries: Rationale, Contents and Key Messages. In *Community-Based Water Law,* edited by B. V. Koppen, M. Giordano, and J. Butterworth. Wallingford, U.K.: CAB International 1–11.

Vaux, H. 2005. Personal communication, 28 June.

Veblen, T. 1934. *The Theory of the Leisure Class.* New York: Modern Library.

Vermillion, D. 1996. *The Privatization and Self-Management of Irrigation: Final Report.* Colombo: International Irrigation Management Institute.

Vijapurkar, M. 2000 Water as a Community Asset. *The Hindu.* http://www.narmada. org/archive/hindu/files/hindu.20000419.05192524.htm, accessed 30 January 2008.

Villarroya, F. and Aldwell, C. R. 1998. Sustainable Development and Groundwater Resources Exploitation. *Environmental Geology* 34(2–3): 111–15.

Vincent, L. 2001. Struggles at the Social Interface: Developing Sociotechnical Research in Irrigation and Water Management. In *Resonances and Dissonances in Development: Actors, Networks and Cultural Reportoires,* edited by P. Hebink and G. Verschoor. Netherlands: Royal Van Gorcum, 65–82.

Vishwanathan, P. K. 1997. Irrigation Projects in Kerala: A Review of Past Performance and Future Perspectives. Paper presented at Dr. T. N. Krishnan Memorial Seminar on Development Experience of South Indian States in a Comparative Setting, Centre for Development Studies, Tiruvananthapuram, India, September.

Von Oppen, M., and Subba Rao, K. V. 1980. *Tank Irrigation in Semi-Arid Tropical India. Part II: Technical Features and Economic Performance.* Economics Program Progress Report 5. Hyderabad, India: ICRISAT.

———. 1987. *Tank Irrigation in Semi-Arid Tropical India: Economic Evaluation and Alternatives for Improvement.* Research Bulletin 10. Hyderabad, India: ICRISAT.

Wade, R. 1975. Administration and Distribution of Irrigation Benefits. *Economic and Political Weekly* 10(44–5): 1741–45.

———. 1982. The System of Administrative and Political Corruption: Canal Irrigation in South Asia. *Journal of Development Studies* 18(3): 287–28.

———. 1984. Irrigation Reform in Conditions of Populist Anarchy: An Indian Case. *Journal of Development Studies* 14(2): 285–303.

———. 1986. Common Property Resource Management in South Indian Villages. Proceedings of the Conference on Common Property Resource Management. Washington, D.C.: National Academy Press, 231–258.

Wallach, B. 1985. British Irrigation Works in India's Krishna Basin. *Journal of Historical Geography* 11(2): 155–74.

———. 1988. Irrigation in Sudan since Independence. *The Geographical Review* 78(4): 417–34.

Wang, J., Huang, J., Blanke, A., Huang, Q., and Rozelle, S. 2007. The Development, Challenges and Management of Groundwater in Rural China. In *The Agricultural Groundwater Revolution: Opportunities and Threats to Development,* edited by M. Giordano and K. G. Villholth. Wallingford, U.K.: CAB International, 37–62.

Warner, J. 2003. Virtual Water, Virtual Benefits? Scarcity, Distribution, Security and Conflict Reconsidered. In *Virtual Water Trade, Proceedings of the International Expert Meeting on Virtual Water Trade,* edited by A. Y. Hoekstra. Value of Water Research Reports Series 12. Delft, Netherlands: IHE, 126–35.

Weissing, F., and Ostrom, E. 1991. Irrigation Institutions and the Games Irrigators Play: Rule Enforcement without Guards. In *Game Equilibrium Models 11: Methods, Morals, and Markets,* edited by R. Selten. Berlin: Springer-Verlag, 188–262.

Whitcombe, E. 1971. *Agrarian Conditions in Northern India.* Berkeley: University of California Press.

Whitcombe, E. 2005. Irrigation. In *The Cambridge Economic History of India, c 1757–c 1970,* volume 2, edited by D. Kumar and M. Desai. Hyderabad, India: Orient Longman, 677–737.

Wijesinghe, M. W. P. 1994. Water lifting devices and management of groundwater resources for irrigation in Sri Lanka. In *Water Lifting Devices and Groundwater*

Management for Irrigation. Report of the Expert Consultation of the Asian Network on Water Lifting Devices for Irrigation Devices, Bangkok, 27 September–1 October 1993. Bangkok: FAO, Regional Office for Asia and the Pacific (RAPA), 223–28.

Willcocks, Sir W. 1984. *Ancient System of Irrigation in Bengal,* Delhi, India: B. R. Publishing Corporation.

Williamson, O. E. 1981. The Economics of Organization: The Transaction Cost Approach. *American Journal of Sociology* 87(3): 548–77.

———. 1985. *The Economic Institutions of Capitalism.* New York: Free Press

———. 1993. Transaction Cost Economics Meets Posnerian Law and Economics. *Journal of Institutional and Theoretical Economics* 149(1): 99–118.

Wilson, K. 2002. Small Cultivators in Bihar and "New" Technology. *Economic and Political Weekly* 37(13): 1229–38.

Wittfogel, K. A. 1957. *Oriental Despotism: A Comparative Study of Total Power.* New Haven, Conn.: Yale University Press.

Wood, G. D. 1999. Private Provision after Public Neglect: Bending Irrigation Markets in North Bihar. *Development and Change* 30: 775–94.

World Bank. 1991. *Irrigation in the Humid Tropics: Project Design Issues in Indonesia and Thailand.* OED Precis 13, December.

———. 2005a. *India's Water Economy: Bracing for a Turbulent Future.* Report 34750-IN. Agriculture and Rural Development Unit, South Asia Region. Washington, D.C.

———. 2005b. *Pakistan–Country Water Resources Assistance Strategy: Water Economy Running Dry,* Report 34081-IN. Agriculture and Rural Development Sector, South Asia Region. Washington, D.C.

———. 2006. *Ethiopia: Managing Water Resources to Maximize Sustainable Growth: A World Bank Water Resources Assistance Strategy for Ethiopia.* Washington, D.C.

World Bank and Government of India Ministry of Water Resources. 1998: *India: Water Resources Management Sector Review Groundwater Regulation and Management Report, World Bank.* New Delhi: Government of India.

World Bank and Swiss Agency for Development Co-operation (SDC). 2000. Middle East and North Africa: Regional Water Initiative Workshop on Sustainable Groundwater Management, Sana, Yemen, June 25–28.

Zhengying, Q. 1994. *Water Resources Development in China.* Beijing: China Water and Power Press, and New Delhi: Central Board of Irrigation and Power.

Zhou, W. 1997. Review of the Irrigation Equipment Manufacture and Supply Sector in China. In *Irrigation Technology Transfer in Support of Food Security: Proceedings of Sub Regional Workshop,* Harare, Zimbabwe, 14–17 April. Water Reports 14. Rome: FAO, 139–48. http://www.fao.org/docrep/W7314E/w7314e0t.htm, accessed 30 January 2008.

INDEX

Note: Page numbers in italics indicate figures and tables. Page numbers followed by an "n" indicate notes.

Accelerated Irrigation Benefits Program, 65
adaptive irrigation, 7–13, *10*
Africa
    canal irrigation projects, 77
    irrigation development context, 18–20
agriculture
    dairy production, 114
    diversification of, 50–52, 75–78, *113*, 113–116
    dry-land, 109–113, *112*
    fruit production, 114–115
    homogeneity of, 75–78
    and poverty, 91
    and scientists' beliefs, 184–186

ahar-pyne systems, 248n
alluvial aquifers, management of, 234
    see also aquifers
anarchy
    cause of, 139
    and fewness, 72–75
    "functioning anarchy" label, 187
    and water control, 69
Angkor Empire, 17–18, 247n
aquifers
    arid alluvial, 159–166, *161*
    communities, 152–153
    community management, 194–197
    confined aquifers, 172–177, *173*, *176*
    cooperative gaming, 172–177, *173*, *176*

aquifers (*continued*)
    hard-rock, 166–171, *168*, 219–222
    hard-rock aquifers, 166–177, *168*,
        173, *176*, 219–222
    institutional dynamics, 153–154,
        154
    and institutions, 151–186
    see also water governance
arid agrarian systems, 53
arid alluvial aquifers, collusive oppor-
        tunism, 159–166, *161*
    see also aquifers
arsenic, 255n–256n
atomistic individualism, Indo-Gangetic
        basin, 155–159, *156*
atomistic irrigation, 29–32,223,
        227,231, *31*
Australia, irrigation development con-
        text, 20–21
authority, and gravity-flow irrigation
        management, 78–81

Babur, 9
    see also Mughal India
bagayat tax, 140
begar, 8
Boserup, Esther, 44–46
Brayne, F.L., 45
British rule, 23–24, 139
Buchanan, Francis, reports on well irri-
        gation, 12
build-neglect-rebuild syndrome, 68–71

CADAs (command area development
        agencies), 71
Cambodia, 17–18, 247n
canal command areas, shrinking of,
        65–66
canals
    Africa, 77
    constructive imperialism, 13–16, *15*
    decline of, *64*, 64–65
    see also gravity-flow irrigation
captivity, and gravity-flow irrigation
        management, 82–83
Cautley, Major Proby, 13, 22
chaos, and water control, 69
charasa, *10*, 10–11

check dams, 174–176, *176*
    see also dams
chud-pon, 81
civil engineering profession, 22–23
Coase, Ronald, 189
collective action, 11–12
collusive opportunism
    arid alluvial aquifers, 159–166, *161*
    see also institutional dynamics
colonial irrigation ideology. *see* con-
        structive imperialism
colonial rule, 23–24, 139
command area development agencies
        (CADAs), 71
command areas, shrinking of, 65–66
community aquifer management,
        194–197
    see also water governance
confined aquifers, cooperative gaming,
        172–177, *173*, *176*
constructive imperialism, 13–16, *15*,
        22–26
cooperative gaming, 172–177, *173*, *176*
    see also institutional dynamics
Cotton, Sir Arthur, 13, 22
crops, homogeneity of, 50–52, 75–78,
        113, 113–116
    see also agriculture
Cubbie Station, 73

dairy production, 114
dams
    check dams, 174–176, *176*
    Sardar Sarovar Dam, 134
Daxi pumps, 223–227, *224*
Deakin, Alfred, 20, 84
depletion of groundwater, 123–125,
        124
desilting, 220–221
development contexts elsewhere,
        16–22
Dhawan, BD, 26, 38, 43, 62, 65, 92,
        103, 108, 130, 142, 250-251n,
        267n.
diesel pumps vs. electric pumps,
        144–148, 158–159, 224–227
direct regulation, 190–191
    see also water governance

distributed governance, 244
diversification
    impact of pump irrigation, 104–105
    and WEMs, 114–115
drought, and pump irrigation, 116
dry-land agriculture. *see* agriculture
dug wells. *see* wells
Dutt, R.C., 32

Easement Act (1882), 139
East Asia, irrigation development context, 17–18
economic instruments, 191–192
    see also water governance
efficiency, impact of pump irrigation, 105–106
electric pumps vs. diesel pumps, 144–148, 158–159, 224–227
electricity
    pump irrigation boom, 110–111
    subsidies, 149–150, 178
    utility companies, 142–148, *145*
energy subsidies. *see* subsidies
energy-irrigation nexus, 232–233
"environment scan," 238–243
exit, 178–180, *179*
    see also institutional dynamics

famine, 15–16
farming. *see* agriculture
fewness, and gravity-flow irrigation management, 72–75
flow irrigation. *see* gravity-flow irrigation
fossil groundwater, 53
    see also groundwater
Foucault, Michael, 18–19
fresh-saline water interface, 129–130
fruit production, 114–115
    see also agriculture
"functioning anarchy" label, 187

Ganga basin, 155–159, *156*
Gezira irrigation scheme, 18–20, 76
gravity-flow irrigation
    deprivation levels, *67*
    Gezira irrigation scheme, 76
    as an irrigation technology, 83–89
    vs. lift irrigation, 61–65, *64, 65*

sustainability factors, 72–83
    see also canals
Green Creeper, 178
Green Revolution, 26
groundwater
    depletion, 123–125, *124*
    extraction, 36–37, *37*
    fossil, 53
    governance. *see* water governance
    management challenges, 125–132, *126, 131*
    recharge programs, 218–223, *219*
    revolution, 206
    socioecologies, 53–56, *54*
    vs. surface water, 38
    usage factors, 37–40
Gujarat, *Jyotirgram* scheme, 212–218, *215, 216, 217*

Habib, Irfan, 7
hard-rock aquifers
    cooperative gaming, 172–177, *173, 176*
    recharge programs, 219–222
    rivalrous gaming, 166–171, *168*
homogeneity, and gravity-flow irrigation management, 75–78
human dynamics, 184–186
hydrogeology, working rules, 38–40
hydropolitics, 137–142

IMT (irrigation management transfer), 70
Indo-Gangetic basin
    atomistic individualism, 155–159, *156*
    WEMs, 168–169
Indonesia, 42
Indus irrigation system, 23–25
industrial agricultural systems, 53–55
informal water economy, 137–142
institutional dynamics
    aquifers, 153–154, *154*
    formal and informal economies, 256n–257n
    local, 227–231, *229*
intensification, impact of pump irrigation, 103–104

irrigation communities
  and captivity, 82–83
  homogeneity of, 75–78
irrigation development contexts elsewhere, 16–22
irrigation governance. *see* water
  governance
irrigation management transfer (IMT),
  70
irrigation services, selling of, 96
ITP (IWMI-Tata Water Policy Program),
  vii–viii
IWMI vii-x, 211-217, 220, 232,
IWRM, and water governance, 198–203,
  201

Jyotirgram scheme (Gujarat), 212–218,
  215, 216, 217

kareze, 250n
Kerala, 51–52
Khmer Rouge, 17–18

Laos, 41
leather bucket, *10,* 10–11
lift irrigation
  vs. gravity-flow irrigation, 61–65,
    64, 65
  see also wells
"Lighted Village" scheme. *see Jyotirgram*
  scheme (Gujarat)
local institutional arrangements,
  227–231, *229*

Malthus, Thomas, 44
Marx, Karl, 6–7
Mexico, groundwater governance in,
  190, 194-197, 199, 210, 204
Mollinga, Peter, 22, 24, 65, 66, 79, 85,
  198, 251n
moral water economy, 180–184
Mughal India, 7–13, *10*
Myanmar, 42

neerkatti, 81
Nehru, Pandit Jawaharlal, on dams, 23,
  87
noise, and water control, 69

North Africa, irrigation development
  context, 16–17
North China Plain, pump irrigation
  boom, 35–36

O'Malley, L.S.S., on well irrigation, 13

Pani Panchayats, 70
participatory irrigation management
  (PIM), 70–71
pastoral tradition, support of, 55
Patidars, 163–164
Persian wheel, *10,* 10–11, 246n
Philippines, 41
PIM (participatory irrigation management), 70–71
  see also IMT (irrigation management
    transfer)
pipes. *see* water transport
population density, 44–46, 56–57
Pot, Pol, 17–18, 247n
poverty, 91, 106
power subsidies. *see* subsidies
power supply, reduction of
  see also Jyotirgram scheme (Gujarat)
Prisoners' Dilemma (PD), 188–189
productivity, impact of pump irrigation, 103
property rights, 192–194
propositions, "environment scan,"
  238–243
public irrigation systems
  lift irrigation vs. gravity-flow irriga-
    tion, *64,* 64–65
  management of, 93–95
  need for, 237
  subsidies, 46–47
  wara bandi system, 66–68
pump irrigation
  and agricultural diversificationty,
    113, 113–116
  benefits, 92
  boom, 40–44, 110–111
  drought, 116
  dry-land agriculture, 109–113
  economic significance, 106–109,
    107
  effects of, 103–106

informal water economy, 137–142
negative aspects, 122–150
other impacts, 116–117
prices, 259n
and poverty, 92, 94, 96-99
reservoirs, 117
river basin reconfiguration, 132–137, *133*
service markets, 95–103
treadle pumps, 115–116
water security, 117–121, *118*, *119*
see also wells
pump revolution, 44–50, *48*, *49*, *50*
pump technology
Daxi pumps, 223–227, *224*
diesel pumps vs. electric pumps, 144–148, 158–159, 224–227

qanat, 250n

rational expectations model, 152
recharge programs, 218–223, *219*, 235
rehabilitation, 68–71
reservoirs
and pump irrigation, 117
underground, 234
resource depletion, 123–125, *124*
rivalrous gaming
hard-rock aquifers, 166–171, *168*
see also institutional dynamics
river basin reconfiguration, 132–137, *133*

Sadguru Foundation, 135
Salinity Control and Reclamation Project (SCARP), 28–29
salinization, 129–130, 178
Sardar Patel Participatory Water Conservation Program, 175
Sardar Sarovar Dam, 134
Schon, Donald, 231–232
scientists, and farmers' beliefs, 184–186
Scott, James C., 243
secondary salinization, 129–130
Sen, Hun, 18
service markets, pump irrigation, 95–103

Sinchai Samitis, 70
small pump irrigation, 26–29, 160
see also wells
smallholder intensive farming system, 55–56
socioecologies of groundwater, 53–56, *54*
soil salinization, 129–130
South Asia, groundwater boom, 34–58, *37*, *48*, *49*, *50*, *54*
Southeast Asia, irrigation development context, 17–18
Spain, groundwater governance in, 190, 194-197, 199, 210, 204,

Sri Lanka, 41, 199
stabilization, impact of pump irrigation, 105
Stamp, Sir William, 26–29
subsidies
canal irrigation, 110
costs, 143
groundwater depletion, *124*, 148
impact on gravity-flow irrigation systems, 87
reduction of, 237, 241
water security, 120
well irrigation, 46
WEMs, *124*
Sudan, irrigation development context, 18–20
summary propositions, 238–243
surface irrigation systems
transaction costs, 73
transformation costs, 73
see also gravity-flow irrigation
surface water vs. groundwater, 38

tank desilting, 220–221
tank irrigation systems, 43, 62
see also gravity-flow irrigation
taxes, 139–141, 143
Thailand, 41
three-phase power, reduction of, 213
see also Jyotirgram scheme (Gujarat)
tokenism, 227
see also local institutional arrangements

tradable property rights, 192–194
transaction costs, 73, 75, 252n
transformation costs, surface irrigation systems, 73
treadle pumps, 115–116
tube wells, 26–29, 160
    see also wells

United States,
    groundwater governance in, 193–199, 201
    irrigation development context, 20–21
utility companies, 142–148, 145

vegetable production, 114–115
Vietnam, 41

Wade, Robert, 60, 65, 81, 83, 85, 87
wara bandi system, 21–22, 66–68
water assemblies, 70
water control, 68–71
water depletion
    groundwater, 123–125, *124*
    WEMs, 127–128, 133
water economy
    creating order in, 209–211
    experiments in, 180–184
    pump irrigation, 137–142
    transformation of, 203–207, *204*
    see also water governance
water extraction mechanisms (WEMs).
    see WEMs (water extraction mechanisms)
water governance
    creating order in, 231–238, *233*
    defined, 198
    instruments of, 189–198

and IWRM, 198–203, *201*
    see also water economy
water security, pump irrigation, 117–121, *118, 119*
water transport, 236–237
water-lifting devices, *10*, 10–11
"water-managed agriculture," FAO definition, 247n
wells
    crowding out, 197–198
        see also water governance
    lift irrigation vs. gravity-flow irrigation, 61–65, *64, 65*
    Mughal India, 9–13, *10*
    recharge programs, 220–222
    see also pump irrigation
WEMs (water extraction mechanisms)
    benefits, 52, 103–106, 111, 120
    density, 48
    diesel pumps vs. electric pumps, 144–148, 158–159
    and diversification, 114–115
    impact on gravity-flow irrigation systems, 37–38
    Indo-Gangetic basin, 168–169
    North China Plain, 36
    ownership, 29–32, 95–103
    subsidies, *124*
    water depletion, 127–128, 133
West Asia, irrigation development context, 16–17
Whitcombe, Elizabeth, 61
Willcocks, Sir William, lectures on irrigation projects, 12–13
Wittfogel, Karl, 6–7, 78, 245n–246n

zamindars, 74, 80–81, 248n